cache
nurturing achievement

Children and Young People's Workforce

Carolyn Meggitt

DYNAMIC
LEARNING

HODDER
EDUCATION

Orders: please contact Bookpoint Ltd, 130 Milton Park, Abingdon, Oxon
OX14 4SB. Telephone: (44) 01235 827720. Fax: (44) 01235 400454. Lines are open
from 9.00 - 5.00, Monday to Saturday, with a 24-hour message answering service.
You can also order through our website www.hoddereducation.co.uk

If you have any comments to make about this, or any of our other
titles, please send them to educationenquiries@hodder.co.uk

British Library Cataloguing in Publication Data
A catalogue record for this title is available from the British Library

ISBN: 978 1 444 135 466

This Edition Published 2011
Impression number   10 9 8 7 6 5 4 3
Year   2014, 2013, 2012

Hachette UK's policy is to use papers that are natural, renewable and
recyclable products and made from wood grown in sustainable forests.
The logging and manufacturing processes are expected to conform to the
environmental regulations of the country of origin.

Cover photo © iStockphoto / Ekaterina Monakhova.
Typeset by Servis Filmsetting Ltd, Stockport, Cheshire
Printed in Dubai for Hodder Education, An Hachette UK Company,
338 Euston Road, London NW1 3BH.

Contents

Acknowledgements

I would like to thank the following people for their contributions: Laura Meggitt (Community Play Specialist) for her valuable insights and for providing many of the early years case studies; Kirsty Meggitt (Recruitment Consultant) for help with the section on using SMART targets in Chapter 2; Gill Hutt (Youth Worker) for help with information on young people's services.

I would also like to thank the editorial team at Hodder Education – in particular Colin Goodlad, Publisher, Chloé Harmsworth, Desk Editor, and Llinos Edwards, Freelance Copy Editor, for all their hard work and support.

This book uses intellectual property/material from books previously co-authored with Tina Bruce and Julian Grenier, who willingly agreed to Carolyn writing this book in order to share what is important for high quality early childhood practice.

Carolyn Meggitt

Photo and artwork credits:

Every effort has been made to trace the copyright holders of material reproduced here. The authors and publishers would like to thank the following for permission to reproduce copyright illustrations:

Figures: 1.01 © Justin O'Hanlon; 1.02 © Andrew Callaghan; 1.03 © Andrew Callaghan; 2.01 © mangostock – Fotolia; 2.02 © Andrew Callaghan; 3.01 © Andrew Callaghan; 3.02 © Andrew Callaghan; 4.01 © Justin O'Hanlon; 4.02 © Justin O'Hanlon; 4.03 © Comstock/ Photolibrary.com; 4.04 © Lev Olkha – Fotolia; 4.05 © 2009 Benjamin Loo – Fotolia; 4.06 © ImageState Media; 4.07 © Creatas/Photolibrary.com; 4.08 © lisalucia – Fotolia; 4.09 © Stock Connection/ SuperStock; 4.10 © saintclair23 – Fotolia; 4.11 © Wojciech Gajda – Fotolia; 4.12 © gwimages – Fotolia; 4.13 © mamahoohooba – Fotolia; 4.14 © Andrew Callaghan; 4.15 © Andrew Callaghan; 4.1 © David Meggitt; 5.01 © Andrew Callaghan; 5.02 © Andrew Callaghan; 5.03 © Andrew Callaghan; 5.04 © Andrew Callaghan; 5.05 © Andrew Callaghan; 6.01 © Andrew Callaghan; 8.01 © Andrew Callaghan; 9.01 © ian west/Alamy; 10.01 © age fotostock/SuperStock; 11.02 © Roman Milert – Fotolia; 12.03 © Gusto Images/Science Photo Library; 13.01 © David Meggitt; 13.02 © Adrian Sherratt/ Alamy; 14.01 © Poster courtesy of Every Disabled Child Matters (EDCM); 14.02 © Andrew Callaghan; 14.03 © 2010 Photononstop/SuperStock; 14.04 © Jaren Wicklund – Fotolia; 15.01 © UpperCut Images/Alamy; 15.02 © Andrew Callaghan; 15.03 © Justin O'Hanlon; 16.01 © Andrew Callaghan; 16.02 © Andrew Callaghan; 17.01 © Andrew Callaghan; 17.02 © David Meggitt; 17.03 © Courtesy Booktrust, used with permission; 17.04 © Andrew Callaghan; 17.05 © Andrew Callaghan; 18.01 © Justin O'Hanlon; 18.02 © Andrew Callaghan; 18.03 © Andrew Callaghan; 18.04 © Justin O'Hanlon; 18.05 © Justin O'Hanlon; 18.06 © Justin O'Hanlon; 18.07 © Justin O'Hanlon; 18.08 © Justin O'Hanlon; 18.09 © Justin O'Hanlon; 18.10 © Andrew Callaghan; 18.11 © Andrew Callaghan.

Section 1 and Section 2 header photos © Justin O'Hanlon.

Figures 9.04 (Just Eat More portion poster) and 9.05 (The eatwell plate) © Crown copyright material as reproduced with the permission of the Controller of HMSO and the Queen's Printer for Scotland.

Illustrations by Barking Dog Art (Figures 1.04, 7.02, 11.04, 11.05, 11.06, 12.01, 12.02, 12.05), Oxford Designers and Illustrators and Kate Nardoni/Cactus Design and Illustration.

Figure 12.04 © Image courtesy of the Meningitis Trust.

SECTION 1

Mandatory Units

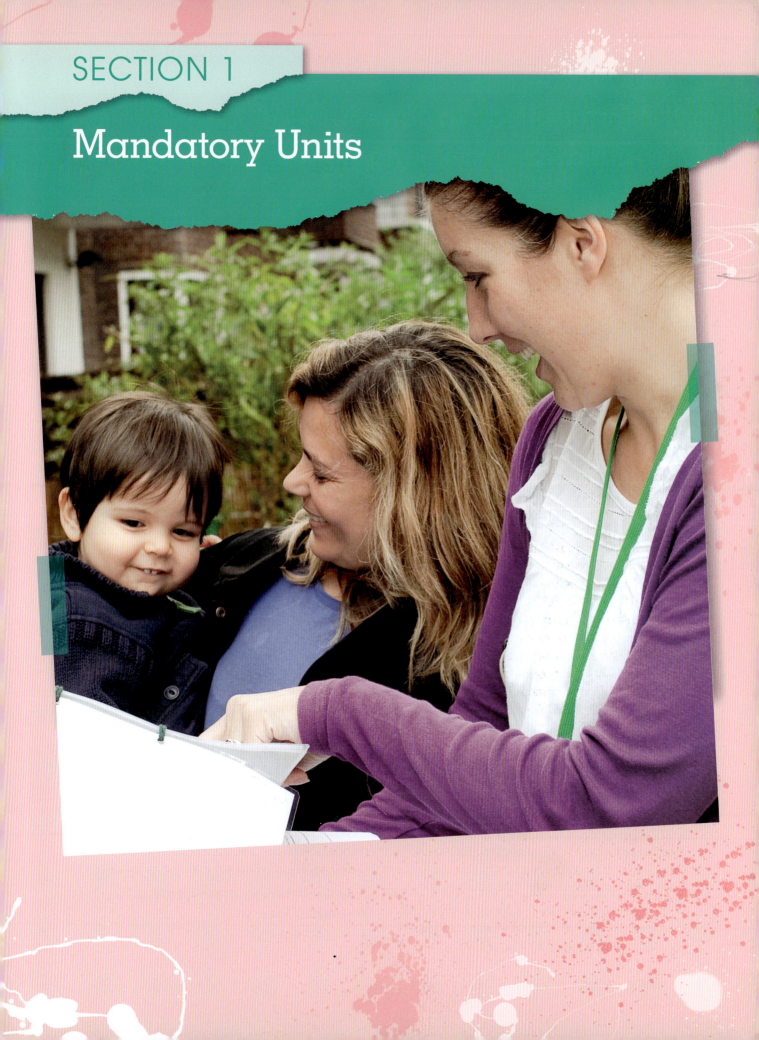

1 Introduction to communication in children and young people's settings: Unit SHC 21

Effective communication is the cornerstone of work in all settings with children and young people. Being able to communicate well helps in forming positive relationships, with colleagues, children and young people and their families.

Learning outcomes

By the end of this chapter you will:

1. Understand why communication is important in the work setting.
2. Be able to meet the communication and language needs, wishes and preferences of individuals.
3. Be able to reduce barriers to communication.
4. Be able to apply principles and practices relating to confidentiality at work.

The importance of communication in the work setting

When working in a Children and Young People's setting you need to be able to communicate effectively with a wide range of other people, such as:

- children and young people
- their parents, families and carers
- colleagues and managers
- different professionals, such as teachers, doctors, nurses and social workers.

These may be **one-to-one** interactions, with a child, young person, parent or carer, or **group** interactions, such as activities with children, case conferences, and staff meetings.

Good communication involves **listening, questioning, understanding** and **responding**.

It is important to remember that there is more to communication than the words being spoken. In fact it is thought that more than 70 per cent of messages are conveyed in **non-verbal** ways. Communication also involves:

- facial expressions
- body language (posture and actions or gestures), which helps to convey meaning
- tone of voice (this can alter the meaning of what has been said; for example, the tone used by someone to say our name instantly tells us whether we are in trouble, being appealed to or just having our attention drawn)
- pauses
- taking turns.

When communicating, it is also important to:

- take account of culture and context, for example where English is an additional language
- build a rapport by showing understanding, respect and honesty.

Reasons why people communicate in work settings

The main reasons why people communicate in work settings are given below, with examples:

1 **To promote relationships and to offer support:** a social worker arranges regular contact with a family 'in need' and builds up a mutual system of support.

2 **To maintain relationships:** a child's key person will ensure that he or she gets to know the child and her family in order to build and maintain a trusting relationship.

3 **To exchange information:** a patient visiting a GP will supply the doctor with information about their symptoms. They will in turn receive information that will enable them to understand more about their medical problem.

4 **To negotiate and liaise with others:** a nursery manager will liaise with other professionals and with parent groups and committees to discuss policies and procedures.

5 **To express needs and feelings:** children and young people should be given opportunities to express themselves freely and to know that adults will acknowledge them and meet their needs.

6 **To develop learning:** children and young people need to receive feedback from practitioners about progress made.

Developing effective communication skills

The most important skills that will improve communication are those of being approachable and an 'effective listener'. Some people are easy to talk to, while others seem to put up a barrier. It is possible to learn the skills that will improve your ability to communicate with other people. These skills are shown in the photo below.

Figure 1.01

Respect for other people's beliefs and views

We all have different ideas about how we conduct our lives. It is inevitable that each practitioner will encounter many people with vastly different backgrounds, beliefs and outlooks on life. Regardless of your own views, you should always respect the views of others. This involves:

- not passing judgement on the way in which other people live
- avoiding stereotyping people on the basis of age, gender, ethnicity or colour
- not trying to impose your views on others.

Only if people feel that their individual values and beliefs are respected will they develop the confidence to express themselves freely and to make choices.

How effective communication affects all aspects of your work

Children and young people will learn to trust and respect you if you communicate effectively with them. You will also develop a better relationship with colleagues, parents and other adults if your communication skills are effective. The following communication skills are all important to the way in which you work with children and young people:

Showing interest in the individual

It is vital to try to establish a rapport with children and young people, their parents and carers, and with work colleagues. This can be achieved by:

- being patient and showing that you have time to listen to their views
- listening carefully to them
- remembering their names, likes, dislikes and personal preferences
- asking relevant questions and not suddenly changing the subject

Case Study   A communication problem

Sumayah is 24 months old, and new to the nursery. Her family are originally from Pakistan but she was born in the UK. Sumayah's father is fluent in English and her mother has a good understanding but sometimes finds it difficult to express what she wants to say. Susie is Sumayah's key person. She gets on well with the family, and appears to have a positive relationship with Sumayah, who has been very happy attending nursery three days a week. However, her colleague, Richard, is uncomfortable when one day Susie makes reference to Sumayah's mum as being 'a Paki' in general conversation.

Later in the same month, Sumayah is given a sausage by accident at lunchtime, despite the fact that her family is Muslim and do not eat pork. The staff on duty notice the error too late and feel guilty. Richard asks Susie if they should fill out an incident form before telling the family. Susie says, 'Oh, I wasn't even going to tell Sumayah's mum! She hardly understands anything anyway, and Sumayah enjoyed that sausage. Anyway, if they're going to live in this country, they have to expect that their children will become English.' Richard is left feeling uncomfortable with concealing information from Sumayah's mum and does not know what to do.

1 What do you think Richard should do?

2 What are the main issues arising from this scenario which need to be addressed?

3 Susie finds it difficult to communicate with Sumayah's mum. How might this impact on the level of care which Sumayah receives? How can Susie be supported to improve communication?

- using **body language** effectively

Using appropriate body language

How you sit and how you use gestures will make a great difference to your interactions with others. To put someone more at ease, adopt an **open posture**: sit with your arms apart, hands open, legs uncrossed and slightly apart, leaning forward – with your body fully facing the other person. This shows that you are ready to communicate and that you are interested in what the other person has to say.

Key term

Body language – Body language is also known as **non-verbal communication**. It includes facial expressions, eye contact, tone of voice, body posture and motions, and positioning within groups. It may also include the way we wear our clothes or the silence we maintain.

Active listening

On the whole we tend not to listen to others as well as we could. Research shows that people tend to listen in 30-second spurts before losing attention. Sometimes we only hear items that we are interested in and do not attend to others. If we are bored and if we dislike the speaker's personality, mannerisms, accent or appearance, we may 'switch off' and follow more interesting thoughts of our own.

Active listening, the listening required in any relationship with children and young people, calls for concentration; it is hard work and tiring. The following skills are important for active listening:

1. **Eye contact:** Maintaining eye contact lets a person know you are listening and that you are interested in the conversation. It is difficult for a person not to pay attention when you make good eye contact. However, it is important to be aware that in certain cultures, mutual eye contact is considered disrespectful.

2. **Posture:** The listener should keep the body and hands neat and relaxed. An occasional nod acts as positive reinforcement; it can encourage the other person when he or she is saying something useful or helpful.

3. **Language:** Sensitive use of certain key words can draw out a lot of basic information. For example: a parent tells you that they are worried because their child refuses to eat properly at home. You could try using open-ended questions – asking: *What* is the problem? *When* did it start? *Who* could help? *Where* should we begin to sort it out? *How* have you managed so far?

Showing warmth

Showing warmth in everyday practice is very important. The person may have personal information to reveal and may well decide not to do so if the practitioner is in any way cold and rejecting. Warmth may be shown **non-verbally** by:

- a warm smile (facial expression)
- open welcoming gestures
- a friendly tone of voice
- a confident manner
- your general appearance.

Showing understanding

A practitioner conveys understanding through empathy, acceptance and a non-judgemental attitude. These are all-important values that underpin all aspects of caring for children and young people.

Understanding is also shown when the practitioner shows knowledge and acceptance of the particular physical, intellectual and social needs of the individual.

Figure 1.02 It is important to convey warmth and understanding when communicating with children

Showing sincerity

Warmth, understanding and sincerity are all shown primarily by the use of **eye contact**, which shows interest and attention. Remember, however, that in certain cultures, the use of eye contact is considered disrespectful. Reassuring the person that all information is strictly confidential also shows sincerity.

Showing the positive value of others

Healthy personal development occurs through forming relationships that provide us with affection, love or respect from others. Such positive regard is **unconditional**: it does not matter how we behave, we are still loved just for being ourselves. If we *do* receive unconditional positive regard then we would also give ourselves unconditional positive regard; in other words, we will have high **self-esteem** or self-worth. If our parents or carers love us *conditionally*, perhaps only showing affection when we get good grades at school, we will constantly seek approval from others as we grow into adulthood.

Showing the positive value of others may be done by using the following non-verbal signals:

- smiling
- calm movements
- listening skills
- eye contact
- open gestures.

Both verbally and non-verbally, the positive value of others may be shown by demonstrating:

- empathy
- freedom from any type of stereotyping or discrimination
- warmth, understanding and sincerity
- assurance of confidentiality, with its boundaries explained
- acceptance and a non-judgemental attitude
- respect for the individual.

Observing the reactions of individuals

You need to be able to observe and to interpret the reactions of those with whom you are communicating. This includes noticing their facial expressions, their body language – and also what the individual is *not* saying. Certain expressions and reactions may have different meanings in different cultures and situations. Nodding one's head means 'Yes' and reflects agreement in most parts of the world – but there are exceptions. In parts of India, for example, nodding the head can actually mean 'No'.

 **Progress check**

Observing an individual's reactions

- Be aware that facial expressions and gestures can have different meanings in different cultures.
- Non-verbal communication can convey just as much as – sometimes more than – verbal communication.
- Some people avoid eye contact if they disagree with you. Others may regard you more intensely because they are having difficulty in understanding you or because they do not want to show their feelings.
- Body posture can indicate an individual's true feelings. For example, a closed posture – arms folded tightly over the chest – can indicate tension or anger. An open posture – sitting with shoulders back in a relaxed posture – indicates self-confidence.

Physical touch is more acceptable in some cultures than others. You need to be sensitive to the ways in which individuals use touch and respond appropriately.

Written communication

Most early years settings have a parent's board where notices are displayed to give information about a wide variety of matters relating to the setting's policies, procedures and activities. There are many occasions when you may need to provide written information about children in your care. For example, you may need to complete a chart in the Baby Room of a nursery to detail an individual child's feeding and sleeping patterns. If a child or young person has an accident in the setting, you will need to record the details in the Accident Report Book.

Meeting the communication and language needs, wishes and preferences of individuals

The way in which we communicate with others should always take account of each individual's needs, wishes and preferences. For example, parents and carers may express a preference to be addressed by their full title, or they may ask to be addressed by their first name.

Empathetic listening

Empathy means being able to 'project' yourself into the other person's situation and experience, in order to understand them as fully as possible. Practitioners need to be able to listen with sympathy and understanding, and give support at the appropriate time. They also need to be able to encourage people who lack confidence that other people will value what they say.

For more information on how to communicate well with children and young people, see p 292, Chapter 17, Unit OP 2.15: Contribute to the support of children's communication, language and literacy.

Communicating with parents and carers

You will find that there are many occasions when you are responsible for passing information clearly to parents and carers. But parents will want to talk, as well as listen, to you. You will need to develop listening skills. Try to set a particular time for parents and carers so that they do not take your attention when you are involved with the children. For some parents this can be very difficult to arrange, especially if they are working.

Guidelines: How to communicate well with parents and carers

- Maintaining eye contact helps you to give your full attention.
- Remember that your body language shows how you really feel.
- Try not to interrupt when someone is talking to you. Nod and smile instead.
- Every so often, summarise the main points of a discussion, so that you are both clear about what has been said.
- If you do not know the answer to a parent's question, say so, and tell them that you will find out. Do not then forget to do this!
- Remember that different cultures have different traditions. Touching and certain gestures might be seen as insulting by some parents and carers, so be careful.
- If the parent speaks a different language from you, use photographs and visual aids. Talk slowly and clearly.
- If the parent has a hearing impairment, use sign language or visual aids.
- When you are talking together, bear in mind whether this is the parent's first child or whether they also have older children.
- If the parent has a disability, make sure that when you sit together you are at the same level.
- Occasionally, parents might become upset and will shout at you. If this happens, do not shout back. You should speak quietly and calmly, showing them that you are listening to them.
- Never gossip or break confidences.

Barriers to communication

When communications are difficult, it is often because of 'barriers' of one kind or another. The first step in overcoming such barriers is to identify them.

Identifying barriers
The physical environment

This may prove a barrier to communication. The design of a building, lack of access for people who use wheelchairs, noise and lack of privacy are all factors that can prevent effective communication. For example, too much background noise can prevent a message from being fully understood. There may be too many people talking at the same time or there may be a lack of privacy.

Disability and impairment

Practitioners need to be trained to recognise the influence of hearing impairment, limited mobility, visual and verbal impairments and conditions such as autism that affect the child's ability to communicate. For example, a child may have a physical impairment such as cleft palate and harelip, or speak with a stammer or stutter.

An additional language

Children and young people's home language must be valued. Adults should recognise that these children and young people whose home language is different from that used in the setting are, most likely, competent communicators at home and need support to develop an additional vocabulary which may only apply in the setting.

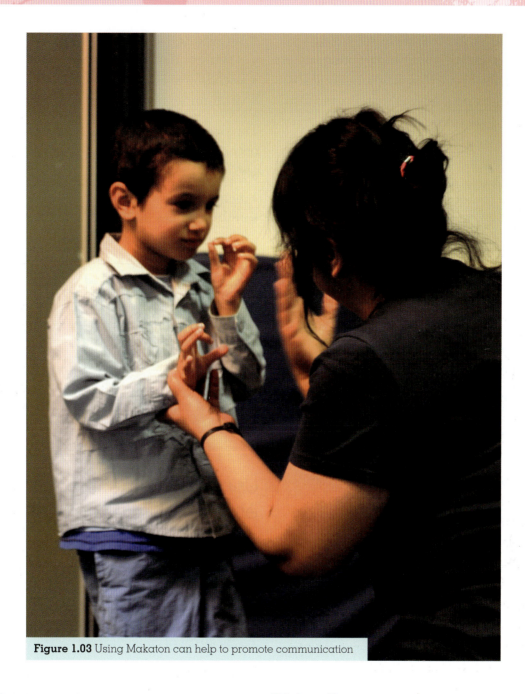

Figure 1.03 Using Makaton can help to promote communication

Attitudes

If practitioners are unaware of the stereotypes and prejudices they hold in their own minds, these will unconsciously act as a barrier to communication. For example, stereotyped thinking can deflect you from seeing someone as an individual with particular life experiences and interests, and so prevent effective communication.

Distractions

A continuous noise outside an interview room is a distraction, but interaction between two people will be inhibited far more by interruptions.

For example: Suppose a young person is telling their personal story to a practitioner when the phone rings or there is a knock at the door. The practitioner takes their attention from the young person and talks for some minutes to the person on the telephone, or the person at the door, about another matter entirely. The young person will feel devalued, that their key communication is unimportant, and therefore that *they* are also unimportant. The young person may feel angry, and when the practitioner at last turns back, might have decided not to reveal any more about themselves. Practitioner/young person communication will have broken down. Any interruption should therefore be dealt with briefly, with the practitioner making it clear to the young person that their problems are the current priority.

Dominating the conversation

Practitioners are there to listen and should put their own concerns to one side. However, they may perhaps unintentionally dominate the conversation in any of three ways:

1 Making the young person's story his or her own story: 'Oh, I'm sorry to hear that happened to you. My own sister/niece/uncle had a similar experience . . .'
2 By assuming responsibility for working out the problem and giving the young person only a minor role. An extreme example would be to set out a treatment or care plan, and then impose it on the young person.
3 By trying to scrutinise every area of the child or young person's life, regardless of the actual service the child or young person may need.

Blocking the other's contribution

During one-to-one, face-to-face interaction, one participant may block communication in a number of ways – both verbally and non-verbally. The practitioner may block the communication of the other person in many *non-verbal* ways, for example:

- a look of boredom
- a yawn

- the slightest expression of disgust
- a smile at the wrong time
- withdrawal of eye contact, turning away
- drumming the fingers or fidgeting.

The practitioner may block the communication of the client *verbally* by, for example:

- changing the subject
- being critical
- misunderstanding
- joking at the client's expense.

Reflective practice: Recognising barriers to communication

Think about a situation in which you have found communication unsatisfactory. Why do you think this occurred? Try to identify any possible barriers and think how you could improve your own communication skills.

Using support or services to enable more effective communication

In order to promote effective communication, practitioners need to know when to call in help from outside and whom to approach when more specialist expertise and help are needed. Support services include:

- **specialist teachers** for children who are learning English as an additional language
- **translation and interpretation services**: these may be provided by local authorities for people who do not speak English, who are blind, who have a visual impairment, or who are deaf or have a hearing impairment
- **advocacy services**: an advocate's role is to represent the wishes and feelings of children and young people to the courts and to provide a view of the child's best interests

- **speech and language therapists:** speech and language therapists assess and treat speech, language and communication problems in people of all ages to enable them to communicate to the best of their ability
- **specific 'sign' languages** – such as Makaton, Signalong and Picture Exchange Communication System (PECS).

Makaton

The Makaton vocabulary is a list of over 400 items with corresponding signs and symbols, with an additional resource vocabulary for the UK National Curriculum. The signs are based on British Sign Language (BSL), but are used to support spoken English. The Makaton Project publishes a book of illustrations of the Makaton vocabulary. Most signs rely on movement as well as position, so you cannot completely learn the signs from the illustrations. Also, in many signs facial expression is important.

If a child at a school or nursery is learning Makaton, the parents or carers should be invited to learn too. The Makaton Project will support schools and parents in this, as they know that everyone involved with the child must use the same signs.

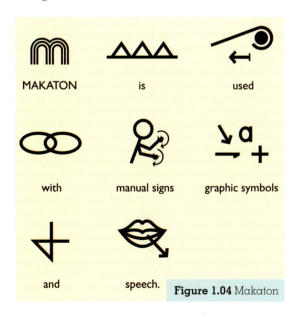

Figure 1.04 Makaton

Signalong

Signalong is a sign-supporting system that is also based on British Sign Language; it is designed to help children and adults with communication difficulties (mostly associated with learning disabilities) and is user-friendly for easy access. The Signalong Group has researched and published the widest range of signs in Britain.

Picture Exchange Communication System (PECS)

PECS begins with teaching children to exchange a picture of an object that they want with a teacher, who immediately gives it to them. For example, if they want a drink, they will give a picture of 'drink' to an adult, who then directly hands them a drink. Verbal prompts are not used; this encourages spontaneity and avoids children being dependent on the prompts. The system goes on to teach recognition of symbols and how to construct simple 'sentences'. Ideas for teaching language structures such as asking and answering questions are also incorporated. It has been reported that both pre-school and older children have begun to develop speech when using PECS. The system is often used as a communication aid for children and adults who have an autistic spectrum disorder.

Research Activity

Different ways of communicating with children

Find out more about methods of communicating with children – such as Makaton, Signalong and PECS. (See useful websites on p 15.)

The importance of effective communication

1. Why is communication so important when working with children and young people?

2. What is meant by non-verbal communication or body language?

3. Why is it important to be aware of the reactions of others when we are communicating with them?

Principles and practices relating to confidentiality at work

The importance of confidentiality

Confidentiality is very important when working in settings with children and young people. Confidentiality is respect for the privacy of any information about a child and his or her family. You will be entrusted with personal information about children and their families, and it is important that you do not abuse this trust. The giving or receiving of sensitive information should be subject to a careful consideration of the needs of the children and their families – for example, a child who is in need of protection has overriding needs which require that all relevant information be given to all the appropriate agencies, such as social workers or doctors.

Key term

Confidentiality – The preservation of secret (or privileged) information concerning children and their families that is disclosed in the professional relationship.

Sharing information

Some information *does* have to be shared, but only with your line manager. For example, if you suspect there may be a child or young person protection issue, this should be shared with your line manager in strictest confidence. Parents and carers need to be aware of this policy from the outset of your partnership so that they understand that, although they may tell you things in confidence, you may have to share the information with your line manager. It is not fair to encourage parents or carers to talk about confidential things with you unless they first understand this.

Some information has to be shared with the whole staff team, such as information about diet, allergy, and if the child or young person is being collected from the setting by someone else. Make sure that children, young people, parents and carers are clear about the sort of information that *cannot* be confidential.

Confidentiality policies

Settings are expected to draw up their own policies on confidentiality. The policy should take into account the Human Rights Act, the Freedom of Information Act and the Data Protection Act. The Human Rights Act protects a person's right to respect for their 'private and family life, home and correspondence', unless this is overridden by the 'public interest'.

The Children Act 2004

If a request for information is received from a professional or agency, you have a duty to disclose confidential information if:

- there are any perceived risks to a child
- the information given would allow appropriate help and services or action to reduce risk to a child.

Progress check

Your role in maintaining confidentiality

Children, young people and their parents and carers need to feel confident of the following points:

- You will not interfere in their private lives, and that any information you are privileged to hold will not become a source of gossip. Breaches of confidentiality can occur when you are travelling on public transport, for example, and discussing the events of your day. Always remember that using the names of children or young people in your care can cause a serious breach of confidentiality if overheard by a friend or relative of the family.
- You will not write anything down about a child that you would feel concerned about showing their parents or carers.
- You understand when the safety or health needs of the child override the need for confidentiality. Parents need to be reassured that you will always put the safety and wellbeing of each child before any other considerations.

In many instances you will be working under the supervision of others and it is likely that parents will pass confidential information directly to a more senior staff member. However, there may be occasions on which *you* are given information and asked to pass it on, or you may hear or be told confidential information in the course of the daily routine. You may be entrusted with personal information about children, young people, parents and staff, either directly (being told or being given written information) or indirectly (hearing staffroom discussions, parental comments or children's conversations) and it is important that you do not repeat any of it at home or to friends. The incidents may be discussed in your teaching sessions among your learner group but you should not identify those concerned and it must be agreed that they are not talked about beyond the group.

The Data Protection Act 1998

Anyone who keeps personal records and data, whether on computer or on paper, should comply with this Act. The purpose for keeping the data should be clear to service users. Information about a child or young person should also be accessible to his or her parent or

Case Study   Lisa

Lisa is a learner on the CACHE Level 2 course and her first placement is in a private nursery. She enjoys most of the work at the nursery, but is unsure how to react when children show behaviour which is unacceptable in the setting – such as name-calling, biting and pulling the hair of other children. Her supervisor has arranged to hold a special evening session on problem behaviour and has encouraged Lisa to attend if she can.

Lisa usually catches the same bus as a fellow learner, Natasha, who is working at a nearby primary school. One day, she pours out all her pent-up feelings of frustration to her on their journey home. She is particularly anxious about Abigail, a three-year-old child who has started biting the other children in her group, and tells Natasha that Abigail has a young, inexperienced mother whose partner has recently left her for another woman. She says she feels sorry for the mother, but that there's no excuse, in her mind, for any child to bite another child, and she thinks the mother is to blame.

Also on the bus that afternoon, sitting directly behind Lisa and Natasha, was Abigail's auntie. She realises that they are talking about her niece, and is very upset. She does not say anything to Lisa, but decides to phone the nursery manager to complain when she gets home. When Lisa arrives at the nursery the following day, she is called in to see her supervisor about the incident and soon realises that she has made a dreadful mistake.

1 Which fundamental principle has Lisa ignored by her behaviour on the bus?

2 Give three examples of information that Lisa spoke about to Natasha.

Case Study   Lisa (cont.)

3 Would the situation be any different if Lisa and Natasha were the only people on the bus, and if so, how?

carer and shared with them. It is not necessary to do this 'on demand'; a convenient time to be able to discuss the information can be arranged.

Information should not be kept for longer than necessary, though accident and incident records need to be kept in case they are required for reference at some time in the future. Records must also be stored securely.

What does personal data cover?

Personal data covers both facts and opinions about a living individual. It covers:

- 'Ordinary personal data' – name, address and telephone number
- 'Sensitive personal data' – relating to racial or ethnic origin, political opinions, religious beliefs, trades union membership, health, sex life and criminal convictions.

Personal data can be held in the following formats:

- computer files, including word-processor, database and spreadsheet files
- paper files
- microfiche, CCTV pictures, audio.

In Practice

Confidentiality

Find out about your setting's confidentiality policy. What sort of personal information does your setting hold with the permission of parents, guardians and carers? What sort of records are *you* expected to keep, and how are they kept accurate and secure?

A breach of confidentiality

This week a lunchtime supervisor at a village primary school was sacked for telling a child's parents that she was sorry their daughter had been attacked in the playground at school. The dinner lady had found a seven-year-old girl tied up by her wrists and ankles, surrounded by four boys, having been whipped with a skipping rope across her legs. The dinner lady had rescued the child and taken the boys to the head teacher. That night she bumped into the parents, who were friends of hers, and offered her sympathy. It instantly became clear that the parents had not been told the story by the school. Their daughter had arrived home traumatised and refusing to talk about what happened, with a note saying only that she had been 'hurt in a skipping-rope incident'. As soon as the school discovered that the dinner lady had told the parents the truth, she was first suspended for several months, and then sacked by the governors for 'breaching pupil confidentiality'.

(Story adapted from the *Guardian*, 24 September 2009)

This news report caused a fresh debate over the complex issue of confidentiality. The dinner lady had not revealed to the parents the names of the children involved in the incident, but was deemed to have breached confidentiality as she had not followed the correct procedure for reporting what she had witnessed.

1. Do you agree with the school governors that the dinner lady had breached confidentiality?
2. What should you do if you witness an incident of bullying in the playground?

How and when to seek advice about confidentiality

Confidential information received by you should not be disclosed unless required by law or to protect the interests or welfare of the child. Always report any concerns directly to your supervisor, teacher or line manager.

Useful resources and websites

www.makaton.org	**Makaton** was developed to help people with learning disability to communicate. It is now widely used with a variety of children with communication difficulties.
www.nyas.net	The **National Youth Advocacy Service** (NYAS) is a UK charity providing children's rights and socio-legal services. It offers information, advice, advocacy and legal representation to children and young people up to the age of 25, through a network of advocates throughout England and Wales.
www.pecs.org.uk	**Picture Exchange Communication** (PECS) uses functional and practical interventions to teach individuals how to communicate, function independently, and be successful in their schools, homes, places of employment and the community.
www.signalong.org.uk	**Signalong** empowers children and adults with impaired communication to understand and express their needs, choices and desires by providing vocabulary for life and learning.

2 Introduction to personal development in children and young people's settings: Unit SHC 22

This Unit will help you to improve your practice by looking at ways of improving your knowledge, skills and understanding. You need to know how to agree a personal development plan, which involves reviewing your progress and making decisions about training and professional development. You will learn the importance of using reflection and feedback in your practice, and how to ensure that you work in accordance with the standards and regulations that apply in your setting.

Learning outcomes

By the end of this chapter you will:

1. Understand what is required for competence in own work role.
2. Be able to reflect on own work activities.
3. Be able to agree a personal development plan.
4. Be able to develop knowledge, skills and understanding.

Competence in your own work role

Your duties and responsibilities

The supervisor, line manager, teacher, parent or carer will have certain expectations about your role, and your responsibilities should be detailed in your job contract. In place of a job contract, learners may be issued with a learner or student job description and guidelines on what to expect from their placement.

As a practitioner, you need to carry out all your duties willingly and to be answerable (or accountable) to others for your work. You need to know about the **lines of reporting** within a work setting and how to find out about your own particular responsibilities. If you are unsure what is expected of you – or if you do not feel confident in carrying out a particular task – then you should ask your line manager or your immediate supervisor for guidance.

Key term

Line of reporting – A vertical route in a hierarchy made up of individuals who report to or are responsible to the next most senior person.

Your duties and responsibilities will vary, depending on what sort of setting you are working in.

Skills required when working with children and young people

Working with children and young people can be physically and emotionally demanding, but also very rewarding. All children and young people should be treated with respect and dignity and their needs must be considered as paramount. This means working within the guidelines of an equal opportunities code of practice, and not allowing any personal preferences or prejudices to influence the way in which you treat children or young people.

There are many skills involved in working with and caring for children and young people that all adults need. These include:

- experience and the support to reflect and learn from experience
- confidence and the ability to respond in the best possible way to the individual child or young person
- really knowing about the child or young person, trusting that knowledge and the judgements that are based on this
- being prepared to learn from the child – for example, by listening to what a child tells you and observing what they do.

Working as part of a team

To meet the needs of all the children and young people, the staff members must work effectively together as a team. The roles and responsibilities of individual team members will depend on the organisation of the work setting. In your role as a learner you will be supporting the work of others. You will usually work under the direction (or sometimes supervision) of a manager or teacher, depending on the setting. There may also be professionals from other disciplines (medicine, social services, dentistry, etc.) who are involved with the families and children or young people you work with. A special school or nursery that cares for children with physical disabilities will have a **multidisciplinary team**; this may include teachers, early years practitioners and assistants, trained special care assistants, physiotherapists, paediatricians and, possibly, social workers.

Effective teamwork is vital in such settings to ensure that:

- everyone knows their individual roles and responsibilities
- parents and primary carers know which team member can deal with any specific concerns.

Induction to your new job

Everyone in the workforce should have an **induction** based on the Common Core of Skills and Knowledge for the Children's Workforce, tailored appropriately to their role and setting. Effective induction is central to good human resources practice and is the foundation of continuing professional development. It applies to practitioners:

- who are newly recruited
- who have been promoted
- whose existing role is changing.

It applies to those who work with children and young people as the main part of their job, and those who come into contact with children and young people for some of the time.

Figure 2.01 Achieving effective teamwork

Key term

Induction – Induction is the process of welcoming new staff members into the workplace and providing them with the information they need to settle into their new role.

Remember – nobody will expect you to know everything at first. Colleagues are there to help you to get the most out of each placement and your trainer or tutor will discuss any concerns you may have. If you are unsure about any aspect of care, or how to speak with a parent, do not be afraid to ask your supervisor or tutor.

Standards underpinning work with children and young people

All early years settings are regulated and inspected and must comply with certain standards. National Standards set out certain principles and values in order to ensure that children and young people receive the best possible opportunity to thrive, develop and grow in the child care setting. Standards that you must be aware of include:

- Regulations, such as The Children Act 2004, The Health and Safety at Work Act, The Care Standards Act 2000 and The Data Protection Act.
- National Occupational Standards: These describe what an individual needs to do, know and understand in order to carry out a particular job role or function. They differ slightly in the four countries of the United Kingdom, where they are monitored by different inspectorates; Ofsted in England, HMIe in Scotland, Estyn in Wales and the Education and Training Inspectorate (ETI) in Northern Ireland.
- National Minimum Standards, such as the Early Years Foundation Stage (EYFS) welfare requirements.
- Codes of practice, policies and procedures relevant to each setting.

The Children Act 2004

The Children Act 2004 was introduced following high-profile enquiries into safeguarding children and young people. The Act's aims were to achieve positive outcomes for children and young people and their families by:

- improving and integrating children's services
- promoting early intervention
- providing strong leadership, and
- bringing together different professionals in multidisciplinary teams.

As this Act affects the way you should work with other professionals to benefit children and their families, it is important that you are aware of its main contents.

National Occupational Standards (NOS)

The NOS describe the values, knowledge, understanding, skills, attitudes and actions that are necessary to do a specific job. These descriptions are written as statements of competence. They enable a common language to be developed among professionals and improve understanding of the variety of tasks that are performed in the relevant occupations. National Occupational Standards are not training courses or programmes of study, but they do provide a foundation for training and form the basis of national qualifications, such as NVQs and SVQs.

Induction standards: The Children's Workforce Development Council (CWDC) induction standards set out what new workers should know, understand and be able to do within six months of starting work.

The Early Years Foundation Stage (EYFS) welfare requirements

The welfare requirements are designed to support providers in creating settings which are welcoming, safe and stimulating, and where children are able to enjoy learning through play, to grow in confidence and to fulfil their potential. Within this statutory framework, there are five welfare requirements that apply to all children and young people's settings:

- Safeguarding and promoting children's welfare
- Suitable people to look after children
- Suitable premises
- Suitable environment and equipment
- Organisation and documentation.

These standards are embedded as principles in the course you are undertaking. As you will be among the most important adults in the children or young people's lives, it is your responsibility to apply them in your everyday practice.

In Practice

Working to meet required standards

Find out about the following as they apply in your home country:

- ❏ Health and Safety legislation
- ❏ The Child Care Act 2004
- ❏ The National Occupational Standards.

Ensuring that personal attitudes or beliefs do not obstruct the quality of your work

Personal attitudes and beliefs

Our beliefs, values and attitudes towards other people develop from early childhood. The way in which we are brought up and the behaviour we see around us will help us to form opinions and to make choices about every aspect of our lives. Children and young people learn moral values by example and by imitation. If a child is made to feel secure and loved within their family, they will develop confidence and self-esteem and find it easier to make close relationships with others. Children whose early life involves unhappy or very weak relationships with others often find it difficult to make close, lasting relationships when they are older.

Attitudes are the opinions and ways of thinking that we have towards other people and their beliefs. These attitudes are shaped by our values. Examples of moral values are:

- truth
- correct conduct
- love
- non-violence
- peace
- justice.

Our attitudes towards others are based on our beliefs and feelings about the world. Negative attitudes towards others may result from assumptions about people and their way of life, which may be very different from our own. Travellers, for example, have often been discriminated against within care settings because of these differences.

Exploring your attitudes and values

Discuss the following moral questions:

1. Should women go out to work when they have young children?
2. Should the armed forces accept gay men and women into their ranks?
3. Should it be against the law to smack a child? Should childminders and teachers have the right to smack a child if the parents consent?
4. Should gay couples (male or female) be allowed to adopt a child?
5. Should men take an equal share with women in bringing up their children?

In pairs, discuss each question in turn, making brief notes on the arguments for and against each question. Then, in the whole group, consider how each answer could affect your attitudes towards parents and children in the work setting.

It is not the task of practitioners to try to change the values and attitudes of others, but we should be prepared to challenge others – or to refer to a superior – if their behaviour shows discrimination. What is most important is that we act as positive role models through our work with children and young people, so that they can learn to imitate our behaviour and express positive attitudes towards others.

The following poem by Dorothy Law Nolte describes the effect our values have on children's development:

Children learn what they live

- If children live with criticism, they learn to condemn.
- If children live with hostility, they learn to fight.
- If children live with ridicule, they learn to be shy.
- If children live with shame, they learn to feel guilty.
- If children live with encouragement, they learn confidence.
- If children live with tolerance, they learn to be patient.
- If children live with praise, they learn to appreciate.
- If children live with acceptance, they learn to love.
- If children live with approval, they learn to like themselves.
- If children live with honesty, they learn truthfulness.
- If children live with fairness, they learn justice.
- If children live with kindness and consideration, they learn respect.
- If children live with security, they learn to have faith in themselves and others.

Figure 2.02 If children live with kindness and consideration, they learn respect

Activity

Exploring moral values

Working in pairs or small groups, identify and list five moral values within the poem above, and for each value, discuss how it can be promoted within the care and education setting. (One example could be the value of appreciation: by praising children every time they have achieved something, however small that thing may be, you are demonstrating your appreciation for them as individuals and promoting their self-esteem.)

Ensuring that personal attitudes do not obstruct the quality of work

An important part of your personal development is self-awareness. Self-awareness means:

- knowing who you are and what you enjoy doing
- being able to recognise your skills, strengths and weaknesses
- being able to recognise your effect on other people.

Key areas for self-awareness include our personality traits, personal values, habits and emotions. Self-awareness helps you to exploit your strengths and cope with your weaknesses. The process of being self-aware can be uncomfortable when you realise that something you have done or said has had a negative impact on someone else. However, unless we face such self-awareness we can never really develop and improve our practice. What is important here is that you have a network of colleagues that you can call upon for support and guidance should you require it.

Self-awareness is also crucial for developing effective interpersonal skills and building effective relationships with children or young people and their families. Additionally, being self-aware allows you to identify your own learning needs and the ways in which those learning needs can be met – and then it is involved in your evaluation of whether those needs have been met.

Being non-judgemental

It is very important to be non-judgemental. It is easy to criticise others and to believe that you would approach things in a better way. However, children, young people and their parents and carers can only learn to trust you if they know that you are not judging their actions.

Reflect on your own work activities

You should get used to reviewing and reflecting on your experiences as part of your everyday learning. In this way, every experience – whether positive or negative – will contribute to your development and personal growth. Ways to reflect include:

- making a record of your thoughts and reflections, to help you to keep track of your ideas and see how far they have developed over a period of time
- working out what you have achieved and what you still need to work on
- recording your thoughts on any difficulties or challenges you are facing
- talking things through with another person, such as another learner or a trusted friend
- asking yourself questions about what you did and thinking about how you could have done it better
- using evidence to support or evaluate any decision – for example, observations or lecture notes.

It is a good idea to develop the habit of *recording* your reflections. This will help you to extend your skills in reflective practice.

Assessing how well your own knowledge, skills and understanding meet standards

Reflecting on your practice helps you to consider how far your own knowledge, skills and understanding meet the standards expected and to identify any gaps. You also need to be able to evaluate your progress.

Self-evaluation

The Self-Evaluation Form (SEF) that settings are required to complete prior to their Ofsted inspection was discontinued in 2010 for maintained schools and nurseries. However, it remains a very useful reflective practice tool for all practitioners. The SEF can be used by practitioners to reflect – in a structured way – about how they:

- implement the themes of the Early Years Foundation Stage framework: A Unique Child, Positive Relationships, Enabling Environment and Learning and Development.
- are guided by the policies and procedures in their setting
- ensure equality of opportunity for all children and young people
- support children with special educational needs and/or disabilities
- seek out the views of all those who use their setting and how they use these views to improve the quality of the provision to meet the children's individual needs.

Appraisals

Appraisals provide an opportunity for you to assess whether you meet required standards and also to identify your own strengths and weaknesses and plan for improvement. Many settings use a Pre-appraisal Form to help

Progress check

Reflective practice

Using **reflective practice** will help you to review and evaluate your own practice. General and specific reflective questions will help to organise this evaluation – for example:

General questions:

- Was my contribution to the planning meeting or activity appropriate?
- Did I achieve my targets? If not, was it because the targets were unrealistic?
- What other methods could be used?
- How can I improve my practice?
- Who can I ask for advice and support?

Specific questions:

- How can I help a young person to make the transition from a pupil referral unit back to his school?
- What is making a child behave inappropriately at meal times?

managers to find out about the learner's experiences and so be better able to conduct an effective appraisal. A self-appraisal form will help you, the learner or employee, to:

- identify areas in your job description in which you feel you have done well
- identify any areas with which you feel less satisfied
- help you to identify areas in which performance could be improved
- support you in developing your skills, knowledge and expertise.

Reflecting on your own work activities

One of the most useful ways to reflect on your activities and experiences in the setting is to keep a Reflective Diary. Reflective Diaries are a personal record of your experiences throughout your placement and so it is important to use them to report thoughts, feelings and opinions rather than simply listing the factual events of the day. Only by reporting personal feelings following an event can experiences be built upon and improved. It is also important to use your Reflective Diary to record positive experiences and achievements as well as the not-so-positive ones.

Agree a personal development plan

A personal development plan will:

- help you to take responsibility for your own career and professional development
- motivate you to develop your own skills
- help you to be aware of your strengths and weaknesses
- help you to decide what training might be required to fulfil your future plans.

Sources of support

Support for your learning and development is very important and may be provided by people within your work setting and by outside agencies.

Before starting a new course of formal study or training, you should discuss the following issues with your manager or supervisor:

- Where is the course held? Is it easily accessible?
- Does the course meet your learning objectives?

In Practice

Keeping A Reflective Diary

Each person will have a different way of keeping a Reflective Diary, but certain factors need to be included. The diary should be written honestly and should provide a useful personal record and a prompt to your memory. It can be used to describe, to reflect on and to evaluate all aspects of your practice:

❑ *Activities that you have provided for children or young people*: Did they enjoy the activity? What went particularly well – or not so well? What would you do to improve the activity for next time?

❑ *Responding to behaviour of children and young people*: Recording your thoughts and feelings will help to build up a range of strategies that you have found effective when dealing with unacceptable or challenging behaviour. You often do not have the time to stand back and reflect when responding to unwanted behaviour as you may have to act swiftly to prevent any harm to children.

❑ *Relationships with colleagues:* How you have communicated with colleagues; the effectiveness of methods used to exchange information and any difficulties in your working relationships.

❑ *Interactions with parents and carers:* How you have communicated with parents and carers; how you exchange information with them and provide feedback about their child's day.

❑ *Teamwork*: Your contribution to the staff team and to staff meetings: Did you feel encouraged to speak up about any work issues?

- How will the course be funded?
- How much time will it take? Will you be able to take time out of work to attend? Will there still be time for you to study?

Agreeing your personal development plan

Your manager or supervisor should work with you to help you draw up your development plan. He or she should give you advice, time and support to draw up your plan – and then should ensure they are available to discuss any problems or ideas you may have.

Who should be involved

You are not expected to be solely responsible for agreeing your own development plan. Your supervisor or line manager, parents, carers and advocates may all help in listing performance targets and supporting you in your decisions about future development issues.

Contributing to your personal development plan

There are six main steps to creating a personal development plan:

1. *Think about your skills, strengths and weaknesses*: Before you can decide which areas you need to develop, you need to identify the skills you already have.
2. *Decide which areas you need to develop*: Think about what you need to do to become more competent in your present work role.
3. *Create the plan*: Think about how you can achieve your objectives, whether you need training, to shadow a colleague or take on a different role. This then should be given a timescale for the achievements of the objectives. Ensure you set yourself SMART targets (see below).
4. *Discuss your plan with others*: It is important to discuss your plan with colleagues, managers, etc., as they may offer advice and support or have suggestions from which you can gain experience or knowledge.
5. *Implement the plan*: If you have researched well and your plan is realistic, then your plan should be straightforward – although you may find that a course you were going to attend has changed dates, for example, and then you would need to change your plan and the timescale.
6. *Review your plan:* If you do not review your plan regularly it becomes irrelevant, you may find situations change and the goal you had set for yourself is no longer relevant. That's why it is important to review regularly so you can think about what you have achieved and what steps to take next.

Your learning targets should be SMART: Each member of a team needs to know exactly what is expected of them. These expectations are called targets or 'objectives'. The targets that are most likely to be achieved are those which are SMART.

Formal support

Training provided by private training companies, colleges and other organisations

Appraisals provided by your line manager, trainer or tutor

Internet e-learning opportunities

Informal support

Training provided in-house (within the setting)

Staff meetings

Discussions with members of the staff team

SMART targets

SMART is an **acronym for:**

Specific	They must be easy to understand and say exactly what you want to happen. Make sure you have thought clearly about what you need to learn or develop.
Measurable	Success can be measured by checking back carefully against the instructions that have been given. Consider how you will know whether you have achieved what you set out to achieve.
Achievable	The targets can be reached with reasonable effort in the time you are allowed.
Relevant	The targets must be appropriate, building on previous strengths and skills. Be realistic about how and when you can achieve things.
Time related	The targets have clearly set deadlines and are reviewed frequently. Timescales help to motivate, so give yourself a realistic timescale.

Progress check

Using SMART targets

Look at the following scenarios and see how SMART targets can help individuals and teams to plan and to achieve their objectives.

1. *Scenario 1*: Paula has been asked if she would organise a display for the nursery room. The only instructions she has been given are: 'Paula, can you put up a nice, colourful display in the nursery room, please?'
2. *Scenario 2*: At a different nursery, Mark has also been asked to organise a display. On Wednesday, he was given these instructions: 'Next Monday we need to create an interactive display for the nursery room. It will be on the theme of Autumn. We've already collected some pine cones and autumn leaves, and we also have some good posters, but I'd like you to plan what else we need and let me have a list of resources by tomorrow lunchtime.'

Develop knowledge, skills and understanding

The opportunities for learning when working with children and young people are endless. You will increase your knowledge and skills every day through interacting with children, young people and their carers or parents. It is important to take every opportunity to learn more – to increase your skills and understanding. For example, parents and carers will soon recognise when someone has learned about the common pattern of development in their child's age group. They will also appreciate when someone has taken the trouble to learn more about their child's particular condition or home background. You will also learn a lot from colleagues and from training opportunities and should always be willing to share any knowledge you have gained.

Activity

Using targets for personal and professional development

Write down in two or three sentences what you hope to achieve through your course, and how you think it will help you in the future.

- What do you want to be able to do, think, feel, understand or know?

- How would this learning be recognised by others?

- What are the steps you need to take to reach the end result?

Now write your Personal Plan and learning targets based on these ideas, using the notes above as a guide.

Accessing support to review your progress and achievements

Work with an appropriate person, such as your tutor or placement supervisor, to express your opinions and develop an individual plan that includes:

- **targets** that clearly show what you want to achieve in your learning, work or personal life, and how you will know if you have met these

- the **actions** you will take (action points) and dates for completing them (deadlines) to help you meet each target

- how to get the support you need, including who will review your progress and where and when this will take place.

Your **tutor or trainer** will help you to discuss your progress; he or she will enable you to reflect on *what* you learned, *how* you learned, and *what* has been successful or unsuccessful. You should also aim to:

- **identify the targets** you have met, by checking your plan to see if you have done what you set out to do

- **identify your achievements** by finding out what you need to do to improve your performance (the quality of your work, and the way you work)

- **use ways of learning** suggested by your tutor or supervisor, making changes when needed to improve your performance.

Learning from experience

Whenever you attempt a new activity with children or young people, you will be learning something new.

The benefits of reflection

Each of the Early Years Foundation Stage Principles into Practice cards has a constructive section on the back entitled 'Reflecting on Practice' which gives the sort of questions and issues practitioners should be considering.

The benefits of feedback

Using feedback to improve your practice

Feedback is structured information that one person offers to another about the impact of their actions or behaviour – in other words, how you are doing in your study or work role. It is vital to the success of most workplace tasks, and is an activity we engage in on a daily basis. Feedback should not be confused with **criticism**, which is often an unprepared reaction to people who are not behaving in the way you want them

Reflective practice: Reviewing your learning activities

You may be asked to plan an activity to implement in your work setting, such as a storytelling session using props or a painting activity. Choose **one** activity that you have carried out with a group of children and then record your answers to the following questions:

1. How suitable was the activity for the group of children?
2. How successful were you in **planning** the task? Did you consider the following factors: safety, space, children's ages and stage of development, supervision and availability of resources?
3. How did the children respond during the activity? Were you able to maintain their interest?
4. How might you improve the activity if you did it again? What would you do differently and why?
5. Write a short summary of the activity – perhaps using a format for Observations (see p 80) – and use your findings to help you prepare for the next activity.

to. Criticism can make the recipient feel undervalued or angry – both unproductive emotions.

The information you hear when receiving feedback from others may be new – and even surprising. You may react with strong emotion. Positive feedback is an offer of information, not a diagnosis of your character or potential, so you should not react angrily or take it personally.

Receiving feedback can:

- help you become aware of your progress – the positive and the negative, what is working and what is not
- give you some ideas to help you plan your own development, in order to reach your full potential
- give you a 'reality check' – you can compare how you think you are, with what other people tell you.

Feedback from a number of different people helps you to make a balanced decision about the information you are hearing. Apart from the feedback you receive through formal appraisals of your performance, you may receive other forms of feedback, such as:

- informal observations by colleagues, or by children and young people
- mentoring: a mentor supports you by modelling good practice and guiding you to look critically at your own practice and to decide how it can be improved
- questionnaires: these are useful in obtaining feedback from young people, parents and carers about the setting

Evaluating your own performance

Self-evaluation is important because it helps you to improve your own practice and to modify plans to meet the learning needs of the children and young people.

Guidelines for receiving feedback

1. **Ask questions**: state what you want feedback about. Be specific about what you want to know. Give the other person time to think about what they want to say.
2. **Listen**: listen attentively and do not interrupt. Ask for clarification if you are not sure that you have understood what you have heard. Try not to be defensive or to reject the information. You need to listen, but not necessarily to agree. Take notes of what is said.

3 **Check**: check what you have heard. Repeat back what the other person has said and ask for examples of what they mean. Give your reactions to the feedback or ask for time to think about it if necessary. Ask for suggestions on how to improve.

4 **Reflect**: feedback is information for you to use – it is not a requirement to change. If you are unsure about the soundness of the feedback, check it out with other people. Work out the options open to you and decide what you want to do. It is up to you to **evaluate** how accurate and how useful the feedback is.

Recording your progress
Compiling a record of achievement

A record of achievement is a collection of the different types of evidence that can be used to show successful completion of the course. Examples of evidence include the following:

- Completed assignments, observations, projects or case studies, including action plans and evaluations. These can be in written form or word processed, although work in the form of audiotape recordings, logbooks or diaries may also be acceptable where they contain evidence of the practical demonstration of skills. Check with your tutor or trainer.
- Past records of achievement, qualifications, work experience or other evidence of 'prior learning'.
- Samples of relevant class or lecture notes, lists, personal reading records or copies of letters written (perhaps regarding work experience, to request information or advice, or related to job or higher education applications).

Progress check

Recording progress

- Do you keep a record of all training days and staff development events you have attended?
- Have you included evidence in your record of personal development activities – certificates of attendance, notes and other information?
- Have you revisited your development plan – reviewed it and reflected on it?

Assessment practice

Your work role

Using the information in this chapter, compile a folder that provides information about:

- the duties and responsibilities of your own work role
- the national standards that influence the way your role is carried out
- the ways you can ensure that your personal attitudes or beliefs do not obstruct the quality of your work

You could include copies of your job description or contract, the main standards applicable in your setting, and evidence of how you ensure that you apply principles of equality and fairness in your work.

Useful websites and resources

Website address	Organisation
www.cache.org.uk	**The Council for Awards in Care, Health and Education (CACHE)** CACHE is the specialist awarding organisation for qualifications in children's care and education.
www.daycaretrust.org.uk	**Daycare Trust** Daycare Trust is a national child care charity that provides information for parents, child care providers, employers, trade unions, local authorities and policy makers.
www.hse.gov.uk	**Health and Safety Executive (HSE)** HSE is a government-funded organisation that works to protect people against risks to health or safety arising from work activities.

The poem on page 20 is by Dorothy Law Nolte, and is taken from Children Learn What They Live *(1998) by Dorothy Law Nolte and Rachel Harris. Workman Publishing Company.*

3 Introduction to equality and inclusion in children and young people's settings: Unit SHC 23

People working in and using public services are morally and legally obliged to abide by the principles of equality, inclusion and anti-discrimination. As a practitioner, you have a role to play in ensuring that in all aspects of your work every person is given real opportunities to thrive, and that any barriers that prevent them from reaching their full potential are removed. The principles of equality and inclusion are at the heart of work with children and young people in every kind of setting.

Learning outcomes

By the end of this chapter you will:

1. Understand the importance of equality and inclusion.
2. Be able to work in an inclusive way.
3. Know how to access information, advice and support about diversity, equality and inclusion.

The importance of equality and inclusion

The rights of children, young people and their families

Children and adults are entitled to the basic human rights of food, health care, a safe home and protection from abuse. However, children and young people are a special case because they cannot always stand up for themselves. They need a special set of rights that take account of their vulnerability and ensure that adults take responsibility for their protection and development.

The rights embodied by the **UN Convention on the Rights of the Child** that particularly relate to care and education are listed here:

- Children have the right to be with their family or with those who will care best for them.
- Children have the right to enough food and clean water for their needs.
- Children have the right to an adequate standard of living.
- Children have the right to health care.
- Children have the right to play.
- Children have the right to be kept safe and not hurt or neglected.
- Disabled children have the right to special care and training.
- Children have the right to free education.

Figure 3.01 Children have the right to play

Defining important principles

Diversity

Diversity refers to the differences in values, attitudes, cultures, beliefs, skills and life experience of each individual in any group of people. In the UK, frameworks emphasise the importance of developing every child's sense of identity and promoting a positive sense of pride in each child's family origins. Starting with themselves, young children can develop a sense of belonging to the local community and begin to understand and respect less familiar cultures.

Equality

Equality does not mean that everyone has to be treated the same. People have different needs, situations and ambitions. Practitioners have a part to play in supporting children and young people to live in the way that they value and choose, to be 'themselves' and to be different if they wish. Every person should have equality of opportunity.

Inclusion

Inclusion is the process of ensuring equality of opportunity for all children and young people, whatever their disabilities or disadvantages. This means that all children and young people have the right to have their needs met in the best way for them. They are seen as being part of the community, even if they need particular help to live a full life within the community.

Discrimination

Discrimination occurs when someone is treated less favourably, usually because of a negative view of some of their characteristics. This negative view is based on stereotypes that do not have a factual basis.

Children may discriminate against other children on account of their differences. This often takes the form of name-calling and teasing, and may be directed at children who are either fatter or thinner than others in the group, or who wear different clothes.

Discrimination in the work setting

Stereotypes and labels can lead to discrimination.

It is important to avoid labelling or stereotyping people. A **stereotype** is a way of thinking that assumes that all people who share one characteristic also share another set of characteristics. Stereotyped thinking can prevent you from seeing someone as an individual with particular life experiences and interests, and lead to negative attitudes, prejudice and discrimination. Examples are:

- **Racism or racial discrimination**: The belief that some 'races' are superior to others – based on the false idea that different physical characteristics (like skin colour) or ethnic background make some people better than others. For example: refusing a child a nursery place because they are black; failing to address the needs of children from a minority religious or cultural group, such as children from traveller families; only acknowledging festivals from the mainstream culture, such as Christmas and Easter.

- **Sexism and sex discrimination**: These occur when people of one gender reinforce the stereotype that they are superior to the other. For example: boys are routinely offered more opportunities for rough-and-tumble play than girls; while some early years workers may encourage girls to perform traditional 'female' tasks such as cooking and washing.

- **Ageism and age discrimination**: Negative feelings are expressed towards a person or group because of their age; in Western society it is usually directed towards older people; however, young people are often excluded because they are thought to be too young to participate. For example, in the UK young people are not permitted to vote until they are 18.

- **Disablism and disability discrimination**: Disabled people are seen in terms of their disability, rather than as unique individuals who happen to have special needs. Children and young people with disabilities or impairments may be denied equality of opportunity with their non-disabled peers. For example: failing to provide children with special needs with appropriate facilities and services; organising activities in a nursery setting in a way that ignores the special physical, intellectual and emotional needs of certain children.

There are many other stereotypes that can lead to discrimination – such as those concerning gay and lesbian groups, people from low socio-economic groups and those who practise a minority religion.

Scenarios: making assumptions

1. Sam, Jason, Laura and Fatima are playing in the role play area. The nursery teacher asks

Sam and Jason to tidy away the train set and trucks, and asks Laura and Fatima to put the dolls and cooking pots away, as it is nearly storytime.

The assumption here is that dolls and cooking utensils are 'girl' playthings, whereas trains and trucks are 'boy' playthings. The teacher is reinforcing this stereotype by separating the tasks by gender.

② Paul's mother arrives at the school open day. She is in a wheelchair, being pushed by Paul's father. The teacher welcomes the parents and then asks Paul's father if his wife would like a drink and a biscuit.

This is a common feature of daily life for people who use wheelchairs. They are often ignored and questions are addressed to their companion, often because the other person is embarrassed by the unusual situation and afraid of making a mistake. The assumption here is that the person in the wheelchair would not be able to understand and reply to what is said to them.

③ Members of staff are having a tea break and discussing a new child who has just started at their school. Julie says, 'I can't stand the way these travellers think they can just turn up at school whenever they feel like it – they don't pay taxes, you know, and they live practically on top of rubbish dumps . . . poor little mite, he doesn't know any different.'

An assumption has been made which is based on prejudice and stereotyped thinking. In this case, travellers are assumed to be 'scroungers' and to live in unhygienic conditions. Such attitudes will be noticed by all the children in the class and may result in the individual child being treated differently, damaging their self-esteem and leading to feelings of rejection.

④ Harry's mother is a registered heroin addict who has been attending a drug rehabilitation programme for the last few months. Whenever Harry behaves in an aggressive way to other children or to staff, one staff member always makes a jibe about his home life: 'Harry, you may get away with that sort of thing where you come from, but it won't work here. We know all about you.'

This is an extreme and very unkind form of stereotyping. It is assuming that, because his mother is a drug user, Harry is somehow less worthy of consideration and respect. By drawing attention to his home life, the member of staff is guilty of prejudice and discriminatory behaviour. There is also a breach of the policy of confidentiality.

Key terms

Anti-discrimination – An approach which challenges unfair or unlawful treatment of individuals or groups based on a specific characteristic of that group, such as colour, age, disability, sexual orientation, etc.

Diversity – The differences in values, attitudes, cultures, beliefs, skills, knowledge and life experience of each individual in any group of people.

Discrimination – Treating a person less favourably than others in the same or similar circumstances.

Equality – Making sure that everyone has a chance to take part in society on an equal basis and to be treated appropriately, regardless of his or her gender, race, disability, age, sexual orientation, language, social origin, religious beliefs, marital status and other personal attributes.

Inclusion – Ensuring that every child, young person, adult or learner is given equal opportunity to access education and care by meeting his or her specific needs.

Inclusive practice – The process of identifying, understanding and breaking down barriers to participation and belonging.

Case Study — The effects of labelling: Harry, my son

When I first met Harry, he was my son. A year later he was epileptic and developmentally delayed. By eighteen months he had special needs and he was a 'special' child. I was told not to think about his future.

My husband and I struggled to come to terms with all this. By the time he was four, Harry had special educational needs and was a 'statemented' child. He was epileptic, developmentally delayed and had severe and complex communication problems. Two years later, aged six, he was severely epileptic, had cerebral palsy and had communication difficulties. At eight he had severe epilepsy with associated communication problems; he was showing a marked developmental regression, and he had severe learning difficulties. At nine he came out of segregated schooling and he slowly became my son again. Never again will he be anything but Harry – a son, a brother, a friend, a pupil, a teacher, a person.

1 How many different labels can you identify in this short account?

2 Why do you think Harry's mother felt she had 'lost' her son?

The effects of discrimination on children and young people's development

Discrimination of any kind prevents children and young people from developing feelings of self-worth or self-esteem. The effects of being discriminated against can last the whole of a child's life. In particular, they may:

- be unable to fulfil their potential, because they are made to feel that their efforts are not valued or recognised by others
- find it hard to form relationships with others
- be so affected by the stereotypes or labels applied to them that they start to believe in them and so behave in accordance with others' expectations. This then becomes a self-fulfilling prophecy: for example, if a child is repeatedly told that he is clumsy, he may act in a clumsy way even when quite capable of acting otherwise
- feel shame about their own cultural background
- feel that they are in some way to blame for their unfair treatment and so withdraw into themselves
- lack confidence in trying new activities if their attempts are always ridiculed or belittled
- be aggressive towards others: distress or anger can prevent children from playing cooperatively with other children.

How practices that support equality and inclusion reduce the likelihood of discrimination

Promoting equality and inclusion

Provide positive images

Books and displays should use positive images of children and young people:

- with disabilities
- from different cultures

- gender roles, such as men caring for small children and women mending the car.

Consider children and young people with special needs

When you are planning an activity, consider how children with special needs can participate fully with other children. This might mean providing ramps for wheelchair users or working with parents to find comfortable ways for a child to sit; for example, a corner with two walls for support, a chair with a seat belt, or a wheelchair with a large tray across the arms.

Learn a sign language

You could learn a sign language such as Makaton or Signalong to help communicate with

In Practice

Practical ways of encouraging cultural diversity

❏ Provide a range of activities which celebrate these differences (for example, make children and young people aware of what is involved in celebrations of religious festivals such as Diwali and Chinese New Year, as well as Christmas and Easter, whether or not there are children and young people in the setting who celebrate these occasions).

❏ Promote a multicultural approach to food provision; for example, parents could be invited into the setting to cook authentic national and regional dishes – Caribbean food, Yorkshire pudding as a dessert, Welsh bara brith, Irish stew, Asian sweets – the list is endless!

❏ Encourage self-expression in solo and in group activities; for example, by providing 'tools' for cooking and eating from other cultures such as woks, chopsticks, griddles.

❏ Celebrate the diversity of language; use body language, gesture, pictures and actions to convey messages to children and young people whose home language is not English.

a child who has a hearing impairment or a learning difficulty.

Promote cultural diversity

It is important to support an environment that is inclusive and promotes cultural diversity.

Planning activities that promote equality of opportunity

Every child needs to feel accepted, and to feel that they belong, in the setting. Try to find out as much as possible about different cultures, religions and special needs. Activities should be planned which enable each child or young person to:

- feel valued as individuals
- explore a wide range of everyday experiences from different cultures and backgrounds
- express their feelings.

Specific activities may include the following:

1. Play with malleable materials such as play dough, sand or clay. Drawing, painting and craft activities help children to express their feelings and are non-sexist activities. Include examples from different cultures, such as papier mâché, origami or weaving.

2. Provide toys which offer a range of play opportunities rather than those which are aimed particularly at one sex or the other; for example, provide a wide variety of dressing-up clothes that can be used by girls and boys.

3. Include dressing-up clothes from different cultures and make sure that superhero outfits are available for both sexes.

4. Extend the pretend/role play area to provide a wide range of play situations, such as an office or shop or a boat.

5. Use books and tell stories in different languages: invite someone whose first

language is not English to come and read a popular storybook, such as *Goldilocks and the Three Bears*, in their language to the whole group; then repeat the session using the English text, again to the whole group.

6. Play music from a variety of cultures – such as sitar music, pan pipes, bagpipes – and encourage children to listen or dance to the sounds.

7. Plan a display and interest table around one of the major festivals from different cultures, such as Diwali, Hanukkah, Easter, Chinese New Year.

8. Use posters that show everyday things from different countries, such as musical instruments, fruit and vegetables, transport and wildlife.

9. Organise the pretend play area to include a variety of equipment commonly found in homes in different cultures, such as a tandoor, wok, chopsticks.

10. Provide dolls and other playthings that accurately reflect a variety of skin tones and features.

11. Arrange cookery activities using recipes from other cultures and in different languages; contact the relevant organisations to find out how to promote cooking skills for children with special needs.

12. Consult young people about the activities they prefer and try to encourage equality of opportunity.

Reflective practice: Promoting equality of opportunity

Think about ways in which you have encouraged equality of opportunity in your work with children or young people. How can you ensure that your practice is not discriminatory? How can you promote equality of opportunity? Write a short account of ways in which you can ensure that no child is treated unfavourably compared with others.

Figure 3.02 All parents were given the opportunity to attend a massage session with their babies

Working in an inclusive way

Every child and young person needs to be included and to have full access to the curriculum and range of experiences, regardless of his or her ethnic background, culture, language, gender or economic background.

Legislation and codes of practice relating to equality, diversity and discrimination

No law can prevent prejudiced attitudes. However, the law can prohibit discriminatory practices and behaviours that flow from prejudice. The laws relating to equality, diversity and discrimination are as follows:

- The Equality Act (2010) (this new Act has simplified the legal structure by bringing together nine different pieces of equality legislation)
- The Special Educational Needs and Disability Act 2001
- The Race Relations (Amendment) Act 2000
- Convention on the Rights of the Child (UN, 1989)
- The Human Rights Act 1998
- The Special Needs and Disability Act (SENDA) 2001.

For further information about legislation relating to disability, see Chapter 14, Unit TDA 2.14: Support children and young people with disabilities and special educational needs.

(Each of the four countries of the UK will have its own legislation relating to equality, diversity and discrimination, so may differ slightly from the titles listed above).

The legislation should have an influence on the way in which organisations provide services and practitioners approach their work. You need to be aware of the law as it stands in relation to promoting equality of opportunity, although you do not need to know the details.

Codes of practice, policies and procedures

Every setting is bound to work within the framework of the law, and this includes codes of practice and policies that are tailor-made for each setting.

- The Early Years Foundation Stage (EYFS) gives guidance that explains how to put the EYFS into action.
- The SEN Code of Practice provides practical advice and guidance to local education authorities, maintained schools, early education settings and others on carrying out their statutory duties to identify, assess and make provision for children's special educational needs.

Every setting must have a Policy on Equal Opportunities that states how the law is interpreted in that particular setting. The procedures that accompany the Policy give guidance on how the policy can be followed.

 Progress check

Understanding and promoting equality of opportunity

Practitioners should:

- know their Equalities Lead Officer or Equalities Coordinator
- receive support and training in this area
- work to improve his or her own practice
- report all incidents of discrimination (an incident is discrimination if it is felt to be discrimination by anyone involved, even an onlooker)
- take active steps to make sure that everyone knows about the services on offer and to involve everyone in all parts of the service.

In Practice

Codes of Practice and Policies

How are the laws relating to equality and inclusion reflected in your setting's policy?

How does the SEN Code of Practice apply to your setting?

How does your setting fulfil its legal responsibility to ensure that every child or young person is included?

Interaction that shows respect

It is important that you recognise the differences between children and young people, and that you *value* those differences. Children and young people should be encouraged not to feel anxious about people who are different from them. We all have different ideas about how we conduct our lives. It is inevitable that each practitioner will encounter many people with vastly different backgrounds, beliefs and outlooks on life. Regardless of your own views, you should always respect the views of others. This involves:

- showing awareness of a child's personal rights, dignity and privacy
- not passing judgement on the way other people live
- never allowing children and young people to poke fun at another child or young person
- avoiding stereotyping people on the basis of age, sex, disability or ethnicity (or colour)
- not trying to impose your views on others.

Many of the traditions practised within families from ethnic minorities are now adopted by Western societies, such as baby massage with natural oils and the carrying of babies in fabric slings.

Use of language

We should be careful to be sensitive in our use of language as it is important not to cause offence and also to avoid labelling others. In general:

- Avoid the article 'the' when referring to individuals with a specific disability. Grouping all individuals together into a disability category promotes the idea that all of these individuals have common attributes.

For example: **Don't say** '*the* blind' or '*the* disabled'. **Do say** 'people who are blind' or 'people who are disabled'.

- Avoid using terms that turn the disability into a personal noun. The child should come before the disability or special need.

For example: **Don't say** that someone is 'spastic' or 'Down's'. **Do say** 'a child who has cerebral palsy', or 'a young person who has Down's syndrome'.

- Avoid terms which have negative implications such as 'afflicted with', 'suffers from', 'is a victim of', 'is confined to. . .' These terms promote negative stereotypes.

For example: **Don't say** 'Robbie's confined to a wheelchair – he suffers from muscular dystrophy.' **Do say** 'Robbie has muscular dystrophy and uses a wheelchair.' (Wheelchairs are liberating to people with disabilities because they provide mobility.)

- Avoid patronising or sensationalising the individual with a disability.

For example: **Don't say** 'You would never know he was blind' or 'She dances well for a girl with a prosthetic leg.'

- Avoid reference to the disability at all unless it is necessary. In the same way, racial identification is being eliminated from news stories when it is not significant.

For example: Itzhak Perlman, the violinist, once said that he would like, just for once, to read a review of his performance which did not mention his disability, especially as it in no way affected his ability to perform.

• Avoid self-projection – that is, always referring to yourself.

For example: 'I would rather die than be blind,' or 'I really admire you, because I don't know what I would do if I couldn't walk any more.'

Reflective practice: Interacting with others

Think about the way you interact with people in your setting:

• Have you made an effort to show respect and courtesy?
• Do you act as a positive role model, showing children and young people how you value and respect differences?
• How could you improve the way you interact with others to demonstrate your promotion of equality and diversity?

Identifying and challenging discrimination in the work setting

The first step in being able to challenge discrimination is to identify when it is taking place. The most obvious and common form of indirect discrimination is when labels are applied to children and young people. While you may believe in private, for example, that Mark is a 'spoilt' child who gets away with the sort of behaviour that you personally think is

unacceptable, you should not initiate or join in any discussion that results in Mark being labelled as a 'difficult' or 'spoilt' child. Equally, you will find some children more likeable than others. What is important is that you are fair in your treatment of all the children and young people in your care. You should treat them all with respect and work towards meeting individual needs. Study the poem on p 20, 'Children learn what they live', and try to develop **positive attitudes** towards all the children you meet, so that they do not feel the effects of discrimination.

Anti-discriminatory practice is a way of working that challenges words or actions that treat people unfairly (or unlawfully) because of their gender, race, disability, age, sexual orientation,

Exploring your assumptions and stereotypes

The following adjectives are often used by adults to describe children:

bossy noisy sissy aggressive lively helpful energetic shy warm lazy cheeky quiet strong clinging moody babyish gentle emotional competitive kind

Use the headings 'girls', 'boys' and 'either boys or girls' to create three columns. Then put the adjectives from the list into the appropriate column, according to whether you think they describe girls, boys, or either girls or boys. Compare your lists with those of a friend.

1. How similar were your choices? Discuss the similarities and the differences.
2. Discuss the reasons why some adjectives are so closely related to gender.
3. Do your lists really apply to all the children you work with or know?

language, social origin, religious beliefs, marital status and other personal attributes.

In Practice

Challenging discrimination

As well as practising anti-discriminatory behaviour yourself, you should never ignore or make excuses for others – children, young people and other adults – if you observe discriminatory or bullying behaviour. The policies and procedures of the setting should always be followed.

❑ Make sure that you criticise the *behaviour*, not the child or young person. Explain *why* the behaviour is unacceptable – using language appropriate to the child's stage of development. A young child can be told that what they have said or done is hurtful and unfair. Young people can be encouraged to use empathy to understand why their behaviour is inappropriate – e.g. ask them 'How would you feel if someone said (or did) that to you?'

❑ Support the child or young person who has been the object of discrimination to maintain their self-esteem by showing sympathy and reassurance.

❑ Refuse to laugh at jokes based on stereotypes. Point out to the person telling the joke that it isn't funny and explain why you object to it.

❑ Always challenge discriminatory remarks made by colleagues or other adults by telling them that you find their remark or behaviour inappropriate.

Information, advice and support about diversity, equality and inclusion

Sources of information and support

As part of your ongoing personal and professional development, you should always be willing to improve your practice by seeking further information and support from a variety of sources.

Colleagues

In most settings, there is a Special Needs Coordinator (SENCO), whom you can approach for information or support when working with a child or young person with additional needs. It is important to get to know the strengths and personal expertise of individual members in your staff team; you will often find that they can offer useful support, having encountered a similar situation before.

Books and journals

Depending on your area of work, journals and magazines can be valuable in keeping you up to date with what is happening in your sector. Early years practitioners can refer to magazines such as *Nursery World*, *EYE*, and *Infant Educator*. Practitioners working with young people can refer to *Children and Young People Now* and *Community Care*. You can find out which books will be useful from your tutor or trainer, and then order them from your local library.

Parents and families

Remember that parents, carers and family members can be a valuable resource if you need further information about an individual child or young person's:

- disability or condition
- home language
- special dietary needs or allergies, and preferences
- cultural preferences.

How and when to seek information and support

No one will expect you to know and understand everything, and you may come across situations that you find difficult or challenging. It is your responsibility to seek advice and support from your tutor or line manager, and to use your experience as a valuable learning opportunity.

Organisations specialising in equality issues

The table below lists the website addresses of organisations who give advice and information about diversity, equality and inclusion. You can also visit your local Citizens Advice Bureau.

Useful websites and resources

Website address	Organisation
www.ageuk.org.uk	**Age UK** Age UK's **Just Equal Treatment** campaign challenges age discrimination and the organisation works to make sure that we all have fair access to health services, insurance and employment.
www.carersuk.org	**Carers UK** Carers UK is the voice of carers. Carers provide unpaid care by looking after an ill, frail or disabled family member, friend or partner.
www.ncb.org.uk	**National Children's Bureau** A charitable organisation that is dedicated to advancing the health and well-being of children and young people across every aspect of their lives, and providing them with a powerful and authoritative voice.
www.direct.gov.uk	**Directgov** Public services all in one place.
www.equalityhumanrights.com	**Equality and Human Rights Commission** An independent body which has a statutory remit to promote and monitor human rights; also to protect, enforce and promote equality across the seven 'protected' grounds – age, disability, gender, race, religion and belief, sexual orientation and gender reassignment.
www.equalities.gov.uk	**Government Equalities Office (GEO)** GEO is a small policy department employing just over 100 staff, which has responsibility within government for equality strategy and legislation. GEO takes the lead on issues relating to women, sexual orientation and transgender equality matters.

4 Child and young person development: Unit TDA 2.1

Learning about child and young person development involves studying patterns of growth and development, from which guidelines for 'normal' development are drawn up. The sequence and stages of development you will study serve simply as a guide as to the way in which the majority of children develop at certain ages. It is important to remember that each child or young person will develop in a unique way – there is no such child as the 'average' child.

Learning outcomes

By the end of this chapter you will:

1. Know the main stages of child and young person development.
2. Understand the kinds of influences that affect the development of children and young people.
3. Understand the potential effects of transitions on children and young people's development.

The main stages of child and young person development

It is important to keep in mind that every child and young person is unique. By looking at the holistic (or integrated) development of children and young people, we can view the whole person – physically, emotionally, intellectually, morally, culturally and spiritually. Physical growth is different from physical development. Physical **growth** means that children and young people grow in height and weight, whereas physical **development** means that children and young people gain **skills** through being able to control their own bodies.

The whole child or young person may be looked at using six headings or aspects. You can remember these as together they make up the acronym **PILESS**:

- **P**hysical development
- **I**ntellectual development
- **L**anguage development
- **E**motional development
- **S**ocial and behaviour development
- **S**piritual development.

Physical development

Physical development is the way in which the body increases in skill and becomes more complex in its performance. Children's physical development follows a pattern:

- **From simple to complex**: a child will stand before he can walk, and walk before he can skip or hop.
- **From head to toe**: physical control and coordination begin with a child's head and works down the body through the arms, hands and back and finally the legs and feet.
- **From inner to outer**: a child can coordinate his arms using gross motor skills to reach for an object before he has learned the fine motor skills necessary to pick it up.
- **From general to specific**: a young baby shows pleasure by a massive general response (eyes widen, legs and arms move vigorously, etc.); an older child shows pleasure by smiling or using appropriate words or gestures.

There are two main areas of physical development:

1 **gross motor skills**: these use the large muscles in the body and include walking, squatting, running, climbing, etc.

2 **fine motor skills**, which include:

- **gross manipulative skills** – single limb movements, usually the arm, for example throwing, catching and sweeping arm movements
- **fine manipulative skills** – precise use of the hands and fingers for pointing, drawing, using a knife and fork, writing, doing up shoelaces, etc.

There are wide variations in the ages at which children acquire physical skills, such as sitting, standing and walking. The rate at which children develop these skills will have an effect on all the other areas of development: for example, on the development of language, understanding, self-confidence and social skills. Once a child has learned to crawl, to shuffle on her bottom, or to be mobile in other ways, she will be more independent and be able to explore things that were previously out of reach. Adults will make changes to the child's environment now that she is mobile, by putting reachable objects out of her way and making clear rules and boundaries.

The senses of a newborn baby

Newborn babies are already actively using all their senses to explore their new environment. They are:

- sight
- hearing
- smell
- taste
- touch.

Visual development

Newborn babies are very near-sighted at first, and they can focus best on things that are within 25 cm (10 inches) of their faces. This means that they can see well enough to focus on their mother's face when being held to the breast. Their vision is quite blurry outside this range but they can follow a light with their eyes and turn toward lights. Sometimes babies appear to have a squint as their eyes may move independently of each other. This is normal, as they are still gaining control of the eye muscles. Newborn babies prefer to look at:

- people's faces and eyes, especially those of their mothers
- bright colours – they will often reach for colourful objects
- light and dark **contrasts** and sharp outlines
- patterns, such as stripes or circles, rather than plain surfaces
- things which are moving: they will focus on and follow a moving ball with their eyes, a skill known as **tracking**.

Hearing

Babies develop a very acute sense of hearing while in the womb. Ultrasound studies have shown that unborn babies as early as 25 weeks' gestation can 'startle' in response to a sudden loud noise. Newborn babies can distinguish different voices and other sounds, and they can also determine from which direction a sound is coming. For example, if a small bell is rung above a newborn baby's head, he will turn his head in the direction of the sound and watch the object making the sound. Newborn babies prefer to listen to:

- **the human voice**, especially female voices. They usually recognise their own mother's voice from the start, since this is the voice they have heard, although muffled, throughout their time in the womb. Newborn babies become quiet when they hear their mother's voice, and they turn their heads toward their mother when she speaks. After about a week or so, most newborn babies will prefer their father's voice to that of other men.
- **soft, melodic speech**: they can tell the difference between a calm, happy tone and an angry voice, and will respond with pleasure to a soft, lilting voice or may cry when they hear a loud, angry voice.

Hearing is an important part of speech development, so it is essential that babies are talked to. Parents and other adults automatically alter the pitch of their voices when talking to babies, and use a lot of repetition.

Touch

Newborn babies are very sensitive to touch. They love to be held close, comforted, cuddled, stroked, and rocked. Newborn babies prefer:

- **stroking of their skin**: this action helps newborn babies to sleep, and it helps to encourage closeness between baby and parent

- the feel of **soft fabrics**
- **skin-to-skin contact** with their parents, and being cuddled.

Babies who are fed but not touched or held often have problems with their physical and mental development. Gentle stroking is especially beneficial for premature babies. Research shows that it leads to increased weight gain, more alertness and activity, and an earlier discharge from hospital.

Taste

Newborn babies also have a well-developed sense of taste. They generally enjoy sweetness and dislike sour liquids. They can detect differences in the taste of their mother's milk, which can change depending on what the mother eats. Babies show that they find tastes pleasant or unpleasant by screwing up their faces and trying to reject the taste from their mouth.

Smell

Newborn babies are sensitive to the smell of their mother, and they can tell it apart from that of other women. They are attracted not just to the smell of milk, but also to their mother's own unique body scent. Breastfed babies are more aware of their mother's smell compared with babies who are bottle-fed. This may be because breastfed babies spend more time in skin-to-skin contact with their mothers compared with babies who are bottle-fed. Babies will also turn away from a smell they find unpleasant.

Communication and language development

Language development is very closely linked with cognitive development, and a delay in one area usually affects progress in the other. Language development is the development of communication skills. These include skills in:

- receptive speech – what a person understands
- expressive speech – the words the person produces
- articulation – the person's actual pronunciation of words.

Babies are born with a need and a desire to communicate with others before they can express themselves through speaking. Learning how to communicate (to listen and to speak) begins with **non-verbal communication**, which includes:

- body language, such as facial expression, eye contact, pointing, touching and reaching for objects
- listening to others talking to them
- making sounds to attract attention
- copying the sounds made by others.

These skills develop as babies and young children express their needs and feelings, interact with others and establish their own identities and personalities.

Intellectual development

Intellectual (or cognitive) development is the development of the mind – the part of the brain that is used for recognising, reasoning, knowing and understanding. It involves:

- what a person knows and the ability to reason, understand and solve problems
- memory, concentration, attention and perception
- imagination and creativity.

Children learn through play. They need opportunities to learn through:

- **Learning to predict**: children learn to predict that something is about to happen. For example, a baby learns to predict that food will soon appear if a bib is tied around his or her neck.

- **Learning the consequences of their actions**: children understand that they can bring about a result by their own actions. For example, a baby learns that if he or she cries, he or she will be picked up and comforted.
- **Asking questions**: as soon as they can talk, children ask questions to try to make sense of their world and gain information. For example, four-year-old children constantly ask the question 'Why?' whereas a child aged two and a half often asks 'Who?' and 'What?'.
- **Understanding concepts**: experiences with real objects help young children to understand concepts and to develop problem-solving skills. For example, mathematical concepts involve understanding number, sequencing, volume and capacity, as well as weighing and measuring. Musical concepts include tempo (speed), rhythm and pitch. To understand the concept of pitch, for example, children need to identify the difference between high and low notes, and this can be promoted using real instruments and musical activities.
- **Repetition**: children learn by repeating activities over and over again. For example, they can learn a song or rhyme by hearing it sung to them many times.
- **Imitation:** Children learn by copying what others do. For example, they learn how to write by copying letters, and in **role play** children are copying the way they have observed others behave in certain situations.

Key term

Role play – A form of pretend play when children engage in, explore and learn about the everyday roles that occur in their familiar experience; the roles carried out by their parents or carers and members of their community.

Figure 4.01 Learning through role play: driving a car

Emotional, social and behavioural development

These three areas of development are very closely linked. Emotional development involves:

- the growth of feelings about, and awareness of, oneself
- the development of feelings towards other people
- the development of **self-esteem** and a **self-concept**.

Social development

Social development includes the growth of the child's relationships with other people. **Socialisation** is the process of learning the skills and attitudes that enable the child to live easily with other members of the community.

The development of social and self-help skills

As early as six months of age, babies enjoy each other's company. When they are together, they look at each other, smile and touch each other's faces. As their social circle widens they learn how to cooperate with each other when they play, and they begin to make friends.

What are social skills?

Children and young people need to develop certain social skills (or ways of behaving) in order to fit in – and to get on well – with the people around them. These social skills include:

- Developing a sense of self and of belonging
- Developing trust
- Learning to separate from their parents
- Playing with other children: sharing and taking turns
- Being able to express their opinions and desires
- Developing skills of caring for and looking after your self (independence)
- Using words to solve conflicts and develop control of emotions
- Learning that it is okay to make a mistake
- Developing confidence and self-respect
- Developing respect for others and feelings of empathy

Figure 4.02

Key terms

Empathy – Awareness of another person's emotional state, and the ability to share the experience with that person.

Socialisation – The process by which children learn what is expected of them in terms of behaviour and attitudes within society.

Behaviour is the way in which we act, speak and treat other people and our environment. (For more information on the development of behaviour, see Chapter 7, Unit MU 2.4: Contribute to children and young people's health and safety.)

Moral and spiritual development

Moral and spiritual development consists of a developing awareness of how to relate to others ethically, morally and humanely. It involves understanding values such as honesty and respect, acquiring concepts such as right and wrong, and taking responsibility for the consequences of one's actions.

Case Study — Christophe

Christophe is new to The Ark nursery. He is two years old and has a brother, Olivier, who is four and a half years old and has started attending pre-school. Christophe's family have recently moved to the UK from France. Monique, the mother, is fluent in English but speaks French to the boys at home, and has employed a French-Canadian au pair to collect the boys from the nursery two days a week. Antoine, the father, also speaks good English, but is very rarely at the nursery.

The boys are both very lively. Olivier soon picks up English phrases and everyone is delighted

Case Study   Christophe (cont.)

and relieved at his speedy progress in becoming bilingual. However, Christophe is struggling with English words and Monique reports that he has stopped speaking so much French. At nursery, Christophe does not say any recognisable words, and will instead 'grunt' answers or start crying. This makes it difficult for nursery staff to communicate with him – he just stares as they address him and does not respond to instructions at all. He can sometimes be quite destructive and refuses to tidy up after tipping over boxes. Staff members try to show him with actions, but Christophe rarely responds. However, apart from his obvious frustration when trying to communicate, Christophe loves to run around and laughs a lot as he watches other children, and joins in their games. He also joins in with different activities.

1 Why do you think Olivier finds the new language so much easier than does Christophe?
2 How has Christophe's difficulty in communicating impacted on other areas of his development?

Key terms

Dynamic tripod grasp – Using the thumb and two fingers in a grasp closely resembling the adult grasp of a pencil or pen.

Echolalia – The tendency of a child to echo the last words spoken by an adult.

Palmar grasp – Using the whole hand to grasp an object.

Pincer grasp – Using the thumb and fingers to grasp an object.

Primitive tripod grasp – Grasping objects by use of the thumb and two fingers.

Telegraphese – The abbreviation of a sentence such that only the crucial words are spoken, as in a telegram – e.g 'Where daddy going?' or 'Shut door'.

The stages and sequence of holistic development from birth to 19 years

The following pages outline the main features of **holistic** child and young person development, the ages shown being those at which the average child performs the specific tasks. Remember, however, that children develop at different rates, and some may be faster or slower to learn certain skills than other children.

Holistic development: The first month

Physical development

Gross motor skills	Fine motor skills
• The baby lies **supine** (on his or her back). • When placed on his or her front (the **prone** position), the baby lies with head turned to one side, and by one month can lift the head. • If the baby is pulled to sitting position, the head will lag, the back curves over and the head falls forward.	• The baby turns his or her head towards the light and stares at bright or shiny objects. • The baby is fascinated by human faces and gazes attentively at carer's face when fed or held. • The baby's hands are usually tightly closed. • The baby reacts to loud sounds but by one month may be soothed by particular music.

Communication and language development

• Babies need to share language experiences and cooperate with others from birth onwards. From the start babies need other people.

• The baby responds to sounds, especially familiar voices.

• The baby quietens when picked up.

• The baby makes eye contact.

• The baby cries to indicate need, e.g. hunger, dirty nappy, etc.

• The baby may move his or her eyes towards the direction of sound.

Intellectual development

Babies explore through their **senses** and through their own activity and movement.

Touch

• From the beginning babies feel pain.

• The baby's face, abdomen, hands and the soles of his or her feet are also very sensitive to touch.

• The baby perceives the movements that he or she makes, and the way that other people move him or her about through his or her senses.

• For example, the baby gives a 'startle' response if they are moved suddenly. This is called the '**Moro**' or startle reflex.

Sound

• Even a newborn baby will turn to a sound. The baby might become still and listen to a low sound, or quicken his or her movements when he or she hears a high sound.

• The baby often stops crying and listens to a human voice by two weeks of age.

Taste

• The baby likes sweet tastes, e.g. breast milk.

Smell

• The baby turns to the smell of the breast.

Sight

• The baby can focus on objects 20 cm (a few inches) away.

• The baby is sensitive to light.

• The baby likes to look at human faces – eye contact.

• The baby can track the movements of people and objects.

• The baby will scan the edges of objects.

Holistic development: The first month (cont.)

- The baby will imitate facial expressions (e.g. he or she will put out their tongue if you do). If you know any newborn or very young babies, try it and see!

Emotional and social development

- A baby's first smile in definite response to carer is usually around 5–6 weeks.
- The baby often imitates certain facial expressions.
- The baby uses total body movements to express pleasure at bathtime or when being fed.
- The baby enjoys feeding and cuddling.
- In the first month babies are learning where they begin and end, e.g. his or her hand is part of them but mother's hand is not.

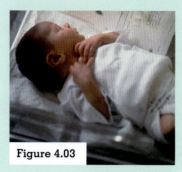

Figure 4.03

Table 4.1 Holistic development: the first month

Holistic development from one to four months

Physical development

Gross motor skills	Fine motor skills
From four to eight weeks: - The baby can now turn from side to back. - The baby can lift the head briefly from the prone position. - Arm and leg movements are jerky and uncontrolled. - There is head lag if the baby is pulled to sitting position.	- The baby turns her head towards the light and stares at bright or shiny objects. - The baby will show interest and excitement by facial expression and will gaze attentively at carer's face while being fed. - The baby will use his or her hand to grasp the carer's finger.
From eight to twelve weeks: - When lying supine, the baby's head is in a central position. - The baby can now lift head and chest off bed in prone position, supported on forearms. - There is almost no head lag in sitting position. - The legs can kick vigorously, both separately and together.	- The baby moves his or her head to follow adult movements. - The baby watches his or her hands and plays with his or her fingers. - The baby holds a rattle for a brief time before dropping it.

Holistic development from one to four months (cont.)

- The baby can wave his or her arms and bring his or her hands together over the body.

Communication and language development

From four to eight weeks:

- The baby recognises the carer and familiar objects.
- The baby makes non-crying noises such as cooing and gurgling.
- The baby's cries become more expressive.

From eight to twelve weeks:

- The baby is still distressed by sudden loud noises.
- The baby often sucks or licks lips when he or she hears sound of food preparation.
- The baby shows excitement at sound of approaching footsteps or voices.

During the first three months:

- The baby listens to people's voices. When adults close to the baby talk in motherese or fatherese (a high-pitched tone referring to what is around and going on) the baby dances, listens, replies in babble and coo.
- The baby cries with anger to show they are tired, hungry, and to say they need to be changed.
- The baby is comforted by the voices of those who are close to them and will turn especially to the voices of close family members.

Intellectual development

- The baby recognises differing speech sounds.
- By three months the baby can even imitate low- or high-pitched sounds.
- By four months the baby links objects they know with the sound, e.g. mother's voice and her face.
- The baby knows the smell of his or her mother from that of other mothers.

Emotional and social development

Four to eight weeks:

- The baby will smile in response to an adult.
- The baby enjoys sucking.
- The baby turns to regard nearby speaker's face.
- The baby turns to preferred person's voice.
- The baby recognises face and hands of preferred adult.
- The baby may stop crying when he or she hears, sees or feels her carer.

Eight to twelve weeks:

- The baby shows enjoyment at caring routines such as bathtime.
- The baby responds with obvious pleasure to loving attention and cuddles.
- The baby fixes his or her eyes unblinkingly on carer's face when feeding.
- The baby stays awake for longer periods of time.

Holistic development from one to four months (cont.)

Figure 4.04

Table 4.2 Holistic development from one to four months

Holistic development from four to six months

Physical development

Gross motor skills	Fine motor skills
• The baby is beginning to use a **palmar grasp** and can transfer objects from hand to hand.	• The baby now has good head control and is beginning to sit with support.
• The baby is very interested in all activity.	• The baby rolls over from back to side and is beginning to reach for objects.
• Everything is taken to the mouth.	• When supine the baby plays with his or her own feet.
• The baby moves his or her head around to follow people and objects.	• The baby holds his or her head up when pulled to sitting position.

Communication and language development

- The baby becomes more aware of others so he or she communicates more and more.
- As the baby listens, he or she imitates sounds he or she can hear, and reacts to the tone of someone's voice. For example, the baby might become upset by an angry tone, or cheered by a happy tone.
- The baby begins to use vowels, consonants and syllable sounds, e.g. 'ah', 'ee aw'.
- The baby begins to laugh and squeal with pleasure.

Intellectual development

- By four months the baby reaches for objects, which suggests they recognise and judge the distance in relation to the size of the object.
- The baby prefers complicated things to look at from five to six months and enjoys bright colours.
- The baby knows that he or she has one mother. The baby is disturbed if he or she is shown several images of his or her mother at the same time. The baby realises that *people* are permanent before he or she realises that *objects* are.
- The baby can coordinate more, e.g. the baby can see a rattle, grasp the rattle, put the rattle in his or her mouth (they coordinate tracking, reaching, grasping and sucking).
- The baby can develop favourite tastes in food and recognise differences by five months.

Emotional and social development

- The baby shows trust and security.
- The baby has recognisable sleep patterns.

Holistic development from four to six months (cont.)

Figure 4.05

Table 4.3 Holistic development from four to six months

Holistic development from six to nine months

Physical development

Gross motor skills	Fine motor skills
• The baby can roll from front to back.	• The baby is very alert to people and objects.
• The baby may attempt to crawl but will often end up sliding backwards.	• The baby is beginning to use a **pincer grasp** with thumb and index finger.
• The baby may grasp feet and place them in his or her mouth.	• The baby transfers toys from one hand to the other and looks for fallen objects.
• The baby can sit without support for longer periods of time.	• Everything is explored by putting it in his or her mouth.
• The baby may 'cruise' around furniture and may even stand or walk alone.	

Communication and language development

- Babble becomes tuneful, like the lilt of the language the baby can hear (except in hearing-impaired babies).
- Babies begin to understand words like 'up' and 'down', raising their arms to be lifted up, using appropriate gestures.
- The baby repeats sounds.

Intellectual development

- The baby understands **signs**, e.g. the bib means that food is coming.
- From eight to nine months the baby shows that he or she knows objects exist when they have gone out of sight, even under test conditions. This is called the concept of object constancy, or the **object permanence test (Piaget)**. The baby is also fascinated by the way objects move.

Emotional and social development

- The baby can manage to feed his- or herself using his or her fingers.
- The baby is now more wary of strangers, sometimes showing **stranger fear**.
- The baby might offer toys to others.
- The baby might show distress when his or her mother leaves.
- The baby typically begins to crawl and this means he or she can do more for him- or herself, reach for objects and get to places and people.
- The baby is now more aware of other people's feelings. For example, he or she may cry if their brother cries.

Holistic development from six to nine months (cont.)

Figure 4.06

Table 4.4 Holistic development from six to nine months

Holistic development from nine to twelve months

Physical development

Gross motor skills	Fine motor skills
• The baby will now be mobile – may be crawling, bear-walking, bottom-shuffling or even walking. • The baby can sit up on her own and lean forward to pick up things. • The baby may crawl upstairs and onto low items of furniture. • The baby may bounce in rhythm to music.	• The baby's pincer grasp is now well developed and he or she can pick things up and pull them towards him or her. • The baby can poke with one finger and will point to desired objects. • The baby can clasp hands and imitate adults' actions. • The baby can throw toys deliberately. • The baby can manage spoons and finger foods well.

Communication and language development

- The baby can follow simple instructions, e.g. kiss teddy.
- Word approximations appear, e.g. hee haw = donkey or more typically mumma, dadda and bye-bye in English-speaking contexts.
- The tuneful babble develops into 'jargon' and the baby makes his or her voice go up and down just as people do when they talk to each other. 'Really? Do you? No!' The babble is very expressive.
- The baby knows that words stand for people, objects, what they do and what happens.

Intellectual development

- The baby is beginning to develop images. Memory develops and the baby can remember the past.
- The baby can anticipate the future. This gives the baby some understanding of routine daily sequences, e.g. after a feed, changing, and a sleep with teddy.
- The baby imitates actions, sounds, gestures and moods after an event is finished, e.g. imitate a temper tantrum he or she saw a friend have the previous day, wave bye-bye remembering Grandma has gone to the shops.

Holistic development from nine to twelve months

Emotional and social development

- The baby enjoys songs and action rhymes.
- The baby still likes to be near to a familiar adult.
- The baby can drink from a cup with help.
- The baby will play alone for long periods.
- The baby has and shows definite likes and dislikes at mealtimes and bedtimes.
- The baby thoroughly enjoys peek-a-boo games.
- The baby likes to look at him- or herself in a mirror (plastic safety mirror).
- The baby imitates other people – e.g. clapping hands, waving bye-bye – but there is often a time lapse, so that he or she waves after the person has gone.
- The baby cooperates when being dressed.

Figure 4.07

Table 4.5 Holistic development from nine to twelve months

Holistic development from one year to two years

Physical development

Gross motor skills	Fine motor skills
At 15 months: - The baby probably walks alone, with feet wide apart and arms raised to maintain balance. He or she is likely to fall over and often sit down suddenly. - The baby can probably manage stairs and steps, but will need supervision. - The baby can get to standing without help from furniture or people, and kneels without support.	- The baby can build with a few bricks and arrange toys on the floor. - The baby holds a crayon in palmar grasp and turns several pages of a book at once. - The baby can point to desired objects. - The baby shows a preference for one hand, but uses either.

Holistic development from one year to two years (cont.)

Physical development

Gross motor skills	Fine motor skills
At 18 months: • The child walks confidently and is able to stop without falling. • The child can kneel, squat, climb and carry things around with him or her. • The child can climb forwards onto an adult chair and then turn round to sit. • The child can come downstairs, usually by creeping backwards on her tummy.	• The child can thread large beads. • The child uses pincer grasp to pick up small objects. • The child can build a tower of several cubes. • The child can scribble to and fro on paper.

Communication and language development

- The child begins to talk with words or sign language.
- **By 18 months**: The child enjoys trying to sing as well as listening to songs and rhymes. Action songs (e.g. 'Pat-a-cake') are much loved.
- Books with pictures are of great interest. The child points at and often names parts of their body, objects, people and pictures in books.
- The child echoes the last part of what others say (**echolalia**).
- The child begins waving his or her arms up and down, which might mean 'start again', or 'I like it', or 'more'.
- Gestures develop alongside words. Gesture is used in some cultures more than in others.

Intellectual development

- The child understands the names of objects and can follow simple instructions.
- The child learns about things through trial and error.
- The child uses toys or objects to represent things in real life (e.g. using a doll as a baby, or a large cardboard box as a car or a garage).
- The child begins to scribble on paper.
- The child often 'talks' to him- or herself while playing.

Emotional and social development

- The child begins to have a longer memory.
- The child develops a sense of identity (I am me).
- The child expresses his or her needs in words and gestures.
- The child enjoys being able to walk, and is eager to try to get dressed – 'Me do it!'
- The child is aware when others are fearful or anxious for him or her as he or she climbs on and off chairs, and so on.

Holistic development from one year to two years (cont.)

Figure 4.08

Table 4.6 Holistic development from one year to two years

Holistic development from two years	
Physical development	
Gross motor skills	**Fine motor skills**
• The child is very mobile and can run safely. • The child can climb up onto furniture. • The child can walk up and downstairs, usually two feet to a step. • The child tries to kick a ball with some success but cannot catch yet.	• The child can draw circles, lines and dots, using preferred hand. • The child can pick up tiny objects using a **fine pincer grasp**. • The child can build tower of six or more blocks (bricks), with longer concentration span. • The child enjoys picture books and turns pages singly.

Communication and language development

- Children are rapidly becoming competent speakers of the languages they experience.
- The child over-extends the use of a word, e.g. all animals are called 'doggie'.
- The child talks about an absent object when reminded of it; e.g. seeing an empty plate, they say 'biscuit'.
- The child uses phrases (**telegraphese**), 'doggie-gone' and the child calls him- or herself by name.
- The child spends a great deal of energy naming things and what they do – e.g. 'chair', and as they go up a step they might say 'up'.
- The child can follow a simple instruction or request, e.g. 'Could you bring me the spoon?'
- The child increasingly wants to share songs, dance, conversations, finger rhymes.

Intellectual development

- The child has improved memory skills, which help his or her understanding of **concepts** (e.g. the child can often name and match two or three colours – usually yellow and red).
- The child can hold a crayon and move it up and down.

Holistic development from two years (cont.)

- The child understands cause and effect (e.g. if something is dropped, he or she understands it might break).
- The child talks about an absent object when reminded of it (e.g. he or she may say 'biscuit' when seeing an empty plate or bowl).

Emotional and social development

- The child is impulsive and curious about their environment.
- **Pretend play** develops rapidly when adults encourage it.
- The child begins to be able to say how he or she is feeling, but often feels frustrated when unable to express him- or herself.
- The child can dress him- or herself and go to the lavatory independently, but needs sensitive support in order to feel success rather than frustration.
- By two and a half years the child plays more with other children, but may not share his or her toys with them.

Figure 4.09

Table 4.7 Holistic development from two years

Holistic development from three years	
Physical development	
Gross motor skills	**Fine motor skills**
• The child can jump from a low step.	• The child can build tall towers of bricks or blocks.
• The child can walk backwards and sideways.	• The child can control a pencil using thumb and first two fingers – a **dynamic tripod grasp**.
• The child can stand and walk on tiptoe and stand on one foot.	
• The child has good spatial awareness.	• The child enjoys painting with a large brush.
• The child rides a tricycle, using pedals.	• The child can use scissors to cut paper.
• The child can climb stairs with one foot on each step – and downwards with two feet per step.	• The child can copy shapes, such as a circle.

Holistic development from three years (cont.)

Communication and language development

- The child begins to use plurals, pronouns, adjectives, possessives, time words, tenses and sentences.
- The child might say 'two times' instead of 'twice'. The child might say 'I goed there' instead of 'I went there'. The child loves to chat and ask questions (what, where and who).
- The child enjoys much more complicated stories and asks for his or her favourite ones over and over again.
- It is not unusual for the child to stutter because he or she is trying so hard to tell adults things. The child's thinking goes faster than the pace at which the child can say what he or she wants to. The child can quickly become frustrated.

Intellectual development

The child develops symbolic behaviour. This means that:

- The child talks.
- The child **pretend plays** – often talking to him- or herself while playing.
- The child takes part in simple non-competitive games.
- The child represents events in drawings, models, etc.
- Personal images dominate, rather than conventions used in the culture, e.g. writing is 'pretend' writing.
- The child becomes fascinated by cause and effect; the child is continually trying to explain what goes on in the world.
- The child can identify common colours, such as red, yellow, blue and green – although may sometimes confuse blue with green.

Emotional and social development

Pretend play helps the child to **decentre** and develop **theory of mind** (the child begins to be able to understand how someone else might feel and/or think).

- The child is beginning to develop a gender role as they become aware of being male or female.
- The child makes friends and is interested in having friends.
- The child learns to negotiate, give and take through experimenting with feeling powerful, having a sense of control, and through quarrels with other children.
- The child is easily afraid, e.g. of the dark, as he or she becomes capable of pretending. The child imagines all sorts of things.

Figure 4.10

Table 4.8 Holistic development from three years

Holistic development from four years

Physical development

Gross motor skills	Fine motor skills
● A sense of balance is developing – the child may be able to walk along a line.	● The child can build a tower of bricks and other constructions too.
● The child can catch, kick, throw and bounce a ball.	● The child can draw a recognisable person on request, showing head, legs and trunk.
● The child can bend at the waist to pick up objects from the floor.	● The child can thread small beads on a lace.
● The child enjoys climbing trees and frames.	
● The child can run up and down stairs, one foot per step.	

Communication and language development

- During this time the child asks why, when and how questions as he or she becomes more and more fascinated with the reasons for things and how things work (cause and effect).
- Past, present and future tenses are used more often.
- The child can be taught to say his or her name, address and age.
- As the child becomes more accurate in the way he or she pronounces words, and begins to use grammar, the child delights in nonsense words that he or she makes up, and jokes using words.

Intellectual development

- At about age four, the child usually knows how to count – up to 20.
- The child also understands ideas such as 'more' and 'fewer', and 'big' and 'small'.
- The child will recognise his or her own name when it is written down and can usually write it.
- The child can think back and can think forward much more easily than before.
- The child can also think about things from somebody else's point of view, but only fleetingly.
- The child often enjoys music and playing sturdy instruments, and joins in groups singing and dancing.

Emotional and social development

- The child likes to be independent and is strongly self-willed.
- The child shows a sense of humour.
- The child can undress and dress him- or herself – except for laces and back buttons.
- The child can wash and dry his or her hands and brush their teeth.

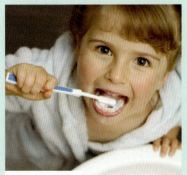

Figure 4.11

Table 4.9 Holistic development from four years

Holistic development from five to eight years

Physical development

Gross motor skills	Fine motor skills
From five years: • The child can use a variety of play equipment – slides, swings, climbing frames. • The child can play ball games. • The child can hop and run lightly on toes and can move rhythmically to music. • The sense of balance is well developed. • The child can skip. **Six and seven years:** • The child has increased agility, muscle coordination and balance. • The child develops competence in riding a two-wheeled bicycle. • The child hops easily, with good balance. • The child can jump off apparatus.	• The child may be able to thread a large-eyed needle and sew large stitches. • The child can draw a person with head, trunk, legs, nose, mouth and eyes. • The child has good control over pencils and paintbrushes. He or she copies shapes, such as a square. • The child can build a tall, straight tower with blocks and other constructions too. • The child can draw a person with detail, e.g. clothes and eyebrows. • The child can write letters of alphabet at school, with similar writing grip to an adult. • The child can catch a ball thrown from one metre with one hand.

Communication and language development

- The child tries to understand the meanings of words and uses adverbs and prepositions. The child talks confidently, and with more and more fluency.
- The child begins to be able to define objects by their function, e.g. 'What is a ball?' 'You bounce it.'
- The child begins to understand book language, and that stories have characters and a plot (the narrative).
- The child begins to realise that different situations require different ways of talking.

Intellectual development

Communication through body language, facial gestures and language is well established, and opens the way into **literacy** (talking, listening, writing and reading).

- The child includes more detail in their drawings – e.g. a house may have not only windows and a roof, but also curtains and a chimney.
- The child will recognise his or her own name when it is written down and can usually write it him- or herself.
- Thinking becomes increasingly coordinated as the child is able to hold in mind more than one point of view at a time. **Concepts** – of matter, length, measurement, distance, area, time, volume, capacity and weight – develop steadily.
- The child enjoys chanting and counting (beginning to understand number). The child can use his or her voice in different ways to play different characters in pretend play. The child develops play narratives (stories), which he or she returns to over time. The child helps younger children into the play.
- The child is beginning to establish differences between what is real and what is unreal/fantasy. This is not yet always stable, so the child can easily be frightened by supernatural characters.

Holistic development from five to eight years (cont.)

Emotional and social development

- The child has developed a stable **self-concept**.
- The child can hide their feelings once they can begin to control them.
- The child can think of the feelings of others.
- The child can take responsibility, e.g. in helping younger children.

Figure 4.12

Table 4.10 Holistic development from five to eight years

Holistic development from eight to eleven years

Physical development

Gross motor skills	Fine motor skills
From eight to nine years: - The child can ride a bicycle easily. - The child has increased strength and coordination. - The child plays energetic games and sports. **From ten to eleven years:** - Children differ in physical maturity. Girls experience puberty earlier than do boys and are often as much as two years ahead of them. - The child's body proportions are becoming more similar to an adult's.	- The child can control his or her small muscles well and has improved writing and drawing skills. - The child can draw people with details of clothing and facial features. - The child is starting to join letters together in handwriting. - The child tackles more detailed tasks such as woodwork or needlework. - The child is usually writing with an established style – using joined-up letters.

Holistic development from eight to eleven years (cont.)

Communication and language development

From eight to nine years:

- The child uses and understands complex sentences.
- The child is increasingly verbal and enjoys making up stories and telling jokes.
- The child uses reference books with increasing skill.

From ten to eleven years:

- The child can write fairly lengthy essays.
- The child writes stories that show imagination and are increasingly legible and grammatically correct.

Intellectual development

From eight to nine years:

- The child has an increased ability to remember and pay attention, and to speak and express their ideas.
- The child is learning to plan ahead and evaluate what they do.
- The child has an increased ability to think and to reason.
- The child can deal with abstract ideas.
- The child enjoys different types of activities – such as joining clubs, playing games with rules, and collecting things.
- The child enjoys projects that are task-orientated, such as sewing and woodwork.

From ten to eleven years:

- The child begins to understand the motives behind the actions of another.
- The child can concentrate on tasks for increasing periods.
- The child begins to devise memory strategies.
- The child may be curious about drugs, alcohol and tobacco.
- The child may develop special talents, showing particular skills in writing, maths, art, music or woodwork.

Emotional and social development

At eight or nine years old:

- The child may become discouraged easily.
- The child takes pride in their competence.
- The child can be argumentative and bossy, but can equally be generous and responsive.
- The child is beginning to see things from another child's point of view, but still has trouble understanding the feelings and needs of other people.

At eleven or twelve years old:

- The child may be experiencing sudden, dramatic, emotional changes associated with puberty (especially girls, who experience puberty earlier than boys).
- The child tends to be particularly sensitive to criticism.
- The child prefers to spend leisure time with friends and continues to participate in small groups of the same sex, but is acutely aware of the opposite sex.
- The child succumbs to peer pressure more readily and wants to talk, dress, and act just like friends do.

Holistic development from eight to eleven years (cont.)

Figure 4.13

Table 4.11 Holistic development from eight to eleven years

The main features of physical development in puberty

From 12 to 16 years

Physical development during adolescence is known as **puberty**. The age at which puberty starts varies from person to person but on average it begins between 9 and 13 in girls and 10 and 15 in boys. Many physical changes occur during puberty.

- **Growth** accelerates rapidly – often called a **growth spurt**. This usually happens in a particular order from outer to inner:
  - the head, feet and hands grow to adult size first, then
  - the arms and legs grow in length and strength, and finally
  - the trunk (the main part of the body from shoulder to hip) grows to full adult size and shape.

This sequence of growth means that, for a brief period, adolescents may feel gawky and clumsy, as they appear to be 'out of proportion'. The average boy grows fastest between 14 and 15. Girls start earlier, growing fastest when 12 and 13. Girls also finish their growth spurt earlier, at 18, while boys need another two years before they finish growing, aged 20.

- **Secondary sex characteristics** develop; these are external traits that distinguish the two sexes, but are not directly part of the **reproductive system**; for example, the growth of pubic hair in both sexes, facial hair and deepened voice for males, and breasts and widened hips for females.

- Primary sex characteristics develop; these are the penis and sperm in males and the vagina and ovaries in females. During puberty, hormonal changes cause a boy's penis and testicles to grow and the body to produce sperm. Girls start to menstruate or have their monthly period. Both these events signal **sexual maturity** – the ability to reproduce.

The main features of physical development in puberty (cont.)

In girls	In boys
The first *external* sign of puberty in most girls is usually breast development – often accompanied by a growth spurt.	The first *external* sign of puberty in most boys is an increase in the size of the testicles and then the penis. This is followed by the growth of pubic and underarm hair. At the same time, the voice deepens and muscles develop. Lastly, boys grow facial hair.
Breasts develop: at first, the nipples start to stick out from the chest (often called 'budding'). Behind the nipple, milk ducts begin to grow. Next, the flat, circular part of the nipple, the areola, rises and starts to expand. Glands that make sweat and scent develop beneath it. The breast begins to fill out, as fat is deposited around the nipple. Some girls feel a tingling sensation or have tender breasts. Initially the breasts stick out in a conical shape. As growth continues they gradually round off into an adult shape.	**Voice breaking:** testosterone causes the voice box – or larynx – to enlarge and the vocal cords to become longer. Sometimes, as the voice changes to become deeper, it may change pitch abruptly, or 'break', at times; the voice box tilts and often protrudes at the neck – as an 'Adam's apple'. (Many boys start to develop breasts in their teenage years, but this disappears as the testosterone levels increase.)
Body size and shape: grows taller. Hips widen as the pelvic bones grow. Fat develops on the hips, thighs and buttocks, and the ratio of fat to muscle increases. The waist gets smaller and the body develops a more curved shape.	**Body size and shape:** grows taller. Body takes on a new, more muscular shape as the shoulders and chest become broader and the neck becomes more muscular.
	Chest hair may appear during puberty – or some years later.
Menstruation: menstruation – having periods – is part of the female reproductive cycle that starts when girls become sexually mature during puberty. During a menstrual period, a woman bleeds from her uterus (womb) via the vagina. This lasts anything from three to seven days. Each period begins approximately every 28 days if the woman does not become pregnant during a given cycle. The onset of menstruation is called the menarche; it can occur at any time between the ages of 9 and 16, most commonly around the age of 12–13. It means that the body is capable of **reproduction**.	**Penile erections:** these occur spontaneously, even from infancy, but during puberty they become more frequent. Erections can occur with or without any physical or sexual stimulation and can cause acute embarrassment.
	Sperm: once the testicles begin to grow they also develop their adult function – producing sperm. Mature sperm is present in the male body towards the end of puberty (most commonly between the ages of 13 and 15) and means that the body is capable of **reproduction**.

In both girls and boys

Pubic hair starts to grow around the genitals, and becomes coarse, dark and curly. In girls, pubic hair forms an upside-down triangle shape; in boys, the hair grows between the legs and extends up from the penis to the abdomen.

Hair grows in the armpits and on the legs.

Sweat: a different kind of sweat is now produced in response to stress, emotion and sexual excitement. It is produced by the apocrine glands, and occurs only in the armpits, the belly button, the groin area, the ears and the nipples. As bacteria break down the sweat it starts to smell strongly – known as BO (body odour).

Oil glands: oil-secreting glands in the skin can become over-active – this can cause skin to become greasier and can also cause acne.

Table 4.12 Physical development in puberty

Holistic development from 12 to 19 years

Communication and language development

From 12 to 19 years

During this period, young people become increasingly independent and spend much of their day outside the home – at school or after-school activities, and with peers.

- The young person has a fast, legible style of handwriting.

- The young person communicates in an adult manner, with increasing maturity.

- The young person understands abstract language, such as idioms, figurative language and metaphors.

- The young person is able to process texts and abstract meaning, relate word meanings and contexts, understand punctuation, and form complex syntactic structures.

Intellectual development

From 12 to 19 years

Around this time, young people experience a major shift in thinking from **concrete** to **abstract** – an adult way of thinking. Piaget described this as the **formal operational stage** of intellectual development. This involves:

- *thinking about possibilities* – younger children rely heavily on their senses to apply reasoning, whereas adolescents think about possibilities that are not directly observable.

- *thinking ahead* – young people start to plan ahead, often in a systematic way; e.g. younger children may look forward to a holiday, but they are unlikely to focus on the preparation involved.

- *thinking through hypotheses* – this gives them the ability to make and test hypotheses, and to think about situations that are contrary to fact.

- *thinking about their own thought processes* – this is known as **metacognition**; a subcategory of metacognition is **metamemory**, which is having knowledge about your memory processes – being able to explain what strategies you use when trying to remember things (e.g. for an exam).

- *thinking beyond conventional limits* – thinking about issues that generally preoccupy human beings in adulthood, such as morality, religion and politics.

They approach a problem in a systematic fashion and also use their imagination when solving problems.

Emotional and social development

- The young person may become self-conscious or worried about physical changes (e.g. too short, too tall, too fat, too thin).

- The young person develops a sexual identity; self-labelling as gay or lesbian tends to occur around the age of 15 for boys and 15 and a half for girls, although first disclosure does not normally take place until after the age of 16 and a half years for both sexes.

- The young person often feels misunderstood.

- The young person can experience wide emotional swings (e.g. fluctuate between emotional peaks of excitement and depths of moodiness).

- The young person wants to become accepted and liked.

- The young person tends to identify more with friends and begin to separate from parents; they are less dependent on family for affection and emotional support.

Table 4.13 Holistic development from 12 to 19 years

Spiritual aspects of a child's development

The first year	Even a tiny baby experiences a sense of self, and of awe and wonder, and values people who are loved by them. Worship is about a sense of worth. People, loved teddy bears, a daisy on the grass grasped and looked at (or put in the mouth!) are all building the child's spiritual experiences. This has nothing to do with worship of a god or gods. Spirituality is about the developing sense of relationship with self, relating to others ethically, morally and humanely, and a relationship with the universe.
One to three years	Judy Dunn's work suggests that during this period children already have a strongly developed moral sense. They know what hurts and upsets their family (adults and children). They know what delights them and brings about pleased responses. Through their pretend play, and the conversations in the family about how people behave, hurt and help each other, they learn how other people feel. They learn to think beyond themselves.
Three to eight years	With the help and support of their family, early years practitioners and the wider community, children develop further concepts like being helpful and forgiving, and having a sense of fairness. By the age of seven years, they have a clear sense of right and wrong – e.g. they realise that it is wrong to hurt other people physically.
Eight to eleven years	By eight or nine years, children continue to think that rules are permanent and unchangeable because they are made up by adults, who must be obeyed and respected. They have a clear idea of the difference between reality and fantasy, and are highly concerned about fairness. By ten and eleven years, children understand that certain rules can be changed by mutual negotiation; often, they do not accept rules that they did not help make. They may begin to experience conflict between parents' values and those of their peers. These concepts become more abstract – such as justice, right, wrong, good versus evil, beauty and nature, the arts and scientific achievements.
Twelve to nineteen years	Young people are able to think beyond themselves more and to understand the perspective of another. They are developing their own ideas and values, which often challenge those of home; they may deliberately flout rules or keep to them only if there is otherwise a risk of being caught.

Table 4.14 Spiritual aspects of a child's development

Assessment practice

Stages of development timeline

Look at Table 4.15. Using the holistic development charts on pp 50–67, for each age group in Column 1, select three significant 'milestones' of development, using each category of development in Columns 2, 3, 4 and 5.

For example, for the age group **Birth to 1 year (Physical development)** you could choose to include the following three milestones:

- At eight to twelve weeks, the baby can now lift head and chest off bed in prone position, supported on forearms.

- At four to six months, the baby is beginning to use a palmar grasp and can transfer objects from hand to hand.

- At nine to twelve months, the baby will now be mobile – may be crawling, bear-walking, bottom-shuffling or even walking.

Age group	Physical development	Intellectual development	Communication and language development	Emotional and social development
Birth to 1 year				
1 to 3 years				
3 to 5 years				
5 to 8 years				
8 to 11 years				
12 to 19 years				

Table 4.15 Development chart

How different aspects of development can affect one another

The areas of development do not work separately – they are interconnected – this is why we talk about holistic development. Even when focusing on one aspect of development, it is important not to forget that we are looking at a whole person. Children and young people need to develop many different skills and this concerns more than one area of development. For example, a group painting activity requires children to use specific physical skills as well as involving aspects of intellectual, language, social and emotional development:

Communication and intellectual development

- Talking about their paintings
- Learning new words about painting: e.g. brush, names of colours, runny, bright etc.
- Using numbers in painting: e.g. people have two legs and two arms
- Making patterns and learning new words to describe them: round, square, straight, zig-zag.

Physical development

- Fine motor skills: holding brush or other tool, picking up paint from small pots etc.
- Awareness of space needed to paint without jogging each other.

Social, emotional and behavioural development

- Taking turns and sharing equipment
- Interested, excited, motivated to learn
- Choosing what to paint, when to paint and how to paint
- Concentrating, knowing which colours or materials they need.

Figure 4.14

Influences that affect children and young people's development

There are very many factors that affect the healthy growth and development of children. These factors work in combination and so it is often difficult to estimate the impact of any single factor on holistic child development.

Background
Parental health and lifestyle

Children who live with one or both parents who have a mental health problem, such as *depression*, sometimes suffer as their parents may lack the necessary support to deal with their condition. Also, some older children may find themselves in the role of carer for younger children.

- **Parents not available to their children:** This may occur when parents have substance misuse and are often absent both physically

Figure 4.15 Factors affecting development

(because they are out looking for drugs) and emotionally (because they are intoxicated). Either way, they are not available to the child. Parents who work long hours may also be unavailable to their children.

- **Poor parenting skills**: Substance misuse is often, but not always, associated with poor or inadequate parenting. This can show itself in a number of ways, including physical neglect, emotional neglect or unpredictable parental behaviour: for example, lurching between 'too much' or 'not enough' discipline and mood swings – being very affectionate or very remote. This leads to inconsistent parenting that can be confusing and damaging to the child. Some parents have poor parenting skills, such as being unable to cook.

Poverty and social disadvantage

Poverty is the single greatest threat to the healthy development of children in the UK. Growing up in poverty can affect every area of a child's development: physical, intellectual, emotional, social and spiritual.

Accident and illness: Children growing up in poverty are four times more likely to die in an accident and have nearly twice the rate of long-standing illness than those living in households with high incomes.

Quality of life: A third of children in poverty go without the meals or toys or clothes that they need.

Poor nutrition: Living on a low income means that children's diet and health can suffer.

Space to live and play: Poorer children are more likely to live in substandard housing and in areas with few shops or amenities, where children have little or no space to play safely.

Growth: They are also more likely to be smaller at birth and shorter in height.

Education: Children who grow up in poverty are statistically less likely to do well at school and have poorer school attendance records.

Long-term effects: As adults they are more likely to suffer ill health, be unemployed or homeless. They are statistically more likely to become involved in offending, drug and alcohol abuse. They are statistically more likely to become involved in abusive relationships.

Health
Infection

During childhood there are many infectious illnesses that can affect children's health and development. Some of these infections can be controlled by childhood immunisations; these are diphtheria, tetanus, polio, whooping cough, measles, meningitis, mumps and rubella. Other infections can also have long-lasting effects on a child's health.

Diet

There are various conditions that may occur in childhood that are directly related to a poor or unbalanced diet:

- **failure to thrive** (or faltering growth) – poor growth and physical development
- **dental caries** or tooth decay – associated with a high consumption of sugar in snacks and fizzy drinks
- **obesity** – children who are overweight are more likely to become obese adults
- **nutritional anaemia** – due to an insufficient intake of iron, folic acid and vitamin B12
- **increased susceptibility to infections** – particularly upper respiratory infections, such as colds and bronchitis.

Sleep

Sufficient sleep is essential for all aspects of children and young people's development. Being tired all the time because of insufficient sleep at night can affect their ability to learn as well as causing emotional, social and behavioural problems. (See Chapter 9 for further information on the importance of sleep and rest).

Environment

Pollution

Pollution of the environment can have a marked effect on the health and development of children and young people. The three main threats to health are **water pollution**, **air pollution** and **noise pollution**. Children are particularly vulnerable to air pollution. This is partly because they have a large lung surface area in relation to their small body size; this means that they absorb toxic substances more quickly than adults do and are slower to get rid of them. The effects of air pollution from factory chimneys, the use of chemical insecticides and car exhausts include:

- **lead poisoning** – children are particularly susceptible to lead poisoning, mostly caused by vehicle exhaust fumes. Even very low levels of lead in the blood can affect children's ability to learn.
- **asthma** – air pollution can act as a *trigger* for asthma and can make an existing condition worse. The incidence of asthma is much higher in traffic-polluted areas.

Housing

Poor housing is another factor that affects healthy holistic development. Low-income families are more likely to live in:

- *homes which are damp and/or unheated* – this increases the risk of infection, particularly respiratory illnesses
- *neighbourhoods which are densely populated*, with few communal areas and amenities – children without access to a safe garden or play area may suffer emotional and social problems
- *overcrowded conditions* – homeless families who are housed in 'hotels' or bed and breakfast accommodation often have poor access to cooking facilities and have to share bathrooms with several other families; often children's education is badly disrupted when families are moved from one place to another.

Accidents

Some accidents have lasting effects on a child or young person's healthy growth and development, and many are preventable (see Chapter 11, Unit PEFAP 001: Paediatric emergency first aid).

Emotional and social factors

A child who is miserable and unhappy is not healthy, although he or she may appear *physically* healthy. Children need to feel secure and to receive unconditional love from their primary carers. Child abuse, although not common, is bound to affect a child's health and wellbeing, and can have long-lasting health implications. See Chapter 6 for information about child abuse.

Opportunities for play

Through play, children bring together and organise their ideas, feelings, relationships and their physical life. It helps them to use what they know and to make sense of the world and people they meet. Play brings together:

- ideas and creativity
- feelings
- relationships
- physical coordination
- spiritual development.

Play helps children to use what they know and understand about the world and people they meet. In this way, you can see how play influences all aspects of child development.

Reflective practice: Supporting parents and carers

The great majority of parents are concerned to do their best for their child, even if they are not always sure what this might be. How might ineffective parenting skills affect a child's development? Find out what support is available for parents in the community.

Recognising and responding to concerns about children and young people's development

Practitioners are ideally placed to recognise when a child or young person's development is not following the expected norms. Often the parents will have expressed their own concerns and you need to respond to these.

At any point in their lives children and young people may need extra support in nursery or school. This may be for any reason, at any time and for any length of time. Some developmental concerns are temporary (such as a hearing impairment that is corrected by an operation) and therefore only require temporary support. (Chapter 5 has information on how to identify and assess development needs.)

The potential effects of transitions on children and young people's development

What are transitions?

A transition is a change from one stage or state to another. Children and young people naturally pass through a number of stages as they grow

 **Progress check**

Concerns about development

The following factors can all affect the way in which a child or young person develops holistically:

- **Family circumstances:** Family breakdown – e.g. separation of parents or arrival of a new partner; a child or young person being a carer for another family member; being looked after by the local authority or recently having left care.
- **Social or emotional problems:** Bereavement; behavioural difficulties; being involved in a bullying situation or subject to some form of discrimination.
- **Disability or health needs:** Hearing or visual impairment; language and communication difficulties; autistic spectrum disorder; chronic illness leading to frequent hospitalisation, and conditions requiring a surgical operation.

A child or young person whose development is giving cause for concern will need to be supported. Practitioners should try to identify the child or young person's particular developmental needs and respond quickly; the sooner the difficulty is identified the more likely that the support offered will be effective. Parents or carers should be consulted and the support needed can then be tailored to the individual child or young person.

and develop. Often, they will also be expected to cope with changes such as movement from nursery education to primary school, from primary to secondary school, or moving house.

You may have just made the transition from secondary school to a tertiary college or sixth form. Along with the excitement of a new course and possibly making new friends, you are likely to have felt some apprehension about the change to your life. This is likely to affect you more if you have experienced many changes in your life.

These changes are commonly referred to as **transitions**.

Expected transitions

Babies experience transitions when they:

- are weaned onto solid food
- are able to be cared for by others, such as at nursery or at a childminder's home
- progress from crawling to walking
- move from needing nappies to being toilet trained.

Children experience transitions when they:

- start nursery or are cared for by a childminder
- start primary school
- move up to secondary school.

Young people experience transitions when they:

- attend college or university
- go through puberty
- leave home, or
- start work.

Adults experience transitions when they:

- get married
- become separated or divorced
- have children
- change jobs
- experience a death in the family, which changes the family structure.

Unexpected transitions

Not every transition is experienced by every child – and not all transitions can be anticipated. These unexpected transitions include:

- Particular and personal transitions may include the following:
- the birth of a new baby in the family (although this is a very common transition, it is not always expected)
- divorce and the split of the family
- adoption
- leaving care
- issues related to sexuality
- the process of asylum
- teenage pregnancy
- disabilities
- family illness or the death of a close relative.
- parental mental health or substance misuse
- the consequences of crime.

Understanding the potential effects of transitions

You need to be able to identify transitions and understand what you can do to support children and young people through them. Before we can fully understand the importance of transitions in children and young people's lives, we need to learn about the concepts of **attachment** and **separation**, and the effects of **multiple transitions** in a child's life.

Attachment

Attachment means a warm, affectionate and supportive bond between a child and his or her carer that enables the child to develop **secure relationships**. When children receive warm, responsive care, they feel safe and secure.

- Secure attachments are the basis of all the child's future relationships. Because babies experience relationships through their senses, it is the expression of love that affects how they develop, and that helps to shape later learning and behaviour.
- Children who are securely attached will grow to be more curious, get along better with other children and perform better in school than children who are less securely attached.
- With children who have a strong attachment to their parent or primary carer, the process of becoming attached to the **key person** is *easier*, not harder, than it is for children with a weaker attachment. Remember, though, that all parents find separation difficult, whether they have formed a strong attachment with their child or not.

Figure 4.16 Babies need to have a strong attachment with their primary carers

Separation

Many of the times that prove to be difficult for children are connected with separation. Going to bed is separation from the main carer and is often a source of anxiety in children. Some young children can be terrified as a parent walks out of the room. How children react to separation is as varied as children's characteristics. For some children each new situation will bring questions and new feelings of anxiety; other children love the challenge of meeting new friends and seeing new things.

The effects of multiple transitions

Children who have had to make many moves or changes may feel a sense of loss and grief. These changes may have a profound effect on their emotional and social development. Reasons for transitions include:

- **Divorce or separation**: children whose parents have separated or divorced may have to live and get along with several 'new' people, such as stepfathers, stepmothers, half-brothers and sisters, etc.
- **Changes in child care arrangements**: children who experience many different child care arrangements; for example, frequent changes from one nanny or childminder to another.

- **Children who are in local authority care** – either in residential children's homes or in foster care.
- **Children whose families have moved house several times**, perhaps for employment reasons, or as travellers.

How transitions may affect children and young people's development and behaviour

Children and young people who have experienced multiple transitions need to feel supported every time they enter a new setting. They may:

- **Feel disorientated**: no sooner have they settled in one place and got to know a carer, than they may be uprooted and have to face the same process again.
- **Feel a sense of loss and sadness**: every time they make a move, they lose the friends they have made and also the attachments they have formed with their carers.
- **Become withdrawn**: they may withdraw from new relationships with other children and with carers, because they do not trust the separation not to happen again.
- **Become more clingy** and need to be shown more affection
- **Have difficulty in sleeping**
- **Experience mood swings**: this is particularly common during puberty
- **Show unacceptable behaviour**: young children may have frequent tantrums; older children and young people may show challenging behaviour
- **Experience changes in appetite**: this can result in obesity, when they eat more food as a means of gaining comfort, or in eating disorders such as anorexia or bulimia – when they restrict their food intake in an effort to gain control over their own changing lives

- **Show risky behaviours**: they may start to self-harm or to abuse alcohol and drugs
- **Play truant from school**: see Chapter 8 for more information on truancy.

As children become older, they start to cope better with being separated from their parents or main carers; however, the way they cope will still depend on their early experiences of separation and how earlier transitions were managed. Children who have had to change schools many times – maybe because of a parent's job being changed – often find it harder to settle in and make new friends and relationships. For more information on supporting children and young people through transitions, please see p 93, Chapter 5.

One expected transition that all young people experience is puberty. Puberty is the physical process where a child's body develops into an adult body and becomes capable of reproduction. We all have to make the transition from childhood into adulthood and almost without exception, everyone experiences some self-doubt. Because there is a very wide variation in the ages at which young people experience

 **Progress check**

Transitions

Choose three **expected transitions** and three **unexpected transitions** that may occur in children and young people's lives. (For example: one *expected* transition for all children is starting school; one *unexpected* transition might be their parents separating or divorcing.)

For each transition, describe:

- the possible effects on the child or young person when experiencing the transition
- how the child or young person could be supported through the transition.

Case Study | A new baby in the family

Sean is two and a half years old. He has been attending nursery for three days a week since he was a baby and is a happy, sociable little boy who interacts well with the other children. Sean's mother is expecting her second child. In the run-up to her due date, Sean is booked in occasionally for extra days and often dropped off by his father or grandparents. He seems to adjust very well to this and talks proudly about becoming an older brother. One Tuesday, after a few days away, Sean attends nursery with the news that he has a new little sister. He brings in photos and seems happy, if a little more tired than usual.

A week later, Sean is brought in by his mother (with his baby sister) for the first time in a few weeks. He becomes clingy and cries inconsolably for twenty minutes after she leaves. Over the following couple of weeks, Sean is brought in and picked up by his father, mother or grandparents. Sometimes he does not know who will be picking him up, or at what time. He is often late to arrive, missing the register time and morning song.

Sean becomes clingy to his key person and sullen when he has to share toys. He sometimes disrupts storytimes by wandering away and has started to have sudden tantrums. One day, Sean is playing with one of his friends, Jemima. They both want the same toy and Sean bites Jemima in frustration when she reaches for it first.

1 Identify all the changes in Sean's behaviour.
2 Why might having a new baby in the family affect Sean's behaviour and development?

puberty, the person who is the first or last one in their peer group to go through the physical and hormonal changes may feel awkward and embarrassed; they may also be teased by others in their group and this increases their feelings of insecurity.

In Practice

Helping children to settle in

This activity will help a child who is new to the setting to realise that he or she is not alone, and that other children also feel shy and alone at times.

❏ **Introduction**: choose a teddy and introduce him to the group, saying something like: 'Teddy is rather shy and a little bit lonely. How can we help him to feel better?'

❏ **Discussion and display**: take photos of teddy – using a digital camera if possible – with different groups of children, and in different places in the nursery (for example, playing in the sand, reading a book, doing a puzzle) and use later for discussion and display.

❏ **Circle time**: in circle time, pass teddy round, and encourage each child to say something to him: 'Hello Teddy, my name is Lara' or 'Hello Teddy, I like chocolate . . .', etc.

❏ **Taking teddy home**: each child takes it in turns to take teddy home. Include a notebook and encourage parents to write a few sentences about what teddy did at their house that evening. The children can draw a picture.

❏ **Storytime**: read and act out the story of *Goldilocks and the Three Bears*, with the different sized bowls, beds and chairs.

❏ **Cooking**: use a shaped cutter to make teddy-shaped biscuits or dough teddies.

❏ **Teddy bears' picnic**: Arrange a teddy bears' picnic where each child brings in a favourite bear.

What does your teddy like to eat? Are there enough plates, biscuits and cups for all the bears?

Progress check

Observing social needs

In your work placement, plan to observe an individual child's social needs during a whole session. Make a checklist that includes the following needs:

- **Interaction with other children**: observe how the child plays; for example, does he play alone (solitary play), alongside others but not with them (parallel play), or actively with other children?
- **Attention from adults**: does the child seek attention from one particular adult, or from any adult? Note the number of occasions a child seeks adult attention and describe the interaction.
- **Self-help skills and independence**: observe the child using self-help skills, such as putting on coat to go outside, washing hands and going to the lavatory.

Identify the stage of social development the child is passing through and list the ways in which you can ensure that their social needs are met within the setting.

Case Study
Supporting young people as they prepare for transitions

The Derby City Pathfinder is an example of targeted youth support. The new multi-agency youth support team aims to help prepare vulnerable young people for transitions and tackle drop-out from post-16 provision to reduce the numbers becoming NEET: NEET stands for **N**ot in **E**ducation, **E**mployment or **T**raining. The team is trialling an early identification tool based on risk factors associated with becoming NEET and identifying those most at risk of failure in the transitions from Key Stages 3 to 4 and leaving school (young people aged 11 to 16). A structured home visit questionnaire has been developed for use with parents and carers of those most at risk and their feedback has been very positive.

Research Activity

Targeted youth support

Find out about targeted youth support in your area. Support provided may include the following areas – all involving transitions:

- Parenting support
- Teenage pregnancy
- Youth homelessness
- Youth justice
- Drug and substance misuse.

The websites www.ecm.gov.uk (for England), www.scotland.gov.uk (for Scotland), www.deni.gov.uk (for Northern Ireland) and www.wales.gov.uk (for Wales) have a range of guidance documents and toolkits relevant to youth support programmes.

5 Contribute to the support of child and young person development: Unit CCLDMU 2.2

As we have seen in Chapter 1, Unit SHC 21: Introduction to communication in children and young people's settings, each child or young person develops in a unique way. When supporting child and young person development you need to learn how to meet each individual's needs. Observing children and young people in a structured way enables you to find out what their individual needs are and how best you can support them – by reflecting their interests and views, providing play opportunities for younger children and through providing challenges to children in a safe environment.

Learning outcomes

By the end of this chapter you will:

1. Be able to contribute to assessments of the development needs of children and young people.
2. Be able to support the development of children and young people.
3. Know how to support children and young people experiencing transitions.
4. Be able to support children and young people's positive behaviour.
5. Be able to use reflective practice to improve your own contribution to child and young person development.

Assessing the development needs of children and young people

Parents, babysitters and practitioners automatically watch the children in their care. They want to know that the children are safe, happy, healthy and developing well. Watching or observing closely can often reassure all concerned that everything is all right, but may also alert them to problems or illness. Any discussion about a child usually relates to what has been seen, heard or experienced, and leads to conclusions about his/her personality, likes and dislikes, difficulties, etc.

Anyone who works with children and young people needs to develop the skill of observing them (sometimes to be written/recorded) to check that a child is:

- **safe** – not in any physical danger from the environment, from itself or from others

- **contented** – there are many reasons why a child or young person might be miserable; some may relate to physical comfort (such as wet nappy, hunger, thirst), emotional comfort (such as main carer is absent, comfort object is lost) or lack of attention and stimulation. A young person might be feeling vulnerable when going through a transition or when experiencing problems at school or at home.
- **healthy** – eats and sleeps well and is physically active (concerns about any of these aspects may indicate that the child or young person is unwell). A young person may show signs of misusing substances, such as alcohol or drugs.
- **developing normally** – in line with general expectations for the child or young person's age in all areas; there will be individual differences but delays in any (for example, crawling, walking or speaking) may show a need for careful monitoring and, perhaps, specialist help. Any particular strength or talent may also be identified and encouraged.

A series of observations – particularly if they are written or recorded – can provide an ongoing record of progress, which can be very useful to parents and other professionals who may be involved with a child or young person's care and education.

Using different observation methods

The importance of careful observations

Observations can provide valuable information about:

- individual children and young people – their progress and how they behave in particular situations

- groups of children and young people – the differences between individuals in the same situations
- adults – how they communicate with children and young people and deal with behaviour
- which activities are successful and enjoyed by children and young people.

What should be recorded?

There is some information that should be included in any observation, but other aspects will depend on the purpose of the observation. If it is to consider the child's fine manipulative skills then the detail will probably be different from an observation that is to find out about a young person's social development – even if the same activity or situation is being observed. You should also record some introductory information (see below).

When you carry out a written observation it is usually because you want to find out something about an individual or a group of children and young people. This provides an **aim**, which should be identified at the start of your work. For example: 'To see what gross motor skills Child R uses in a PE lesson and consider how confident he is on the apparatus.'

A clear aim explains what you want to find out and the activity or context that you have decided will best show you. This is better than saying you will watch Child R in a PE lesson. The aim you identify should affect what information you write in your introduction and in the actual observation.

As well as an aim, your observation should also have the following:

- date carried out
- start and finish times
- who gave permission
- where it took place (setting)

- number of children or young people present
- number of adults present
- age of child/children or young people
- names or identification of children or young people (remember confidentiality)
- method used (brief reason for choice)
- signature of supervisor or tutor.

How should it be recorded?

Your tutors will have their own preferences for how they want you to present your work but, generally, each observation should include the following sections: **Introduction**; **Actual observation**; **Evaluation**; **Bibliography**.

Introduction

In this section you must state where the observation is taking place (for example, at the sand tray in a reception class) and give some information about what is happening (for example, the children had just returned to the classroom from assembly). If there is any relevant information about the child, you might include it here (for example, Child R has been ill recently and has missed two weeks of school). Include information that is relevant to your aim – it may be important to know whether he is of average build if you are dealing with physical skills, but not particularly relevant if you are dealing with imaginative play.

Actual observation

There are many different methods of recording and your tutors will help you decide which one is best – perhaps a 'chart' format, a checklist, or a written record describing what you see as it happens. Remember only to write what you see and, if appropriate, hear. Do not write your judgements, opinions, assessments, and so on. Make sure you include information about other children, young people or adults involved, if it is relevant.

When recording your observation, remember to maintain **confidentiality** by using only a child's or young person's first name or initial, or some other form of identification (such as 'Child R'). You may use 'T' or 'A' for 'teacher' or 'adult'.

Evaluation

An evaluation is an assessment of what you have observed. This section can be dealt with in two parts.

1. You need to look back at your recorded information and summarise what you have discovered. Example: 'Child R was looking around the classroom and fidgeting with his shoelaces during the story, and appeared bored and uninterested. However, he was able to answer questions when asked, so he must have been listening for at least part of the time.' This is a review of what you saw.

2. You then need to consider what you have summarised, and compare your findings to the 'norm', 'average' or 'expected' for a child of this age and at this stage of development. What have you yourself learned about this particular child/group of children, and how has this helped you to understand children's development more widely? Use relevant books to help you and make reference to them – or quote directly if you can find a statement or section that relates to what you are saying or the point you are making. Your tutor or assessor wants to know what you understand, not information he or she could read in a book, so use references carefully.

As observation of children and young people can help carers to plan for individual needs, try to suggest what activity or caring strategy might be needed next. You may also, in this section, give your opinion as to reasons for the behaviour, and so on; but take care not to jump to conclusions about the role of the child's background, and never make judgements about the child or the child's family.

Techniques for observations

Types of observation

This chapter looks at six different types of observation.

Narrative

Perhaps the most common form of observation is the narrative or descriptive observation. This type attempts to record everything that happens, as it happens, with plenty of detail. Methods that fit into the 'narrative' framework are:

- descriptive/running record
- detailed
- target child
- diary description
- anecdotal record
- tape and transcript (may be considered to fit into this category so long as the section is focused upon, and the tape used for evaluation purposes is continuous and not a series of edited extracts).

Time sampling

This is specific, selected information recorded at chosen time intervals. A chart format is most often used.

Event sampling

This involves specific actions, incidents or behaviour observed whenever they occur. A chart format is most often used.

Diagrammatic

These provide a visual and accessible display of collected information or, in the case of growth charts, information plotted in the context of identified 'norms'. They could take the form of:

- pie charts
- bar graphs
- flow diagrams
- sociograms
- growth charts.

Checklists

This type of observation is carried out with a pre-prepared list of skills or competencies that are being assessed, and is often used for 'can do' checks in the context of a structured activity.

Longitudinal study

Usually a collection of observations and measurements taken over a period of time using a variety of recording methods.

Sharing of information

Most settings provide clear guidance (sometimes in a booklet or sheet written especially for learners) about working with children and young people. Some settings now also have an Observations Policy. As a learner, you should also be given information that will help you understand what a particular setting is trying to achieve and how it goes about it. You will always need to gain *permission* to carry out an observation, and your tutor or placement supervisor may wish to read your work. This is not only to check it through, but also out of interest, to find out more about the children, activity or safety aspects that you observed. Remember, information accurately observed by you can be just as valuable to the setting as that gathered by staff.

Cooperation between professionals requires sharing of information. However, in a work setting observations and records must be kept confidentially and access given only to certain people; these may include the individual child's parents or legal guardian, supervisor, teacher or key worker and other involved professionals (such as the health visitor).

Remember: any information about a child may be shared only if the parent or legal guardian gives consent.

The importance of confidentiality and objectivity

Maintaining confidentiality is an important aspect of your role, but it is particularly important when carrying out observations, especially those that are written and recorded. For your own training and assessment purposes, the identity of the child or young person and setting is not important. They must, therefore, be protected (see below). You are developing your observational and record-keeping skills as you learn more about children and young people in general, children and young people as individuals, and the various work settings.

Objectivity in observations

When you record your observational findings you need to be as objective as possible. This means that you must record *factual information* – what you actually see and hear – rather than information you have already begun to interpret.

By including plenty of detail to describe what you see, you are providing yourself (and any reader) with much information for analysis. For example, the first extract in the case study below presents a much fuller picture of the situation than the second, and may lead you to a different conclusion about G's interest and attention. It is often difficult to describe facial expressions and actions accurately, which is why many learners produce work in the style of Observation B rather than in the style of A.

Observation A

'. . . G is sitting on the floor with her legs crossed and her left hand in her lap. She is twiddling her hair with her right hand and staring at a picture on the wall display behind the teacher's head.

Progress check

How to maintain confidentiality in your observation

- Ensure you have permission for making an observation – from your supervisor and the parent/main carer (this is confirmed by an authorising signature).
- Use codes rather than names to refer to the individuals involved – you should never use a child's first name. An initial or some other form of identification (such as Child 1) is sufficient. (You may use 'T' or 'A' for 'teacher' or 'adult'.)
- Understand and abide by policies and procedures in the setting.
- Take extra care when sharing observations with fellow learners – they may have friends or family involved in a work setting and could easily identify individuals.
- Never discuss children, young people or staff from your work setting in a public place (such as when sitting on a bus or in a café).
- Never identify individuals when talking at home about your daily experiences (they could be neighbours' children).

Case Study   Observations

Read the two brief examples below and identify where the observer has substituted a conclusion or interpretation for what was actually seen.

She is smiling. The teacher says 'G, what do you think will happen to the cat next?' G stops fiddling with her hair and looks at the teacher. 'I think it will hide,' she says and laughs as she turns to N next to her . . .'

Observation B

'. . . G is sitting cross-legged on the floor in front of the teacher. She is fiddling with her hair and looking bored. The teacher asks her a question,

'G, what do you think will happen to the cat next?' G says, 'I think it will hide . . .'

Supporting assessments of developmental needs

Having observed children and young people, practitioners can work out the best way to assess the developmental needs of each individual child or young person. In the Early Years Foundation Stage (EYFS), observation, assessment and planning make up one of the commitments under the heading of 'Enabling Environments'.

Each setting will have its own method of assessment, including:

- EYFS Assessment Framework (England) Early Intervention (Scotland), Cymorth (Wales), and Sure Start (Northern Ireland).
- Curriculum frameworks in schools
- Common Assessment Framework (see below).

Other professionals and specialists involved in observation and assessment

Health visitors oversee infant health, referring to paediatricians when necessary. They monitor weight, diet, general growth and development, usually until the child begins school. School Health Services, child health clinics and family health centres also use observations and assessments to monitor children's health and development. Sometimes, a child or young person is being helped by more than one agency. For example, a young person who is overweight will be at school and also under the care of a dietician. In these cases, the professionals will work together to assess the child's development, in partnership with parents, using the Common Assessment Framework (CAF). The CAF is useful in the following ways:

- *Assessment*: It helps to assess the child or young person in a holistic or all-round way. It

is just as important, using the example of an overweight young person, to find out how physically active he or she is at home and at school, as it is to find out what he or she is eating.

- *Parents and carers*: The CAF also looks at the support offered to the child or young person, including relationships, stimulation and responding to the child's needs.
- *Family and environment*: The CAF takes a wider look at the overall family and environment, and the overall capacity of the parents to support the child or young person's development now and over time.
- *Plan of action*: It will be used to agree an integrated plan of action, involving the parents, to meet the child or young person's needs.

How to meet identified developmental needs

Having observed and assessed the child or young person, you need to decide how best their needs can be met. You will need to refer to the relevant section of normative development to work out which area of development needs to be supported and then decide how this can be done. This involves:

- *Finding out about their interests and opinions*: Children and young people need to know that their interests and opinions are valued. This means showing respect for their interests and showing that you value their contributions. You can find out from parents and carers about the activities most enjoyed by young children. Older children and young people should be consulted about their preferences.
- *Providing challenging activities:* Children and young people need to feel engaged in activities – they may find activities that are too easy for them boring and unexciting. By planning activities that challenge them, you will be

helping them to feel a sense of achievement and supporting their progress.

- *Being prepared to be flexible when planning activities:* Planning activities should be a flexible process. You need to be prepared to alter your plans to take into account the individual preferences of children and young people. In this way, you will promote an atmosphere of trust and respect. Also, when you consult a young person about what they want to do at a particular time you can often support him or her to take ownership of the activity.

Case Study — The Early Morning Boxing project

The Early Morning Boxing project is for young people with issues such as aggression or drug and alcohol misuse. Young people work with qualified boxing coaches through twice-weekly intervention. This allows key workers to focus on issues like reducing smoking or cannabis use in order to achieve the training schedule. The programme is also positive in coaching young people who would not usually get up early in the morning to change their sleeping pattern. If a young person is using cannabis until the early hours of the morning, they soon realise that they have to change their habits in order to achieve their goals.

Supporting the development of children and young people

Planning activities to support children's holistic development

When deciding what activities and experiences will be offered to children, staff in a work setting must consider safety, space, children's ages and stage of development, supervision and availability of resources. Most work settings plan activities around well-chosen themes or topics. In early years settings and primary schools, these are usually relevant to the children themselves and, perhaps, the time of year – common ones are 'Ourselves', 'Autumn', 'Festivals' (such as Christmas, Diwali, Hanukkah, Chinese New Year), 'Growth' and 'Nursery Rhymes'.

Adult-led activities

These are planned, prepared and often initiated by adults. A water activity might be planned that focuses particularly on 'force' or 'pressure'. The adult may have selected the equipment that lends itself to using water under pressure – squeezy bottles, thin plastic tubing, a water pump – and allowed children to use it in their own way, or played alongside the children, talking about what was happening and questioning them so that they express their ideas.

Research Activity

Supporting young people with identified needs

Every local authority runs programmes for young people to support them and to help them achieve their potential. Find out the range of activities for young people in your local area. A useful website is www.nya.org.uk (The National Youth Agency).

Even when an activity is adult-led, it should always involve *active participation* by the children. Activities that have an 'end product' (such as a model or a special occasion card) must allow for children's experimentation and creativity, so that each one is different and original. There is absolutely no value in directing every aspect of a task. You should not aim for all the children's work to look the same or 'perfect' (your idea of what the finished article should look like). Ownership is very important: children need to feel that their work is their own. What children learn from doing the activity – practical skills, understanding of materials, textures, sounds, and so on – is far more important than the finished article. Young children should also be able to choose whether or not to make a card or a model.

Child-initiated activities

These occur when children make their own decisions, without suggestion or guidance from adults, about the way in which they use the equipment and resources provided for them. For example, although an adult may have chosen which construction materials to set out (such as wooden blocks), two children may decide to work together to build a castle for 'small world' figures or 'play people'. This, then, is a child-initiated activity.

Structured activities

These should be carefully planned to develop a particular aspect of understanding or skill. They are structured in that there are resources, carefully chosen, and usually a sequence of tasks, or steps, that may lead to a desired learning outcome or objective. An adult usually leads, supervises and monitors children's responses.

 In Practice

A simple sorting activity

The aim of this activity is to find out whether children can identify and sort all the blue objects from a selection of objects of different colours.

Ask the children individually to find something blue and to put it in the sorting 'ring' with other blue things – this ensures that all children participate, and enables the adult to find out if the child has understood the task and can carry it out.

❏ For this task the child has to know what 'blue' means and be able to distinguish objects of that colour from others.

❏ Some children may not realise that there are different shades of blue that are still 'blue'.

❏ Adults working with children on an activity such as this need to talk to them. Asking questions and enjoying a chat together help adults check each child's understanding.

Spontaneous activities

These can be stimulated by natural events – a hailstorm, snow, a rainbow, puddles – or by an experience a child has had and wants to share with you (such as the arrival of a new baby, a new pet, a birthday). The excitement generated by such occurrences makes the learning opportunities too good to let pass without capitalising on them. Planned activities can be postponed to another time in order to make the most of spontaneity. Other spontaneous activities arise when children make their own decisions about how they use the play equipment – perhaps arranging chairs to pretend they are travelling on a bus.

The adult role during an activity

The most obvious role is that of ensuring safety by supervising effectively. Regardless of age and setting, there are always some activities that must be supervised. These include:

Figure 5.01 Children love to splash in puddles

- cooking
- tasting
- activities involving living things
- those involving equipment that could be dangerous if wrongly used
- physical – particularly those involving climbing frames and/or gymnastic equipment.

Another role is to encourage children and young people to try new things and to express their ideas. This involves the adult showing a genuine interest in the children's activities and talking with them about the activities they are involved in. It is important that children experiment themselves, explore the materials and use them in creative ways rather than follow an adult's directions. Asking 'open' questions (see Chapter 1, Unit SHC 21: Introduction to communication in children and young people's settings, for more information on effective communication) encourages children to put their thoughts into words, and the adult can extend their vocabulary by offering the new words in context and at the right time.

When to intervene

You *must* intervene when:

- children are likely to harm themselves
- children could hurt others
- there is a risk of damage to property or equipment

. . . **play is becoming rough or too boisterous** – sometimes just a look or a word will be enough to remind them of acceptable behaviour.

. . . **children deserve praise** – for effort, acceptable behaviour, achievement.

. . . **you notice the children are experimenting and you see an opportunity to develop their understanding,** e.g. rolling toy cars down a slope and talking about which one is fastest. Questioning – 'Why do you think the blue one reached the carpet first?' encourages them to express their ideas – they may be on the wrong track 'because it's blue' or they might think of a reason that could be tested 'because it has more wheels than the red one' or 'because its wheels are bigger'.

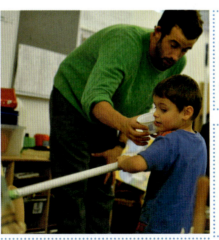

. . . **some children appear to be excluded from an activity** – this may result from strong personalities 'taking over'. Just talking to the group and asking what each is doing may be enough to solve the problem.

. . . **children are experiencing difficulties** – this may result in them losing concentration and not managing to persevere with what they are trying to do. A little encouragement and praise for their efforts can give them the confidence to try again.

. . . **children become frustrated** – offer support to help them through the difficult stage and move them on to the next step, e.g. if they are having trouble joining two pieces of Lego assist them by calming them and then, perhaps, holding one piece firmly while they fit the other. DO NOT take both pieces and do it for them.

. . . **children are losing interest** – talk to them about the activity, ask questions that might prompt them to try something new or creative OR suggest they move to another activity.

Figure 5.02 Adults may choose to intervene when. . .

- children are behaving unacceptably (for example, showing discrimination by name-calling, physical aggression or spitefulness).

The important thing to remember is that children learn best by finding answers for themselves with encouragement and support. The adult role is *not* to take control of the activity away from the children and 'do the difficult bits' for them.

Chapter 1, Unit SHC 21: Introduction to communication in children and young people's settings, discusses the principles of effective communication with children.

Helping children to learn: Scaffolding

Jerome Bruner, a psychologist, believed in the importance of scaffolding in helping children to learn. Adults can help develop children's thinking by being like a piece of scaffolding on a building. At first, the building has a great deal of scaffolding (adult support of the child's learning), but gradually, as the children extend their competence and control of the situation, the scaffolding is progressively removed until it is no longer needed.

Scaffolding can be described as anything a teacher can provide in a learning environment that might help a child or young person to learn. This includes anything that allows the learner to grow in independence – such as:

- clues or hints
- reminders
- encouragement
- breaking a problem down into smaller steps
- providing an example.

The same scaffolding may be provided to all learners, or teachers may offer customised scaffolding to individual learners.

Scaffolding an activity

Daniel and his father were out shopping. Daniel stopped walking and was obviously struggling to zip up his jacket, and was becoming increasingly frustrated. His father stood behind him and – using his own hands to guide Daniel's – helped him to insert the end of the zip into the metal fitting. When Daniel had managed to slot it in, he was easily able to pull the zip up by himself and was delighted.

In class, think about the following scenarios and discuss how you could scaffold the child's learning:

- learning to ride a two-wheeled bike
- learning how to tie shoelaces.

How to encourage concentration and attention in children and young people

An important part of the learning process is being able to concentrate and to keep one's attention focused on one activity at a time, without being distracted by other things. We all use our attention and concentration skills everyday, often without really noticing them. These skills help us to:

- select and focus on what is important (such as what the teacher is saying)
- ignore irrelevant things that we do not need to pay attention to (such as what you can hear going on outside), and
- maintain our effort or attention over time (such as concentrate for the necessary amount of time).

Sometimes we need to pay attention to more than one thing at a time. This may require certain skills – for example, copying work from the board while the teacher is explaining the information being given.

Figure 5.03 (A–E) The practitioner is 'scaffolding' this child's attempts to walk unaided

There are two types of concentration required in different situations:

1. **Active concentration**: construction, creative activities, imaginative play, sand and water play, problem-solving in maths and science, and literacy activities.
2. **Passive concentration:** watching television or videos, listening to stories, sitting in assemblies, etc.

Some children can concentrate passively for fairly long periods, while others are better able to concentrate actively when building a model or taking part in imaginative play.

Difficulties with attention and concentration

All children and young people have times when they find it difficult to concentrate. This could be because they:

- are too tired or unwell
- are unable to focus in a busy environment, with other children talking to them or around them
- are easily distracted by things going on around them
- are easily distracted by thoughts or feelings which are unrelated to the task at hand (day-dreaming)
- are easily overwhelmed by large amounts of information
- are emotionally distressed
- have attention deficit hyperactivity disorder (ADHD – see Chapter 14, Unit TDA 2.15: Support children and young people with disabilities and special educational needs).

Promoting self-reliance

Children and young people need to learn to be capable and independent in order to learn new skills. The child who is self-reliant will be more active, independent and competent; he or she

In Practice

Helping children and young people to concentrate

There are many ways in which you can help children to concentrate. These include the following:

- ❏ **Minimise distractions**: children need a quiet area for activities which require more concentration; carpets and rugs can be used to keep noise levels down.
- ❏ **Respond to individual needs**: some children react inappropriately when they feel rushed in their learning – others become bored and may disrupt others if given too much time for one activity.
- ❏ **Time activities appropriately**: avoid situations where the children or young people are passive listeners for long periods of time. Keep activities brief or structure them into short blocks; provide a clear beginning and end.
- ❏ **Provide children with hands-on activities**: for example, experiments, orienteering activities, projects, etc.
- ❏ **Use children's names and make eye contact**: when giving instructions, grab the child's attention by calling their name and making eye contact.
- ❏ **Use memory games** and encourage participation in classroom discussions and other collaborative activities.
- ❏ **Use songs and rhymes**: these will improve memory and concentration.
- ❏ **Use praise and positive feedback**: children benefit from having targets to improve their concentration and incentives or rewards when they reach them.

will have the confidence necessary to cope with situations on his/her own and to become an effective learner. All children should be allowed and encouraged to do the things that they can do from an early age – and be praised and rewarded for their efforts.

Allow children to do things for themselves

Even very young children begin to show an interest in doing things for themselves.

- Encourage independence by letting children do things for themselves as soon as they express a desire to do so.
- Focus on the effort made by the child and avoid being critical of the 'end product'.
- Always praise children for doing things on their own. As children grow and mature, they will naturally want to do more and more for themselves.
- Encourage children to help with challenging tasks. This helps to promote self-confidence.
- Encourage children to try to do new things and to face new challenges; this will promote self-confidence. Remember to choose tasks that children can accomplish.

Encourage children to make decisions

Children learn to make positive choices by being given choices. At first, choices should be kept simple, like allowing children to choose what to wear out of two outfits. As children get older, encourage them to make more and more complex decisions.

Be a positive role model for responsibility and independence.

Children learn by watching adults. Let children see you making decisions without wavering, and also taking care of responsibilities in an appropriate manner.

Help and encourage children to solve their own problems

Problem-solving is a skill that must be learned. Encourage children to think of their own solutions to their problems. The ability to solve problems is a skill that will be useful throughout children's lives. It will also help in the development of confidence and independence.

Encourage children to take risks

Taking risks involves facing potential failure. Many parents – and other adults – try to shield children from the disappointment of failure. However, children need to take risks in order to grow. Children must experience failure in order to learn how to cope with it.

Be there to provide support, when needed

Even the most independent-minded children need adult support on certain occasions. Make an effort to be available to the children in your care and to provide support when needed. Children who are secure in their relationships will have the confidence needed to explore the world.

Praise children

Children should receive praise when they display responsible and independent behaviour. Adults who praise such behaviour are letting children know that they notice and appreciate their efforts.

Give children responsibilities

One of the best ways for children to learn how to behave responsibly is to be given responsibilities. Make sure that the tasks assigned to the children match their capabilities. Take the time to show them how to do their assigned tasks properly. However, how well children perform a task is not as important as what they are learning about responsibility.

Figure 5.04 This child enjoys responsibility for pouring water for others at lunchtime

The importance of consulting the child when supporting children's learning

It is important to recognise that young people have a right to participate in the key decisions that affect their lives. Article 12 of the United Nations Convention on the Rights of the Child states that children and young people should have the opportunity to express their views on matters that concern them, and to have those views taken into account when decisions are made. It is generally agreed that participation by young people results in real benefits for themselves and for the organisations that consult them. These benefits include:

- skills development – communication, negotiation and teamwork
- educational experience
- promoting a sense of responsibility for oneself and others

- being enjoyable and sociable
- raising self-esteem.

Recent research into consultation with pupils found that children's learning experiences could be enhanced if tasks were more closely aligned with the social worlds in which they lived – both inside and outside the classroom. Children said they found it helpful when teachers used materials, objects and images with which they were already familiar.

Motivation to learn

Being able to make decisions about their activities is a very important aspect in children's active learning because it ensures that learning is matched to what they *want* to do and achieve. It also enables children to be in control and independent.

Supporting children and young people experiencing transitions

For a description of the transitions commonly experienced by children and young people, see pp 73–8, Chapter 4, Unit TDA 2.1: Child and young person development.

The first few days at a nursery or playgroup can be very daunting for some children. They may not have been left by their parents or primary carers before and some children will show real distress. You need to be able to recognise their distress and to find ways of dealing with it. Children show their distress at being separated from their carer by crying and refusing to join in with activities. Parents too can feel distressed when leaving their children in the care of others; they may feel guilty because they have to return to work, or they may be upset because they have never before been separated from their child.

You can help a child to settle in by doing the following:

- **Trying to plan for the separation**: nursery staff can help by visiting the child and their parents at home. This gives both parents and children the opportunity to talk about their fears and help them to cope with them. When children know in advance what is going to happen and what will not happen, they can think about and get used to their feelings about it. Parents can be encouraged to prepare their child for the change by:
  (a) visiting the nursery with their child so that they can meet the staff
  (b) reading books about starting at a nursery or going to hospital, and
  (c) involving their child in any preparation, such as buying clothing or packing a 'nursery bag'.

- **Encouraging parents to stay with their child until the child asks them to leave**: this does not mean that the parents should cling to their child. Children can always sense a parent's uncertainty. Although young children do not have a very good sense of time, parents and carers should make it very clear when they will be back, saying for example, 'I'll be back in one hour.'

- **Allowing the child to bring a comforter**, such as a blanket or a teddy bear, to the nursery. If it is a blanket, sometimes the parent can cut a little piece and put it in the child's pocket if they think there will be any embarrassment. Then the child can handle the blanket and feel comforted when feeling lonely. This object is often called a **transitional object** as it helps the child to make the transition from being dependent on family for comfort to being able to comfort him- or herself.

- **Having just one person to settle the child**: hold and cuddle the child and try to involve him or her in a quiet activity with you, such as reading a story. Most child care settings now employ a key person who will be responsible for one or two children during the settling-in period.

- **Contacting the parent or primary carer** if the child does not settle within 20 minutes or so. Sometimes it is not possible to do this, and you will need to devise strategies for comforting and reassuring the child. Always be honest with parents regarding the time it took to settle their child.

Other transitions

Where children are facing other transitions or changes in their lives – such as bereavement or loss or the arrival of a new sibling – their key person will need to be especially sensitive to their feelings and always take time to talk with them

Figure 5.05 A happy reunion for mother and child

Key terms

Transition – Any significant stage or experience in the life of a child or young person that can affect his or her behaviour and/or development.

Transitional object – Often a soft toy or blanket to which a child becomes attached, a transitional object is used by a child to provide comfort and security while he or she is away from a secure base, such as mother or home.

Comfort objects

Do you remember having a special comfort object? What did this object mean to you? Using examples from your settings, discuss how, in early childhood, such objects help to comfort young children coping with separation and transitions.

Reflective practice: Transitions

How does your setting help children to cope with transitions? Does it have a settling-in policy? Find out how children new to the setting are helped to separate from their parents or carers.

about how they are feeling. Opportunities should be provided for children to express their feelings in a safe and unthreatening environment. For example, some children may be encouraged to use play dough to release pent up feelings of frustration; others may choose to use role play.

The role of the key person

Each family is allocated a key person at nursery who gets to know them well, and this helps everyone to feel safe. A baby or young child knows that this special person and the important people at home often do the same things for them; they:

- help the child manage through the day
- think about the child
- get to know the child well
- sometimes worry about the child
- get to know each other
- talk about the child.

The key person role is defined as a special emotional relationship with the child and the family.

Support children and young people's positive behaviour

For information on how to support children and young people's positive behaviour, see Chapter 8, Unit TDA 2.9: Support children and young people's positive behaviour.

Using reflective practice to improve your own contribution to child and young person development

It is important to be consistent in the way we react to behaviour from the children which is unacceptable in the setting. We should not underestimate the impact which our own mood and our own behaviour can have on the children in our care. By reflecting on our own behaviour we can learn more about the factors influencing behaviour generally and how to promote positive behaviour in children and young people.

Useful websites and resources

www.teachingexpertise.com	Resources for early years professionals to support children's development and learning needs.

Reflective practice: Thinking about your own behaviour

Ask yourself the following questions:

- Do I know why the child or young person is behaving as he or she is?
- Have I considered the child or young person's needs? Is he or she tired, hungry, or simply needing a hug?
- Have I talked with and listened to the child or young person?
- Have I been consistent in dealing with unacceptable behaviour, and set a positive role model?
- Would it be appropriate for a child to say or do what I have just said or done?
- Is there anything I could change in the physical environment to create a more relaxed, comfortable environment, one that is conducive to meeting the child or young person's needs?

Assessment practice

Transitions

1. Explain what is meant by the term 'transition'. Why is it important to be able to identify when a child is going through a transition?

2. Describe the different transitions that a child or young person may experience. Give examples of how each type of transition might affect the person.

3. Explain how you could support a child through the transition phase.

6 Safeguarding the welfare of children and young people: Unit TDA 2.2

Safeguarding children and young people's welfare means protecting them from harm and ensuring their wellbeing and quality of life. It also means helping children to grow up into confident, healthy and happy adults.

Learning outcomes

By the end of this chapter you will:

1. Know about the legislation, guidelines, policies and procedures for safeguarding the welfare of children and young people including e-safety.

2. Know what to do when children or young people are ill or injured, including emergency procedures.

3. Know how to respond to evidence or concerns that a child or young person has been abused, harmed or bullied.

Safeguarding children and young people

Safeguarding and promoting the welfare of children is defined as:

- protecting children from maltreatment
- preventing impairment of children's health or development
- ensuring children are growing up in circumstances consistent with the provision of safe and effective care.

Child protection is a part of safeguarding and promoting welfare. It refers to the activity that is undertaken to protect specific children who are suffering, or are likely to suffer, significant harm. Safeguarding children is broader than the previous term, child protection, as it also encompasses the *prevention* of child abuse and neglect.

Legislation, guidelines, policies and procedures

Laws and guidance

A number of laws and statutory guidance documents govern the ways in which children in the UK are safeguarded. The laws are slightly different in each of the UK countries.

In England and Wales:

- the Children Act 1989
- the Children Act 2004
- Working Together to Safeguard Children 2006.

In Scotland:

- the Children (Scotland) Act 1995
- Protection of Children (Scotland) Act 2003.

In Northern Ireland:

- The Children (Northern Ireland) Order 1993.

The Children Act 1989 (England and Wales), Children (Northern Ireland) Order 1993

These Acts were introduced in an effort to simplify the laws affecting children. They emphasise the importance of the **principle of paramountcy** – which means that a child's welfare is paramount when making any decisions about his or her upbringing.

The Children Act 2004

The Children Act 2004 was prompted by the Lord Laming inquiry into the horrific history of abuse and eventual death of Victoria Climbié in February 2002. The inquiry report revealed major failings within the different child protection systems and procedures with which the eight-year-old girl came into contact. Victoria Climbié died despite being known to four London boroughs, two hospitals, two police child protection teams and the National Society for the Prevention of Cruelty to Children.

Working Together to Safeguard Children 2006

This followed on from The Children Act 2004 and confirmed the intention to oblige all agencies and services to work together to minimise risks and to anticipate what might threaten the welfare of children and young people.

'The support and protection of children cannot be achieved by a single agency . . . Every service has to play its part. All staff must have placed upon them the clear expectation that their primary responsibility is to the child and his or her family'.

Lord Laming (2003)

The Safeguarding Vulnerable Groups Act 2006

This Act was passed as a result of the Bichard Inquiry arising from the Soham murders in 2002 – when the schoolgirls Jessica Chapman and Holly Wells were murdered by Ian Huntley (a school caretaker). The inquiry questioned the way employers recruit people to work with vulnerable groups, and particularly the way background checks are carried out. Scotland set up its own similar authority linked to the Independent Safeguarding Authority (see p 98).

Statutory guidance documents

Statutory guidance documents are produced by each relevant government department to explain the duties contained in the different Acts in non-legal language. They serve to clarify for everyone who works with children and young people precisely what their duties are in the protection of children from abuse. Remember that these guidance documents may refer to law that does not necessarily apply to your area of the UK.

Policies and procedures

All settings working with children and young people provide the following:

- A policy – reviewed annually – that sets out the responsibilities for practitioners for the protection of children and young people under the age of 18
- Training on safeguarding for all those working in – or involved with – the setting
- A named senior staff member with responsibility for safeguarding arrangements

- A duty to inform the Independent Safeguarding Authority of any person involved with the setting who is a threat to children and young people
- Arrangements to work with the Local Safeguarding Board
- Procedures that include risk assessment within the setting to ensure that the policy works in practice
- The Criminal Records Bureau (see below) checks on all adults who have regular unsupervised access to children under the age of 18.

 Progress check

A safeguarding policy

Find out about the policy and procedures in your workplace relating to child protection and safeguarding.

The roles of different agencies involved in safeguarding the welfare of children and young people

The Integrated Children's System

Local child protection registers are being phased out and replaced by the new Integrated Children's System. The Integrated Children's System is designed to help social services managers and practitioners, together with colleagues from other agencies, to improve outcomes for children in need and their families. It builds upon previous developments such as the Assessment Framework and the Looking After Children materials, and offers a single approach to undertaking the key processes of assessment, planning, intervention and reviewing based on an understanding of children's developmental needs in the context of their families and communities.

(See also p 178, Chapter 10, Unit MU 2.9: Understand partnership working in services for children and young people.)

The Criminal Records Bureau

The Criminal Records Bureau (CRB) carries out checks on anyone who wishes to work with children, young people, elderly people or individuals who might otherwise be classed as vulnerable. The CRB is able to provide information about whether or not an individual has a criminal conviction or has been charged with a criminal conviction which has expired. This information is gathered from a number of sources and collated by the CRB who will provide the applicant with what is known as a 'disclosure'.

The Independent Safeguarding Authority (ISA)

The ISA introduced the controversial Vetting and Barring Scheme, which would require *anyone* working or volunteering with children and vulnerable adults to register with the ISA. The Scheme was planned to come into force in July 2010, but has been halted by the present government.

The Child Exploitation and Online Protection (CEOP) Centre

This is the UK's national law enforcement agency that focuses on tackling the sexual abuse of children and runs the **ThinkUKnow** internet safety scheme. This scheme highlights the importance of online safety (**e-safety**) to children and parents and also encourages them to use the 'Report Abuse' button, which can be used to get help and advice and to report illegal online behaviour.

The NSPCC

The NSPCC (The National Society for the Prevention of Cruelty to Children) helps end cruelty to children in the UK in a range of different ways:

- *Helping children through ChildLine*: ChildLine is the UK's free, confidential helpline for children and young people. Trained volunteers provide advice and support, by phone and online, 24 hours a day. Children can also receive advice by text.
- *Services for children and families*: Projects in local communities offer a range of services for children who have experienced, or are at risk of, abuse.
- *Advice for adults and professionals*: NSPCC helplines, general enquiries and specialist advice and information for adults and professionals in order to help them protect children.
- *Research*: NSPCC looks at the issues around abuse in order to develop services, campaigns and other new ways to end cruelty to children.
- *Consultancy services*: NSPCC works with organisations and professional networks to help them do everything they can to protect children. If necessary, they will use their authorized person status to intervene when a child is at risk.

What to do when children or young people are ill or injured, including emergency procedures

Occasionally a child or young person may arrive at the setting apparently healthy and happy, yet later he or she may be showing signs and symptoms of a serious illness, or may have an accident and need treatment. You need to make sure that you know the signs and symptoms of the more common illnesses and injuries – and when to send for medical help.

General signs and symptoms of illness in children

When children feel generally unwell, you should ask them if they have any pain or discomfort and treat it appropriately. Take their temperature and look for other signs of illness, such as a rash or swollen glands. Often, feeling generally unwell is the first sign that the child is developing an **infectious disease**. Some children can also show general signs of illness if they are anxious or worried about something, either at home or at school.

Common signs and symptoms of illness in children are:

- **Loss of appetite** – the child may not want to eat or drink; this could be because of a sore, painful throat or a sign of a developing infection.
- **Lacking interest in play** – the child may not want to join in play, without being able to explain why.
- **Abdominal pain** – the child may rub his or her tummy and say that it hurts. This could be a sign of gastroenteritis.

- **Raised temperature (fever)** – a fever (a temperature above 38°C) is usually an indication of viral or bacterial infection, but can also result from overheating.
- **Diarrhoea and vomiting** – attacks of diarrhoea and/or vomiting are usually a sign of gastroenteritis.
- **Lethargy or listlessness** – the child may be drowsy and prefer to sit quietly with a favourite toy or comfort blanket.
- **Irritability and fretfulness** – the child may have a change in behaviour, being easily upset and tearful.
- **Pallor** – the child will look paler than usual and may have dark shadows under the eyes; a black child may have a paler area around the lips, and the conjunctiva (the lining of the eyelids) may be pale pink instead of the normal dark pink.
- **Rash** – any rash appearing on the child's body should be investigated. It is usually a sign of an infectious disease.

High temperature (fever)

The normal body temperature is between 36°C and 37°C. A temperature of above 37.5°C means that the child has a fever. Common sense and using the back of your hand to feel the forehead of an ill child are almost as reliable in detecting a fever as using a thermometer.

A child with a fever may:

- look hot and flushed; the child may complain of feeling cold and might shiver (this is a natural reflex due to the increased heat loss and a temporary disabling of the usual internal temperature control of the brain)
- be either irritable or subdued
- be unusually sleepy
- refuse their food
- complain of thirst.

Children can develop high temperatures very quickly. You need to know how to bring their temperature down to avoid complications such as dehydration and febrile convulsions.

 Progress check

How to recognise general signs of illness in a child

If you can answer 'Yes' to any of these questions, then the child could be ill and the child's parents or doctor should be informed:

- Is the child complaining of not feeling well?
- Does the child appear lethargic (more than usual)?
- Does the child have skin rashes, itchy skin or scalp?
- Does the child appear to have a fever? And if so, is their temperature above 38°C?
- Does the child vomit?
- Does the child have an abnormal stool (such as diarrhoea)?
- Does the child have a severe cough?
- Is the child not urinating?
- Is the child refusing to eat or drink the amount that is normal for the child (especially when offered favourite foods)?
- Does the child appear or behave differently from normal?

How to respond when a child or young person is ill or injured

The responsibility of caring for a child who becomes ill is enormous; it is vital that carers should know the signs and symptoms of illness and when to seek medical aid. When a child is taken ill or is injured, it is vital that the parents or guardians are notified as soon as possible.

If a child becomes ill while at nursery, he or she may have to wait a while to be taken home; meanwhile you should:

- offer support and reassurance to the child, who may feel frightened or anxious.

Research Activity

Reducing a child's temperature

Write a one-page (A4) leaflet showing the following information:

- the normal body temperature
- what is meant by fever, or raised temperature
- how to take
  - (a) a baby's temperature
  - (b) a child's temperature
- how to reduce a child's temperature.

- always notify a senior member of staff if you notice that a child is unwell; that person will then decide if and when to contact the child's parents.

A member of staff – preferably the child's key person – should remain with the child all the time and keep them as comfortable as possible.

You must deal with any incident of vomiting or diarrhoea swiftly and sympathetically to minimise the child's distress and to preserve their dignity. All child care settings have an Exclusion policy that lets parents know when it is safe for their sick child to return to the nursery or group.

Treatment for common injuries is detailed in Chapter 12, Unit MPII002: Managing paediatric illness and injury.

What to do in case of serious illness or injury

- **Call for help**: Stay calm and do not panic! Your line manager or designated First Aider will make an assessment and decide whether the injury or illness requires **medical help**, either a GP or an ambulance. He or she will also **contact the parents** to let them know about the nature of the illness or injury.
- **Stay with the child** and comfort and reassure him or her.
- **Treat the injury or assess the severity of the illness** and treat appropriately. You are not expected to be able to diagnose a sudden illness, but should know what signs and symptoms require medical treatment.
- **Record exactly what happens** and what treatment is carried out.

What to do when an accident happens

If a child has had an accident, they are likely to be shocked and may not always cry immediately. They will need calm reassurance as **first aid** is given, together with an explanation of what is being done to them and why. Parents must be informed and the correct procedures for the setting carried out. If the child needs emergency hospital treatment, parental permission will be needed.

If you work in a setting with others such as a day care facility or school, there is likely to be a designated person who is qualified in first aid, and they should be called to deal with the situation.

Remember! It is essential that you do not make the situation worse. It is better to do the minimum to ensure the child's safety such as putting them into the **recovery position**. The only exception to this is if the child is not breathing or there is no heartbeat.

Recognising the need for urgent medical attention

A child or young person who has sustained a serious injury or illness will need to be seen urgently by a doctor. Serious conditions include:

- a head injury or any loss of consciousness
- a wound that continues to bleed after first aid treatment is given
- fracture or suspected fracture, burns and scalds, foreign bodies
- life-threatening incidents: for example, seizures, poisoning, choking, **anaphylaxis**, loss of consciousness, respiratory and cardiac arrest.

Key Terms

Anaphylaxis – A severe allergic reaction that affects the whole body. It can lead to anaphylactic shock.

Anaphylactic shock – A potentially fatal immune response when the body system literally shuts down. The most common cause is a severe allergic reaction to insect stings and certain drugs.

For further information, see Chapter 12, Unit MPII002: Managing paediatric illness and injury.

How to get emergency help

- **Assess the situation:** stay calm and do not panic.
- **Minimise any danger to yourself and to others** – for example, make sure someone takes charge of other children at the scene.
- **Send for help:** notify a doctor, hospital, parents, etc. as appropriate. If in any doubt, call an ambulance: **dial 999**.
- Be ready to **assist** the emergency services by answering some simple questions:
  (a) your name and the telephone number you are calling from
  (b) the location of the accident – try to give as much information as possible (familiar landmarks such as churches or pubs nearby)
  (c) explain briefly what has happened – this helps the paramedics to act speedily when they arrive
  (d) tell them what you have done so far to treat the casualty.

What to do in the event of a non-medical incident or emergency

Types of emergency

There are many different types of emergency (apart from a medical emergency when a person is seriously injured or ill), and it is important to know what procedures to follow; for example:

- if a child goes missing
- in case of fire
- if there is a security incident.

Missing children

Strict procedures must be followed to prevent a child from going missing from the setting. However, if a child *does* go missing, a procedure must be followed; for example:

1. The person in charge will carry out a thorough search of the building and garden.
2. The register is checked to make sure no other child has also gone astray.
3. Doors and gates are checked to see if there has been a breach of security whereby a child could wander out.

4 The person in charge talks to staff to establish what happened.

5 If the child is not found, the parent is contacted and the missing child is reported to the police.

In case of fire

In the case of fire or other emergency, you need to know what to do to safely **evacuate** the children and yourselves. Follow these rules for fire safety:

- No smoking is allowed in any child care setting.
- Handbags containing matches or lighters must be locked securely away out of children's reach.
- The cooker should not be left unattended when turned on.
- Fire exits must be clearly signed.
- Fire drills should be carried out regularly; registers must be kept up to date throughout the day.
- Fire exits and other doors should be free of obstructions on both sides.
- Instructions about what to do in the event of a fire must be clearly displayed.
- You should know where the fire extinguishers are kept and how to use them.
- Electrical equipment should be regularly checked for any faults.

Evacuation procedures

A plan for an escape route and the attendance register must be up to date so that everyone – children and staff – can safely be accounted for at the meeting point of safety. The attendance record must be taken by the person in charge when the building is evacuated. Clearly written instructions for fire drills and how to summon the fire brigade must be posted in a conspicuous place in the setting.

Security issues and violence

Early years settings and schools should be secure environments where children cannot wander off without anyone realising. But they also need to be secure so that strangers cannot enter without a good reason for being there. Occasionally you might encounter a problem with violence – or threats of violence – from a child's parents or carers. Your setting will have a policy that deals with this issue.

How to respond to evidence or concerns that a child or young person has been abused, harmed or bullied

It is very important in all suspected cases of abuse that early years practitioners follow procedures that are regarded as good practice and which fulfil the legal requirements. This includes suspicions of child abuse or neglect from your own observations, and disclosure or allegation – either from a child who tells you they have been abused, or from a parent or other adult who communicates their concerns about the abuse of a child to you.

Your role in enabling children to protect themselves

You have an important role to play in safeguarding children from abuse. You should always do the following:

- **Listen to them** and take their concerns seriously; often when a child has been bullied or abused in another way, he or she will try to put into words what has happened – they need to know that you are there to listen and,

Case Study — Problem at home time

Megan is a three-year-old child who attends a nursery group three mornings a week. Her parents recently separated and are now living apart. Megan is usually collected at the end of the nursery session by her mother, Kirsty, but occasionally – usually on a Friday – her father, Dan, and his new female partner collect her because she stays with them at weekends. Megan's mother has spoken to the nursery manager about this arrangement and has agreed that she will always inform the staff on the days when Dan will be collecting Megan. One Friday, Dan turns up unexpectedly – and ten minutes early – to collect her from nursery and explains that it was a last-minute arrangement between himself and Kirsty that he should collect Megan, because they were going away on holiday. Megan seems very excited about going away. Her father insists that Kirsty is happy about it and is clearly angry to be questioned and impatient to get away as they have a train to catch.

Discuss the scenario above in class and answer the following questions:

1 Should the staff at the nursery consent to Megan's father taking Megan from the nursery?

2 What are the main issues involved in this case study?

3 What would you do if you were in charge?

Try to think around the problem; if you decide to contact Megan's mother, what if you cannot get in touch?

most importantly, you will believe what they tell you.
- Encourage children to think about their own **personal safety**; for example, never allowing

In Practice

Policies and procedures

Find out what policies and procedures apply to your setting. Make sure you know what your role is in keeping children safe and healthy.

Progress check

Safeguarding children in early years settings and schools

An early years setting or school keeps children safe by:

- having effective procedures around safe recruitment, management and its general operating policy; for example, if children are encouraged to speak out when they feel unhappy or uncomfortable, they will be much less vulnerable to abuse.
- ensuring that children's intimate care – nappy-changing, toileting, dressing and undressing – is coordinated by a key person. This reinforces the child's right to privacy, and the child would not then expect that just anyone could take them aside and undress them.

them to leave the setting with anyone other than the person designated to collect them.
- Create opportunities for children to **express their feelings**; they need to know that it is OK to feel sad or afraid.
- Aim to **increase children's confidence** by praising them for any achievements and showing a genuine interest in what they have to say.
- **Observe children**: keep regular records of children's behaviour – you are in a strong position to note any changes of behaviour or signs of insecurity which could be a result of child abuse.

You need to be aware of the indicators of child abuse as outlined below. However, it is

Figure 6.01 Observing children in the setting is an important aid to understanding children's development

important not to jump to conclusions. If you have any cause for concern, you should always talk to your immediate superior or to the head of the nursery or school. Every child care setting has a **policy** for dealing with suspected child abuse.

If you suspect child abuse in the home setting, then you should contact your local Social Services or the National Society for the Prevention of Cruelty to Children (NSPCC).

Allegation of abuse

If a child or young person tells you he or she has been abused, this is called an allegation of abuse or a safeguarding allegation. (It used to be known as disclosure.) You should do the following:

- Reassure the child, saying that you are glad that they have told you about this.

- Believe the child; tell the child that you will do your best to protect them, but do not *promise* that you can do that.
- Remember that the child is not to blame, and that it is important that you make the child understand this.
- Do a lot of listening; do not ask questions.
- Report your conversation with the child to your immediate superior.
- Write down what was said by the child as soon as possible after the conversation.

 **Progress check**

Guidelines for recording suspicions of abuse and allegations of abuse

Table 6.1 lists the factors of which you should make a record *as soon as possible* after the observation or conversation.

Factors to record after the observation or conversation	
The child's name	The child's address
The age of the child	The date and time of the observation or the allegation
A concise, objective and factual record of the observation: for example, if a child has physical injuries, these should be clearly recorded on a body outline figure. You should only record the facts as you see them and not draw any conclusions about the possible cause of the injury	An objective record of the allegation: write down what the child or young person has told you, using their own words. Note also your own responses. Avoid making judgements and interpretations
The name of the person to whom the concern was reported, with date and time	The name(s) of any other person(s) present at the time

Table 6.1 Factors to record as soon as possible after the observation or conversation

Confidentiality

These records must be *signed* and dated and kept in a separate confidential file. As a general rule, information about a child protection issue should only be shared with people on a *'need to know'* basis. This means that only staff working directly with the child or the parents will have access to any information about an allegation or investigation. Gossip and hearsay must be avoided. Names and identities must never be disclosed outside the group designated as having a 'need to know'.

Guidelines for reporting child abuse or neglect

Report the indicators that have led you to suspect child abuse or neglect to your designated **safeguarding and child protection officer**. Your line manager will help you to follow the correct procedures, but you should know them too. You will need to continue to keep carefully written observations. This is because you may be required to make a report, and for this you must have written evidence.

Types of child abuse

The categories of child abuse are:

- physical
- emotional
- neglect
- sexual.

Physical abuse

Physical abuse, or non-accidental injury (NAI), involves someone deliberately harming a child. This may take the form of:

- bruising – from being slapped, punched, shaken or squeezed
- cuts – scratches, bite marks, a torn frenulum (the web of skin inside the upper lip)
- fractures – skull and limb fractures from being thrown against hard objects
- burns and scalds – from cigarettes, irons, baths and kettles.

Often the particular injuries can be explained easily, but you should always be suspicious if a child or young person has any bruise or mark that shows the particular pattern of an object (such as a belt strap mark, teeth marks or the imprint of an iron). Also look out for behavioural disturbances in the child, such as aggression towards others or a withdrawn attitude.

Emotional abuse

Emotional abuse occurs when a child or young person consistently faces threatening ill-treatment from an adult. This can take the form of verbal abuse, ridiculing, mocking and insulting the child. It is difficult to find out how common this form of abuse is, because it is hard to detect. However, signs of emotional abuse include:

- withdrawn behaviour – child may not join in with others or appear to be having fun
- attention-seeking behaviour
- low self-esteem and confidence
- stammering and stuttering
- tantrums beyond the expected age
- telling lies, and even stealing
- tearfulness.

Emotional neglect means that children do not receive love and affection from the adult. They may often be left alone without the company and support of someone who loves them.

Neglect

Physical neglect occurs when the adult fails to give their child what they need to develop physically. They often leave children alone and unattended. Signs of physical neglect include:

- being underweight for their age and not thriving
- unwashed clothes, which are often dirty and smelly
- poor skin tone, dull, matted hair and bad breath; a baby may have a persistent rash from infrequent nappy changing
- being constantly tired, hungry and listless or lacking in energy
- frequent health problems, and prone to accidents
- low self-esteem and ineffective social relationships – delay in all areas of development is likely because of lack of stimulation.

Sexual abuse

There is much more awareness today about the existence of sexual abuse. Sexual abuse means that the adult uses the child or young person to gratify their sexual needs. This could

involve sexual intercourse or anal intercourse. It may involve watching pornographic material with the child. Sexual abuse might also mean children being encouraged in sexually explicit behaviour or oral sex, masturbation or the fondling of sexual parts. Signs of sexual abuse include the following:

- bruises or scratches as in a non-accidental injury or physical injury
- itching or pain in the genital area
- wetting or soiling themselves
- discharge from the penis or vagina
- low self-esteem and lack of confidence
- may regress and want to be treated like a baby
- poor sleeping and eating patterns
- withdrawn and solitary behaviour.

 **Progress check**

Child abuse

- What are the four categories of child abuse?
- What should you remember to do, if a child makes an allegation to you? What should you avoid doing?

Bullying

Bullying usually includes:

- deliberate hostility and aggression
- a victim who is less powerful than the bully or bullies
- an outcome which is always painful and/or distressing.

Key term

Bullying – Persistent ill-treatment that is intended to hurt the person on the receiving end, physically or emotionally.

Bullying can be:

- **physical**: pushing, kicking, hitting, pinching, and any other forms of violence

Possible signs of bullying	
Suddenly asking for money (to pay the bully)	Not wanting to go to school, changing their route to school or playing truant
Suddenly feeling ill in the mornings	Starting to perform badly at school
Developing unexplained cuts and bruises	Becoming aggressive to younger children
Constantly 'losing' schoolbooks and possessions	Coming home hungry (bully has taken dinner money)
Having nightmares or crying themselves to sleep	Becoming withdrawn, stammering and lacking confidence
Developing fears of particular children	Refusing to say what's wrong (frightened of the bully)
Threatening or attempting suicide	Becoming distressed and anxious, may stop eating

Table 6.2 Possible signs of bullying

- **verbal**: name-calling, sarcasm, spreading rumours, threats
- **emotional**: excluding (refusing to speak to the child), tormenting (hiding books, threatening gestures), ridicule, humiliation
- **racist**: racial taunts, graffiti, gestures
- **sexual**: unwanted physical contact, abusive comments, homophobic abuse
- **online/cyber**: setting up 'hate websites', sending text messages, emails and abusing people via their mobile phones.

Signs that a child or young person is possibly being bullied

A child may show by his or her changed behaviour that he or she is being bullied. If the child shows some of the signs shown in Table 6.2, he or she may be a victim of bullying.

Cyberbullying and young people

Cyberbullying is when one person or a group of people try to threaten, tease or embarrass someone else by using a mobile phone or the internet. A 2009 survey by the **Beatbullying** charity of more than 2,000 young people aged 11 to 18 found that text messages, prank mobile phone calls and content posted on social networking sites were at the heart of a 'growing epidemic.' The research found that one in three young Britons have been the victims of cyberbullying and teenage girls were four times more likely to be bullied in this way than boys. The findings coincide with the launch of a new nationwide social networking site, **CyberMentors**, backed by celebrities and politicians. CyberMentors allow trained schoolchildren to provide help and advice for their peers in an effort to keep children and young people safe online.

Anti-bullying policy

Head teachers must by law have a policy to prevent all forms of bullying among pupils. Challenging bullying effectively will improve the safety and happiness of pupils, show that the school cares and make clear to bullies that the behaviour is unacceptable.

As with the other forms of child abuse, children and young people who are being bullied need to know that they will be taken seriously and that those adults in whom they confide will help them to resolve the situation. If you suspect a child is being bullied – or if the child confides in you that something is wrong – you need to listen carefully and follow the guidelines for recording and reporting detailed on p 106 above.

The importance of e-safety for children and young people

The internet has become an everyday tool in family life, whether accessed from a computer, mobile phone or other device. It is used for online banking, buying and selling goods, finding information and for socialising with others. It also has a darker side, however, with 'cyber crime', inappropriate material and illegal activity taking place online, affecting both adults and children.

What is e-safety?

This new term, 'e-safety', is concerned with the safeguarding of children and young people in the 'digital' world and ensuring that they feel safe when accessing new technology.

What are the risks?

Child sex abusers find the internet a convenient place to participate in a range of child sexual abuse activity – including contact with children – as they can remain anonymous. They feel a sense of security by operating from the safety of their own homes, and have also been known to set up fake email accounts and chat 'personas' to mask their real identity online.

What is online grooming?

The Sexual Offences Act 2003 defines online grooming as:

> 'A course of conduct enacted by a suspected paedophile, which would give a reasonable person cause for concern that any meeting with a child arising from the conduct would be for unlawful purposes.'

Adults who want to engage children or young people in sexual acts, or talk to them for sexual gratification, often:

- lie and pretend to be younger than they really are, or pretend to be people other than themselves
- seek out young people who desire friendship
- use a number of grooming techniques, including building trust with the child through lying about who they are
- try to engage the child in more intimate forms of communication – including compromising a child with the use of images and webcams
- use blackmail and guilt as methods of securing a meeting with the child.

The adult sex abuser who grooms children online uses a number of techniques, which include:

- swapping child abuse images in chat rooms or through instant messages with other adults or young people
- swapping personal information of children or young people that they have collected with other sex abusers
- taking part in online communities such as blogs, forums and chat rooms with the intention of grooming children, collecting sexually explicit images and meeting children to have sex.

What are the consequences?

Young people often feel more confident when chatting on the internet than they do in other situations, and can be tempted to say and do things that they would not even consider if they were meeting someone face to face. The consequences of this freedom include the young person:

- becoming drawn into repeated contact and intimacy online with a stranger; IM (instant messaging) is a more intimate area than a chat room and the young person feels a sense of trust because a 'friend of a friend' knows them

- giving out personal information such as mobile numbers and pictures of themselves
- being groomed when this information is misused; other sex abusers may respond when the young person's image is posted on a website.

Progress check

e-safety for children and young people

- Find out what child protection services your Internet Service Provider (ISP) offers. Most ISPs provide free software to help in child protection.
- Use special internet filtering software, 'walled gardens' – and use a child- or family-friendly search engine (such as the CBBC Safe Search) with younger children to bookmark favourite sites for children to use.
- Families should keep their computer in a communal area of the house, where children's viewing of internet sites can be supervised.
- Teach children *never* to give out their personal details such as names, schools, phone numbers, email addresses, or photos of themselves, to online friends.
- Children love to chat, but make sure they use only moderated chat rooms, and encourage them to tell you if they feel uncomfortable, upset or threatened by anything they see online.
- Remember that what is acceptable for a teenager is not necessarily suitable for a child of primary school age.
- Have clear rules about making and meeting with online friends safely (such as taking someone with them, meeting in a public place).
- All schools should have an e-Safety Policy and an e-Safety Coordinator who will be able to advise you where to look for more support.

It is not realistic to forbid use of the internet. Children use computers and games consoles at friends' houses and at school, so education about using them safely is essential.

How to respond to evidence or concerns about a colleague

All early years settings and schools are required to have a policy to deal with allegations made against staff. This will cover cases where a child makes a disclosure, or an adult is seen or overheard behaving in an inappropriate way. But there are other examples that might give rise to a concern, without a specific allegation being made, for example:

- a child who seems fearful of a particular member of staff
- a member of staff seeming to try to develop a very close relationship with a child – for example, offering small presents and special treats, or arranging to meet the child outside the setting or school
- a parent expressing a general concern about how a member of staff relates to their child, without being able exactly to say what is wrong.

In cases like these, you will need to discuss your concerns with the staff member responsible for safeguarding. Discussions like these are awkward, but it is important to share any concerns you have – the child's welfare is paramount.

Whistle-blowing

Sometimes a person inside an organisation knows that something is going wrong and is being covered up. It may be that someone has:

- harmed a child or put a child at risk of harm
- displayed behaviour involving or related to a child that might constitute a criminal offence, or
- behaved in a way that raises concern about the adult's suitability to work with children.

If a member of staff has spoken to the manager, head teacher or other appropriate person and made clear that a situation is dangerous and illegal, and no action is taken, it is necessary to 'blow the whistle' and report the concerns directly to an outside body, such as the local Children's Services, OFSTED or the NSPCC. In general, employees who blow the whistle are

Case Study

Karen, a cause for concern time

Karen has been working at your nursery for two years and has recently qualified as an early years practitioner. You and Chloe have just joined the nursery, which has seen a huge staff turnover in the last year. The room-leader, Sarah, is very efficient, but because the nursery manager is on maternity leave, she is increasingly called out of the room. Sarah leaves Karen in charge as she knows the routine and is qualified. Karen is very authoritative and quite organised. She has positive relationships with parents but she can be sharp with staff – often referring to the fact that she has stuck by the nursery when many staff have come and gone. As Karen is left more and more often in charge, she becomes irritable and frequently loses her temper, often shouting at the children.

One day, a little boy, Jacob, will not sit down to lunch. He gets up and runs around the tables, laughing and treating it as a game. In the end, Karen loses her temper and grabs him. She forces Jacob hard into a bucket chair and slams the chair towards the table. Unbeknown to Karen, Jacob was clutching the chair arms and his fingers get trapped between the chair and the table. He howls and looks frightened. Karen looks embarrassed, but tells him that he should not have been running around, and leaves it at that.

1 What concerns would you report to your manager?

2 What do you think could be done to ensure that nothing like this happens again?

legally protected against being bullied, sacked or disciplined, if they have acted in good faith.

The principles and boundaries of confidentiality and when to share information

Chapter 1, Unit SHC 21: Introduction to communication in children and young people's settings, deals with the principles and boundaries of confidentiality. If you have any reason to think that a child might be at risk of harm, you should first report your concerns to your line manager or teacher, as detailed on p 106.

Coping with stress

How can learners release their feelings about their work with children in a professional manner?

Useful websites and resources

www.kidscape.org.uk	**Kidscape** is the first charity in the UK established specifically to prevent bullying and child sexual abuse.
www.beatbullying.org	**Beatbullying** works with children and young people across the UK to provide them with all-important opportunities to make positive and lasting changes to their lives and outlook.
www.baspcan	**The British Association for the Study and Prevention of Child Abuse and Neglect (BASPCAN)** is a registered charity that aims to prevent physical, emotional and sexual abuse and neglect of children by promoting the physical, emotional and social wellbeing of children.
www.everychildmatters.gov.uk/ workingtogether	**Working Together to Safeguard Children** is the government's guide to inter-agency working to safeguard and promote the welfare of children.
www.nspcc.org.uk	**The National Society for the Prevention of Cruelty to Children (NSPCC)** campaigns against cruelty to children, and runs ChildLine, the free, confidential helpline for children and young people. The NSPCC also offers services to support children and families, and can investigate cases where child abuse is suspected.
www.bullying.co.uk	**BullyingUK** is a charity offering help and advice for victims of bullying, their parents and school.

7 Contribute to children and young people's health and safety: Unit MU 2.4

Safety is a basic human need. When working with children and young people, you need to know how to provide a safe, healthy environment. This involves knowing how to assess risks to children's safety and to ensure that any such risks are minimised. A fine balance must be achieved which allows children to explore their environment and to learn for themselves but also ensures that the environment in which children are playing and learning is as safe and healthy as possible.

Learning outcomes

By the end of this chapter you will:

1. Know the health and safety policies and procedures of the work setting.

2. Be able to recognise risks and hazards in the work setting and during off-site visits.

3. Know what to do in the event of a non-medical incident or emergency.

4. Know what to do in the event of a child or young person becoming ill or injured.

5. Be able to follow the work setting procedures for reporting and recording accidents, incidents, emergencies and illnesses.

6. Be able to follow infection control procedures.

7. Know the work setting's procedures for receiving, storing and administering medicines.

Health and safety policies and procedures of the work setting

Health and safety legislation and policy aim to make sure that all workers, children, young people and families are safe and protected from harm when in work or using services. You do not need to be an expert in this area, but you should be aware of the legal issues and national and local guidance relating to health and safety, and know where to go and who to ask for advice and support.

The most relevant laws relating to health and safety in settings for children and young people in the UK are listed in Table 7.1.

Health and Safety Legislation

Health and Safety at Work Act 1974

Employers have a duty to:

- make your workplace as safe as they are able to.

- display a Health and Safety Law poster or supply employees with a leaflet with the same information. This is available from the Health and Safety Executive.

- decide how to manage health and safety. If the business has five or more employees, this must appear on a written Health and Safety Policy.

As an employee, you have a duty to:

- work safely. If you are given guidance about how to use equipment, you should follow that guidance. You should not work in a way that puts other people in danger.

Fire Precautions (Workplace) Regulations 1997

Fire Officers must check all child care premises while they are in the first registration process. They will advise what is needed to make the workplace as safe as possible.

- Evacuation procedures should be in place, known to all the adults, and practised regularly using all available exits at different times, so that everyone can leave the building quickly and safely if an emergency occurs.

- Some exits may be locked to prevent children wandering away or intruders entering, but adults must, in the case of an emergency, quickly open them.

- Designated fire exits must always be unlocked and kept unobstructed. Fire extinguishers should be in place and checked regularly. A fire blanket is needed in the kitchen.

Childcare Act 2006, Regulation of Care (Scotland) Act 2001 and National Standards

The Care Standards Act 2000 sets out 14 minimum standards that settings for children and young people must meet. The different inspectorates – Ofsted (in England), HMIe (in Scotland), Estyn (in Wales) and ETI (in Northern Ireland) – are responsible for registering nurseries, childminders, playgroups, after-school clubs, crèches and play schemes.

Control of Substances Hazardous to Health Regulations 1994 (COSHH)

Things such as bleach or dishwasher powders, some solvent glues and other materials in your setting can be hazardous. You should have a Risk Assessment that tells you what these things are and what to do to minimise the risks involved. Any new person coming to the team must be made aware of what to do.

Reporting of Injuries, Diseases and Dangerous Occurrences Regulations 1995 (RIDDOR)

An accident book must be kept in which incidents that happen to staff are recorded. If an incident occurs at work that is serious enough to keep an employee off work for three or more days, employers will need to fill in the relevant paperwork and send the report to the Health and Safety Executive. They may investigate serious incidents and give advice on how to improve practice if needed.

Health and Safety (First Aid) Regulations 1981

Employers should make sure that at least one person at each session has an up-to-date first aid qualification and is the 'Appointed' first aider. In settings regulated by Ofsted, HMIe, Estyn or ETI there is also a requirement for a staff member to be trained in 'Paediatric First Aid'. Methods of dealing with incidents for adults and children are not the same, particularly where resuscitation is involved. Recommendations also change. For this reason, first aid qualifications must be renewed every three years.

Food Handling Regulations 1995

If you prepare or handle food, even something as basic as opening biscuits or preparing food for a snack, you need to comply with Food Handling Regulations. These cover what might be seen as common-sense things:

- Washing your hands before preparing food

- Making sure the surfaces and utensils you use are clean and hygienic

- Making sure food is stored safely at the correct temperature

- Disposing of waste hygienically.

But it also includes knowledge of safe practices in the use of chopping boards, having separate sinks for hand washing and preparing foods, how to lay out a kitchen, and so on. There should always be people who have completed a Basic Food Hygiene certificate available to ensure guidance is properly carried out.

Health and Safety Legislation

Personal Protective Equipment at Work Regulations 1992

Under these regulations, employers must make sure that suitable protective equipment is provided for employees who are exposed to a risk to their health and safety while at work. This is considered a last resort, for the risk should be prevented wherever possible. In children and young people's settings, the most important piece of personal protective equipment that is provided will be gloves, to be used when dealing with body fluids.

Employees and learners should be made aware of the need to use these when changing nappies or dealing with blood spillage or vomit. Good hygiene protects both adults and children.

Table 7.1 Health and Safety Legislation

There are a number of documents giving guidance on safe practices when working with children, young people and parents. The most relevant document is the *Guidance for Safe Working Practice for the Protection of Children and Staff in Education Settings* (2005). Although the focus is on those working in education, much of the guidance provides useful advice for practitioners working in a non-education setting.

Policies and procedures

Every child care and education setting will have **policy documents** covering such areas as:

- safety
- health and hygiene
- safety at arrival and departure times, and on outings
- prevention of illness and first aid
- fire prevention
- staffing ratios and supervision.

In group settings, a member of staff is usually nominated as being responsible for health and safety. In a childminder's home or if you are working as a nanny, you can contact the local Childminding Association or nanny agency for information on health and safety.

Lines of responsibility and reporting

Your setting's health and safety policy will contain the names of staff members responsible for health and safety. All practitioners are responsible for health and safety in any setting. Your responsibilities include:

- taking reasonable care for **your own safety** and that of others.
- working with your employer in respect of **health and safety** matters.
- knowing about the **policies and procedures** in your particular place of work – these can all be found in the setting's **health and safety** policy documents.
- not intentionally damaging any health and safety equipment or materials provided by the employer.
- **reporting all accidents**, incidents and even 'near misses' to your manager. As you may be handling food, you should also report any **incidences of sickness** or diarrhoea.
- **reporting any hazards** immediately you come across them.

Apart from your legal responsibilities, knowing how to act and being alert and vigilant at all times can prevent accidents, injury, infections and even death – this could be in relation to you, your fellow workers, or the children or young people in your care.

Understanding safety issues relevant to the care of children and young people

The likelihood of different types of accidents occurring depends on:

- **The age and developmental capabilities** of the child or young person: for example, bicycle accidents are more likely in older children; accidents involving poisoning are more common in younger children; young people may have access to drugs and alcohol.
- **The environment**: indoor or outdoor, child-aware or not. For example, toddlers visiting childless relatives are more likely to find hazards (such as trailing electrical flexes, loose rugs or unsecured cupboards containing potentially dangerous cleaning products) than in a household with children.
- **The degree of supervision** available: for example, inquisitive toddlers with little appreciation of danger need more supervision in an environment that is not child-aware. At the same time, the adult may be less aware of potential dangers due to distractions; for example, holding an adult conversation with a friend, talking on the phone (especially mobile phones) or in a busy shopping centre where there is a lot of visual stimulation.

Preventing accidents

Accidents are the most common cause of death in children between the ages of one and fourteen years old. The pattern of accidents varies with the child's age, in keeping with the child's stage of development, and their exposure to new hazards.

Table 7.2 shows the most common injuries to children and young people, and the age group that is most vulnerable to those injuries.

Identifying risks in the setting

Babies and young children

Babies and young children are at particular risk of harm because they:

- lack any appreciation of danger
- are naturally inquisitive
- love to explore and test the boundaries of their world.

You need to help young children to explore within safe boundaries, but to adjust those boundaries according to their capabilities and increasing skill. Useful skills to employ when dealing with inquisitive toddlers include recognising the value of **distraction** – guiding attention away from something dangerous and towards something potentially more interesting, physically removing the child: 'Harry, come with me – I want to show you something . . .'

Even so, no environment – however carefully planned and designed – can ever be totally without risk to children.

Older children and young people

This group face different risks. They are more likely to travel to school independently and need to be aware of the principles of road safety. They also need to be aware of the risks involved in using the internet (see p 109 for information on e-safety).

Risks and hazards in the work setting and during off-site visits

Children and young people need a safe but challenging environment

Practically every human activity involves a certain degree of risk, and children need to learn

Choking and suffocation	High-risk age	Burns and scalds	High-risk age
Use of pillows Unsupervised feeding Play with small parts of toys Plastic bags Peanuts Cords and ribbons on clothes	Under one year	Matches, lighters, cigarettes Open fires and gas fires Baths Kettles and irons Cookers Bonfires and fireworks	From nine months on, when children are newly mobile
Falls	**High-risk age**	**Poisoning**	**High-risk age**
Stairs Unlocked windows Bouncing cradles left on worktop or table Pushchairs and high chairs Climbing frames	Under three years	Household chemicals, e.g. bleach and disinfectant Medicines Berries and fungi Waste bins Vitamins	One to three years
Electric shocks	**High-risk age**	**Road accidents**	**High-risk age**
Uncovered electric sockets Faulty wiring	Under five years	Running into the road Not wearing child restraints in cars Playing in the road Cycling	All ages up to 16 years
Drowning	**High-risk age**	**Cuts**	**High-risk age**
Unsupervised in the bath Ponds and water butts Swimming pools, rivers and ditches	Under four years	Glass doors Knives, scissors and razor blades Sharp edges on doors and furniture	One to eight years

Table 7.2 Common injuries to children and young people

how to cope with this. For example, when a child first learns to walk, he or she will inevitably fall over or knock into things. This is a valuable part of their learning and a natural part of their development.

Children who are sheltered or overprotected from risk and challenge when young will not be able to make judgements about their own strengths and skills, and will be poorly equipped to resist peer pressure in their later years. Also, a totally risk-free environment lacks challenges and stimulation; this leads inevitably to children becoming bored and displaying inappropriate behaviour. Simply being *told* about possible

dangers is not enough: children need to see or experience the consequences of not taking care. An important aspect of teaching children about risk is to encourage them to make their own **risk assessments** and think about the possible consequences of their actions. Rather than removing objects and equipment from the environment in case children hurt themselves, adults should teach children how to use them safely. It is important to strike the right balance: protecting children from harm while allowing them the freedom to develop independence and risk awareness.

The risk assessment process

Risk assessment is a method of preventing accidents and ill health by helping people to think about what could go wrong and devising ways to prevent problems. The flow chart below shows how to carry out a risk assessment.

What is the difference between a risk and a hazard?

In the child care setting a hazard may be a substance, a piece of equipment, a work procedure or a child's condition. Examples of hazards in child care settings are shown in Table 7.3.

Key Terms

Hazard – A source of potential harm or damage, or a situation with potential for harm or damage.

Risk – The possibility of suffering harm or loss; danger.

Risk assessment – The assessments that must be carried out in order to identify hazards and find out the safest way to carry out certain tasks and procedures.

The most important factor in preventing accidents is *you*!

Look for hazards

↓

Decide who might be harmed and how

↓

Weigh up the risk: a risk is the likelihood that a hazard will cause harm

↓

Decide whether existing precautions are enough

↓

If not, decide what further precautions are needed to reduce risk

↓

Record your findings

Figure 7.01 The risk assessment process

Hazards in child care settings	
Toys and play equipment	Chemical hazards, such as cleaning materials and disinfectants
Biological hazards, such as airborne and blood-borne infections	The handling and moving of equipment and of children
Unsupervised children	Security of entry points and exits
Administration of medicines	Visual or hearing impairment of children

Table 7.3 Hazards in child care settings

Risk is defined as the chance or likelihood that harm will occur from the hazard. The likelihood is described as 'the expectancy of harm occurring'. It can range from 'never' to 'certain' and depends on a number of factors.

Example 1: A door

The main entrance to a nursery or primary school may present a **hazard**. The **risks** are that:

- a child might escape and run into the road, or go missing, or
- a stranger might enter the building.

The likelihood of the **hazard** of the entrance/door posing a **risk** will depend on a number of factors:

1. the security of the entrance – can it only be opened by using a key pad or entry phone system, and is the door handle placed high up, out of a child's reach?
2. policies and procedures being known to parents and other visitors, for example at collection times.

Example 2: A damaged or uneven floor surface

This may present a **hazard**. The **risk** is that someone may trip over and become injured.

The likelihood of the **hazard** of the damaged floor posing a **risk** will depend on a number of factors:

1. the extent of the unevenness or damage
2. the number of people walking over it

3. the number of times they walk over it
4. whether they are wearing suitable footwear
5. the level of lighting.

Safe working practices: protecting children from common hazards

All areas where children play and learn should be checked for hygiene and safety at the start of every session and again at the end of each session – but do be alert at all times. Look at your setting's written **policy** for health and hygiene issues. Find out from your manager how to clean toys and other equipment, and remember that many objects (plastic toys and soft toys) end up in children's mouths, which is a way of passing on and picking up an infection.

Remember that *you* could also be a risk to children's health. For example, if you have a heavy cold or have suffered from diarrhoea or vomiting within the previous 24 hours, you must not attend for work as you could pass on a serious infection to the children.

The indoor and outdoor setting should be made as accident-proof as possible. Remember that playing should be fun and is an important part of growing up. Your role is to make sure that it stays fun and does not lead to a serious accident.

The following guidelines apply both to the home setting and to nursery and other group settings:

Safety guidelines for playing indoors

- Try to keep very young children out of the kitchen, even when an adult is there.
- Put them in a playpen or high chair if there is no alternative; or you could try putting a stair gate in the doorway.
- Put safety film over glass doors and beware of children playing rough-and-tumble games near glass doors or low windows.
- Encourage children not to play on the stairs or in the main walkways in group settings.

In a flat or maisonette

- Always supervise children on balconies – they may be tempted to climb up or over the railings.

Playing with toys

- Keep toys and other clutter off the floor so that no one trips up; use a toy box such as a large, strong cardboard box.
- Choose toys suitable for the child's age and stage of development. Keep toys for older children away from younger brothers or sisters to prevent them from choking on small parts. Follow the manufacturer's instructions.
- Check the toys in family homes and group settings. Go through the toy box regularly and clear out any broken and damaged toys. Do not hand them on to jumble sales or charity shops, where they could cause injury to another child.

Safety guidelines for playing outdoors

If there is a garden or outdoor play area:

- Make sure the children cannot get out on their own: block up gaps in the fence and keep the gates locked.

- Set up garden toys properly and check they are stable with no loose nuts and bolts.
- Have something soft under climbing frames – regularly watered grass is fine, but dried earth can be as hard as concrete.
- Watch children at all times in the paddling pool and empty it straight away after use.
- **Remember, small children can drown in just a few inches of water**.
- Cover, fence off or fill in the garden pond to keep small children away.

Playgrounds are good places for children to run around and play, but some are safer than others. You should always do the following:

- Teach children to use the equipment properly – make sure they understand your instructions; for example, teach children never to run in front of or behind children using swings.
- Keep a close eye on very young children at all times.
- Avoid old, damaged or vandalised equipment which could hurt a child.
- Keep to playgrounds with safety surfaces.
- Check for rubbish such as broken glass or even syringes, particularly if young people or adults meet there. (If these problems persist, contact the playground owners.)
- Watch out for nearby hazards such as roads and streams.
- **Always be aware of children with special needs**, for example, those with mobility problems or a visual impairment.
- Whenever children are **playing with or near water** – even indoors at the water play area – they must be supervised at all times.

Safety and hygiene guidelines: checking equipment regularly

- **Floors and surfaces**: floors and surfaces must be checked for cleanliness.

- **Plastic toys**: throw out any plastic toys that have cracks or splits in them, as these cracks can harbour germs. Also check for splits and cracks when you clean them; plastic toys such as Duplo® bricks should be washed weekly.
- **Metal equipment**: check tricycles, pushchairs and prams for rust and/or broken hinges or sticking-out screws, etc.
- **Wooden equipment**: check wooden blocks or wheeled carts for splinters and rough edges; remove any which are damaged and report this to your supervisor.
- **Dressing-up clothes and soft toys**: all toys and play equipment should be cleaned at least once a week. This includes dressing-up clothes and soft toys – and you should always remove from the nursery any toy that has been in contact with a child who has an infectious illness. Particular care should be taken to keep hats, head coverings and hairbrushes clean in order to help prevent the spread of head lice.
- **Water tray**: water trays should be emptied daily, as germs can multiply quickly in pools of water.
- **Sandpit**: check that sandpits or trays are clean and that toys are removed and cleaned at the end of a play session; if the sandpit is kept outside make sure it is kept covered when not in use.
- **Home area**: the home area often contains dolls, saucepans and plastic food; these need to be included in the checking and in the regular wash.
- **Ventilation**: adequate ventilation is important to disperse bacteria or viruses transmitted through sneezing or coughing. Make sure that windows are opened to let in fresh air to the nursery – but also make sure there are no draughts.
- **Outdoor play areas**: these should be checked before any play session for litter, dog or cat faeces or any other object which could cause children harm.

Your role in preventing accidents

There are different views on whether the environment should be made 'toddler-proof' by removing all potentially dangerous items and ensuring adult supervision at all times, or whether by helping children to develop skills, including self-control, they can be encouraged to recognise and manage a degree of risk appropriate to their capabilities. The guidelines contained in Table 7.4 will help you to ensure that children in your care are protected from some common hazards. For further information on accident prevention, visit the website for CAPT (see 'Useful websites and resources' at end of this chapter).

Maintaining and promoting the personal health and safety of the child

Children who play closely together for long periods are more likely than others to develop an infection – and any infection can spread quickly from one child to another and to the adults who care for them. Good hygiene will help to prevent infection and the spread of disease. Being clean also increases self-esteem and social acceptance, and helps to prepare children in skills of independence and self-caring.

Here, as elsewhere, you should be a positive role model with your personal hygiene and by wearing the right clothes. You should help children to develop good **personal hygiene routines**, for example by encouraging children to keep their face clean by using a clean flannel.

Preventing burns and scalds	Preventing poisoning
• Never carry a hot drink through a play area or place a hot drink within reach of children.	• Make sure that all household chemicals are out of children's reach.
• Make sure the kitchen is safe for children – kettle flexes coiled neatly, cooker guards used and saucepan handles turned inwards.	• Never pour chemicals or detergents into empty soft drink or water bottles.
• Make sure the kitchen is inaccessible to children when no one is in it.	• Keep all medicines and tablets in a locked cupboard.
• Never smoke in child care settings, and keep matches and lighters out of children's reach.	• Use childproof containers. • Teach children not to eat berries or fungi in the garden or park.
Fire safety	**Preventing falls**
• In the case of fire or other emergency, you need to know what to do to evacuate the children and yourself. You should also always practise fire safety.	• Babies need to be protected from falls, so close supervision is needed. All children will trip and fall at some time, but children should not be put at risk of *serious* injury.
• Remember that no smoking is allowed in any child care setting.	• Never leave a baby unattended on a table, work surface, bed or sofa.
• Keep handbags containing matches or lighters securely away out of children's reach.	• Make sure young children cannot climb up near windows – and ensure window catches are used.
• The nursery cooker should not be left unattended when turned on.	• Always clean and dry a floor where children are playing.
• Fire exits and other doors should be free of obstructions on both sides.	• Make sure that clutter is removed from floors.
• Ensure that you know where the fire extinguishers are kept and how to use them.	• Make sure you know how to use safety equipment, such as stair gates, reins and harnesses, adjustable changing tables and car seats.
• Regularly check electrical equipment for any faults.	• Use safety gates when working in home settings.

Table 7.4 Guidelines to protect children from hazards

Teach children how and when to wash their hands

The chief way of preventing the spread of infection is through the washing of hands. Regular hand washing should be practised and promoted within all early years settings.

- Teach children **how** to wash and dry their hands.
- Make sure they always wash their hands **before eating and drinking**.
- Make sure they always wash their hands **after going to the toilet**.
- Make sure they always wash their hands **after playing outdoors**.
- Make sure they always wash their hands **after handling pets or other animals**.
- Make sure they always wash their hands **after blowing their nose**.

How to wash our hands effectively

We all think we know how to wash our hands but many of us do not do it properly. Figure 7.02 shows how we often miss certain parts of our hands – particularly our thumbs and between our fingers – when washing them.

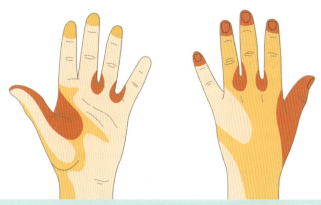

Figure 7.02 Parts commonly missed when washing hands: red = parts most commonly missed; orange = parts sometimes missed; cream = parts rarely missed.

A step-by-step guide to effective hand washing:

1. Wet your hands thoroughly under *warm* running water and squirt liquid soap onto the palm of one hand.
2. Rub your hands together to make a lather.
3. Rub the palm of one hand along the back of the other and along the fingers. Then do the same with the other hand.
4. Rub in between each of your fingers on both hands and around your thumbs.
5. Rinse off the soap with clean running water.
6. Dry hands thoroughly on a clean dry towel, paper towel or air dryer.

This should take about 15–20 seconds.

Remember: 1,000 times as many germs spread from damp hands as from dry hands.

Teach children how to play safely

Children need a safe environment, so that they can explore and learn and grow. As they develop, children need to learn how to tackle everyday dangers so that they can become safe adults. You have an important role, not only in ensuring that children are kept as safe and secure as possible, but also in teaching them to be aware of safety issues. Every opportunity should be made to teach children about different aspects of keeping themselves and others safe. Above all, children should be taught:

- **road safety**: how and when to cross roads safely (even *with* adults holding onto them)
- **fire safety**: never to play with matches, lighters, cigarettes, sparklers, etc.
- **water safety**: not to play near ponds and rivers (ideally young children should be taught how to swim)
- **food safety**: how germs spread and the importance of hand washing
- **play safety**: for example:
  - to carry things carefully
  - never to run with anything in their mouths – this includes sweets and other food
  - never to run while carrying a glass, scissors, or other pointed objects; if a child falls she can stab herself with something as simple as a pencil
  - never to throw sand
  - to take turns when using bikes, slides and climbing frames.

Always give reasons for the safety message:

- 'You mustn't throw sand because you'll hurt your friend.'
- 'Never run into the road, because you could be hit by a car.'

- 'Don't run with a stick in your hand as it would hurt you if you fall.'

When teaching young children about safety, you will need to find ways to communicate with each child according to their needs.

Repetition
Children learn best by doing or practising things – over and over again – but first you have to make the activity enjoyable.

Adapt your approach
Think about the message which you are trying to convey, and adapt your approach accordingly; for example, make sure that *all* children in the group can join in and benefit from the activity.

Modify the message
Think about who you are talking to; children with hearing difficulties, for example, will need both children and adults to face them so that they can see any signs and lip-read, if the hearing loss is severe.

Use real-life examples
Children remember what they have seen and/or experienced themselves – so, if a child has had sand thrown in his eyes, this would be a good moment to teach other children about the dangers of throwing sand.

Practise sun safety

Strong sun can easily burn the skin. For people with fair skin, the more sunshine that they are exposed to, the more likely they are to develop skin cancer later on in life. Sunburn is especially bad; it is painful, and sunburnt children may be especially prone to skin cancer later in life. Follow these guidelines:

- Keep children out of the sun between 11 am and 2 pm. This is the time to let them read, do some drawing or play with toys and games.
- Cover the children up. It is better to wear some clothes than nothing at all. The most protection comes from clothes that are loose, long-sleeved and are made of tightly woven materials, such as T-shirts.
- Provide floppy sun hats. Try to shade the head, face, neck and ears.
- Coat children with sun cream. Choose a high sun protection factor (SPF), as anything less than factor 8 gives little protection for children. Sun cream will not last all day so apply more from time to time, especially if the children are in and out of the water.

Note that babies under six months old should be kept out of direct sunlight altogether. Written permission to use sun cream on a child is needed from parents or carers.

Keep children safe during meal and snack times

One of the most common accidents in babies and children under five is choking. Babies are most at risk from choking when left unsupervised either eating or playing. Young children are most at risk of choking when they are tired, crying or running around. Half of all cases of choking in children under four years old involve food (only six per cent of cases were due to toys).

- **Never** leave a child propped up with a bottle or feeding beaker.
- **Always** supervise babies and young children when eating and drinking. If a toddler goes to the toilet – or leaves the table for any reason – during meal or snack time, make sure an adult accompanies him or her. (Accidents in nursery settings have occurred when a child chokes silently on food when no adult is present.)
- **Never** give peanuts to children under four years old as they can easily choke or inhale them into their lungs, causing infection and lung damage.
- Make sure you know what to do if a child is

choking (see Chapter 11, Unit PEFAP 001: Paediatric emergency first aid).

Keep children and young people safe on outings

Any outing away from the children's usual setting – for example, trips to farms, parks and theatres – must be planned with safety and security issues as a top priority. Many schools now employ an Educational Visit Coordinator to oversee the safety of school trips.

Each setting must consider the following points:

- *Planning*: Visit or find out about the place beforehand and discuss any particular requirements – for example, what to do if it rains, or specific lunch arrangements.
- *Contact numbers*: A copy of the children's contact information should be taken on the outing, and the person in charge should regularly check the names of the children against the day's attendance list.
- *Permission*: The manager or head teacher must give permission for the outing, and a letter should be sent to all parents and guardians of the children.
- *Informing parents*: Parents should be informed of what is involved on the outing, such as what the child needs to bring (for example, packed meal, waterproof coat), spending money if necessary (state the advised maximum amount). Also inform parents that *no* glass bottles or sweets should be brought.
- *Supervision*: Arrange adequate adult supervision. There should always be trained staff on any outing, however local and low-key. The adult-to-child ratio should never exceed one to four. If the children are under two years old or have special needs, then you would expect to have fewer children per adult.

Swimming trips should be attempted only if the ratio is one adult to one child for children under five years old. The younger the children, the more adults are required, particularly if the trip involves crossing roads, when an adult must be available to hold the children's hands.

- *Transport*: If a coach is being hired, check whether it has seat belts for children. By law, all new minibuses and coaches must have seat belts fitted, and minibus drivers have to have passed a special driving test.

What to do in the event of a non-medical incident or emergency

For information on what to do in the event of a non-medical incident or emergency, please refer to p 102, Chapter 6, Unit TDA 2.2: Safeguarding the welfare of children and young people.

How to recognise when a child or young person is ill or injured

Everyone who works with children should attend a first aid course. There are now specialist courses, such as St John Ambulance's Early Years First Aid and the British Red Cross's First Aid for Child Carers. The Sure Start Childcare Approval Scheme for nannies requires candidates to hold a relevant paediatric First Aid Certificate. Chapter 12, Unit MPII002: Managing paediatric illness and injury, covers the first aid measures you need to understand.

Occasionally a baby or child may arrive at nursery or school apparently healthy and happy, yet later he or she may be showing signs and symptoms of a serious illness, or may have an accident and need treatment.

The signs and symptoms of common childhood illnesses

Young children are not always able to explain their symptoms, and may display non-specific complaints such as headache, sleeplessness, vomiting or an inability to stand up. Babies have even less well-developed ways of showing how they are feeling – they may simply cry in a different way, refuse their feeds or become listless and lethargic. In most infectious illnesses, there will be fever. Detection of symptoms relies on the child being able to describe how they are feeling.

General signs and symptoms of illness in babies

Babies and very young children are not able to explain how they are feeling to their carers, so it is important to recognise some of the general signs that accompany illness. Some babies may cry in a 'strange' way – or one that is different from their usual cry (when hungry or thirsty, for example). They may refuse feeds or become unusually listless or lethargic. If the baby has an infection, there will be a raised temperature (or fever).

Some of the common signs of illness in babies are:

- **Raised temperature or fever**: the baby may look flushed or be pale but will feel hot to the touch. Black babies – and those with dark skin tones – may look paler than usual and their eyes may lose sparkle. Occasionally a very high temperature may trigger a seizure (fit) or febrile convulsion.
- **Refusing feeds/loss of appetite**: a young baby may refuse feeds or take very little. An older baby may want only milk feeds and refuse all solids.

- **Diarrhoea**: persistent loose, watery or green stools can quickly dehydrate a baby. This means that the baby is losing important body salts.
- **Vomiting**: if persistent or projectile (so forceful that it is projected several feet from the baby) and not the more usual **possetting**.
- **Excessive and persistent crying**: if the baby cannot be comforted in the usual way or if the cry is very different from usual crying.
- **Lethargy or 'floppiness'**: the baby may appear to lack energy and lack the normal muscle tone.
- **Dry nappies**: if the baby's nappies are much drier than usual because he or she has not passed urine, this could be a sign of **dehydration**.
- **Persistent coughing**: coughing in spasms lasting more than a few seconds. Long spasms often end with vomiting.
- **Difficulty with breathing**: if breathing becomes difficult or noisy with a cough, the baby may have bronchitis or croup.
- **Discharge from the ears**: ear infections may not show as a discharge, but babies may pull at their ears and may have a high temperature.
- **Sunken anterior fontanelle**: a serious sign of dehydration, possibly after diarrhoea and vomiting. The anterior fontanelle is a diamond-shaped soft spot at the front of the head just above the brow, measuring about four to five cm across. It remains visible in babies up to 12 to 18 months. In dehydrated babies, this area is sunken and more visible.
- **Seizures (also called convulsions or fits)**: during a seizure the baby either goes stiff or else jerks his or her arms or legs for a period lasting up to several minutes. The eyes may roll upwards, the skin and lips may become

In Practice

Observing babies

Observe a baby's head, so that you can identify the anterior fontanelle and understand how it should appear in healthy babies. (It is normal in young babies for the anterior fontanelle to bulge slightly when the baby is crying, but this should be temporary).

blue. The baby may dribble and will be unresponsive to you.

Identifying signs of illness in babies and children with different skin tones

Both within and between different ethnic groups there is a wide variety of skin tones and colours affecting the way skin looks during illness. When dark-skinned children are ill they may show the following signs:

Skin appearance

Normal skin tone and sheen may be lost; the skin may appear dull and paler or greyer than usual. You must pay attention to those parts of the body with less pigmentation – the palms, the tongue, the nail beds and the **conjunctiva** – the insides of the bottom eyelids. All of these will be paler than usual.

Rashes

In children with very dark skin, raised rashes are more obvious than flat rashes.

Bruising

The discoloration that is obvious in pale skin may not be easily observed in darker-skinned children. When bruised, the skin may appear darker or more purple when compared with surrounding skin.

Jaundice

In a fair-skinned child, gently press your finger to his forehead, nose, or chest, and look for a yellow tinge to the skin as the pressure is released. In a darker-skinned child, check for yellowness in his gums or the whites of his eyes.

When urgent medical attention is needed

It is important to be aware when a child or young person needs urgent medical attention. You need to be aware of the following signs and symptoms, which are always cause for concern, and which indicate that the child needs to be seen urgently by a doctor. If a baby, child or young person:

- Has a life-threatening incident: for example, seizures, poisoning, choking, **anaphylaxis**, loss of consciousness, respiratory and cardiac arrest.
- Has a high temperature of 38.6° C (101.4 ° F) that is not lowered by measures to reduce fever, and appears ill.
- Has convulsions (fits), or is limp and floppy.
- Has severe or persistent vomiting and/or diarrhoea, seems dehydrated or has projectile vomiting.
- Is unconscious, cannot be woken, is unusually drowsy or may be losing consciousness.
- Has symptoms of **meningitis:** very stiff neck, fever, headache, purplish rash that does not fade under pressure. (See pp 219–20 for information on meningitis.)
- Has wounds that will not stop bleeding and may need sutures.

- Is pale, listless, and does not respond to usual stimulation.
- Cries or screams inconsolably and may have severe pain.
- Has bulging **fontanelle** (soft spot on top of head – of a baby) when not crying.
- Appears to have severe abdominal pain, with symptoms of shock.
- Develops purple-red rash anywhere on body.
- Passes bowel motions (stools) containing blood.
- Has an asthma attack that does not respond to use of an inhaler.
- Has a suspected ear infection.
- Has been injured, e.g. by a burn which blisters and covers more than 10% of the body surface.
- Has inhaled something, such as a peanut, into the air passages and may be choking.
- Has swallowed a poisonous substance, or an object, e.g. a safety pin or button.
- Has bright pink cheeks and swollen hands and feet (in a baby – could be due to hypothermia).
- Has difficulty in breathing.
- Has sustained a head injury and has symptoms of headache, confusion, vomiting, problems with vision.

Your role and responsibilities

During your training, you should never be left alone with a group of children. Your duty is to tell someone immediately if you find a child who is in need of urgent medical attention, and then follow their instructions. You might be asked to stay with the other children to comfort and reassure them – or to fetch the first aid kit. If you do find that you are alone with a child or young person who needs first aid, try to stay calm and follow the first aid procedures: checking the immediate area for safety, then checking for breathing and giving first aid treatment when necessary (See Chapter 11 First Aid).

Procedures for reporting and recording accidents, incidents, emergencies and illnesses

Reporting to parents or carers

All accidents, injuries or illnesses that occur to children in a group setting must be reported to the child's parents or primary carers. If the injury is minor (such as a bruise or a small graze to the knee) the nursery or school staff will inform parents when the child is collected at the end of the session; or they may send a notification slip home if someone else collects the child. The parents are notified about:

- the nature of the injury or illness
- any treatment or action taken
- the name of the person who carried out the treatment.

In the case of a major accident, illness or injury, the child's parents or primary carers must be notified as soon as possible. Parents need to know that the staff are dealing with the incident in a caring and professional manner, and to be involved in any decisions regarding treatment.

The Accident Report Book

Every workplace is, by law, required to have an Accident Report Book and to maintain a record of accidents. Information recorded includes:

- name of person injured
- date and time of injury
- where the accident happened (for example, in the garden)
- what exactly happened (Kara fell on the path and grazed her left knee)
- what injuries occurred (a graze)

- what treatment was given (graze was bathed and an adhesive dressing applied)
- name and signature of person dealing with the accident
- signature of witness to the report
- signature of parent or guardian.

One copy of the duplicated report form is given to the child's parent or carer; the other copy is kept in the Accident Report book at the early years setting.

If you are working in the family home as a nanny, you should follow the same reporting procedure, even though you do not have an official Accident Report Book.

Reporting and recording when a child becomes ill

If a child becomes ill while in a group setting, you should **first** report it to your manager or supervisor and then record the following details in the child's Daily Record:

- when the child first showed signs of illness
- the signs and symptoms: for example, behaviour changes, a high temperature or a rash
- any action taken, for example taking the temperature or giving paracetamol (with parental permission agreed beforehand)
- progress of the illness since first noticing it: for example, are there any further symptoms?

Infection control procedures

The legislation relating to care of children and young people states that children must be cared for in an environment that is safe and hygienic, that all play equipment must be kept clean, and that staff must take measures to control the spread of infection.

Your responsibility for promoting a healthy hygienic environment

Staff with infections can place children and others at risk, therefore staff suffering from particular conditions must be **excluded** from their work in accordance with Health Protection Agency guidelines.

- Any member of staff who handles food and becomes sick with diarrhoea, vomiting or infected skin problems must report this to his or her supervisor.
- Any member of staff with diarrhoea or vomiting should be excluded from work until at least 48 hours after symptoms have stopped. Staff with infected wounds or skin infections on exposed parts of their bodies should be similarly excluded until the lesions are healed, or they have been advised that it is safe to return to work by the GP.
- Any member of staff with other conditions that could spread infections, such as the common cold, should take sensible precautions. Staff should inform their supervisor.

In Practice

Infection control policy

Find out about the infection control policy in your own setting.

- ❏ When should you wear protective clothing?
- ❏ When should you wear gloves?
- ❏ How should you dispose of waste?
- ❏ Which conditions should you report to your supervisor and not attend for work?

When to wear protective clothing

It is recommended that a new disposable plastic apron and gloves be worn:

- during nappy changing
- when cleaning up blood or body fluid (faeces, urine and vomit) spills.

Procedure for nappy changing

- The nappy changing area must be separate from food preparation and eating areas.
- The changing surface should be smooth, non-absorbent and easy to clean.
- Place a disposable covering (paper roll) on the area where you will place the child's bottom.
- Put on a plastic apron and disposable gloves after assembling all equipment and preparing child.
- Dispose of soiled nappy into an individual nappy sack before placing into a bin lined with a plastic liner. The bin should have a secure lid, and be operated by a foot pedal.
- Non-disposable nappies should be placed directly into a plastic bag to give to parents. Solid faecal matter may be disposed of into the toilet.
- Never rinse or wash non-disposable nappies, because the risk of splashing may cause microbes (germs) to spread to staff or children.
- If a child needs to be washed completely, use a sink with running water; thoroughly clean and disinfect the sink after use.
- Remove gloves after disposing of nappy and cleaning bottom. Put on clean nappy.
- Dispose of paper towel.
- Clean changing area using a detergent spray or soap and water, and dry surface. Alternatively, an appropriate wipe may be used.
- Wash hands.

- If creams are used they should be supplied by parents, and be for that individual child's use only.

Procedure for cleaning up blood or body fluid spillages

- Put on disposable gloves and plastic apron.
- Use paper towels to mop up any excess and dispose of them in a plastic bag.
- Do not use a mop to clean up spillages.
- Wash area with hot water and detergent using a disposable cloth, and dry using paper towels.
- Discard apron and gloves into disposable bag and dispose of appropriately in a bin.
- Always wash your hands thoroughly after removing gloves and aprons.
- If staff clothing is contaminated by body fluid spillages, clothes should be changed as soon as possible and placed in a plastic bag and sealed. These clothes should be washed at the highest temperature possible for the item. Correct hand washing and drying are essential after touching the clothes.

Procedures for receiving, storing and administering medicines

Most nurseries have a policy on the giving of medicines. This usually states that *no drugs* will be given to the child while at nursery. However, there are certain exceptions to this rule. For example, if a child has a condition (such as asthma) that requires an immediate response, or has a condition (such as eczema or glue ear) that requires long-term medication, parents should discuss this with the nursery manager or supervisor.

Medicines prescribed by a doctor and paracetamol may be given to these children only after the parent's or carer's written consent is

In Practice

Disposal of waste

You should always:

❏ Protect yourself from infection by wearing a protective apron and disposable gloves.

❏ Protect children by keeping them away from spillages at all times.

❏ Dispose of waste safely and hygienically – in special bins.

❏ Clean up spillages that could cause infection, using special solutions. If children are likely to come near the affected area, ask another member of staff to keep them away while you deal with the incident.

❏ Wrap children's soiled clothes in a polythene bag and give them to the parents when they arrive.

❏ Empty a used potty immediately after use, and clean appropriately.

Progress check

The importance of good hygiene in children's settings

- Why is good hygiene so important in early years settings? Give three reasons.
- When should children wash their hands?
- Why should children's toys and playthings be checked for hygiene and regularly cleaned?
- How should you dispose of a soiled nappy in an early years setting?
- When preparing and serving food and drinks for children, you must follow the rules of food hygiene. State three important ways in which you can prevent infection from food or drink.

obtained. The consent should be on a form that includes the following details:

- the child's name
- the name of the medicine to be given
- the precise dose to be given
- the time it should be given, or if given irregularly, parents must detail the precise circumstances or symptoms that would mean the medicine should be given
- how it should be given – that is, oral medicine, skin cream, eye drops, inhaler, etc.
- parent's name and signature and the date signed.

All medicines must be stored in their original containers, be clearly labelled and be kept in a locked cupboard inaccessible to the children. The only exception to this is **inhalers for asthma,** which should be easily available to the particular child at all times. If you give any medicine to a child you must record the details on a special form or book; these include the child's name, date, time, dose given. You must then sign it and ask another member of staff to sign as witness.

The parents will then sign the record book to acknowledge that the medicine has been given. If there is any problem with giving the medicine – for example, if the child refuses it or is sick shortly after – this should also be recorded. Always make sure that you understand how and when to give a child's medicine; if in doubt, ask your manager or supervisor.

Useful websites and resources

www.capt.org.uk	**The Child Accident Prevention Trust (CAPT)** is committed to reducing the number of children and young people killed, disabled or seriously injured in accidents.
www.sunsmart.org.uk	**SunSmart** gives advice about preventing sunburn which can lead to skin cancer.

8 Support children and young people's positive behaviour: Unit TDA 2.9

Behaviour is the way in which we act, speak and treat other people and our environment. Children and young people whose early social and emotional development is positive are more likely to make friends, settle well into school and understand how to behave appropriately in different situations. They have strong self-esteem and a sense of self-worth, but also have a feeling of empathy for others. They understand what the boundaries are, and why they are necessary. Behaviour has a significant impact on current and later success for children and young people, in terms of their social skill development, education and employment.

Learning outcomes

By the end of this chapter you will:

1. Know the policies and procedures of the setting for promoting children and young people's positive behaviour.

2. Be able to support positive behaviour.

3. Be able to respond to inappropriate behaviour.

The setting's policies and procedures for promoting positive behaviour

Every setting should have a behaviour policy. This should be specific to the aims and needs of the setting and include guidelines for promoting positive behaviour of both children *and* adults involved with the setting. A behaviour policy will help all staff to learn how to promote positive behaviour, by explaining that children need to develop positive skills and attributes:

- self-respect and self-esteem
- consideration and **empathy** for others
- social skills such as negotiation and problem-solving.

Key term

Empathy – The ability to understand and share the feelings of another.

The policy should also include guidance in two important areas:

1 promoting appropriate behaviour in the children and young people in the setting

2 discouraging inappropriate behaviour in the setting.

Specific procedures for staff to follow which help in achieving these aims should also be included, such as:

- **Being a positive role model**: showing the children and young people what is appropriate behaviour in the setting, by setting a positive example in your own behaviour.
- **Showing respect** to children, young people and other adults: by the way you listen, your facial expression, your body language and by what you say.
- **Praising children and young people**: when they have shown positive and appropriate behaviour – for example, when they have been helpful to another child.
- **Organising the environment**: to make it easier for children and young people to understand why they need to be patient or to take turns.
- **Intervening calmly**: to stop children and young people hurting each other or behaving in an unsafe way.
- **Setting boundaries**: supporting children and young people in learning what sort of behaviour is acceptable and what is not.
- **Giving a simple explanation or alternative** to the child who is finding it difficult to observe boundaries.

The policy should also detail the strategies that will definitely *never* be used in the setting and also explain why; for example:

- Adults will not hit or shake children or young people – this is against the law. It is a misuse of your adult strength and is contrary to the ground rules for children and young people's behaviour.
- Adults will not use verbal humiliation or insults – this would undermine children and

young people's self-esteem and would be an example of inappropriate behaviour.

In Practice

Behaviour policy

Find out about the policy and procedures in your setting. Why is it important for settings to have a behaviour policy?

Codes of conduct

Each behaviour policy applies to a particular setting and so will vary according to the type of setting. The Early Years Foundation Stage requires that 'children's behaviour must be managed effectively and in a manner appropriate for their stage of development and particular individual needs'. Schools are also legally required to have policies and procedures in place to identify and prevent bullying. Codes of conduct generally form part of a setting's behaviour policy. These relate to the behaviour of staff as well as to the behaviour of children and young people.

The code of conduct for staff in a children or young people's setting may provide extra guidance for staff on dealing with inappropriate behaviour:

- keeping calm when dealing with inappropriate behaviour
- listening to both sides of the story when there is conflict and apologising if you have made a mistake
- being consistent when dealing with inappropriate behaviour
- making sure that you do not make any negative comments in front of the children or young people.

The main features of a code of conduct for children and young people deal with issues such as fairness and taking turns, playing safely and not bullying. The code may be negotiated with older children and young people and will also describe use of the following measures to promote positive behaviour.

Rewards and sanctions

Most settings have ways of rewarding positive behaviour and of using sanctions to discourage inappropriate behaviour. The use of rewards and sanctions is discussed in the next section.

Dealing with conflict and inappropriate behaviour

Everyone working with children and young people needs to be clear about what is meant by inappropriate behaviour; this is why it is so important to have a behaviour policy. Practitioners must follow the code of conduct by dealing with conflict in a fair and consistent way.

Anti-bullying

Bullying is a complex issue that mostly affects older children and young people. The setting's policy should include guidance on how to prevent bullying.

Attendance

The importance of regular attendance is usually part of a school's code of conduct, although not always in an early years setting.

The importance of being fair and consistent

It is important that everyone in the setting is both fair and consistent when dealing with children's and young people's behaviour. When you are fair and consistent in your response to inappropriate behaviour, the child's sense of security and knowledge of right from wrong will be reinforced. The adult response to

inappropriate behaviour should be the same, every time that behaviour occurs.

Consistency in applying the boundaries is important, especially in the work setting, where children and young people need to relate to several adults. They will check that the rules have not changed and that they still apply whichever adult is present. If you are supervising an activity, the children will expect you to apply the same rules as other staff. It undermines your own position if you allow unacceptable behaviour and another staff member has to discipline the children you are working with.

Setting rules and boundaries

If children and young people are to understand what is regarded as acceptable behaviour at home, in the work setting and in society, then they must be given very clear and consistent guidelines. Work settings will have a policy relating to behaviour and discipline, which all staff should follow and which is regularly reviewed.

Rules

The policy will explain the rules that are applied, and how children and young people will be helped to understand and learn to keep them. In most cases the rules are simple and reflect the concerns for safety and for children and young people to be considerate of others and their environment. They should be appropriate for the age and stage of development of the children or young people and for the particular needs of the work setting. Rules apply to the forms of behaviour that are encouraged, and cover physical, social and verbal aspects.

Rules – or targets – should be realistically set for the child or young person's age and stage of development. Examples of rules for a child aged four to five years are to:

- say 'please' and 'thank you'
- share play equipment
- tidy up
- be quiet and listen for short periods (such as story- or register time).

Boundaries

These are the limits within which behaviour is acceptable – they identify what may, and may not, be done or said. Children and young people need to understand the consequences of not acting within those boundaries. It is important that the boundaries are appropriate for the age and stage of development.

Examples of boundaries for young children are that they may:

- play outside – but must not tread on the flowerbeds
- watch television – but only until tea is ready
- use the dressing-up clothes – if they put them away when they have finished.

Examples of boundaries for older children and young people are that they may:

- use the internet – but only for agreed periods
- visit their friends' houses – as long as they always let you know where they are.

How to support positive behaviour

The ways in which children and young people behave will depend to a large extent on their developmental stage. Before looking at how to support positive behaviour, we need to understand what is expected behaviour at certain ages.

Stages of behavioural development

The following stages of behavioural development are, of course, linked only loosely to the ages shown. As with any normative measurements, they serve only as a rough guide to help understand children and young people's behaviour and how best to respond to it. Much will depend upon children and young people's experiences and the way in which they have been helped to develop effective relationships.

Aged one to two years

At this age, children:

- have developed their own personalities and are sociable with close family and friends
- still become shy and anxious when parents or carers are out of sight
- are developing their speech, and can attract attention by calling out or crying
- can become possessive over toys, but can often be distracted to something else
- are discovering that they are separate individuals
- are self-centred (see things from their own point of view)
- are gaining mobility, improving their ability to explore their surroundings – this results in conflicts, often regarding safety
- begin to understand the meaning of 'No', and firm boundaries can be set
- can be frustrated by their own limitations, but resist adult help (perhaps saying 'me do it').

Aged two to three years

Children now:

- are developing greater awareness of their separate identities
- are not yet able to share easily
- are developing their language abilities; they begin to communicate their needs and wishes more clearly and to understand 'in a minute'

Figure 8.01 Children and young people need to know what behaviour is expected of them; they need boundaries

- can still be distracted from the cause of their anger
- have tantrums (usually when parents or main carers are present) when frustrated – possibly caused by their efforts to become self-reliant (such as feeding or dressing themselves) or having ideas that the adult does not want them to carry out
- experience a range of feelings – being very affectionate and cooperative one minute and resistant the next

- are aware of the feelings of others and can respond to them.

Aged three to four years

Children at this age:

- are very aware of others and imitate them – especially in their play; their developing speaking and listening skills allow them to repeat swear words they hear

- are more able to express themselves through speech and, therefore, there is often a reduction in physical outbursts; however, they are still likely to hit back if provoked
- can be impulsive and will be less easily distracted
- become more sociable in their play and may have favourite friends
- can sometimes be reasoned with and are just becoming aware of the behaviour codes in different places or situations
- like and seek adult approval and appreciation of their efforts.

Aged four to five years

Children now:

- can behave appropriately at mealtimes and during other 'routine' activities and may begin to understand why 'Please' and 'Thank you' (or their equivalents) are important
- are able to share and take turns, but often need help
- are more aware of others' feelings and will be concerned if someone is hurt
- are becoming more independent and self-assured, but still need adult comfort when ill or tired
- will respond to reason, can negotiate and be adaptable, but can still be distracted
- are sociable and becoming confident communicators able to make more sense of their environment; there will continue to be conflicts that they cannot resolve on their own and with which they will need adult help
- can sometimes be determined, may argue and show aggression.

Aged five to six years

Children at this age:

- understand that different rules apply in different places (such as at home, school,

grandparents' house) and can adapt their behaviour accordingly
- are developing control over their feelings – they argue with adults when they feel secure and need to feel there are firm boundaries in place
- will respond to reason and can negotiate, but are less easily distracted – anger can last longer and they need time to calm down
- are able to hide their feelings in some situations
- can cooperate in group play, but are not yet ready for team games
- may show off and boast (for example, when they celebrate an achievement)
- will continue to need adult support to resolve conflicts
- will share and take turns, and begin to have an understanding of what is 'fair' if given an explanation.

Aged six to eight years

Children now:

- can quickly adapt behaviour to suit the situation
- can play games with rules
- can argue their viewpoints
- are growing in confidence and becoming independent
- are developing some moral values and understanding of 'right' and 'wrong'
- can be friendly and cooperative
- can control how they feel much of the time but there are still times when they want to do things their way and quarrels develop.

Aged eight to 12 years

Between these ages, children:

- enjoy playing and inventing games with rules
- tend to be cooperative and enjoy being given responsibility
- tend to be closely attached to parental figures

- make friends often with same-gender peers, usually based on proximity, common interests and hobbies; girls tend to have fewer, but emotionally closer, friends than boys.

Aged 12 to 19 years

Children and young people:

- often question rules at home and try to push the boundaries
- may show *avoidance* behaviours (such as truanting, bullying and behaving disruptively in class), often caused by low self-esteem; some may experience bullying themselves.

Linking behaviour to child development

When assessing children and young people's behaviour it is important to bear these developmental stages in mind and to view the behaviour in the context of overall development. Here are two examples:

1. It is well known that **tantrums** are a common, even expected, feature of a two-year-old child's behaviour. There is bound to be some cause for concern, however, if they are a regular feature of a six-year-old child's behaviour. However, some adults have unrealistic expectations of children and young people and express surprise when inappropriate behaviour occurs.
2. A five-year-old child becomes fidgety and whines during a Christmas pantomime. The adults will view the occasion as a treat and may feel resentment that their child is complaining, but it is reasonable that a five-year-old should lose concentration, be unable to sit still for a lengthy period or understand all of what is going on.

Factors affecting behaviour

It is well known that behaviour is commonly affected by certain factors. There are some factors that stem from the children and young people themselves:

- illness
- accident and injury
- tiredness.

Other factors result from their situations:

- arrival of a new baby
- moving house
- parental separation or divorce
- change of carer – either at home or in a setting
- loss or bereavement
- change of setting – such as transition from home to nursery or nursery to school.

Individual children and young people will respond to these situations differently but *regression* is common (usually temporary) when they revert to behaviour that is immature for them. Events that they do not understand will leave them confused, leading to frustration and aggressive outbursts, or they may blame themselves, which could result in withdrawn behaviour and the development of inappropriate habits through anxiety.

Generally, any factor that causes stress may result in the child:

- needing more comfort and attention
- being less sociable
- being unable to cope with tasks that they would normally manage
- being subject to mood swings
- being unable to concentrate (this includes listening to instructions) and less able to cope with challenging situations and difficulties.

The benefits of encouraging and rewarding positive behaviour

Positive behaviour management is about using positive rather than negative approaches to encourage children and young people to behave appropriately. Promoting positive behaviour involves:

- setting clear boundaries, which are applied in a calm and consistent way
- encouraging children and young people to make their own choices about behaviour – and to understand the negative consequences if they choose inappropriate behaviour
- setting 'positive' rules rather than 'negative' ones. Negative rules tend to begin with the word 'Don't', and tell children and young people what they must not do, but do not guide them as to what they may or should do.

Skills and techniques for supporting and encouraging positive behaviour

In trying to understand behaviour, it is helpful to note whether there are particular incidents or situations that seem to trigger inappropriate behaviour. Some of these can be avoided altogether by minor changes in routine or approach, but others, such as siblings teasing each other, will occur frequently; children and young people therefore need to be given strategies and support to be able to cope with them effectively. It is important never to reject the child but only what the child has done (for example, 'That was an unkind thing to say' rather than 'You are unkind').

The A-B-C of behaviour

- **Antecedent:** what happens before, or leads up to, the observed behaviour.

- **Behaviour:** the observed behaviour – what the child says and how he or she acts (this is any behaviour, both positive and negative).
- **Consequence:** what happens following the observed behaviour.

Part of your role as a practitioner is to observe children and young people's behaviour, whether or not you make a written record, so that you can contribute to discussions about a child's behaviour and develop positive practice in managing inappropriate aspects. In your work setting you should try to see not only how other staff and parents deal with incidents, but also which methods seem to be effective with which children or young people.

Using rewards

There are different forms of reward:

- verbal praise (such as 'Well done')
- attention – this could be non-verbal (smile of approval, a nod)
- stars or points (for older children) leading to certificates or for group recognition
- sharing success by telling other staff and parents
- own choice of activity or story
- tangible rewards such as stickers.

Rewards work on the principle of **positive reinforcement** – based on the idea that if children and young people receive approval and/or a reward for behaving acceptably, they are likely to want to repeat that behaviour. If one child is praised (for example, for tidying up) others are often influenced to copy or join in so that they, too, will receive praise and attention. For young children, the reward must be *immediate* so that they understand the link between it and the positive behaviour. It is of little value to promise a treat or reward in the future. Similarly, star charts and collecting points are not appropriate for children younger than five years old.

There are problems associated with rewards in that some children and young people may behave in a particular way purely to receive the reward rather than from an understanding of the need to consider safety, others and their environment or enjoying what they have achieved for its own sake. The *type* of reward also needs to be considered; for example, is it desirable for children and young people to be given sweets as rewards? Some parents may have strong views about this.

Rewards might work in the short term, but do not always succeed in the long term. They might even undermine lifelong learning by encouraging children and young people to seek reward, rather than be disposed to learn because something is interesting.

Providing an effective role model

Children learn about positive behaviour – such as sharing and saying 'thank you' – by watching others. They can also learn about inappropriate behaviours – such as being unwilling to share and swearing – from watching adults. You need to act as a positive role model for children and young people. You can do this by modelling positive behaviour. Children will try to copy your behaviour, so you need to show positive behaviour at all times.

Involving children and young people in decision-making

Children and young people can be involved in helping to devise basic classroom rules, which can then – if wanted – be posted on the wall; some examples are given below.

Golden Rules for positive behaviour

Staff at a nursery drew up a short set of Golden Rules, after discussing them with the children:

Case Study — Using rewards

In primary school a new head teacher introduced the regular practice of listening to children read to her. This involved children being sent individually to her office where she would reward them with a jelly bear if they read well or tried hard. One mother was surprised, when talking to her daughter about the school day, that she was upset to have read to her class teacher instead of to the head teacher. The girl explained that everyone was asking to read to the head teacher and she was not chosen – so she missed out on a jelly bear!

The parent was alarmed, firstly that sweets were being given as a reward without parents knowing, and secondly that children were not rewarded by the experience itself and the head teacher's appreciation of children's efforts.

- We take care of our things.
- We share with each other.
- We walk inside.
- We listen when someone is talking.
- We are kind to each other.

They illustrated the Rules with photos of children behaving appropriately and also showed the relevant Makaton symbols.

Classroom rules for positive behaviour

- We arrive with the correct equipment for the lesson.

- We keep unkind words to ourselves.

- We take turns to contribute to teaching and learning.

- We have a right to learn.

- We have a responsibility to respect the rights of others.

- We recognise our own responsibility for our education.

Youth workers consulted the young people in their youth centre and involved them in drawing up a set of rules. They called it The Respect Code:

The following are the examples of behaviour that we – young people and staff – would consider unacceptable at the centre.

- Using your power, strength or authority to intimidate others

- Abusive language

- Racist, homophobic, sexist language

- Possession of, and taking of, drugs or any illegal substances

- Fighting and violent behaviour

- Disrespectful behaviour towards anyone at the centre

- Deliberate damage to property

- Possession of, and taking of, alcohol – or entering the premises after having taken alcohol.

How to respond to inappropriate behaviour

Inappropriate behaviour conflicts with the accepted values and beliefs of the setting and of society. Inappropriate behaviour may be demonstrated through speech, writing, non-verbal behaviour or physical abuse and includes:

- attention-seeking
- aggression (both physical and verbal) towards others
- self-destructive behaviour or self-harming.

Attention-seeking

Children will do just about anything to get the attention they crave from parents and carers. This is often shown through *disruptive* (making noises, not responding to an instruction) or *aggressive* behaviour and needs managing as identified below. Sometimes children who are trying to please can be just as disruptive. Those who desperately want adults to notice them will call out, interrupt, ask questions and frequently push in front of other children to show something they have made or done.

Strategies for dealing with attention-seeking behaviour

Children who seek attention challenge patience but with some reminding about turn-taking, and clear expectation that they will do so, they can learn to wait for their turn. It is important to give attention when they have waited appropriately so that they are encouraged to do so again. Practitioners could try the following strategies:

- *whenever possible ignoring attention-seeking behaviour*, unless their attention is drawn to it (perhaps by another child) as the message sent then is that it is acceptable to behave in that way

Case Study   A lack of consistency

Callum is in nursery class. He is an energetic, popular and sociable boy, aged two-and-a-half years. The room leader, Joanne, has a particular soft spot for Callum as she was friends with his mum before he started at the nursery. Lately, Callum has begun to disrupt the class by running around during quieter times and mealtimes. He has recently dropped his afternoon nap at Mum's request, and is very noisy and boisterous when the other children are trying to sleep. Joanne is usually in the office during this naptime after lunch, and leaves Fiona in charge of the running of the room. Fiona adopts a firm line with Callum. She takes him aside, gets down to his level and tells him clearly why he cannot make noise and run around, and what behaviour she expects from him. She also takes the opportunity to go with him to find quiet games to play while the others are asleep. This works well for a little while, but usually Callum needs a few reminders before he accepts. Occasionally, as a treat, he is allowed to go and play outside with the pre-school children (if they have room for him) but Fiona will not allow this unless Callum is behaving well.

However, Fiona has noticed that when Callum is being disruptive and Joanne is in the room, she adopts a different approach. First Joanne will tell him to stop, but when he does not respond, she leaves the room – taking him with her to 'help' her run errands, saying to the other staff members that he is bored and that is why he is not behaving well. Fiona views this as rewarding inappropriate behaviour, and finds that after it has happened a few times, Callum becomes increasingly difficult to control, and becomes easily upset and tearful. He stops responding so positively to Fiona's technique, and requires one-to-one attention at a time when staff members are trying to settle ten other children for their naps, as well as supply play for the few children who, like Callum, no longer have daytime naps.

1 What do the staff need to do to rectify this situation?

2 Why do you think that Callum is now becoming upset easily?

3 Do you think that Callum's 'treat' of running errands is making him happy in the long run?

4 Why is it unfair on children when there is inconsistency in discipline techniques?

- *giving attention and praise* to another child who is behaving acceptably
- *distracting the child's attention* – distraction is particularly appropriate with younger children) or removing him or her to another activity or group
- *expressing disapproval* – verbally and/or non-verbally through body language, facial expression (frowning) and shaking of the head

- *using a sanction* – withdrawal of a privilege (such as removing a toy or activity).

Physical aggression

This usually results from strong feelings that are difficult to control. Whatever the cause – and it may be provocation – the adult should deal with it calmly and ensure that the needs of all the children and young people involved are met. A child who has lost control frightens herself and the other children and young people.

Strategies for dealing with aggressive behaviour

Time out: This involves the child who has been aggressive being taken to an identified place away from the incident – a corner or chair, where the child can be given a quiet activity, such as reading a book. 'Time out' allows for a calming-down period and for other children and young people to be reassured. This method can work but needs positive follow-up by a staff member to explain that the behaviour was unacceptable, explain why and suggest how the child might have behaved otherwise; for example, asked instead of snatched, or listened to the apology for the model being broken. (See p 147 for more information on using Time Out as a sanction).

How to respond when a child bites

This is when a child biting is inappropriate. Try to think why the child has bitten. Ask the following questions to help you to understand why it has happened:

- When and where did it happen?
- Who with?
- What happened before?
- What happened afterwards?
- How do you think the child feels?

Many settings develop a 'biting policy' and produce a leaflet with guidelines to support both parents and practitioners. It is not when a baby bites down as a reflex action or a young child uses their mouth to explore new objects.

Strategies for dealing with a child who bites

- Comfort and take care of child who has been bitten, in a 'low-key' calm way. Tell the bitten child, 'That must be sore, let's get a cold cloth'.

Case Study   Aidan's behaviour

Aidan had recently started in the reception class and displayed inappropriate behaviour in many different ways and situations. On arrival in the playground in the mornings, with both his parents and younger sister, he would walk around poking and kicking other children. This caused anger among other parents, upset among the children, and ill feeling towards his parents who would shout at him before grabbing him, holding him by the hand and telling him off loudly. The staff discussed this with the parents and it was agreed that, in the short term, Aidan should be brought to school ten minutes later than everyone else. Every morning the father would deliver him to the classroom door with the instruction, 'Behave.'

Aidan always said that he would; however, he did not really understand what 'behave' meant in terms of his own actions. His teacher made a point of reminding him, throughout the day, of what behaviour was expected and explained what that meant for him; for example, 'When I ask you to "sit nicely", this means sitting still without touching any other child or anything.' It was also an opportunity to reinforce the rule for other children. Improvement was very gradual. Only one aspect of behaviour was dealt with at a time. He was given one-to-one support when available and observations were recorded to monitor progress and plan future strategies.

1 How did Aidan's teacher help him to change his behaviour?

2 In pairs produce some simple rules for four-to-five-year-olds in a reception class that give clear guidance about what they should do – rather than what they should not do. For example, DO walk sensibly in the classroom (instead of DO NOT run in the classroom).

- To the biter, say firmly, but gently, 'It's not OK to bite, because biting hurts. If you want to bite, you can bite a biscuit or a toy, but I can't let you bite Martha.'
- Encourage the biter to 'make amends' in some way – to help get the cold cloth or a teddy for comfort.

 Progress check

Managing the behaviour of a child who bites

- Try to offer positive attention and affection to the 'biter' throughout the day.
- Provide snacks and drinks regularly.
- Make sure there is more than one of a favourite toy so there is a smaller chance of the child becoming frustrated.
- Arrange the room to make space for play.
- Show the child how to negotiate and take turns.
- Be aware of any changes taking place at home, and help the child to deal with these by talking sensitively with them about it.

 Progress check

Dealing with tantrums

- **Try to avoid them** – if you can anticipate them, try distracting the child with a game or another activity.
- **Try to ignore them** – apart from safety concerns, try to give as little attention as possible during the tantrum.
- **Be consistent** – if children and young people think, from past experience, that the adult will not keep the boundary firmly, they will continue to tantrum; clear boundaries are essential.
- **A firm hug** may help the child feel secure and under control until the child calms down – this is useful in situations where you cannot walk away.
- **Talk about them** – this may help older children and young people to express their feelings calmly.
- **Provide experiences and activities** that the child finds interesting; this usually helps children and young people to become involved in positive ways.
- **Do not give in and let the boundary go** – this almost certainly leads to *more* rather than *fewer* tantrums because children and young people are confused by inconsistency.

Temper tantrums

These are usually associated with two-year-olds but can occur in older children or young people. In fact, many people would not describe tantrums as inappropriate behaviour in toddlers. They may happen particularly when a child is ill or tired, but often build from a confrontational incident when he or she is asked to do something, or not to do something and a battle of wills begins! Temper tantrums often involve shouting and crying, refusal to cooperate and mounting anger – shown through kicking, hitting, screaming, stamping – and, on occasions, self-harm. In younger children tantrums can be over very quickly but in older ones can take longer to reach a peak and longer to calm down afterwards.

Unacceptable language

This includes swearing and name-calling that often result from children and young people repeating what they have themselves heard. Sometimes they are unaware that it is unacceptable in one setting but not another. In these cases they need to be told firmly not to say those words 'here' – you cannot legislate for language they may use at home or criticise their families. Some children and young people will deliberately use unacceptable language to shock or seek attention. In these cases you should state the rule calmly and firmly.

Name-calling

Name-calling must always be challenged and dealt with firmly, particularly if it is discriminatory (regarding race, creed, disability, family background, appearance, etc.). Explain that it is hurtful and that we are all different. This behaviour is best combated through positive example and through anti-discriminatory practices in the work setting, which will help children and young people to value other people as individuals.

Truancy

A truant is a child aged between 5 and 16 who fails to attend school and does not have a legitimate reason for being absent. Every year hundreds of thousands of UK students play truant. Some of the reasons that students engage in truancy include:

- Being bullied at school
- Problems in the family home
- Undiagnosed behavioural or emotional problems
- General dislike of school
- An inability to do coursework or to ask for help
- Peer pressure
- Exclusions that leave them with little interest in attending school.

Children who miss school are missing out on social interaction, which can affect their ability to make friends. The instances of truancy may be limited to one or two individuals in a school or can be attributed to a gang of pupils who have the same disliking for school. Sometimes the children or young people who are playing truant are placed in the care of a *learning mentor* who may be able to help them learn and to establish the underlying cause of truancy. Parents may have to sign up to a parenting contract. This written agreement is entered into by the parents of the child playing truant and also the local authority and school. The agreement is not a legal document, but it may help parents to understand and deal with any behavioural issues that their child may have.

Self-harming

'Deliberate self-harm' is a term used when someone intentionally injures or harms themselves. This can take a number of forms including:

- cutting or burning
- taking overdoses of tablets or medicines
- pulling out hair or eyelashes
- scratching, picking or tearing at skin, causing sores and scarring
- head-banging.

There are many reasons why a child or young person deliberately self-harms. Young people who are depressed, have an eating disorder or other serious mental health problem are at greater risk, as are young people who take illegal drugs or excessive amounts of alcohol. Self-harm is often kept secret, but the young person may often appear withdrawn or irritable, and may refuse to wear short sleeves or to take off clothing for sports, because of scarring on their arms. Self-harming usually signals some emotional difficulty that needs expert intervention. Staff and parents need to discuss their concerns and agree a common approach based on the advice they are given.

The use of sanctions

A sanction is designed to discourage inappropriate behaviour. To be effective, however, it must also protect the practitioner's relationship with the child and safeguard the child's self-esteem. Examples of sanctions to be used with young children include:

- A non-verbal signal: for example, a frown or shake of head can be very effective.
- A minute's withdrawal (timed with a timer to ensure fairness) from the activity or group.
- Time out: It is important that 'time out' is used appropriately, and only when essential (see below).

When children misbehave, the adult responsible at the time should deal with it and, whenever possible, issue rebukes and sanctions in private. Children should always receive a warning before a sanction is imposed, to give them the chance to cooperate.

Time out

Time out involves removing the child from whatever they are doing and insisting that he or she sits in a safe place and takes part in a quiet activity for a period of time. The supervising adult in these circumstances should:

- *ignore the child, offering no eye contact or conversation*: This gives the child time to calm down – to think and reflect on his or her behaviour.
- *time the Time Out:* The length of time out should ideally match the age of the child; for example, for a three-year-old child use three minutes.
- *invite the child to return:* The child should be invited to return after the Time Out, and to agree to behave appropriately if he or she wants to rejoin the wider group.
- *praise the child:* If the child then behaves appropriately in the next few minutes, the adult should offer approval and praise.

Examples of other sanctions

Sanctions often used in schools with young people include the following (from least severe to most severe):

- a verbal warning
- pupil moved to another seat
- punishment exercise
- pupil moved to another classroom
- detention
- referred to a senior member of staff
- excluded from class.

Reflective practice: Rewards and sanctions

What kinds of reward systems have you observed in schools and nursery settings? How did the children respond to them? Were some rewards more effective than others? How did children respond to sanctions or to you threatening to use them?

Referring inappropriate behaviour to others

Sometimes the behaviour management strategies outlined above fail to be effective, or are only effective for a short period of time. If inappropriate behaviour is linked to the child or young person's development, is temporary and capable of being managed within the setting, then there is no need to refer to a professional.

When to refer

Practitioners may need to refer the following types of inappropriate behaviour:

- behaviour that is inappropriate for the child's stage of development: e.g. a child over four years old who continues biting, or an older child who hits other children or is physically aggressive in other ways
- Self-harming behaviour
- Bullying.

There are other professionals who may be called upon to help all those involved. It is useful for senior practitioners to attend meetings which everyone to contribute information about a child; these will help to create an overall view of progress, development and behaviour and it is here that recorded observations will be especially useful. It is important to follow correct procedures for reporting incidents.

Professionals who may become involved include the following:

- **Health visitors** work primarily with children up to five years and their families, checking for healthy growth and development.
- **Play therapists** have specialist training and work with children through play to help them feel emotionally secure.
- **Paediatricians** are doctors who specialise in the care of children and young people up to the age of 16, to check for normal development and diagnose difficulties.
- **Educational psychologists** assess children and young people who have special needs, and give advice, particularly for those with emotional and behavioural difficulties.

- **Child psychiatrists** work with children and young people and their families to help them to express their thoughts and feelings.

Assessment practice

Promoting children and young people's positive behaviour

Check that you know what the policies and procedures are for promoting positive behaviour in your work setting. Describe the boundaries and rules used in your setting to promote positive behaviour, and explain why staff should apply these consistently and fairly.

Sharing experiences

Discuss how staff in your setting deal with inappropriate behaviour. Do you feel that the methods used are generally effective?

9 Contribute to the support of positive environments for children and young people: Unit MU 2.8

All environments in which children and young people spend time should be positive environments. This can be achieved by promoting inclusion and equality, and through approaches to developing positive relationships and behaviour. A positive environment helps children to become independent and to have the confidence to learn new skills and gain a sense of belonging.

Learning outcomes

By the end of this chapter you will:

1. Know the regulatory requirements for a positive environment for children and young people.

2. Be able to support a positive environment that meets the individual needs of children and young people.

3. Be able to support the personal care needs of children and young people within a positive environment.

4. Understand how to support the nutritional and dietary needs of children and young people.

The regulatory requirements for a positive environment for children and young people

All settings that provide care and education for children and young people must be registered with the appropriate authority:

1. **The Early Years Register:** All early years practitioners – such as childminders, day nurseries, pre-schools and private nursery schools – providing for children from birth to the 31 August following their fifth birthday (known as the early years age group) must register on the Early Years Register and deliver the Early Years Foundation Stage (EYFS) or The Foundation Phase in Wales. The EYFS is the statutory framework for the early education and care of children in the early years age group. The EYFS includes requirements for the provision of young children's welfare, learning and development that all providers must meet, as well as good practice guidance.

2 General Childcare Register (GCR): The GCR has two parts:

- *Compulsory part*: Providers of child care for children from 1 September following their fifth birthday (for example, the end of the Foundation Stage) up to the age of eight, and where at least one individual child attends for a total of more than 2 hours in any one day, are required to register on the compulsory part of this register, unless they are exempt. Care that is provided in the child's home is exempt from compulsory registration.

- *Voluntary part*: Providers of child care to children aged eight and over, or care that is exempt from compulsory registration, can now choose to be registered on the voluntary part of the register if they meet the requirements.

The different inspectorates – Ofsted (in England), HMIe (in Scotland), Estyn (in Wales) and ETI (in Northern Ireland) – are responsible for regulating and inspecting all settings with children under the age of 16 for more than two hours each day.

The Early Childhood Environment Rating Scale (ECERS)

In the UK, many providers of early years care and education use The Early Childhood Environment Rating Scale.

The ECERS enables settings to evaluate their environment and provision, and to identify clear steps for development in order to improve outcomes for children. Providers rate their environment against the indicators in the following seven areas:

- Space and furnishings
- Personal care routines
- Language and reasoning
- Activities
- Interaction
- Programme structure
- Provision for parents and staff.

Providers can then use the ECERS to fill in the Self-Evaluation Form (SEF) required by Ofsted and other inspectorates, all of which need to see a positive environment where children's needs are being met.

What is a positive environment?

Children and young people need an environment that is not just safe, healthy and hygienic, but also one that enables them to develop and learn – and is reassuring and welcoming. To provide for all their needs (physical, intellectual, language, emotional and social), the environment should:

- take account of each child and young person's **individual needs** and provide for them appropriately
- **be stimulating**; it should offer a wide range of activities that encourage experimentation and problem-solving
- provide opportunities for all types of **play** and activity
- encourage positive social interaction
- encourage physical development.

Key term

Positive environment – An environment that supports every child and young person's learning and development in a challenging but achievable way.

Regulatory requirements underpinning a positive environment

The regulatory requirements for settings that have children and young people under 16 in the setting for more than two hours a day are detailed in Ofsted's National Standards. They include the following requirements:

Clean and well-maintained	Appropriate rest areas
Adequate ventilation: locks and toughened glass on windows	Outdoor and indoor surfaces should be stable, non-slippery and easily cleanable.
All areas well lit for full visibility: plugs covered and current breakers for all electrical equipment	Clear telephone communication, with emergency numbers available
Adequate space and storage	Appropriate outdoor space with suitable equipment: soft area under climbing equipment
Adequate security: all external doors and gates locked and coded as appropriate; handles and door locks out of reach of children	Welcoming: access points must be kept clear, unlocked and made known to all children and adults, including visitors, in the case of an emergency evacuation
Appropriate temperature: 15–18°C; babies' rooms 20–22°C	Appropriate kitchen and laundry facilities
Safe and adequate supply of hot, cold and drinking water	Safe and appropriate play equipment
Sole use of premises during session	Appropriate toilet facilities
Safe supply of gas and electricity	Safe outings and use of transport
Appropriate supervision: the legal requirements for registered settings are: • Under 2: 1 adult to 3 children • Over 2 and under 3: 1 adult to 4 children • 3–5 years: 1 adult to 8 children • School reception class (full day): 1 adult to 13 children	Awareness of fire safety: regular fire drills etc. Smoke alarms and emergency equipment available Fireguards in front of fire and radiators covered
Adequate insurance	Appropriate plants

It is your responsibility as a practitioner to help to ensure the safety of the children and young people in your setting. Your manager will be responsible for providing equipment and premises that comply with safety requirements – and also for making sure that all repairs and inspections of equipment are carried out by suitably qualified people.

Assessment practice

A positive environment for children and young people

1 Describe what is meant by 'a positive environment'.

2 Describe the regulatory framework in your area that underpins a positive environment.

Supporting a positive environment that meets the individual needs of children and young people

There is a variety of settings that provide care for children and young people. These include:

- **The home environment**: children who are cared for at home (by a nanny) or in a childminder's home (a home learning environment) may not have access to special child-sized equipment or the wide range of activities that can be provided in a purpose-built nursery setting.

- **Children's Centres:** Children from birth to five years old and their families and carers are offered a wide range of services.
- **Pre-school or play groups**: staff may have to clear away every item of equipment after each session because the hall or room is used by other groups – for example, when the sessions take place in a village hall.
- **Purpose-built nurseries and infant schools**: these usually have child-sized chairs, basins, lavatories and low tables. Such provision makes the environment safer and allows children greater independence.
- **Crèches**: often provided in or near carers' workplaces, crèches provide day care for children up to the age of five.
- **Extended Care**: for children and young people aged four to 16 years.
- **Youth Clubs and Youth Activities:** for young people aged 11 to 16 years.

Maintaining the environment so that it is safe, hygienic, reassuring and attractive is part of *everyone's* role, wherever children and young people are being cared for. Where children are able to see that the care of their environment is important and shared between all adults, they are provided with positive role models to influence their own attitudes.

Welcoming children and young people to the setting

You can help to promote a sense of belonging by:

- greeting children individually by name and with a smile when they arrive
- marking their coat pegs with their names and their photographs
- naming their displayed work

- ensuring that their cultural backgrounds are represented in the home corner, in books, displays and interest tables
- providing routines for children; children like their environment to be predictable. They feel more secure and comfortable when their day has some sort of shape to it. Most early years settings have a daily routine, with fixed times for meals, snack times and outdoor play.
- Ensuring that young people feel welcome by establishing a rapport: being friendly and interested in what they have to say and encouraging them to ask questions.

In Practice

Helping children to feel valued

Children and young people and their families need to feel that they matter and that they are valued for themselves. You can help by doing the following:

- ❏ Establish a positive relationship with parents and carers; always welcome and listen to them.
- ❏ Squat or bend down to the children's level when you are talking with them.
- ❏ Praise, appreciate and encourage children.
- ❏ Be responsive to children's needs.
- ❏ Use positive images in the setting.
- ❏ Provide support for children who may be experiencing strong feelings, for example, when settling in to a new nursery or when they are angry or jealous.
- ❏ Encourage children who use them to bring in their comfort objects, such as a favourite teddy or a piece of blanket.
- ❏ Encourage the development of self-reliance and independence.
- ❏ Ensure that children who have special needs are provided with appropriate equipment and support.

Reflective practice: Welcoming children and young people

Think about the way you welcome children or young people into your setting:

- Do we look interested when a child or young person is talking to us?
- How do we make sure that the child knows we are listening and that we consider that what he or she has to say is important to us?
- Do you recognise and understand the ways in which body language is used by both you and the child or young person?
- Think of the ways in which you could improve how you welcome a child or young person into the setting. You could use a Reflective Diary to record your reflections.

Providing opportunities for choice in activities

The EYFS requires that children have an active role in setting up and choosing what activities they engage in. Creating a comfortable child-friendly environment means planning both the **physical layout** and the **organisation of activities**. It involves:

- considering health and safety before anything else; for example, fire exits and doors should be kept clear at all times
- giving children the maximum space and freedom to explore; rooms should be large enough to accommodate the numbers of children and be uncluttered
- ensuring that the room temperature is pleasant – neither too hot nor too cold (between 18°C and 21°C)
- making maximum use of natural light; rooms should be bright, airy and well-lit
- enabling access to outdoors; this should not be restricted to certain times and seasons

- ensuring displays are clearly visible; interest tables should be at child height where possible, and include items that can be safely handled and explored
- available space being divided appropriately to suit the range of activities offered.

How to encourage decision-making and active involvement

Children and young people need opportunities to make choices and to take control of some aspect of their lives, and to develop their preferences and dislikes. Being able to make decisions:

- reduces feelings of aggression and frustration
- builds self-esteem
- helps them to feel confident and take on responsibility
- helps them to learn skills of negotiation.

Involving children and young people in decision-making lets them know that they are important to you: that what they think and feel is important to you and to the setting as a whole.

In an early years setting, you can encourage children to make choices by providing the following opportunities:

- choosing which activities to put out
- deciding where to sit at snack time
- deciding what to have at snack time
- choosing the story at storytime
- choosing when to go outside.

In a young people's setting you can encourage young people to make choices by providing the following opportunities:

- planning and setting up an activity of their own choice
- making decisions about the way the setting is organised
- developing their own code of conduct or behaviour agreement

 **Progress check**

Encouraging children and young people to engage in activities of their choice

- Very young children need to be supported to make their own decisions. You could start the process by giving them a simple choice to make between two things. For example, 'Would you like to do thread these beads or play with the play dough?'
- Explain the activities on offer and encourage children to discuss the options available to them.
- Make sure that activities and equipment are clearly and appropriately stored and labelled, so that children can access them independently.
- Older children and young people can be encouraged to plan and implement their own activities.

Provision of equipment

Always remember that you, the practitioner, are the child's most valuable resource. (One of the principles that underpins the **Every Child Matters** Framework is that 'caring adults count more than resources or equipment'.) Most early years settings provide a wide variety of equipment:

- **Sand** – wet and dry: equipment in boxes on shelves nearby, labelled and with a picture of contents – these may be 'themed' such as items with holes/clear plastic/red.
- **Water**: activities that require water or hand washing should be near the sink and with aprons nearby. Equipment can be stored as for sand.
- **Clay and play dough**: cool, airtight storage; selection of utensils for mark-making, moulding, cutting.
- **A quiet area**: for looking at books and reading stories, doing floor puzzles; ideally carpeted with floor cushions.
- **Puzzles, small blocks and tabletop games**: stored accessibly close to tables and carpeted area.

- **Technology**: computer, weighing balance, calculators, tape recorders, etc.
- **Cookery**: measuring equipment, bowls, spoons and baking trays.
- **Art work**: tabards/aprons, brushes, paints and other materials within easy reach.
- **Domestic play**: dolls, cots, telephones, kitchen equipment, etc.
- **Make-believe play**: box of dressing-up clothes – these should be versatile and have simple fastenings.
- **Small world toys**: animals, cars, people, farms, dinosaurs, train and track, etc.
- **Construction**: blocks for building, small construction blocks such as Duplo®, Mobilo®, Stickle Bricks®; a woodwork area.
- **Writing/graphics**: with a variety of paper and different kinds of pencils and pens.
- **Workshop**: glue, scissors, masking tape, found materials such as cardboard from boxes, egg-boxes.
- **Interest table**: with interesting objects for children to handle.
- **Growing and living things**: such as fish aquarium, wormery, growing mustard and cress; ensure appropriate conditions, for example, away from direct sunlight.

A variety of **outdoor** play equipment is needed:

- **Outdoor space**: with safe equipment for climbing and swinging, a safety floor surface, wheeled toys, balls and bean bags
- **Garden**: plants and a growing area, a wild area to encourage butterflies, a mud patch for digging.

Supervision

Supervision is important, and separate areas indoors can be divided at child height so that children can focus attention and not be distracted, yet still be overseen by an adult. Storage units, low-level screens and display surfaces can all be used to divide space effectively without 'shutting off ' some activities. The role play area can become quite noisy and needs to be set up away from similar activities, such as small world play, train track, construction, etc. In school settings, particularly, where there will be more 'directed' and 'structured' activities, this can lead to rising noise levels and disruption.

Displaying children's work

Work settings would be dull and uninteresting places without displays. They can give a lot of information to children, parents and visitors about the setting's values and curriculum. Displays are created for a range of purposes and, sometimes for different audiences. Most settings have a notice board for parents and carers, usually sited near the entrance. This is used to update general information and news about the usual routine and forthcoming events. Often there will be named photographs of staff members and perhaps the week's menus.

Most displays reflect the activities and learning that take place:

- Some will be used as **learning resources** – alphabet and number friezes, days of the week, word banks (lists of commonly used words to consolidate reading and support writing, particularly in school settings), children's birthdays, etc. – and remain on display indefinitely.
- Others will be of **work done by the children** themselves showing their ideas, of their own or about a topic or different materials – for example, string painting, finger painting, collage, etc. These displays show that we value all the children's efforts.

Creating attractive displays needs careful consideration and can be time consuming. Factors to take into account include:

- size of space available
- themes/materials/colour schemes of adjacent displays
- location of space (some are very tricky, having thermostat controls or pipes in awkward places or involving corners!)
- availability of materials
- age and stage of development of children – this affects content and also what kinds of labels/titles/lettering you use.

There are many different types of display.

Wall display

The most usual type of display found in early years settings is a straightforward wall display. Boards of varying shapes and sizes are often placed on otherwise plain walls so that displays can be created and changed frequently to provide interest.

Window display

The use of windows for displays is also common. Paint (with a little washing-up liquid added so it can be easily washed off) is used to create colourful window displays – often of well-known characters from cartoons, stories or television or of animals or seasonal pictures. Sometimes pieces of art or craftwork may also be attached to windows, particularly if the materials lend themselves to having light behind them – for example, 'stained glass' windows or tissue paper pictures. Remember that the sunlight will fade the colours after a short time.

'Mobile' or 'hanging' display

Mobile or hanging displays can be used effectively, especially in very large rooms. Hanging or suspending shapes or pictures from a hoop or the ceiling needs careful thought. Having them at an appropriate height for the children may cause difficulties for staff! Also, you may have to consider security or alarm systems, which can be set off by moving objects. Such displays can be useful in identifying particular areas of a work setting, for example story characters over the book area, solid or flat shapes over the maths or numeracy area, etc.

Tabletop display

Tabletop displays (sometimes referred to as **interactive displays**) give you the opportunity to use objects or artefacts that will engage the children's interest. Interest objects should be attractively and appealingly displayed to encourage children to interact with them. Posing a question (for example, 'How many blue shapes can you find?') will invite children to use the display as an extra activity. If working with very young children, you must explain what they might do and, perhaps, take them to the display and handle the objects with them.

These displays are often accompanied by an upright board or display space that can be used for interesting pictures, photographs or posters and your own titles to add interest. Older children may appreciate related fact and storybooks to use for research.

Providing activities and resources to meet the individual needs of children and young people

Children's needs change all the time, according to their stage of development and their individual circumstances. The provision of activities and resources should always be planned with the individual child in mind, and this involves *assessing* their needs on a regular basis. Children with particular needs should have the same opportunities for playing and learning as other children. Settings may need to adapt their room

layout to improve access, for example for children or young people who use wheelchairs or have a visual impairment. They may need to work with parents to find out how the child can be encouraged to participate fully with other children within the setting. Any setting must take into account the particular needs of each child, in addition to the basic care and education needs of all children. This might involve:

- providing ramps for wheelchair users
- providing thick pencils and brushes for children with poor fine motor skills
- positioning children so that they learn effectively; for example, by making sure the light falls on the adult's face, so that a child wearing a hearing aid is able to lip-read and a child with a visual impairment can use any residual eyesight to see facial expressions
- adapting standard equipment; for example by having a tray on the table so that objects stay on the table, and a child with a visual impairment does not 'lose' objects that fall off
- providing the opportunity to learn sign languages; for example, Makaton or PECS (see Chapter 14, Unit TDA 2.15: Support children and young people with disabilities and special educational needs)
- helping children to maintain good posture, appropriate muscle tone and ease of movement, and promoting skills in independent mobility
- helping children to manage eating and drinking; there is a wide range of specialist aids for eating and drinking, such as angled spoons and suction plates
- promoting relaxation and support to help children manage stress and anxiety; some settings use a sensory room, but a quiet, comfortable area will benefit all children.

Activities that promote use of the senses

Smelling

Encourage children to develop their sense of smell by pointing out everyday smells – for example, baking and cooking smells, peeling an orange. Play guessing games, where you ask them to put their hands over their eyes and guess the object from sniffing it. Other activities include using 'scratch and sniff' books and taking advantage of unplanned opportunities, such as when grass has just been cut.

Tasting

Some nursery settings provide tasting sessions, where each child is given a piece of food and invited to express their feelings about it. This is an opportunity to learn new words and to state their own preferences.

Touching

Most (but not all) young children love to get their hands dirty. Most settings provide a sandpit or tray (both wet and dry). Children can also be encouraged to sift through some other substances, such as cornflour, oatmeal, pasta or gravel. Outside, children can be encouraged to find pine cones, flowers or leaves or flowers that are smooth, flat or spiky.

Hearing

Teaching children simple songs, especially with accompanying movements, is a good way to promote sensory development. Two-year-olds and even slightly younger children begin to learn pitch during this time. The ability to hear and reproduce specific sounds (words, rhymes and pitch) is enhanced when you sing a nursery rhyme such as Incey Wincey Spider.

Seeing

Babies love to look at moving images, such as a line of washing blowing in the breeze. Recognition and matching games help to promote children's ability to differentiate between colours, shapes, and sizes of objects.

Praising and encouraging individual achievements

Growing up requires an enormous amount of learning – emotional, social and intellectual. Strong incentives are therefore necessary for children and young people to continue through the difficulties that they will inevitably encounter. The most effective incentives are praise and recognition sustained over time.

Self-fulfilling prophecy

Children feel like failures when they cannot live up to the unrealistic hopes of their parent, carers and people who matter to them, and are less likely to repeat their efforts. The lower the expectation of the parent or carer, the lower the level of effort and achievement of the child; this is sometimes called a self-fulfilling prophecy. You need to have realistic expectations of each child.

Intrinsic motivation

If you make children feel anxious when they have not succeeded, they will avoid activities likely to lead to failure. It is important to praise children appropriately when they try hard or have achieved something new, however small it might seem. This will motivate children to greater effort and lead to the desire to achieve something for its own sake; this is called intrinsic motivation.

Activity

A natural treasure basket

Babies learn about their environment using all their senses – touch, smell, taste, sight, hearing and movement. A treasure basket is a collection of everyday objects chosen to stimulate the different senses. Babies have the chance to decide for themselves what they want to play with, choosing in turn whichever object they want to explore.

1 Choose a sturdy basket or box – one that does not tip over too easily.

2 Fill the basket with lots of natural objects – or objects made from natural materials – so that the baby has plenty to choose from. Examples include:

- fir cones
- pumice stone
- woollen ball
- feathers
- large seashells
- fruit such as apple, lemon
- wooden pegs
- large pebbles
- large walnuts
- brushes
- small baskets
- gourds.

3 Make sure that everything you choose for the basket is clean and safe; remember that babies often want to put everything into their mouths.

4 Make sure that the baby is seated comfortably and safely, with cushions for support if necessary.

5 Sit nearby and watch to give the baby confidence. Only talk or intervene if the baby clearly needs attention.

6 Check the contents of the basket regularly, cleaning objects and removing any damaged items.

Write an **observation** of the activity, noting the following:

- the length of time the baby plays with each item
- what he or she does with it
- any facial expressions or sounds made by the baby.

Supporting personal care needs

Caring for skin, hair and teeth

As children grow and become involved in more vigorous exercise, especially outside, a daily bath or shower becomes necessary. Most young children love bath time and adding bubble bath to the water adds to the fun of getting clean.

Note: Children should NEVER be left alone in the bath or shower, because of the risk of drowning or scalding.

In Practice

How to give praise and encouragement to children and young people

❏ **Verbal praise or encouragement:** whenever children and young people attempt a new skill, whether they succeed or not, praise them and urge them to try again. Encouragement is the most important factor in helping them towards independence.

❏ **Displaying children's work:** when children know their ideas and their work are valued, they are affirmed. They know they can achieve.

❏ **Sharing positive feedback:** begin with some unconditional positive praise – 'You did that well,' or 'It was really good the way you . . .' Then give the positive feedback – 'This part could be improved if you . . .' or 'How do you think you could improve this part?' Then finish with further unconditional praise – 'I really enjoyed reading that' or 'Keep it up – well done.'

❏ **Non-verbal:** for example, maintain eye contact – get down to the child's level and smile or make a thumbs-up gesture.

❏ **Highlighting positive aspects:** praise should highlight the positive things children do or the way in which children use the qualities or attributes they possess. Most importantly, praise should focus on children's effort and perseverance.

❏ **Sharing time or circle time:** encourage children to put themselves forward by saying what they are good at and how proud they are of themselves.

Guidelines: Caring for children's skin and hair

- Wash face and hands in the morning (note that Muslims always wash under running water).
- Always wash hands after using the toilet and before meals; dry hands thoroughly – young children will need supervision. Use individual or paper towels.
- After using the toilet, girls should be taught to wipe their bottom from front to back to prevent germs from the anus entering the vagina and urethra.
- Wash hands after playing outside, or after handling animals.
- Nails should be scrubbed with a soft nailbrush and trimmed regularly by cutting straight across. Never cut into the sides of the nails as this can cause sores and infections.
- Find out about any special skin conditions such as eczema or dry skin, and be guided by the parents' advice concerning the use of soap and creams. Parent or carer permission is required if using cream or oils.
- Each child should have their own flannel, comb and brush that should be cleaned regularly.
- Skin should always be dried thoroughly, taking special care of such areas as between the toes and under the armpits; black skin tends to dryness and may need massaging with special oils or moisturisers.
- Babies' and young children's hair should ideally be washed during bath time, using a specially formulated mild baby soap or shampoo. (Adult shampoos contain many extra ingredients, such as perfumes and chemicals – all of which can lead to irritation of children's delicate skin.)
- Hair usually only needs washing twice a week. Children with long or curly hair benefit from the use of a conditioning shampoo that helps to reduce tangles. Hair should always be rinsed thoroughly in clean water and not brushed until it is dry – brushing wet hair damages the hair shafts. A wide-toothed comb is useful for combing wet hair.
- Afro-Caribbean hair tends to dryness and may need special oil or moisturisers; if the hair is braided (with or without beads), it may be washed with the braids left intact, unless otherwise advised.

- Rastafarian children with hair styled in dreadlocks may not use either combs or shampoo, preferring to brush the dreadlocks gently and secure them with braid.
- Regular combing and brushing will also help to prevent the occurrence of **head lice** (see below).

Head lice

Head lice are a common affliction. Anybody can get them but they are particularly prevalent among children. Table 9.1 gives information on head lice.

Young people: Caring for the skin

Acne is a common skin condition that usually affects teenagers and young adults. However, it can develop at any age. It is most common on the face, but can also occur on the back, chest, shoulders and neck. Acne consists of blackheads and whiteheads (comedones). *Acne vulgaris* is a more serious condition that consists of larger pimples and pustules or large cysts. Permanent scarring can occur after these spots have gone.

Head lice information	
They are tiny insects with six legs.	They only live on human beings; they cannot be caught from animals.
They have mouths like small needles that they stick into the scalp and use to drink the blood.	They are unable to fly, hop or jump.
Head lice are not the same as nits. **Nits** are the egg cases laid by lice. Nits may be found 'glued' on to the hair shafts; they are smaller than a pinhead and are pearly white.	They are between 1 and 4 mm in size – slightly larger than a pin head.
Head lice live on, or very close to, the scalp, and they do not wander down the hair shafts for very long.	They are caught just by coming into contact with someone who is infested. When heads touch, the lice simply walk from one head to the other.
Head lice do not discriminate between clean and dirty hair, but tend to live more on smooth, straight hair.	

Table 9.1 Information on head lice

Activity

Prevention and treatment of head lice

1 Find out how to prevent head lice.

2 Find out how to treat an individual child with head lice.

3 Prepare a fact sheet to give to parents which explains:

- what head lice are and why children are particularly susceptible
- how head lice can be prevented
- the different methods of treatment and where to obtain them.

Less serious acne can also scar unless proper care is taken.

What causes acne?

The ducts of the sebaceous (oil) glands become blocked with dirt, bacteria and dead skin cells. The sebaceous glands produce an oily substance called **sebum**; they are connected to a hair-containing canal called the follicle. Sebum travels to the surface of the skin through the opening of the follicle. The oil seems to stimulate the lining of the wall of the follicle, causing cells to shed more rapidly and stick together, plugging the opening to the skin's surface. This causes whiteheads and blackheads.

The mixture of oil and cells also helps **bacteria**, which are normally present on the skin, to grow in the follicle. The bacteria produce chemicals that can cause the wall of the follicle to break. When this wall is broken the sebum, bacteria and shed skin cells escape, forming skin cysts.

Teenagers are more at risk of acne as the increase of hormone levels during **puberty** can lead to the sebaceous glands enlarging and producing more sebum. Factors that can lead to acne include stress, diet, or taking hormones or corticosteroids. For women, the onset of menstrual periods, pregnancy, and oral contraceptive pills can also affect the skin.

Facts about acne

- **Acne is *not* caused by dirt**: the blackness of a blackhead is not dirt; it is due mainly to dried oil and shed skin cells in the openings of the follicles. Wash twice a day with mild soap. Always wash in the evening to remove the dirt from the day. An antibacterial soap product can also be used. Do not wash too often as excess washing may actually aggravate acne.
- **Greasy hair adds to skin surface oil and can contribute to clogging pores**: ensure that hair is always clean and tied back from face to avoid irritation. Do not attempt to hide spots under a fringe as this will irritate them further.
- **Do not pick, squeeze or scratch the spots**: more redness, swelling, inflammation and scarring may result.
- **Avoid oil-based cosmetics**: use water-based make-up sparingly and ensure it is removed properly in the evening. Look out for cosmetics that are labelled 'non-comedogenic' as these do not block the pores.
- **Exposure to sun**: some people have found that exposure to the sun can reduce acne.
- **Foods**: there is no evidence that specific foods, such as fried foods or chocolate, can cause acne. However, it could help the skin to avoid fatty or sweet foods. Skin will always benefit from a healthy diet that includes drinking plenty of water. Some people find that their acne seems to become worse when they eat certain foods. If that is the case, those particular foods should be avoided.

If acne persists, seek medical advice; a doctor will be able to prescribe various treatments depending on the severity and type of acne.

Care of children's teeth

Care of the first 'milk' teeth is as important as for permanent teeth, since it promotes good habits and encourages permanent teeth to appear in the proper place. Every time the child eats sweet things, acid is produced which attacks the enamel of the tooth. Saliva protects the teeth from this and more saliva is produced during meals. The protective effect lasts for about half an hour so the more frequently the child eats sweets or sugary drinks, the more exposure to acid the teeth have. After the child's first birthday, children can be taught to brush their own teeth; but they will need careful supervision. You can help by following these guidelines:

Guidelines: Caring for children's teeth

- Babies under one year should have their teeth brushed with a soft brush once or twice a day using gentle toothpaste.
- Drinks should be given after meals, with water between meals. Bottles and cups should not contain fizzy or sweetened drinks, and fruit juice should be limited to mealtimes.
- Babies should not be allowed to have constant access to a bottle or cup.
- Babies should be encouraged to drink from a cup between 12 and 15 months.
- Support children to brush their teeth after meals: show them how to brush up and away from the gum when cleaning the lower teeth and down and away from the gum when cleaning the upper teeth. (Younger children will need help in brushing the back teeth.)
- Crusty bread, crunchy fruit and raw vegetables such as carrot or celery help to keep teeth healthy and free of **plaque** – a substance that builds up on the teeth attracting bacteria and causing tooth decay.
- Sweets may be given after meals if at all.
- Take children regularly to the dentist so that they get used to the idea of having their mouth looked at.

The use of dummies

Parents often have strong views about the use of soothers and dummies. These are only likely to be harmful to tooth development if they are used constantly and habitually, or if they are sweetened, which is likely to cause decay. Dummies should be sterilised regularly and changed if they have been dropped on the floor. Dummies should *never* be sucked by adults before giving to babies as this merely transfers bacteria from adult to child and can cause stomach upsets.

Equipment for physical care

There is a wide variety of equipment that may be used when physically caring for children. Children will find it easier to be independent in their hygiene routines if they are provided with suitable equipment, such as a step stool that enables them to reach the washbasin, or a child-sized toothbrush.

The importance of rest and sleep

Rest and sleep are important for our health and wellbeing. By the end of their first year, most babies are having two short sleeps during the day – before or after lunch and in the afternoon – and sleeping through the night, although there is much variation between individual children. It is important to have 'quiet periods', even if the baby does not want to sleep.

When we sleep, we rest and gain energy for a new day. But sleep does more than that. When we dream, we process all the events of our daily life. After a night without enough sleep we often feel exhausted and irritable, but after a good night's sleep we feel rested, refreshed and full of energy. It is important to parents that their child sleeps through the night, as it influences the entire family's life and wellbeing. Children need more sleep than adults because the brain is developing and maturing and they are growing physically as well.

Sleep is important to child health:

- It rests and restores our bodies.
- It enables the brain and the body's metabolic processes to recover (these processes are responsible for producing energy and growth).
- During sleep, growth hormone is released; this renews tissues and produces new bone and red blood cells.

- Dreaming is believed to help the brain sort out information stored in the memory during waking hours.
- Children vary enormously in their need for sleep and rest. Some children seem able to rush around all day with very little rest; others will need to 'recharge their batteries' by having frequent periods of rest. You need to be able to recognise the signs that a child is tired; these may include:

  (a) looking tired – dark rings under the eyes and yawning
  (b) asking for their comfort object
  (c) constant rubbing of the eyes
  (d) twiddling their hair and fidgeting with objects
  (e) showing no interest in activities and in their surroundings
  (f) being particularly emotional – crying or being stubborn
  (g) withdrawing into themselves – sucking thumb and appearing listless.

Guidelines: Establishing a routine for rest and sleep

- Children will only sleep if they are actually tired, so it is important that enough activity and exercise are provided. Some children do not have a nap during the day but should be encouraged to rest in a quiet area.
- When preparing children for a daytime nap, rest or bedtime sleep, you need to:

  (a) treat each child uniquely; every child will have his or her own needs for sleep and rest
  (b) find out all you can about the individual child's sleep habits; for example, some children like to be patted to sleep, while others need to have their favourite **comfort object**
  (c) be guided by the wishes of the child's parents or carers; some parents, for example, prefer their child to have a

morning nap but not an afternoon nap, as this fits in better with the family's routine
  (d) reassure children that they will not be left alone and that you or someone else will be there when they wake up
  (e) keep noise to a minimum and darken the room
  (f) make sure that children have been to the toilet – children need to understand the signals which mean that it is time for everyone to have a rest or sleep.

- Provide quiet, relaxing activities for children who are unable, or who do not want, to sleep; for example, jigsaw puzzles, a story tape or reading a book.

Different views about sleep and rest

There are cultural differences in the way in which parents or carers view bedtime and sleep routines. In some cultures it is normal for children to sleep with parents and to have a much later bedtime in consequence. Some families who originate from hot countries where having a sleep in the afternoon is normal tend to let their children stay up in the evening. Such children are more likely to need a sleep while in day care; as long as the overall amount of sleep is sufficient for the child, it does not matter.

It is always worth discussing bedtime routines with parents when toddlers are struggling to behave well. Some areas have sleep clinics managed by the health visiting service to help parents whose children have difficulty in sleeping.

Even after they have established a good sleep routine, children's sleep patterns can become disrupted between the ages of one and three years. There are thought to be a number of factors for this, including developmental changes and behavioural issues.

Supporting personal care routines to meet individual needs and promote independence

Children and young people need to learn to be capable and independent in order to learn new skills. The child who is self-reliant will be more active, independent and competent: he or she will have the confidence necessary to cope with situations on their own and to become an effective learner.

How to promote self-reliance

Encourage independence

Allow children and young people to do things for themselves. Even very young children begin to show an interest in doing things for themselves. Encourage independence by letting children do things for themselves as soon as they express a desire to do so.

Focus on the effort made by the child and avoid being critical of the 'end product'. Always praise children for doing things on their own. As children grow and mature, they will naturally want to do more and more for themselves.

Give challenges to the children

Encourage children to help with challenging tasks and to try new things. This helps to promote self-confidence. Remember to choose tasks that children can accomplish.

Encourage children to make decisions

Children learn to make good choices by being given choices. At first, choices should be kept simple, like allowing children to choose what to wear out of two outfits. As children become older, encourage them to make increasingly complex decisions.

Be a positive role model

Be a positive role model for responsibility and independence. Children learn by watching adults. Let children see you making decisions without wavering, and also taking care of responsibilities in an appropriate manner.

Encourage problem-solving

Help and encourage children to solve their own problems. Problem-solving is a skill that must be learned. Encourage children to think of their own solutions to their problems. The ability to solve problems is a skill that will be useful throughout children's lives. It will also help in the development of confidence and independence.

Encourage children to take risks

Taking risks involves facing potential failure. Many parents and other adults try to shield children from the disappointment of failure. However, children need to take risks to grow. Children must experience failure in order to learn how to cope with it. Always assess each risk, and support and supervise the child.

Be there to provide support, when needed

Even the most independent-minded children need adult support on certain occasions. Make an effort to be available to the children in your care and to provide support when needed. Children who are secure in their relationships will have the confidence needed to explore the world.

Praise children

Children should receive praise when they display responsible and independent behaviour. Adults who praise such behaviour are letting children know that they notice and appreciate their efforts.

Give children responsibilities

One of the best ways for children to learn how to behave responsibly is to be given responsibilities. Make sure that the tasks assigned to the

Progress check

Guidelines for promoting self-reliance skills throughout childhood

Babies

- Encourage babies to cooperate when getting them dressed and undressed – for example, by pushing their arms through sleeves and pulling off their socks.
- Provide finger foods from about eight months and tolerate mess when babies are feeding themselves.
- Set out a variety of toys to encourage them to make choices.

Children aged from two to four years

- Provide a range of activities – both indoors and outdoors.
- Encourage children to help tidy away toys.
- Allow children to have a free choice in their play.
- Encourage children in self-care skills – washing hands, brushing hair and getting dressed; be patient and provide them with adequate time.
- Build choice into routines such as meal and snack times.
- Encourage children to enjoy simple cooking activities.

Children aged from five to eight years

- Provide activities that promote problem-solving skills, such as investigating volume and capacity in sand or water play.
- Allow children to take responsibility for set tasks – for example, wiping the tables, caring for plants, etc.
- Encourage them to learn specific skills – such as using scissors and threading large needles.
- Allow children the opportunity to make choices, and encourage them to assess risks when supervised.

Children aged from eight to 12 years

- Allow children to choose – for example, the choice of playing sports, musical instruments, a dance class, or nothing at all.
- Encourage them to set goals and work towards achieving them.
- Provide opportunities for them to plan and organise their own activities.
- Allow children to make mistakes and to learn from them.
- Encourage them to ask for support – but avoid taking over completely.

Young people aged 13–16 years

- Allow them to take some control over their own learning, deciding what to learn and how.
- Assist them in creating learning goals that are consistent with their interests and future aspirations.
- Provide opportunities for them to demonstrate their skills and achievements – for example, organising fundraising events or a display board.

children match their capabilities. Take the time to show them how to do their assigned tasks properly. However, how well children perform a task is not as important as what they are learning about responsibility.

From birth, babies and children need to be encouraged to 'have a go' even if their early efforts are not always successful. You have an important role in helping to develop self-reliance at all stages of children's development.

Supporting personal care routines

One aspect of children's need for love and security is the need for **routine** and predictability. This is why having daily routines is so important in all aspects of child care. By meeting children's need for routine, parents and carers are helping the child to:

- feel acknowledged
- feel independent
- increase self-esteem.

Routines can be very useful in helping babies and toddlers to adapt both physically and emotionally to a daily pattern, particularly around mealtimes and bedtimes; routines will suit both children and adults caring for them. It will prove especially helpful during times of **transition** and change in their lives, such as starting nursery or moving house. If certain parts of the day remain familiar, they can cope better with new experiences. Having routines for everyday activities also ensures that care is consistent and is of a high quality.

All settings that provide care and education for children have **routines** for daily activities. This does not mean that every day is the same; rather, it means that there is a recognised structure to the child's day, which will help children to feel secure and safe. Such routines include:

- **hygiene** – changing nappies and toileting older children; ensuring there is a hand-washing routine after messy activities and before eating and drinking.
- **health and safety** – tidying away toys and activity equipment; making regular checks on equipment for hazards.
- **safety at home times** and trips away from the setting – ensuring there is a correct ratio of adults to children, permission from parents and contact numbers, etc.

- **meal and snack times**: serving of meals and drinks under close supervision (see Chapter 16, Unit TDA 2.14: Support children and young people at meal and snack times).
- sleep and rest
- outdoor play.

Supporting hygiene routines

All children and young people benefit from regular routines in daily care. You need to encourage children to become independent by helping them to learn how to take care of themselves. Ways of helping children to become independent include:

- supporting children to wash and dry their hands before eating or drinking
- making sure that children always wash and dry their hands after going to the toilet and after playing outdoors
- providing children with their own combs and brushes and encouraging them to use them every day
- providing a soft toothbrush and teaching children how and when to brush their teeth
- ensuring that you are a positive role model for children; for example, when you cough or sneeze, you always cover your mouth
- devising activities which develop an awareness in children of the importance of hygiene routines (for example, you could invite a dental hygienist or dental nurse to the setting to talk to children about daily teeth care)
- making sure that children are provided with a healthy diet and that there are opportunities for activity, rest and sleep throughout the nursery or school day.

Planning routines to meet individual needs

Anyone looking after children should be able to adapt to their individual needs, which will change from day to day. You therefore need to be flexible in your approach and allow, whenever feasible, the individual child to set the pattern for the day – as long as all the child's needs are met. Obviously, parents and carers have their own routines and hygiene practices and these should always be respected (for example, Muslims prefer to wash under running water; Rastafarians wear their hair braided and so may not use a comb or brush).

Whenever you are caring for children, you should always treat each child as an individual. This means that you should be aware of their individual needs at all times. Sometimes a child

may have special or additional needs; children may need specialist equipment or extra help with play activities. Routines may need to be adapted to take into account individual needs and preferences.

Toilet training

The development of bowel and bladder control

Children will not achieve control over their bowel or bladder function until the nerve pathways that send signals to the brain are mature enough to indicate fullness. This usually happens between two and three years of age, with most children achieving control by four years. Gaining control over these basic functions is a major milestone that relies on both psychological and physical readiness.

Toilet training should be approached in a relaxed, unhurried manner. If the potty is introduced too early, or if a child is forced to sit on it for long periods of time, they may rebel and the whole issue of toilet training becomes a battleground.

Toilet training can be over in a few days or may take some months. Becoming dry at night takes longer, but most children manage this before the age of five. There is no point in attempting to start toilet training until the child shows that he or she is ready, and this rarely occurs before the age of 18 months.

Guidelines: Toilet training

- Toilet training must be discussed with the parents or carers, and the decision on when to start agreed.
- Parents must not feel pressured into toilet training their child. However, children do exhibit certain signs and behaviours that will indicate that they are developmentally ready to consider training – that is, they are likely to

In Practice

Everyday routines for babies and young children

- ❏ Be patient – even when pressed for time, try to show children that you are relaxed and unhurried.

- ❏ Allow time for children to experiment with different ways of doing things.

- ❏ If you work directly with parents or carers, encourage them to make a little extra time in the morning and evening for children to dress and undress themselves. Children could be encouraged to choose their clothes the night before from a limited choice; the choosing of clothes to wear is often a fertile ground for disagreements and battles of will.

- ❏ Resist the urge to take over if children are struggling, since this deprives them of the sense of achievement and satisfaction of success.

- ❏ Show children how to do something and then let them get on with it. If they ask for help, they should be shown again. If adults keep doing things for children that they could do for themselves, they are in danger of creating 'learned helplessness'.

- ❏ Offer praise and encouragement when children are trying hard, not just when they succeed in a task.

achieve control successfully and without too much difficulty; parents may find this information helpful.

- You should understand how to recognise the **signs** that children are ready to be toilet trained, which include:
  - (a) ability to pull down pants
  - (b) has bowel movements at regular times, for example after breakfast
  - (c) is willing to sit on the toilet or potty without crying or fuss
  - (d) shows an interest in using toilet or potty and will usually pass urine if placed on it
  - (e) has a word or gesture to indicate a wet or soiled nappy.
- Anticipate when the child is likely to need the toilet – such as after meals, before sleep and on wakening.
- Give children praise on going successfully to the toilet, and have a practical and sympathetic attitude to 'accidents'.
- Demonstrate that using the toilet is a normal activity that everyone does when they are old enough to manage it.

There are different opinions on using a potty or placing the child straight on the toilet. Privacy must be considered within the nursery setting and the potty placed in a cubicle if the child is used to a potty; however, if the toilet is 'child-sized' then they can be encouraged to use it. Aids such as clip-on seats and steps are available to enable children to use an adult-sized toilet and still feel safe – some children are anxious about falling down the toilet.

Dealing with accidents

Even once a child has become used to using the potty or toilet, there will inevitably be occasions when they have an 'accident', that is, they wet or soil themselves. This happens more often during the early stages of toilet training, as the child may still lack the awareness or the control to allow enough time to get to the potty. Older children may become so absorbed in their play that they simply forget to go to the toilet.

You can help children when they have an accident by doing the following:

- Not appearing bothered; let the child know that it is not a big problem, just something that happens from time to time.
- Reassure the child by using a friendly tone of voice and offering a cuddle if they seem distressed.
- Be discreet; deal with the matter swiftly – wash and change them out of view of others and with the minimum of fuss.
- If older children want to manage the incident themselves, encourage them to do so, but always check tactfully afterwards that they have managed.
- Always follow safety procedures in the setting; for example wear disposable gloves and deal appropriately with soiled clothing and waste.

Other developmental areas and gaining control

As we have seen before, all the areas of development are closely linked with each other, and the stages of development reached in one area will have an effect on the way in which independence in toilet needs is reached.

Physical development

A child with a spinal injury or other physical disability may not receive the messages to the brain that tells them that their bladder is full; independence is therefore restricted.

Cognitive and language development

Children who have communication difficulties may need the support of a signed language such as Makaton or Signalong in order to signal their toilet needs.

Emotional and social development

If a child is feeling insecure or under stress, this may affect the rate at which they gain control over their bladder and bowel function. Sometimes, children who have previously been both dry and clean may begin to have more 'accidents'. This is known as regression and is usually a temporary response to an emotional upset, for example the birth of a sibling in the family.

Signs of illness or abnormality

When you help children to use the potty or the toilet you should always be alert to any problems they may have. All observations should be reported to the child's parents, or, if not appropriate, to your immediate supervisor. Some of the signs to look for are:

1 **Diarrhoea**: some nursery-age children are prone to bouts of diarrhoea, which is not usually a sign of infection but a result of the immaturity of the nervous system affecting the speed of digestion.
2 **Constipation**: a child may have difficulty and feel pain when passing a motion.
3 **Pain when passing urine**: this may be caused by a bladder infection (cystitis) and will require treatment.
4 **Rashes around the nappy and genital area**: nappy rash or thrush may cause red spots around the nappy area.
5 **Bruising or other marks**: these could indicate abuse (see Chapter 6, Unit TDA 2.2: Safeguarding the welfare of children and young people, for further information).

The importance of balancing periods of physical activity

Physical play

Physical play promotes a child's health. Physical play links with all other areas of a child's

In Practice

Changing nappies in a group setting

Nappy changing is an important time and you should ensure that the baby feels secure and happy. Chatting and singing should be built into the procedure to make it an enjoyable experience. Each setting will have its own procedure for changing nappies. The following is an example:

❏ Nappies should be checked and changed at regular periods throughout the day.

❏ A baby should never knowingly be left in a soiled nappy.

❏ Collect the nappy and the cream needed. Put on apron and gloves. Ensure that you have warm water and wipes.

❏ Carefully put the baby on the changing mat, talking to and reassuring him or her.

❏ Afterwards dispose of the nappy and discard the gloves.

❏ Thoroughly clean the nappy mat and the apron with an anti-bacterial spray.

❏ Wash your hands to avoid cross-contamination.

❏ Record the nappy change on the baby's nappy chart, noting the time, whether it was wet or dry and whether there had been a bowel movement. Note any change you have observed, for example in the colour or consistency of the stools or if the baby had difficulty in passing the stool. Also note whether there is any skin irritation or rash present.

❏ Check nappy mats for any tears or breaks in the fabric and replace if necessary.

❏ **Never** leave a baby or toddler unsupervised on the changing mat.

development. The brain works better if children have plenty of fresh air and exercise. This is why both indoor and outdoor play are very important.

Through physical play children learn to challenge gender stereotypes. Boys and girls can

Case Study — Toilet training

Jack is 25 months old. He is an intelligent little boy, who is healthy in all areas of his development. His mother, Monica, is a good friend of Priya, mother of Jasmine who is 22 months old and attends the same class as Jack. Jasmine loves to play with the older girls in pre-school when the classes join up, and has recently begun to potty-train herself. She has had a couple of 'accidents' when distracted or excited, and still wears a nappy for nap times, but generally has been very successful. Monica brings Jack in one day and expresses her concern that he has no interest in using the potty – he will do so when asked, but rarely does anything but sit. Jack's key worker reassures Monica that Jack will begin to use it in his own time, but she is unconvinced and decides to start putting him in pants. This starts off well – members of staff take Jack to use the potty regularly and he occasionally uses it. However, he never expresses a need to use the potty. Gradually, as the nursery gets busier, Jack has 'accidents' more frequently. This begins to distress him, especially when his own spare clothes run out and he has to use the nursery's stock.

1 Why do you think Monica is so concerned about Jack not using the potty?

2 What do you think nursery staff could do to minimise Jack's distress?

enjoy playing ball games such as football play scenarios, running and climbing. Children need to be encouraged in these activities. It helps if children wear clothes and shoes that allow freedom of movement.

During physical play, children and young people also:

- learn through their **senses**
- coordinate their **movements**
- develop their **muscles**
- learn about pace and keeping going (**stamina**)
- learn how to use space in a **coordinated** way
- learn to challenge gender stereotypes.

Manipulative play

Children need plenty of opportunities to play using manipulative skills. This particularly encourages children to use their hands, which are very important in human development.

Boys and girls can enjoy manipulative play. Manipulative play links with the Early Years Foundation Stage Framework, with the area of learning called physical development.

When children and young people spend periods of time in the setting, they also need opportunities for rest and quiet. Babies may need to have a sleep. Young children can listen to music or read in a calm environment. Young people enjoy chatting and generally socialising. Some settings also include relaxation exercises in their programme of activities, and yoga is becoming a popular relaxing activity.

Figure 9.01 Using fine manipulative skills and concentration

Physical development
Coordinates movements (fine manipulative and gross motor)

Develops muscles

Develops stamina

Helps children to use space in a coordinated way

Learn through the senses

Learn through movement

Language development
There are endless opportunities, e.g. adults need to give children words they need (vocabulary), such as fast, slow, up, down, nearly, a good landing.

Ideas (cognitive development)
e.g. children develop understanding of:
- timing
- awareness of space
- reasons why things happen, e.g. if I jump from the second step I need to push off harder and to bend my knees when I land, otherwise I will fall.

Relationships (social development)
Children who play physically learn to be sensitive and aware of others, to give them enough space, take turns and share.

They cooperate with each other so that they can all have fun together.

During rough-and-tumble play, they bond with each other emotionally.

This physical play is usually for short periods and can often end quickly, and sometimes in tears!

Physical play

Feelings (emotional development)
When a child falls over but gets back on the climbing frame, they are becoming resilient.

When children shout 'Look at me – I am high up', as they climb, it builds their confidence and gives them high self-esteem.

Children who have plenty of time for free movement in a safe physical environment have opportunities to become adventurous.

Figure 9.02 Aspects of physical play

Relationships (social development)
Children talking about what they are doing with each other and passing each other and passing each other materials they need – sharing and co-ooperating.

Children learn to challenge gender stereotypes.

Physical development
Using fingers and thumbs (pincer movements)

Hand-eye coordination

Develops hand muscles

Language development
Adults and children talk together as they use materials. Does it fit? Do you have enough? It's too big, will you pass me the scissors please?

Manipulative play

Ideas (cognitive development)
Children solve problems as they make models, paint, draw, etc.

They think ahead, estimate sizes, use shapes and make choices.

They develop ideas of their own.

Feelings (emotional development)
Helps resilience

Builds confidence and high self-esteem

Helps children to persevere (keep going)

Figure 9.03 Manipulative play

The nutritional and dietary needs of children and young people

During childhood we develop food habits that will affect us for life. Many adults suffer from some disorder that is related to the diet, for example, tooth decay, heart disease or cancer. Establishing healthy eating patterns in childhood will help to promote normal growth and development, and will protect against later disease. As an early years practitioner, you need to know what constitutes a good diet and how it can be provided.

Government guidance on a balanced diet

A healthy diet consists of a wide variety of foods to help the body to grow and to provide energy. It must include enough **nutrients** (proteins, fats, carbohydrates, vitamins, minerals and fibre) as well as **water**, to fuel and maintain the body's vital functions.

Schools and local authorities must meet the nutritional standards laid down by the government to help improve the quality of food that children eat. These are shown in Table 9.2 and illustrated by the eatwell plate (see Figure 9.05).

1 medium apple

2 broccoli florets

2 halves of canned peaches

1 handful of grapes

1 medium banana

3 heaped tablespoons of peas

1 medium glass of orange juice

7 strawberries

3 whole dried apricots

5 A DAY

Just Eat More (fruit & veg)

3 heaped tablespoons of cooked kidney beans

16 okra

NHS

Figure 9.04 The Just Eat More portion poster for the NHS 5 A DAY programme

The eatwell plate

Use the eatwell plate to help you get the balance right. It shows how much of what you eat should come from each food group.

Figure 9.05 The eatwell plate

Children need a varied **energy-rich** diet for good health and growth. For balance and variety, choose from the five main food groups (see Table 9.2).

Basic food safety

In promoting the health of young children it is important that you understand the basics of food safety as they generally apply to you in the work setting. Your role may involve serving children's food and drinks and supervising them when they are eating and drinking. Often you will have to prepare simple snacks for the children.

You need to be confident that you are doing everything in your power to provide children with food and drink that are safe to eat, free from illness-causing bacteria. As you progress in your career, you may become more involved in food preparation and will then be required to attend an accredited food hygiene course.

Young children are particularly vulnerable to the bacteria that can cause food poisoning or gastro-enteritis. Bacteria multiply rapidly in warm, moist foods and can enter food without causing the food to look, smell or even taste bad. It is therefore very important to store, prepare and cook food safely, and to keep the kitchen clean.

The prevention of food poisoning

- Store food safely.
- Keep food cold. The fridge should be kept as cold as possible without actually freezing the food (1–5°C or 34–41°F).
- Cover or wrap food with food wrap or microwave cling film.

Food groups	Main nutrients	Types to choose	Portions per day	Suggestions for meals and snacks
1. Bread, other cereals and potatoes All types of bread, rice, breakfast cereals, pasta, noodles, and potatoes (beans and lentils can be eaten as part of this group)	Carbohydrates (starch), fibre, some calcium and iron, B-group vitamins	Wholemeal, brown, wholegrain or high-fibre versions of bread; avoid fried foods too often (e.g. chips). Use butter and other spreads sparingly	FIVE All meals of the day should include foods from this group	One portion = • 1 bowl of breakfast cereal • 2 tbsp pasta or rice • 1 small potato Snack meals include bread or pizza base
2. Fruit and vegetables Fresh, frozen and canned fruit and vegetables, dried fruit, fruit juice (beans and lentils can be eaten as part of this group)	Vitamin C, carotenes, iron, calcium folate, fibre and some carbohydrate	Eat a wide variety of fruit and vegetables; avoid adding rich sauces to vegetables, and sugar to fruit	FOUR/FIVE Include 1 fruit or vegetable daily high in Vitamin C, e.g. tomato, sweet pepper, orange or kiwi fruit	One portion = • 1 glass of pure fruit juice • 1 piece of fruit • 1 sliced tomato • 2 tbsp of cooked vegetables • 1 tabsp of dried fruit – e.g. raisins.
3. Milk and dairy foods Milk, cheese, yoghurt and fromage frais (this group does not contain butter, eggs and cream)	Calcium, protein, B-group vitamins (particularly B12), vitamins A and D	Milk is a very good source of calcium, but calcium can also be obtained from cheese, flavoured or plain yogurts and fromage frais	THREE Children require the equivalent of one pint of milk each day to ensure an adequate intake of calcium	One portion = • 1 glass of milk • 1 pot of yogurt or fromage frais • 1 tbsp of grated cheese, e.g. on a pizza Under 2s – do not give reduced-fat milks, e.g. semi-skimmed – they do not supply enough energy
4. Meat, fish and alternatives Lean meat, poultry, fish, eggs, tofu, quorn, pulses – peas, beans, lentils, nuts and seeds	Iron, protein, B-group vitamins (particularly B12), zinc and magnesium	Lower-fat versions – meat with fat cut off, chicken without skin, etc. Beans and lentils are good alternatives, being low in fat and high in fibre	TWO Vegetarians will need to have grains, pulses and seeds; vegans avoid all food associated with animals	One portion = • 2 fish fingers (for a 3-year-old) • 4 fish fingers (for a 7-year-old) • baked beans • chicken nuggets or a small piece of chicken
5. Fatty and sugary foods Margarine, low-fat spread, butter, ghee, cream, chocolate, crisps, biscuits, sweets & sugar, fizzy soft drinks, puddings	Vitamins and essential fatty acids, but also a lot of fat, sugar and salt	Only offer small amounts of sugary and fatty foods. Fats and oils are found in all the other food groups	NONE Only allow children to eat fatty and sugary foods sparingly, e.g. crisps, sweets and chocolate	Children may be offered foods with extra fat or sugar – biscuits, cakes or chocolate – as long as they are not replacing food from the four main food groups

Table 9.2 Food groups

- Never refreeze food that has begun to thaw.
- Do not use foods that are past their sell-by or best-before date.
- Always read instructions on the label when storing food.
- Once a tin is opened, store the contents in a covered dish in the fridge.
- Store raw foods at the bottom of the fridge so that juices cannot drip onto cooked food.
- Thaw frozen meat completely before cooking.
- Always wash hands in warm water and soap and dry on a clean towel before handling food and after handling raw foods, especially meat.
- Wear clean protective clothing that is solely for use in the kitchen.
- Keep food covered at all times.
- Wash all fruits and vegetables before eating. Peel and top carrots and peel fruits such as apples.
- Never cough or sneeze over food.
- Always cover any septic cuts or boils with a waterproof dressing.
- Never smoke in any room that is used for food.
- Keep work surfaces and chopping boards clean and disinfected; use separate boards for raw meat, fish, vegetables, etc.
- Make sure that meat dishes are thoroughly cooked.
- Avoid raw eggs. They sometimes contain *Salmonella* bacteria, which may cause food poisoning. (Also avoid giving children *uncooked* cake mixture, home-made ice creams, mayonnaise, or desserts that contain uncooked raw egg.) When cooking eggs, the egg yolk and white should be firm.
- When reheating food, make sure that it is piping hot all the way through, and allow to cool slightly before giving it to children. When using a microwave, always stir and check the temperature of the food before feeding children, to avoid burning from hot spots.
- Avoid eating leftovers – they are a common cause of food poisoning.

Keeping the kitchen safe

- Teach children to wash their hands after touching pets, going to the toilet, and before eating.
- Clean tin-openers, graters and mixers thoroughly after use.
- Keep flies and other insects away – use a fine mesh over open windows.
- Stay away from the kitchen if you are suffering from diarrhoea or sickness.
- Keep the kitchen clean – the floor, work surfaces, sink, utensils, cloths and waste bins should be cleaned regularly.
- Tea towels should be boiled every day and dishcloths boiled or disinfected.
- Keep pets away from the kitchen.
- Keep all waste bins covered, and empty them regularly.
- Keep sharp knives stored safely where children cannot reach them.

 **Progress check**

Good food hygiene

When serving food and clearing away after meals and snacks, you should observe the rules of food hygiene:

- Wash your hands using soap and warm water and dry them on a clean towel.
- Wear clean protective clothing.
- Ensure any washing-up by hand is done thoroughly in hot water, with detergent (and use rubber gloves).
- Cover cups/beakers with a clean cloth and air-dry where possible.
- Drying-up cloths should be replaced every day with clean ones.
- Never cough or sneeze over food.

Assessment practice

Food safety

Design a poster which describes **basic food safety** when providing food and drink to children and young people. Try to make the poster as eye-catching as possible and avoid including too much text. Focus on including images – for example, cartoons - and captions that demonstrate:

- the importance of hand-washing

- preventing cross-infection when preparing food – for example, using separate chopping boards for each type of food meat, fish, poultry and vegetables

- how to store food safely

- wearing aprons.

Useful websites and resources

www.education.gov.uk	**Department for Education:** provides up-to-date information about the curriculum in England.
www.scotland.gov.uk	**Learning and Teaching Scotland:** provides up-to-date information about the curriculum in Scotland.
www.deni.gov.uk	**Northern Ireland Department for Education:** provides up-to-date information about the curriculum in Northern Ireland.
www.learning.wales.gov.uk	**Welsh Department for Education and Training:** provides up-to-date information about the curriculum in Wales.
www.ican.org.uk	**ICAN** is a charity that supports speech, language and communication development.
www.ncb.org.uk	**National Children's Bureau:** a leading national voluntary organisation acting as a resource, and providing information and support in relation to policy issues to children and young people from birth to 19 years.
www.montessori-uk.org	**Montessori Society AMI (UK)**
www.steinerwaldorf.org.u	The **Steiner Waldorf Schools Fellowship** website
www.high-scope.org.uk	**HighScope UK**
www.reggioemiliaapproach.net	The **Reggio Emilia approach** to Pre-school Education
www.schoolfoodtrust.org.uk	The **School Food Trust** This organisation applies to schools in England, but their website gives links to policies for the rest of the UK.

10 Understand partnership working in services for children and young people: Unit MU 2.9

In this Unit you will learn about the many different professionals who work with children and young people. You will also find out how these partners work together to meet the needs of children, young people, and their parents or carers.

Learning outcomes

By the end of this chapter you will:

1. Understand partnership working within the context of services for children and young people.

2. Understand the importance of effective communication and information sharing in services for children and young people.

3. Understand the importance of partnerships with carers.

Partnership working within the context of services for children and young people

What is partnership working?

Partnership working refers to formal ways of working together. It is often also referred to as **integrated** or **multi-agency** working. A partnership can be formed between a number of individuals or organisations with a shared interest. Partnerships are often formed to address specific issues, and they may be for the short or long term. The key principles of partnership working are openness, trust and honesty, agreed shared goals and values, and regular communication between partners.

The importance of partnership working

Before partnership working became the accepted and desired way of working, the parents of a child with additional needs would probably face many different appointments with several different people, none of whom would have spoken to each other and all of whom would expect the parents to give them a detailed breakdown of their child's disability. Partnership working is designed to cut across this by bringing together professionals with a range of skills to work across their traditional service boundaries.

Every Child Matters (ECM)

Partnership working is a holistic approach to child care and education and is an important feature of the government's **Every Child Matters** Framework:

The five outcomes for ECM are:

- Be healthy.
- Be safe.
- Enjoy and achieve.
- Make a positive contribution.
- Achieve economic wellbeing.

Working in partnership, when done well, enables partners to:

- ensure that everyone communicates about the whole child
- prevent problems occurring in the first place
- support children, young people and families with additional needs
- help to secure improved outcomes.

Services for children and young people

There are many different services for children and young people. These include:

- Children's Centres
- Health Centres and Clinics
- hospital play specialists
- play therapists
- Early Support Family Service
- portage workers
- educational psychologists
- school health service
- social services
- paediatric dieticians
- Youth Development Service

- voluntary organisations, e.g. Barnardos, NSPCC.

Systems of partnership working

In order to meet the needs of families accessing support from a range of professionals, the following systems of partnership working have been developed:

Multi-agency panels, or the Team Around the Child (TAC)

Practitioners remain employed by their home agencies but meet on a regular basis to discuss children and young people with additional needs who would benefit from multi-agency input.

Multi-agency teams

These are made up of practitioners seconded or recruited into the team, making it a more formal arrangement than a multi-agency panel. The team works with universal services (those available to every child) to support families and schools as well as individual children and young people.

Integrated services

Extended schools and Children's Centres provide integrated, multi-agency services that are flexible and meet the needs of young children and their families. In Children's Centres, staff work in a coordinated way to address the needs of children, young people and families, providing services such as:

- integrated early learning and full day care
- family support
- health services
- outreach services to children and families not attending the Centre, and
- access to training and employment advice.

The role of the lead professional

The lead professional is someone who acts as a single point of contact whom the child and their

Key term

Extended school – A school that provides a range of services and activities, often beyond the school day, to help meet the needs of its pupils, their families and the wider community.

family can trust, and who is able to support them in making choices and in navigating their way through the multi-agency system. Part of the role of the lead professional is to arrange Team Around the Child (TAC) meetings.

Identifying relevant partners in the work setting

As you are working with children and young people, you may already know other professionals in your setting who provide support for children, young people and their families. Table 10.1 shows potential partners in different work settings.

Key terms

Portage workers – Education support workers who visit families of pre-school children in their homes.

Connexions – Through multi-agency working, Connexions was set up as part of the **Every Child Matters** Framework to provide impartial information, advice and guidance (including careers advice and guidance) to young people aged 13 to 19. Connexions's personal advisers help to remove barriers to learning and progression, and ensure that young people make a smooth transition to adulthood and working life.

Partners working in early years settings	Partners working in social work and social care
• Playgroups	• Portage workers
• Children's Centres	• Foster carers (including private foster carers)
• Day nurseries	• Children and families social workers
• Nursery schools	• Registered managers of children's homes
• Nursery classes in primary schools	• All residential child care workers
• Registered childminders	• Family centre and day centre workers
• Nannies	• Children and Family Court Advisory and Support Service (CAFCASS) family court advisers
	• Support workers
Partners working in young people's workforce	**Other partners include those working in:**
• Learning mentors	• Children's Trusts
• Education welfare officers	• Lead inspectors of registered children's services
• Behaviour and education support teams	• Anyone who works with children and young people in the voluntary sector, including volunteers
• Education psychologists and therapists	
• Connexions personal advisers	
External agencies who may be involved – but not always working directly as partners	
• Teachers	
• Police officers	
• Health service professionals	
• Play specialists	

Table 10.1 Partners in different settings

Research Activity

Find out how a Portage worker could help a two-year-old child who has Down's syndrome with severe language delay and moderate hearing loss.

How multi-agency teams work

Within multi-agency teams, practitioners share a sense of team identity and are generally line-managed by the team leader, though they may maintain links with their home agencies through supervision and training.

Features of multi-agency teams include the following:

- There is a dedicated team leader.
- There is a good mix of education, health, social care, youth justice and youth work staff.
- The people who work in the team think of themselves as team members. They are recruited or seconded into the team, either full or part time.
- The team works at a range of levels – not just with individual children and young people, but also small-group, family and whole-school work.
- The team is likely to share a base, though some staff may continue to work from their home agencies.
- There are regular team meetings to discuss case working as well as administrative issues.

Behaviour and Education Support Teams (BESTs)

These are multi-agency teams bringing together a complementary mix of professionals from the fields of health, social care and education. The aim of a BEST is to promote emotional wellbeing, positive behaviour and school attendance, by identifying and supporting those with, or at risk of developing, emotional and behavioural problems. **BESTs:**

- work with children and young people aged five to 18, their families and schools, to intervene early and prevent problems developing further
- work in targeted primary and secondary schools, and in the community, alongside a range of other support structures and services
- have a minimum of four to five staff members, who between them have a complementary mix of education, social care and health skills in order to meet the multi-faceted needs of children, young people and their parents.

A typical BEST may include the following professionals:

- behaviour support staff
- clinical psychologists
- education welfare officers
- educational psychologists
- health visitors
- primary mental health workers
- school nurses
- social workers/family workers
- speech and language therapists.

Schools with BESTs include those with high proportions of pupils with, or at risk of developing, behavioural problems, usually demonstrated in levels of exclusions and attendance.

Early Support

Early Support is the central government mechanism for achieving better coordinated family-focused services for very young disabled children (those under three) and their families. Families receive coordinated support through

Children and young people's setting	Services/Professionals
Children's Centre Integrated local settings set up by Sure Start to provide holistic care to young children and their families	Family information services Play specialists Speech and language therapists Stay and Play Group Toy library Jobcentre Parenting classes, e.g. basic skills, English as an additional language (EAL) Child and family health service Outreach and family support
Nursery School Local authority provision for young children	Early education Extended care
School Local authority provision for children aged 5 to 16	Education Extended care: breakfast and after-school clubs Behaviour and Education Support Team (BEST) Counselling services
Youth work Work with young people aged 13–19 Settings vary – school, youth clubs or often outreach work	Education welfare officer Counselling services Drug Action Team Youth offending team worker Primary mental health worker Police and community safety

Table 10.2 Provision of services in work with children and young people

key person/worker systems, better sharing of information between agencies, family support plans and family-held records. For more information, see Chapter 14, Unit TDA 2.15: Support children and young people with disabilities and special educational needs.

Progress check

Partners in your work setting

Look at the lists of partners in Table 10.2 and find out which partners work or have connections with your setting. (There may be some partners that are not in this list.) List each partner and write a brief paragraph on their role in supporting children and young people.

The characteristics of effective partnership working

Partnership working aims to keep children, young people and their families at the centre of decision-making in order to meet their needs and improve their lives. To achieve this, practitioners need to know how to use a variety of tools and processes, including:

- sharing information
- early intervention
- common assessment processes, and
- supporting information and communication technology (ICT) tools.

To work successfully on a multi-agency basis you need to be:

- clear about your own role
- aware of the roles of other professionals

Case Study — Supporting vulnerable children and young people

Kids Company was founded by Camila Batmanghelidjh in 1996. It uses a *multidisciplinary approach* that combines health, housing, emotional wellbeing, mental health, arts, sports, youth justice, education and employment. These interventions are designed to strengthen, supplement or substitute the child's parenting experience. Kids Company employs a broadly skilled team of professionals working at street level, and operates through two street-level centres and a therapy house in South London, as well as a drop-in provision in Camden, North London. Unlike traditional approaches, the organisation creates a unique *'wraparound'* model of care for each child, so that all their issues are addressed by one team, in one place, without the need for referrals or waiting periods. Their

aim is to first stabilise each young person by meeting their *practical needs*, before helping them to address *emotional and behavioural difficulties*. Once the young person has achieved some sense of stability and calm, staff members help them to identify talents and interests and so develop aspirations for the future. 'We believe that no child is born a criminal or a killer. In our experience, violent behaviour in children is typically evidence of the harm that they have been exposed to. All too often children are penalised for society's failures in care, when ultimately the responsibility lies with adults who fail to care robustly enough. We are relentless in our love, doing whatever it takes to protect children struggling to survive their childhood.'

Research Activity

Investigating services for young people in your area

Find out what services are available for young people in your area. These might include:

- Youth Inclusion and support panel
- Youth Development Service
- Detached Youth Work
- Connexions
- Behaviour and Education Support Teams
- Youth Offending Teams.

For each service, write a brief paragraph that describes its aims.

- confident about your own standards and targets, and
- respectful of those that apply to other services.

Each profession has its own jargon and set of rules. You do not need to know about these in depth, but should always be willing to learn from other professionals and to respect the contribution of others working with children, young people and families.

Barriers to partnership working

There are various potential barriers to effective partnership working.

Information sharing

Problems mostly occur around *when* and *how* to share information. Practitioners may be unclear about their individual roles and responsibilities, and worry that they might misjudge the situation and be disciplined for sharing information inappropriately.

Communication difficulties

Often there are differences in the cultures of different agencies, and this can lead to difficulties in understanding the specialist terminology and language used by other professionals. Already you will have noticed that there is a whole set of acronyms commonly used in early years settings – for example, TAC, SEN, BES, EYFS, ECM, CAF – and each profession has a set equally as long! A list of relevant acronyms can be found at the back of this book.

Lack of support

Not knowing whom to contact for advice and support with information sharing can create barriers to effective working of the partnership. This often leads to a lack of confidence.

The fear of the 'new'

Some practitioners may feel threatened by new approaches that require them to work differently and to work across service boundaries. They feel out of their 'comfort zone'.

Lack of understanding of different agency roles

If practitioners do not fully understand the roles and responsibilities of other services and practitioners, they may lack trust and worry that a different agency may not treat the matter confidentially, or even that other practitioners may make things worse for the child, young person or family.

Assessment practice

Partnership working

How does multi-agency working operate in your area? Find out who would be the relevant partners in your own work setting. Try to visit one agency – such as a Children's Centre or a Connexions department, and find out how referrals are made and how often the multi-agency team meets. Collect as much written information as possible.

The importance of effective communication and information sharing

Communication in a multi-professional team

It has been common for the professionals in different agencies – health, social services, child care and education – to keep their observations and records to themselves. The **Every Child Matters** programme is prompting professionals to work together more, and in closer collaboration with parents.

In working with other professionals, practitioners must:

- understand what information other organisations can offer and share with individuals, families, carers, groups and communities
- work effectively with others to improve services offered to individuals, families, carers, groups and communities.

Children's Trusts comprise multi-professional teams of social workers, early years workers, learning mentors, education welfare officers, and nurses. Supportive and effective relationships need to be developed with all these professionals and with parents too. The need for each practitioner to have effective communication and teamwork skills is therefore important. See Chapter 1, Unit SHC 21: Introduction to communication in children and young people's settings, for information on developing effective communication skills.

Why clear and effective communication is required

Effective communication between partners is important to make sure that everyone will:

- Share information in a clear way that focuses on the individual child or young person
- Work towards the same aim: achieve the best positive outcomes for the child or young person and his or family.

The EYFS Guidance states: 'It is vital to ensure that everyone is working together to meet the emotional, health and educational needs of children in all settings that they attend and across all services provided.'

Think about these examples that show why clear and effective communication is needed:

- A young person is in foster care and attends more than one setting – school and extended care.
- A child has sickle cell anaemia and attends school but is often in hospital for weeks at a time. Hospital play specialists, hospital teachers and the child's class teacher are all involved in the child's care and education.
- A child with a severe visual impairment attends a mainstream school and has daily support from a dedicated learning support assistant.

- A young child with special educational needs attends a Children's Centre and is also visited at home by a Portage worker.

Policies and procedures in the work setting for information sharing

Every setting should have policies that encourage effective and clear communication when sharing information. Policies and procedures should include policies relating to:

- Multi-agency working:
- Managing transition from one setting to another
- Ensuring continuity of care between settings and carers.

All policies should be available to those who have an interest and they may be shared with colleagues, parents, carers and other settings, as well as with other agencies and services.

Statutory guidance

The government produced a *Guide to information sharing* (2008) for all practitioners working with children and young people. This outlined the important Acts that can be used to develop an information sharing policy in children and young people's services:

- The Data Protection Act 1998 provides a framework to ensure that information is shared appropriately
- The Children Act 2004 on the duty to safeguard and promote the welfare of children
- *Working Together to Safeguard Children* (HMG, 2006): the statutory guidance that sets out how organisations and individuals should work together to safeguard and promote the welfare of children
- *What to do if you are worried a child is being abused* (HMG, 2006)

- The Education and Inspections Act 2006, which sets out the duty to promote the well-being of pupils to governing bodies of maintained schools
- The Child Health Promotion Programme (DH, 2008)
- Local Safeguarding Children Board (LSCB) policies, procedures, protocols and guidance.

The Guidance document also outlined Seven Golden Rules for information sharing.

Information sharing: The Seven Golden Rules

1 Remember that the Data Protection Act is not a barrier to sharing information but provides a framework to ensure that personal information about living persons is shared appropriately.
2 Be open and honest with the person (and/or their family where appropriate) from the outset about why, what, how and with whom information will, or could, be shared and seek their agreement, unless it is unsafe or inappropriate to do so.
3 Seek advice if you are in any doubt, without disclosing the identity of the person where possible.
4 Share with consent where appropriate and, where possible, respect the wishes of those who do not consent to share confidential information. You may still share information without consent if, in your judgement, that lack of consent can be overridden in the public interest. You will need to base your judgement on the facts of the case.
5 Consider safety and wellbeing: Base your information-sharing decisions on considerations of the safety and wellbeing of the person and others who may be affected by their actions.
6 Necessary, proportionate, relevant, accurate, timely and secure: Ensure that the information you share is necessary for the purpose for which you are sharing it, is shared only with those people who need to have it, is accurate and up to date, is shared in a timely fashion, and is shared securely.
7 Keep a record of your decision and the reasons for it – whether it is to share information or not. If you decide to share, then record what you have shared, with whom and for what purpose.

The Common Assessment Framework (CAF)

The Common Assessment Framework (CAF) is also an important method of communicating with other agencies and professionals. The CAF is a key component of the **Every Child Matters** programme and is used by practitioners to assess the additional needs of a child and their family – which will help to identify which services will meet their needs. The CAF has three elements:

1 **A simple pre-assessment checklist**: to help practitioners identify children or young people who would benefit from a common assessment.
2 **A three-step process** (prepare, discuss, deliver) for undertaking a common assessment: to help practitioners gather and understand information about the needs and strengths of the child, based on discussions with the child, their family and other practitioners as appropriate.
3 **A standard form**: to help practitioners record and, where appropriate, share with others the findings from the assessment, in terms that are helpful in working with the family to find a response to unmet needs.

Confidentiality: conflicts and dilemmas

Confidentiality is an important principle in children's and young people's settings as it imposes a boundary on the amount of personal information and data that can be disclosed without **consent**. Confidentiality arises where a person disclosing personal information reasonably expects his or her **privacy** to be protected, such as in a relationship of trust. It is useful to understand fully the meaning of the terms 'consent', 'disclosure' and 'privacy'.

Consent

Consent means agreement to an action based on knowledge of what the action involves and its likely consequences.

Example: information on a child should only be collected and stored with the consent of the child's parents – and they should have free access to this information on request. The only exceptions to the rule of consent are the very small number of cases where the child might otherwise be at risk of immediate and significant harm if you shared a piece of information with the parent.

Allegation

A safeguarding allegation means the giving out of information that might commonly be kept secret, usually voluntarily or to be in compliance with legal regulations or workplace rules. (Allegation used to be known as disclosure.)

Example: a child tells an adult information that causes him or her to be concerned about the child's safety and wellbeing.

Privacy

Privacy refers to the right of an individual or group to stop information about themselves from becoming known to people other than those to whom they choose to give the information.

Example: when former prime minister Tony Blair's ex-nanny wrote a book about life at No 10

Downing Street, the Blairs took swift legal action to prevent details being leaked to the press. Tony Blair stated that 'We will do whatever it takes to protect our children's privacy.'

The right to confidentiality is not absolute

In partnership working, private information about the child or young person may often be shared with other professional persons within the partner network. The obligation to preserve the child's confidentiality then binds all professionals equally. Records should only show information that is essential to provide the service, and in many instances should be available to the scrutiny of the child and his or her family. (For example, patients have the right to see their medical records).

Practising confidentiality when working with young people

The need to gain a young person's trust and to build a positive relationship with him or her often leads to misunderstandings. To maintain a trusting relationship, practitioners should:

- Be explicit with young people regarding the *boundaries* within which they work; the boundary will normally exclude information which, if withheld, may leave someone exposed to danger (complying with Safeguarding procedures).
- Not lie on behalf of young people – and it is important that they make them aware of this. For example, if a practitioner witnesses first-hand a serious assault, he or she may be obliged to contact the police or to answer truthfully if questioned later by the police.
- Be aware that young people may assume that, through implication, confidentiality goes further than it actually does. It may be necessary to remind the young person that if

he or she insists on telling the practitioner sensitive information – for example, about an illegal practice or abuse by a family member – then the practitioner may need to inform the relevant authorities.

- Understand that they may need to make a 'tactical withdrawal', so that they do not witness an anticipated incident. It is OK to say to a young person, 'If you do that, I can't continue to work with you.'

Case Study | Confidential information?

During a coffee break, practitioners are openly chatting about Harry, a child that you know. Apparently, the people he lives with are not his parents, but his grandparents – although they look young enough to be his parents. They are bringing Harry up because their daughter (his mother) was judged to be unable to look after her child. This all happened a few years ago when Harry was very young, and he had spent some time in social care before his grandparents gained custody. One practitioner noted that Harry always calls them Mummy and Daddy.

1 Is this information confidential? If so, why?
2 Should you inform your line manager of the situation?

Recording and storing information

Every setting must provide clear policies and procedures about the recording and storing of information. These are governed by the Data Protection Act 1998. Anyone who keeps records, whether on computers or on paper, should comply with the Data Protection Act. It should be clear to service users (in this case, parents or guardians) for what purpose the data is being kept. Information about a child should also be accessible to his or her parent or carer and shared with them. It is not necessary to do this 'on demand'. A convenient time to be able to discuss the information can be arranged.

Information should not be kept for longer than necessary, although accident and incident records will need to be kept in case they are needed for reference at some time in the future. Records must also be stored securely. See also Chapter 1, Unit SHC 21: Introduction to communication in children and young people's settings, for further information on confidentiality and the Data Protection Act.

Preparing records and reports

Keeping good records is an essential part of any work with children, young people and families. Good practice in the area of record-keeping is based on the following principles. Records and reports should:

- **Be legible and grammatically correct**: handwriting must be neat and care should be taken to ensure that records are free from spelling and grammar errors.
- **Help to ensure that children's needs are met**: for example, observation records help to identify children's needs and can inform future practice.
- **Help to safeguard the health and wellbeing** of the child or young person: any concern about the child's health or wellbeing should be recorded and reported to the line manager.
- **Help to provide continuity of service**: so that another member of staff can take over in the event of the practitioner being ill or unavailable.

- **Provide evidence of the practitioner's work**: this will go towards compiling a portfolio of work.
- **Contain information that practitioners can use** to monitor and evaluate their work in order to improve their practice.
- **Help managers monitor and evaluate** the quality and performance of the service to children and young people.

Certain reports that you may write will be a statutory requirement within the EYFS Framework and must be made available to any Ofsted inspection. These include accident reports, reporting of illnesses or injuries and any report of concerns about a child.

Electronic recording and storing of information

If information is kept on computers or sent by email, steps must be taken to ensure that it could not fall into the hands of unauthorised people (for example, by the use of encryption software).

The **e-Nabled Common Assessment Framework (eCAF)** enables authorised, trained practitioners from across the children's workforce to electronically store and share Common Assessment Framework (CAF) information quickly and securely, and to work together to build a holistic picture of a child or young person's needs. The system reduces the need for children, young people and families to repeat their story for different services.

Assessment practice

Recording and storing information

Find out about the methods used to record and store information about the children and their families in your setting. What information is held? How are such records kept secure? Who has a right to see the documents held in your setting?

Reflective Practice: Recording information

Think about the last time you wrote a report or record in your work setting. Were you clear about its purpose? Did you have to obtain consent from the child's parents? Evaluate the usefulness of the document.

Referrals to different agencies

Most children and families who need additional support can obtain it through one of the professionals working in a school or community health setting such as a family worker, health visitor or personal adviser.

Many local authorities have set up a **multi-agency referral panel (MARP)** or something similar. This comprises a team of local professionals from a variety of backgrounds. The panel usually includes a:

- health visitor
- social worker
- school attendance officer
- school nurse
- psychologist
- youth worker.

The panel meets regularly to work together to produce a holistic solution to an individual child's circumstances. Because each individual has different needs, and possibly a variety of problems, different agencies agree to take the lead on different aspects of a case. No case is closed unless everyone is happy with the outcome.

Who can make a referral for a multi-agency service?

Children and young people may be able to access support from the multi-agency service by requests initiated by:

- practitioners
- parents and carers
- the child or young person themselves.

The need to obtain consent

Before making a referral, practitioners are expected to obtain the informed consent of the parent, carer or the young person to the provision of services. The language they use in these discussions will need to be clear and sensitive to cultural differences and perceptions of behavioural and mental health issues.

The Multi-agency Referral Form

Often the Common Assessment Framework form (CAF) is used as supporting evidence for the referral – meaning that there is no need to duplicate the information contained in the CAF assessment on a separate referral form. If not supported by a CAF assessment, then the referrer should use the Multi-agency Referral Form to make detailed notes about the individual child's needs, any other issues they are aware of, and what they have done so far to meet those needs.

The importance of partnerships with carers

Working with parents and carers is an essential aspect of work with children and young people. You can strengthen and build on this responsibility so that parents experience an increase in enjoyment of their children and an understanding of child development. Remember that it takes time and regular communication to build positive relationships with parents that are founded on mutual trust and respect.

There are many reasons why it is valuable to involve parents or carers in the work setting:

- Parents are the first and primary educators of their children.
- Parents know their children better than anyone else.
- Children and young people benefit from the extra attention, particularly one-to-one help.
- A range of different skills can be brought to the work setting, such as music, sewing, drawing, cooking, etc.
- Parents and carers who do not share the same language or culture as the work setting can extend the awareness and knowledge of staff, children and young people about the way other people live, cook and communicate.
- Parents and carers can help by sharing lots of books with children from an early age, and by hearing and helping their child read when they start school.
- Involving parents and carers in the play and learning experiences of their children can help to counteract any negative feelings parents may have about education systems, arising perhaps from memories of their own school days.

In most instances you will be working under the supervision of others and it is likely that carers will pass confidential information directly to a staff member. However, there may be occasions on which you are given information and asked to pass it on, or that you may hear or be told confidential information in the course of the daily routine. This issue is dealt with in the section on confidentiality (see Chapter 1, Unit SHC 21: Introduction to communication in children and young people's settings), and as long as you follow guidelines, procedures and practices that apply to the work setting, you will be doing the right thing.

Remember that lines of management are in place in most work settings, and you should follow them if you need to check your understanding or to ask advice. Try to be aware of the ways in

Research Activity

Parent partnership services

Every local authority has a department of Parent Partnership Services. Find out:

- what type of service is provided in your area by PPS
- how practitioners and families can access the support provided by these services in your area.

which staff members relate to and communicate with parents, and try to identify which methods seem to be most effective.

Understanding and respecting the needs of parents and carers

Different approaches

You need to be aware of the wide variety of parenting and family approaches.

Full-time employment

Some parents and carers who are in full-time employment may have a different attitude towards their child settling into the setting from those who have chosen to place their child in a nursery or playgroup on a part-time basis to widen the child's experience.

Individual needs

Every situation and family must be treated individually and the family's needs met through a flexible approach; for example, parents who are dealing with a large family or with disabled family members will have different priorities from a lone-parent family with one child.

Transition to school

Schools often have to deal with children who have had no experience of early childhood education or nursery care, as well as with those who have been in day nurseries from a few months old. Some parents whose children have been in full-time day care find the school's 'staggered' intake – when children attend on a part-time basis at first – both unnecessary and inconvenient, especially if they work. However, most children take time to adapt to a full school day, as this includes a long lunchtime period with less supervision than they are used to, and no facilities for an afternoon rest.

Referral by Social Services

When children or young people have been placed in a child care setting on the advice of a social worker, there may be some resentment from carers. They may feel that their rights and responsibilities have been overridden. It is important that a positive relationship between carers and the setting is established as soon as possible, with a clear understanding that the interest of the child or young person is everyone's main concern. In these situations there will usually be regular meetings involving parents and carers, staff and other professionals to discuss the child's progress. Young people will be invited to attend, as their opinions are important to any decision made.

Starting the relationship: making parents and carers welcome in the setting

Parents and carers start off in an unequal relationship with child care staff. Some carers may feel very anxious, as they are not familiar with the building, the staff or the rules and relationships within the setting. Other factors may increase their uncertainty and feelings of helplessness. For example:

- they may speak a different language from that spoken in the setting
- they may be under emotional pressure about leaving their child
- they may have other worries – for example, about getting to work, financial problems, etc.

You need to be able to see things from a carer's point of view and to do everything possible to make them welcome in the setting. Some useful ideas include the following:

Names accurately recorded

First of all, make sure that you have the parents' or carers' names accurately recorded. Find out how they want to be addressed – do not assume that their surnames will be the same, or the same as the child's.

Greeting

Make a point of greeting parents and smiling at them.

Name badges

These are useful so that parents know to whom they are talking, and also about whom their children are talking.

Photos

A board with staff names and regularly updated photos could be put in the reception area and in newsletters.

Key person

Parents and carers need to know which staff member will be working most closely with their child. Most nursery settings have an identified key person, who will be responsible for keeping notes and records of progress for a small number of children; these key workers will be the main point of contact for the families of those children.

In many nursery settings the children are cared for in groups according to age and/or development, and there may be one supervisor for each group. The manager or supervisor of a nursery or the head teacher in a primary school would still retain overall responsibility.

The importance of effective communication

Ongoing communication with parents and carers is essential if children and young people's needs are to be met. For many parents there can be regular and informal communication when children and young people are brought to, or collected from, the work setting. However, it is unusual for both parents to perform this task and, therefore, it is often the same parent who has contact. The methods below can usually work for both parents and care workers.

Finding ways to communicate with parents can sometimes be difficult, especially when staff may not feel confident themselves.

- **Regular contact with the same person**: always meet and greet parents and the child or young person when they arrive. At the start, it is very important that parents meet the same practitioner – preferably their child's teacher or key person – on a daily basis.
- **A meeting place for parents**: ideally, there should be a room that parents can use to have a drink and a chat together.

Exchanging routine written information

Information that applies in the longer term should ideally be given in writing – for example, information concerning food allergies or medical conditions, such as asthma or eczema. As well as telling staff, notices may need also to be attached to a child's own equipment, lunchbox or displayed in particular areas, for example food

Figure 10.01 Parents need to be made welcome in the setting

preparation, nappy-changing. In a school setting, the class teacher should ensure that any other adults involved in the child's care receive information as appropriate.

Copies of all letters received and sent and a record of all communication should be kept for future reference.

Verbal information

Routine information can be – and often is – exchanged verbally. This usually happens at the start and end of the session, when parents and their child's key worker chat informally.

Talking with parents and carers

Always let parents know about their child's positive behaviour and take the opportunity to praise the child in front of their parents. Then if

you need to share a concern with them, they will already understand that you are interested in their child's welfare and are not being judgemental. (Many adults associate being called in to see the person in charge with their own experiences of a 'telling-off'.)

Recording information and passing on messages

You will need to record some information the parent has talked to you about – especially if you are likely to forget it! You should always write down a verbal message which affects the child's welfare, so that it can be passed on to other members of staff; for example, if someone else is collecting the child, a favourite comfort object has been left at home, or if the child has experienced a restless night. The person delivering the message also needs confirmation

Written information	How and when it is used
Formal letter	Welcome letter prior to admission to the setting To give information about parents' evenings or meetings To alert parents to the presence of an infectious disease within the setting To advise parents about any change of policy or staff changes
Email	To give information about an event To respond to a request from parent or colleague
Newsletters	To give information about future events – fundraising fairs, open forums and visiting speakers, etc.
Notice boards	To give general information about the setting, local events for parents, support group contact numbers, health and safety information, daily menus, etc.
Activity slips	To inform parents about what their child has been doing
Admission form	All parents fill in an admission form when registering their child. This is confidential information and must be kept in a safe place where only staff have access to it
Home books	To record information from both staff and parents. Home books travel between the setting and the home and record details of the child's progress, any medication given, how well they have eaten and slept, etc.
Accident slips	To record information when a child has been ill or is injured when at the setting
Suggestions box	Some settings have a suggestions box where parents can contribute their own ideas for improving the service
Policy and procedure documents	These official documents should be openly available, and parents should be able to discuss them with staff if they have any concerns

Table 10.3 Exchanging routine written information

that it will be acted upon. Where there are shift systems in operation, a strict procedure for passing on messages needs to be established.

Telephone calls

Information received or delivered by telephone should be noted in a diary so that action can be taken.

Difficulties in developing and sustaining partnerships with carers

Parents and carers who may not want to become involved

Many parents will want to become involved in their child's setting, especially if there is an open, welcoming atmosphere and a place to meet other parents. However, there will always

be some parents who do not want to participate. There could be a number of reasons for this reluctance. These include:

- working full-time or having other daytime commitments
- feeling that they have nothing of value to contribute
- not being interested in spending time with other people's children
- lacking confidence or feeling shy.

It is important that parents do not feel pressured into becoming involved. You should always respect parents' decisions and not assume that this shows a lack of interest in their children.

Some early years settings have a drop-in facility for parents that helps support those feeling isolated and experiencing problems, while a

Case Study — Communicating with parents

The parents of three-year-old Thomas have been anxious about their son's appetite since he was ill with a virus. Staff at the day nursery have been observing Thomas, keeping written records and taking photographs, at snack and mealtimes over a period of a week. They have made sure the food is attractively presented, includes some of Thomas's favourite items and that he is offered small portions. They have noticed a great improvement and want to share their findings with his parents and discuss how he is at home.

Five-year-old Charlotte has recently become withdrawn from both adults and other children.

For the past week or so she has needed encouragement to complete work tasks which are within her capability and when she has had free-choice activity, she has tended to sit alone in the books area with a soft toy. This represents a change in Charlotte's behaviour and the teacher wants to discuss her concerns with the parents.

1 In each case, what method would you use to contact the parents?
2 Explain what you would say/write and what you would arrange in order to deal with each situation.

family support group, with a skilled family worker on hand, can help people with parenting skills and other issues.

Barriers to communication: how you can help

Time constraints

There may be several children arriving at the same time, which puts pressure on staff at a busy time. Parents may be in a rush to get away when bringing their children. It is important that you do not interpret this as a lack of interest. Greet them with a friendly nod and pass on any information as briefly as possible.

Not seeing parents or carers regularly

When someone other than the parents brings and fetches the child, staff will need to find other ways to maintain regular communication.

Body language and non-verbal communication

Be aware of how parents may be feeling at a particular time, even when they do not mention anything specific; for example, if a parent does not make eye contact, it may be that they are depressed.

Written communication

Unless sent in the post, there is a chance that some letters and other written notes may not reach the parent. Also, some parents might have difficulty reading and writing and not want to seek help. The **notice board** can also be used to display a general letter sent to all parents.

Making messages clear

Remember that we understand messages not only from what is said but also from *how* it is said – our tone of voice, gestures and facial expressions can change the meaning of a message. The person on the receiving end of a written message has no such clues. It is important to give careful consideration to the wording of any letter and try to make sure that it cannot be misinterpreted.

When English is not the parent's first language

You can help by signing or – where possible – by involving bilingual staff or translators. Notice boards can display signs in picture form – for example, showing the activities the child will be doing during the session. Having written information in a number of different languages is also helpful.

Useful websites and resources

www.childrens-centres.org	**Together for Children:** working in partnership with the Department for Education (DfE) to support local authorities (LAs) in their delivery of Sure Start Children's Centres.
www.cwdcouncil.org.uk/championing-children	**Children's Workforce Development Council** – Championing Children
www.connexions-direct.com	**Connexions:** Support, advice and personal development service for 13- to 19-year-olds in England.
www.parentpartnership.org.uk	**Parent Partnership Services (PPS)** are statutory services offering information advice and support to parents and carers of children and young people with special educational needs (SEN).
www.portage.org.uk	**National Portage Association**
www.nya.org.uk	**The National Youth Agency (NYA)** works in partnership with a wide range of public, private and voluntary sector organisations to support and improve services for young people. Their particular focus is on youth work and they believe that by investing in young people's personal and social development, young people are better able to live more active and fulfilling lives.

11 Paediatric emergency first aid: Unit PEFAP 001

Everyone who works with children should be qualified in first aid techniques. There are now specialist courses, such as the St John's **Early Years First Aid** (paediatric) and the British Red Cross's **First Aid for Child Carers**. Childminders must have attended a training course within six months of registration and must hold a current paediatric first aid certificate at the point of registration. Once you have learned how to respond to an emergency you never lose that knowledge, and this means that you could save a life one day. This chapter explains the major first aid techniques and provides valid competence to meet the requirements of Ofsted.

Learning outcomes

By the end of this chapter you will:

1. Understand the role of the paediatric first aider.
2. Be able to assess an emergency situation and act safely and effectively.
3. Be able to provide first aid for an infant or a child who is unresponsive and breathing normally.
4. Be able to provide first aid for an infant or a child who is unresponsive and not breathing normally.
5. Be able to provide first aid for an infant or a child who has a foreign body airway obstruction.
6. Be able to provide first aid to an infant or a child who is wounded and bleeding.
7. Know how to provide first aid to an infant or a child who is suffering from shock.

The role of the paediatric first aider

First aid is an important skill. By performing simple procedures and following certain guidelines, it may be possible to save lives by giving basic treatment until professional medical help arrives. Also remember that practice makes perfect. If you have memorised some of the most basic procedures – and, more importantly, practised them – you will be able to react quickly and efficiently.

The key aims of first aid can be summarised in three key points:

1. **Preserve life**: The overriding aim of all medical care, including first aid, is to save lives.

2. **Prevent further harm**: This is also sometimes called **prevent the condition from worsening**. It covers both external factors – such as moving a patient away from any cause of harm – and applying first aid techniques to prevent worsening of the condition, such as applying pressure to stop a bleed from becoming dangerous.

3. **Promote recovery**: First aid also involves trying to start the recovery process from the illness or injury, and in some cases might involve completing a treatment, such as in the case of applying a plaster to a small wound.

The responsibilities of a paediatric first aider

Every emergency situation is unique, but the aims of first aid remain the same. Your responsibilities are to:

- assess the emergency situation
- maintain your own safety
- contact the emergency services
- give accurate and useful information to the emergency services
- support the casualty physically and emotionally
- appreciate your own limitations
- know when to intervene and when to wait for more specialist help to arrive.

How to minimise the risk of infection to yourself and others
Basic hygienic measures in first aid

- Wash your hands with soap and water before and immediately after giving first aid. If gloves are available for use in first aid situations, you should also wash your hands thoroughly before putting the gloves on and after disposing of them. (Plastic bags can be used when gloves are unavailable.)
- Avoid contact with body fluids when possible. Do not touch objects that may be soiled with blood or other body fluids.
- Be careful not to prick yourself with broken glass or any sharp objects found on or near the injured person.
- Prevent injuries when using, handling, cleaning or disposing of sharp instruments or devices.
- Cover cuts or other skin-breaks with dry and clean dressings.
- Chronic skin conditions may cause open sores on hands. People with these conditions should avoid direct contact with any injured person who is bleeding or has open wounds.

First aid equipment

There is no mandatory list of items to put in a first aid box. All first aid boxes should have a white cross on a green background. Guidelines published by the National Association of Child Minders, NCMA, as well as Ofsted and experienced paediatric first aid trainers, recommend that the first aid box in a child care setting should contain the items listed in Table 11.1.

Large nurseries and schools may have more than one first aid box, and the contents will vary according to individual needs; for example, a nursery setting will have a larger number of small adhesive dressings or plasters.

- The first aid box must be a strong container that keeps out both dirt and damp.
- It should be kept in an accessible place, but one that is out of the reach of children.
- All employees should be informed where the first aid box is kept, and it should only be moved from this safe place when in use.

Items for the first aid box	
1 first aid guidance leaflet	1 packet hypoallergenic plasters – in assorted sizes
1 large sterile wound dressing	3 medium sterile wound dressings
1 pair disposable gloves	2 triangular bandages
10 individually wrapped wipes	5 finger bob bandages (no applicator needed)
2 sterile eye pads	4 safety pins
1 pair of scissors	

Table 11.1 Items to be contained in a first aid box

- Supplies must be replaced as soon as possible after use.

It is recommended that you do not keep tablets and medicines in the first aid box.

Accident reports and incident records

Chapter 7, Unit MU 2.4: Contribute to children and young people's health and safety, describes the recording and reporting procedures of accidents in early years settings (see p 115). If a pupil is injured while at school, the staff are obliged by law to record the injury in the **Pupil Accident Book**. An accident record must be completed immediately following an incident, providing as much information as possible.

For many incidents it is only necessary to complete an accident record, but in some circumstances the Reporting of Injuries, Diseases and Dangerous Occurrences Regulations 1995 (RIDDOR) require you to report an incident to the Health and Safety Executive.

Definition of an infant and a child for the purposes of first aid treatment

- An infant is under one year old.
- A child is aged from one year to puberty.

Research Activity

Accident and incident reporting

Find out about policies and procedures relating to first aid in your work setting. In particular, find out the following:

- Where is the first aid kit kept, and is it easy to reach quickly?
- Who is responsible for replenishing the first aid box?
- Where is the Accident Report Book kept?
- In what circumstances do you have to report an incident or accident at your work setting to the Health and Safety Executive?

How to assess an emergency situation and act safely and effectively

The primary survey

At the scene of any accident, your first thought should always be safety, both for yourself and the victim. There is already one casualty; do not make yourself another. Firstly look around and **survey the scene**: is it safe? Look for any potential hazards; these could be anything that puts either of you at risk, from falling objects and running engines to oncoming traffic. Only when

D	Danger	Firstly, ensure that neither you nor the casualty is in any danger. Make the situation safe and *then* assess the casualty.
R	Response	If the casualty appears **unconscious**, check this by shouting: 'Can you hear me? Open your eyes,' while gently tapping their shoulders. (See below for how to check for a response in infants and children.) If there is a **response**: if there is no further danger, leave the casualty in the position found and summon help if needed. Treat any condition found and monitor vital signs: level of response, pulse and breathing. Continue monitoring the casualty either until help arrives or he or she recovers. If there is **no response**: shout for **help**. If possible, leave the casualty in the position found and open the airway. If this is not possible, turn the casualty onto their back and open the airway. Check for other life-threatening conditions such as severe bleeding, and treat as necessary.
A	Airway	**Open the airway** by placing one hand on the casualty's forehead and gently tilting the head back. Then lift the chin using two fingers only. This will move the casualty's tongue away from the back of the mouth.
B	Breathing	Look, listen and feel for **no more** than ten seconds to see if the casualty is breathing normally. Look to see if the chest is rising and falling. Listen for breathing. Feel for breath against your cheek. If the casualty is **breathing normally**, place them in the **recovery position**.
C	Circulation	If the casualty is **not breathing normally** or if you have any doubt whether breathing is normal, begin **CPR (Cardiopulmonary Resuscitation)**. Check for other life-threatening conditions such as severe bleeding, and treat as necessary.

Table 11.2 DRABC

you are sure that it is safe should you take action and begin to carry out first aid.

If you happen to come across a casualty, you will need to **assess the situation** before doing anything else. It can be useful to remember **DRABC**, which stands for Danger, Response, Airway, Breathing and Circulation; see Table 11.2.

When and how to call for help

1 **Assess the situation**: stay calm and do not panic.

2 **Minimise any danger to yourself and to others:** for example, make sure that someone takes charge of other children at the scene.

3 **Send for help**: notify a doctor, hospital, parents, etc. as appropriate. If in any doubt, call an ambulance: dial 999. Be ready to assist the emergency services by answering some simple questions:

- your name and the telephone number from which you are calling
- the location of the accident; try to give as much information as possible, for example, familiar landmarks such as churches or pubs nearby
- explain briefly what has happened; this helps the paramedics to act speedily when they arrive
- tell them what you have done so far to treat the casualty.

First aid for an infant or a child who is unresponsive and breathing normally

A child's heart and/or breathing can stop as a result of lack of oxygen (for example, choking), drowning, electric shock, heart attack or other serious injury. If an infant or child has collapsed you need to find out firstly if they are conscious or unconscious.

- **Can you get a response**? Check if conscious.
  - (a) For an infant: call their name and try tapping them gently on the sole of their foot
  - (b) For a child: call their name and try tapping them gently on their shoulders.

If there is no response, you need to **check for breathing**.

- **Open the airway** for both infants and children: place one hand on the forehead and *gently* tilt the head back. Then using your other hand, lift the child's chin. Take a quick look and remove any *visible* obstructions from the mouth and nose.
- **Look, listen and feel** for normal breathing: place your face next to the child's face and listen for breathing. You can do this while looking along the child's chest and abdomen for any movement. You may also be able to feel the child's breath on your cheek. Allow up to ten seconds to check if the child is breathing or not.

If the infant or child is unconscious but breathing normally, place him or her into **the recovery position** – see below.

The recovery position

If a child is unconscious this means that they have no muscle control. If the child is lying on their back, their tongue will be floppy and may fall back, partially obstructing the airway. Any child who is breathing and who has a pulse should be placed in the recovery position while you wait for medical assistance. This safe position allows fluid and vomit to drain out of the child's mouth so that they are not inhaled into the lungs.

Recovery position for an infant (from birth to approximately one year)

Cradle the infant in your arms, with his head tilted downwards to prevent him from choking on his tongue or inhaling vomit.

Recovery position for a child (from one year onwards)

1. Place arm nearest to you at a right angle, with palm facing up.
2. Move other arm towards you, keeping the back of their hand against their cheek.
3. Get hold of the knee furthest from you and pull up until foot is flat on the floor.
4. Pull the knee towards you, keeping the child's hand pressed against their cheek.
5. Position the leg at a right angle.
6. Make sure that the airway remains open by tilting the head back, then check breathing by feeling and listening for breath.

In Practice

The recovery position
In pairs, practise placing each other in the recovery position you would use for a child.

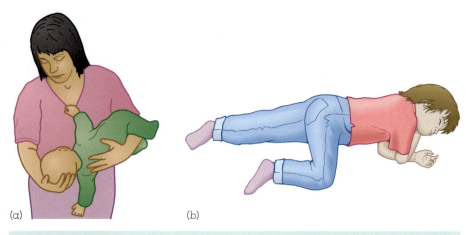

(a)   (b)

Figure 11.01 (a) The recovery position for an infant; (b) The recovery position for a child

Continuous assessment and monitoring of an infant or a child in your care

Remember your **ABC** and continue to monitor the infant or child in your care until you can hand over to a doctor or paramedic.

- **A is for AIRWAY:** check that the airway remains open. Always monitor a child while in recovery position.
- **B is for BREATHING:** check that breathing is normal and regular.
- **C is for CIRCULATION**: check the pulse (*if you are trained and experienced*) but ensure you take no more than ten seconds to do this:
  (a) *In a child over one year*: feel for the carotid pulse in the neck by placing your fingers in the groove between the Adam's apple and the large muscle running from the side of the neck.
  (b) *In an infant*: feel for the brachial pulse on the inner aspect of the upper arm by lightly pressing your fingers towards the bone on the inside of the upper arm and hold them there for five seconds.

In Practice

Taking the pulse

In pairs, practise taking each other's pulse – both the *radial* pulse at the wrist and the *carotid* pulse in the neck.

First aid for an infant or a child who is unresponsive and not breathing normally

An infant or child who is unresponsive and not breathing normally will need to be given Cardiopulmonary Resuscitation (CPR). CPR is a combination of rescue breaths and chest compressions. This keeps the vital organs alive until the ambulance service arrives and starts advanced life support.

Send for help: If you have carried out the checks above, the child is not breathing normally and you have someone with you, send them to **dial 999** for an ambulance immediately. If you are alone, give one minute of CPR – *then* call an ambulance. If the casualty is under one year old, take the infant with you while you call an ambulance.

CPR: Resuscitation for a infant who is not breathing (from birth to one year)

- **Open the airway** by gently tilting the infant's head back and lifting the chin.
- Give FIVE **rescue breaths** by placing your mouth over their **mouth and nose,** and blow gently for about one second, until you see the chest rise.
- Place two fingers on the centre of the infant's chest, and give 30 **chest compressions** by pressing down about a third of the depth.
- Then give TWO rescue breaths, followed by 30 chest compressions.
- Continue this cycle of breaths and compressions for one minute.

If not already done, **call for an ambulance** now and continue the above cycle until help arrives or the infant starts to breathe.

CPR: Resuscitation for a child who is not breathing (from one year onwards)

- **Open the airway** by gently tilting the child's head back and lifting the chin.
- Pinch the child's nose. Give FIVE **rescue breaths** by placing your mouth over their mouth and blow steadily until you see the chest rise.
- Place one hand on the centre of the child's chest and lean over the child. Give 30 **chest compressions** by pressing down about a third of the depth of the chest.
- Then give TWO rescue breaths, followed by 30 chest compressions.
- Continue this cycle of breaths and compressions for one minute.

If not already done, **call for an ambulance** now and continue the above cycle until help arrives or the child starts to breathe.

When to administer CPR

CPR should only be carried out when an infant or child is unresponsive and not breathing normally.

If the infant or child has any signs of normal breathing, or coughing, or movement, **DO NOT** begin to do chest compressions. Doing so may cause the heart to stop beating.

How to administer CPR using an infant or a child manikin

The techniques of giving CPR should never be practised on a child. Infant and child manikins are designed to give a very close experience to the 'real thing' and should always be used to practise on.

How to deal with an infant or a child who is experiencing a seizure

A seizure is caused by a sudden burst of excess electrical activity in the brain, causing a temporary disruption in the normal message-passing between brain cells. This results in the brain's messages becoming temporarily halted or mixed up. Seizures can happen at any time and generally last a matter of seconds or minutes, after which the brain usually returns to normal. Seizures are also called **convulsions** or **fits**.

The most common causes of seizures in young children are high fever (known as a **febrile convulsion** or seizure), epilepsy, head injury and poisoning.

Febrile convulsions are covered in Chapter 12, Unit MPII002: Managing paediatric illness and injury. They are not classified as epilepsy.

Figure 11.02 An infant resuscitation manikin

What happens during an epileptic seizure

During an epileptic seizure, the child:

- suddenly falls unconscious, often with a cry (caused by a tightening of the voice muscles)
- becomes stiff, often arching the back
- may stop breathing and the lips turn blue
- begins convulsive movements: the limbs make rhythmic jerks, the jaw may be clenched and the breathing noisy
- may show saliva – frothing – at the mouth
- may lose bladder or bowel control.

Then the muscles relax and breathing becomes normal. Usually in just a few minutes the child regains consciousness and may fall into a deep sleep or appear dazed. The child will not remember anything about the seizure when they come round, and will need time to recover. Recovery time varies from minutes for some children to hours for others.

What to do if a child has a seizure

- Protect the child from injury by moving any furniture or other solid objects out of the way during a seizure.
- Make space around the child and keep other children away.
- Loosen the clothing around the child's neck and chest, and cushion their head.
- Stay with the child until recovery is complete.
- Be calmly reassuring.

DO NOT do the following:

- Restrain the child in any way.
- Try to put anything in their mouth.
- Try to move them unless they are in danger.
- Give the child anything to eat or drink until they are fully recovered.
- Attempt to bring them round.

Call an ambulance only if:

- It is the child's first seizure and you do not know why it happened.
- It follows a blow to the head.
- The child is injured during the seizure.

- The seizure is continuous and shows no sign of stopping – a very rare condition called *status epilepticus*.

Choking: First aid for a child who has a foreign body airway obstruction

What is choking?

Choking is when a child struggles to breathe because of a blockage in the airway.

Children under three years are particularly vulnerable to choking because their airways are small and they have not yet developed full control of the muscles of their mouth and throat.

What causes choking?

Usually, choking in small children is caused when a small foreign object is blocking one of the major airways. This may be a small toy which they have put in their mouth and inadvertently swallowed, or a small piece of food they have not chewed properly.

Symptoms

Choking often begins with small coughs or gasps as the child tries to draw in breath around the obstruction or clear it out. This may be followed by a struggling sound or squeaking whispers as the child tries to communicate their distress. The child may thrash around and drool and their eyes may water. They may flush red and then turn blue. However, if a small item gets stuck in a infant or toddler's throat, you may not even *hear* them choking – they could be silently suffocating as the object fills their airway and prevents them from coughing or breathing.

The difference between a mild and a severe airway obstruction

If the blockage of the airway is mild, the child should be able to clear it; if it is severe they will be unable to speak, cough or breathe, and will eventually lose consciousness. You need to act promptly if there is any difficulty with breathing.

How to treat an infant or a child who is choking

For an infant who is choking:

- First check inside the infant's mouth. If you can **see** the obstruction, try to hook it out with your finger, but do not dig around in the hope of finding it as you risk pushing it further down. If this does not work, **act quickly**.
- Lay the infant down along your forearm, supporting her head and neck with your hand. The infant's head should be lower than her bottom.
- Give up to **five back blows**, between the shoulder blades with the heel of your hand.
- Check the infant's mouth and pick out any obstructions.
- If the infant is still choking, give up to five **chest thrusts** (as for CPR), pushing inwards and upwards
- Check the mouth again. If still choking, give three full cycles of back blows and chest thrusts, checking the mouth after each cycle.
- Call an ambulance if the infant is still choking and repeat cycles of back blows and chest thrusts until medical aid arrives. If the infant loses consciousness, start CPR.

For a toddler or older child who is choking:

- **First check inside the child's mouth**. If you can **see** the obstruction, try to hook it out with your finger, but do not dig around in the hope of finding it as you risk pushing it further down. If this does not work, **act quickly**.

- Sit down and put the child face down across your knees with head and arms hanging down (or **stand** an older child leaning forward). Keep the child's head lower than the chest.
- Give up to **five sharp back blows** between the shoulder blades with the heel of your hand.
- Check the mouth again and remove any obstruction. If the child is still choking, give **abdominal thrusts**:
  - (a) Place a clenched fist above the belly button.
  - (b) Grasp your fist with your other hand.
  - (c) Pull upwards and inwards up to five times.
- Check the mouth again. If the child is still choking, give three full cycles of back blows and abdominal thrusts, checking the mouth after each cycle.
- Call an ambulance if the child is still choking, and repeat cycles of back blows and abdominal thrusts until medical aid arrives. If the child loses consciousness, start CPR.

The procedure to be followed after administering the treatment for choking

The child may experience difficulties after having treatment for choking – for example, a persistent cough or difficulties with swallowing or breathing. It is important to monitor and assess the child's condition and to seek medical help if the problem persists.

First aid for bleeding and wounds

In most cases bleeding stops quickly. However, if it is severe, you may need to control it to prevent **shock**.

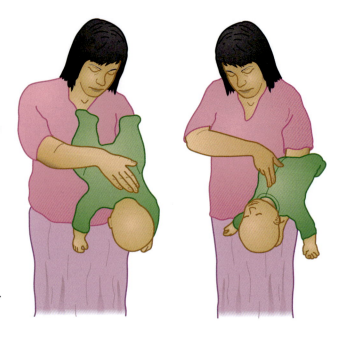

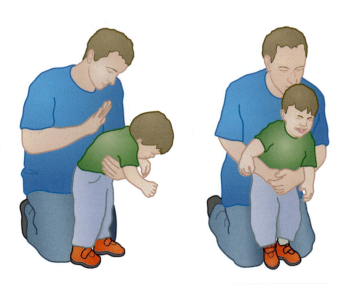

Figure 11.03 How to treat an infant or child who is choking

The types and severity of bleeding and the effect on an infant or a child

Even tiny amounts of blood can seem like a lot to a child. Any bleeding may frighten children because they are too young to realise that the blood loss will stop when clotting occurs. When a child loses a large amount of blood, he or she may suffer shock or even become unconscious.

Safe and effective management for the control of minor and major external bleeding

Bleeding: Cuts, grazes and nosebleeds

For minor cuts and grazes:

1. Sit or lay the child down and reassure them.
2. Clean the injured area with cold water, using cotton wool or gauze.
3. Apply a dressing if necessary.
4. Do not attempt to pick out pieces of gravel or grit from a graze. Just clean gently and cover with a light dressing if necessary.
5. Record the injury and treatment in the **Accident Report Book** and make sure that the parents/carers of the child are informed.

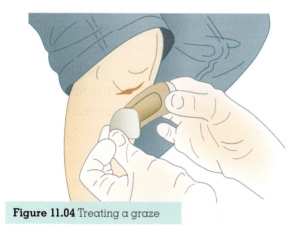

Figure 11.04 Treating a graze

Nosebleeds

Bleeding from the nose usually occurs when tiny blood vessels inside the nostrils are ruptured, either by a blow to the nose, or as a result of sneezing, picking or blowing the nose.

- Sit the child down with her head well forward.
- Ask her to breathe through her mouth.
- Pinch the fleshy part of her nose, just below the bridge.

- Reassure her and tell her not to try to speak, cough or sniff as this may disturb blood clots.
- After ten minutes, release the pressure. If the nose is still bleeding, reapply the pressure for further periods of ten minutes.
- If the nosebleed persists beyond 30 minutes, seek medical aid.

Figure 11.05 Treating a nosebleed

Severe bleeding

When a child is bleeding severely, your main aim is to stem the flow of blood. If you have disposable gloves available, use them. It is important to reduce the risk of cross-infection.

- **Summon medical help** – dial 999 or call a doctor.
- Try to stop the bleeding:
  - (a) **Apply direct pressure to the wound**: wear gloves and use a dressing or a non-fluffy material, such as a clean tea towel.
  - (b) **Elevate the affected part if possible**: if the wound is on an arm or leg, raise the injured limb above the level of the heart.
- **Apply a dressing**: if the blood soaks through, DO NOT remove the dressing, apply another on top and so on.
- Keep the child warm and reassure them.
- DO NOT give anything to eat or drink.

- Contact the child's parents or carers.
- If the child loses consciousness, follow the ABC procedure for resuscitation.

Always record the incident and the treatment given in the Accident Report Book. Always wear disposable gloves if in an early years setting, to prevent cross-infection.

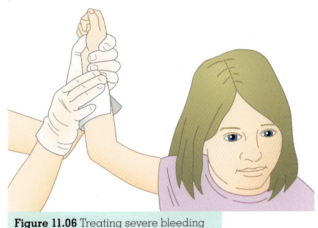

Figure 11.06 Treating severe bleeding

Objects in wounds

Where possible, swab or wash small objects out of the wound with clean water. If there is a large object embedded:

- Leave it in place.
- Apply firm pressure on either side of the object.
- Raise and support the wounded limb or part.
- Lay the casualty down to treat for shock.
- Gently cover the wound and object with a sterile dressing.
- Build up padding around the object until the padding is higher than the object, then bandage over the object without pressing on it.

If you *suspect* there may be something embedded in the wound, make sure you do not press on the object. Instead press firmly on either side of the object and build up padding around it before bandaging to avoid putting pressure on the object itself.

First aid for an infant or a child who is suffering from shock

Shock is a life-threatening condition that occurs when vital organs do not get enough oxygen due to reduced blood circulation. The most common cause of shock is severe blood loss, but it can also be caused by loss of other body fluids as in the case of severe burns or dehydration caused by prolonged vomiting and diarrhoea. When treating someone for shock, it is important to remember that there could be internal bleeding following an injury.

How to recognise and manage an infant or child suffering from shock

Early signs and symptoms of shock in an infant or a child

After an initial adrenaline rush, the body withdraws blood from the skin in order to maintain the vital organs – and the oxygen supply to the brain drops. The infant or child will have:

- pale, cold, clammy skin that is often grey-blue in colour, especially around the lips
- a rapid pulse, becoming weaker
- shallow, fast breathing.

Symptoms as shock progresses

In an infant

The anterior fontanelle is drawn in (depressed).

In an infant or a child

An infant or a child may show:

- unusual restlessness, yawning and gasping for air
- thirst
- loss of consciousness.

Treating shock

The treatment is the same for an infant and a child.

- If possible, ask someone else to **call an ambulance** while you stay with the child. Lay the child down, keeping her head low to improve the blood supply to the brain. Treat any obvious cause, such as severe bleeding.
- **Raise the child's legs** and support them with pillows or on a cushion on a pile of books.
- **Loosen any tight clothing** at the neck, chest and waist to help with the child's breathing. **For an infant**: hold the infant on your lap while you loosen her clothing and offer comfort and reassurance.
- **Cover the child with a blanket** or coat to keep her warm. Never use a hot-water bottle or any other direct source of heat.
- **Reassure the child:** keep talking to her and monitoring her condition while you wait for the ambulance. If the infant or child loses consciousness, open her airway, check her breathing and be prepared to give rescue breaths.
- **Do not give the child anything to eat or drink:** if she complains of thirst, just moisten her lips with water.

How to recognise and manage an infant or child suffering from anaphylactic shock

Anaphylactic shock is a severe and life-threatening allergic reaction that may occur following an insect sting or after eating certain foods, such as peanuts. The reaction can be rapid, developing within seconds or minutes of contact with the 'trigger'. Triggers include:

- nuts
- shellfish
- eggs
- wasp and bee stings
- certain medications.

During an anaphylactic reaction, chemicals are released into the blood that widen (dilate) blood vessels and cause blood pressure to fall. Air passages then narrow (constrict), resulting in breathing difficulties. In addition, the tongue and throat can swell, obstructing the airway. An infant or child with anaphylactic shock will need urgent medical help as this can be fatal.

The following **signs and symptoms** may come all at once and the child may rapidly lose consciousness:

- high-pitched wheezing sound
- blotchy, itchy, raised rash
- swollen eyelids, lips and tongue
- difficulty speaking, then breathing
- abdominal pain, vomiting and diarrhoea.

If you suspect an infant or child is suffering from anaphylactic shock, follow the steps below:

1 **Call an ambulance**. If the child has had a reaction previously, she will have medication to take in case of more attacks. This should be given as soon as the attack starts, following the instructions closely.

Assessment practice

Paediatric emergency first aid

As you complete each section of your first aid course, prepare a folder that includes the following information:

- The responsibilities of a paediatric first aider – including the need to protect yourself and others from infection.
- How to use first aid equipment appropriately.
- How to complete an accident report.
- How to recognise and manage an infant or a child who is suffering from shock.
- How to recognise and manage an infant or a child who is suffering from anaphylactic shock.

2 **Help the child into a comfortable sitting position** to relieve any breathing problems and loosen any tight clothing at her neck and waist. Comfort and reassure her while you wait for the ambulance.

3 **If the child loses consciousness**, open her airway, check her breathing and be prepared to start rescue breaths.

12 Managing paediatric illness and injury: Unit MP II002

In children, illness or injury may happen very quickly, although recovery is usually just as rapid. As a practitioner, you need to know about these illnesses and injuries so that you understand when to seek medical help and how best to support the child.

Learning outcomes

By the end of this chapter you will be able to provide first aid to an infant or a child:

1. with a suspected fracture or a dislocation
2. with a head, a neck or a back injury
3. with conditions affecting the eyes, ears or nose
4. with a chronic medical condition or sudden illness
5. who is experiencing the effects of extreme heat or cold
6. who has sustained an electric shock
7. with burns or scalds
8. who has been poisoned
9. who has been bitten or stung.

First aid for an infant or a child with a suspected fracture or a dislocation

A fracture is a broken bone, but in babies and children it can be difficult to tell the difference between broken bones and muscle or joint sprains and strains. If in doubt, *always* treat the injury as a possible fracture (broken bone) and get the child to hospital for X-rays. Your chief aim as a first aider is to *prevent further injury*; do this by keeping the child still and then ensuring that they get safely to hospital.

Common types of fractures

Children's bones are soft and pliable and do not break as easily as the harder bones of an adult. The most common type of fracture in infants and children is the greenstick fracture, but there are also other types of fracture.

- **Greenstick fracture:** the bone bends and splits but does not break (just like a green stick). There is little damage to the surrounding tissue.
- **Open fracture:** the broken end of the bone breaks through the skin and may stick out.
- **Closed fracture:** the bone is broken but does not damage the skin.

- **Hairline fracture:** the bone is only partially fractured. These fractures can be difficult to detect on X-rays.

Leg bones can be fractured by impact, twisting or direct blows. A broken leg is a serious injury as it can cause serious internal bleeding because of the rich blood supply in the thighbone. If the shinbone breaks it may protrude through the skin and this could cause infection.

Arm bones can be fractured by a direct blow or by a fall onto an outstretched hand.

A collarbone can be fractured when a child falls on her shoulder or on an outstretched hand. It is the bone most often fractured in childhood. This is because the collarbone does not completely harden until adulthood.

How to manage a fracture

If you suspect that a child has a fracture, always call for an ambulance. While waiting for the ambulance:

1. Make sure the child is comfortable, and give plenty of reassurance.
2. Encourage the child to remain as still as possible: unless it is absolutely necessary, do not move the child.

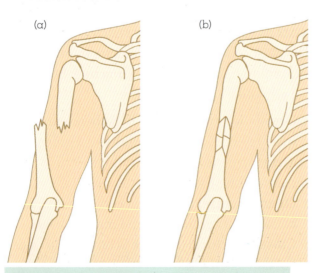

(a)   (b)

Figure 12.01 (a) an open fracture; (b) a closed fracture

Leg injuries

1. Keep the injured limb supported, using your hands to hold it very still.
2. Ask a colleague to fetch something soft (such as rolled-up towels or blankets) and place them between the child's knees and ankles.
3. Make a splint: in order to keep the leg as still as possible, create a splint. Do this by gently bandaging the good leg to the bad leg, above and below the injury. Also, try bandaging the legs together at the knees and ankles.

Arm and collarbone injuries

Immobilise the affected area by putting on the appropriate sling and keep the arm close to the body.

Treat wounds

If the broken bone has pierced the skin or there is a wound leading to the break, treat it as if there is an embedded object in the wound (see p 208, Chapter 11, Unit PEFAP 001: Paediatric emergency first aid). Control the bleeding and loosely cover the wound with a dressing to prevent infection.

Signs of shock

Look out for signs of shock including pale, cold and clammy skin, rapid then weak pulse, fast and shallow breathing, sweating and complaints of nausea and thirst. If you suspect shock, lay the child down and carefully raise their legs above the level of their heart. Make sure you keep the child warm.

Important: DO NOT attempt to straighten a broken limb and **DO NOT** give the child anything to eat or drink (in case he or she needs to have an operation).

How to manage a dislocation

A dislocation is a separation of the end of a bone and the joint it meets. The bone is displaced from its proper position. The shoulders are especially prone to dislocation injuries. Fingers, hips, ankles, elbows, jaws, and even the spine can be dislocated. The elbow is a common dislocation site in toddlers.

A dislocated joint is swollen, misshaped, usually very painful, and discoloured. The principles of managing a dislocation are the same as for managing a fracture – that is, get the child to hospital, immobilise and support the affected area.

How to apply a support sling or an elevation sling

See Figure 12.02, which shows how to apply a support sling and an elevation sling.

In Practice

Supporting arm and collarbone injuries

In pairs, practise applying a support sling and an elevation sling using a triangular bandage.

First aid for an infant or a child with a head, a neck or a back injury

Children are very active in their play and have little sense of danger, so it is not surprising that they are prone to head injuries. Also, their heads are relatively large in proportion to their bodies and therefore more vulnerable to damage than adult heads. Bangs and knocks to the head are common in childhood and are rarely serious. Some common causes are:

- falling out of a cot or from a bed
- falling from a tree or climbing frame

(a) Support sling:
1) **Hold the child's injured** arm across their chest. Slide a triangular bandage between their arm and their chest so that the longest edge of the bandage is parallel to their uninjured side.
2) **Bring the lower half** of the bandage up over the injured arm and take the point around the back of your child's neck. Tie the end together in a knot over the hollow above their collarbone.
3) **Tuck the two ends** of the bandage under the knot – it's more comfortable. Fold the bandage over at the child's elbow and fix it in place with a safety pin. Get your child to hospital.

(b) Elevation sling:
1) **Place triangular bandage**
   Put the fingertips of the hand on the injured side on the other shoulder. Hold one end of the bandage at your child's fingertips, and drape the long edge down the body. The point should be below the elbow on the injured side.
2) **Gather bandage, tie sling**
   Take the bandage under the child's elbow so that it supports the arm on the injured side. Bring the bandage across the child's back. Tie it on the uninjured side with a reef knot, making sure that a few fingers are visible.

Figure 12.02 (a) Support sling; (b) Elevation sling

- falling from windows or down the stairs
- road traffic accidents.

The scalp and forehead have a very rich blood supply, so even a small cut can cause serious bleeding.

The greatest risk of any injury to the head is brain haemorrhage, or bleeding *inside* the skull, which can lead to brain damage.

How to recognise head injuries

If the head injury is mild, there may be no other symptoms except a slight headache and a bump at the site of the injury. More serious head injuries include **concussion, skull fracture and cerebral compression.**

You will not be expected to *diagnose* the child's type of head injury, but you do need to be able to give first aid following an assessment of the child's condition.

Concussion

This is usually caused by a blow to the head that 'shakes' the brain inside the skull, but it can also result from indirect force, such as landing heavily on the feet. It is characterised by a brief period of unconsciousness or a dazed feeling after the injury. Signs and symptoms of concussion include:

- short period of being dazed and confused; may briefly lose consciousness
- dizziness and nausea when the child recovers consciousness
- brief loss of memory
- generalised headache.

Skull fracture

A skull fracture is serious because there is a risk that the brain may be damaged either *directly* by fractured bone from the skull or *indirectly* by bleeding inside the skull. A child with a possible skull fracture may also have a neck (spinal) injury. Signs and symptoms of a skull fracture include:

- a bruise or wound on the head
- soft area or depression on the scalp
- bruising or swelling behind one ear
- bruising around one or both eyes
- clear (straw-coloured) fluid (which is cerebrospinal fluid) or watery blood coming from the nose or ear
- blood showing in the white of the eye

- progressive deterioration in the child's level of response.

Cerebral compression

This is a serious life-threatening condition and the child will need urgent medical or surgical treatment. Signs and symptoms of cerebral compression include:

- history of head injury
- severe headache
- deteriorating level of consciousness
- the pupils of eyes may be unequal in size
- weakness and/or paralysis down one side of body or face
- noisy breathing, which becomes slower
- high temperature and flushed face.

How to manage a head injury

If you suspect that a child may have a head injury you should **check the child's level of** response. Is he alert and responding normally? Does he respond to your voice? Does he respond to pain? Is he unconscious?

If the child is conscious:

- Help him to lie down – **do not** turn his head in case there is a neck injury.
- Control any bleeding from the scalp by applying pressure *around* the wound. Look for and treat any other injuries.
- **Dial 999** for an ambulance.
- If there is any discharge from an ear, cover the ear with a sterile dressing or clean pad, lightly secured with a bandage. **Do not** plug the ear.
- Monitor and record **vital signs** – level of response, pulse and breathing – until medical help arrives.

If the child is unconscious:

- Open the airway and check for breathing. If the child is breathing, try to maintain the airway in the position the child was found.

- Be prepared to give chest compressions and rescue breaths if needed.
- **Dial 999** for an ambulance.
- Monitor and record **vital signs** – level of response, pulse, and breathing – until medical help arrives.

Key terms

Cerebrospinal fluid – A clear, colourless fluid that flows around the brain and spinal cord to provide nourishment and protection.

Concussion – Concussion is a change in mental status caused by trauma (shock). It is accompanied by confusion, loss of memory and sometimes loss of consciousness.

Vital signs – These refer to the most basic functions of the body that are necessary to maintain life – for example, body temperature, pulse, respiration (breathing), and blood pressure.

 Progress check

When to call an ambulance

You should get urgent medical advice if a child has had a head injury and:

- loses consciousness (even for a few moments)
- becomes drowsy or confused
- vomits persistently
- has seizures
- has fluid coming from the ears or nose.

How to manage a suspected spinal injury

As first aiders we cannot confirm or rule out a spinal injury. All we can do is *suspect* it, based on the warning signs and on what has happened. In any serious head injury, *always* assume the spinal cord is also injured. The most important thing you can do is **to make sure the child does not move**. This is because any movement can damage the spinal cord even more and lead to a

more serious and permanent injury. Even if the child *is* able to move, if a spinal injury is suspected they should be kept absolutely still and an ambulance should be called immediately. It is the task of medical professionals (at the hospital) to confirm or rule out a spinal injury, usually with X-rays and scans.

First aid for an infant or a child with conditions affecting the eyes, ears or nose

How to manage an infant or a child with foreign bodies in their eyes, ears or nose

Foreign bodies in the eye

A foreign body – such as an eyelash or a speck of dirt – can usually be removed quite easily:

- Sit the child down facing the light and ask her to look up, down, left and right.
- If you can see the object, tilt the child's head back and try to flush the object out out using a jug of water.
- If this fails, use a damp cotton wool swab or handkerchief to lift the object off the eye.
- For objects that are under the upper eyelid, carefully lift the upper eyelid down over the lower eyelid.
- If you cannot remove the object, cover the eye with a clean pad and seek medical assistance.

Important: if the foreign body is metal or glass, or it is embedded in the child's eye, do not try to remove it. Take the child to hospital immediately.

Foreign bodies in the ear

Children often insert objects – such as beads – into their ears. It is important to remove any foreign object as it could cause infection or damage the eardrum if left in.

- If the object is a hard one like a plastic bead, do not try to remove it as you could end up pushing it further in. Take the child to hospital where it can be removed safely.
- If an insect flies into the child's ear, try flushing it out with warm water.
- If this fails, take the child to hospital and reassure him that the object will soon come out.

Foreign bodies in the nose

Young children often push a small object up their nose and then forget about it. After two or three days, the object will cause a nosebleed or a smelly discharge from the nose. The child might develop difficulty in breathing and swelling of the nose.

- Encourage the child to breathe through his mouth and check his nose.
- Take the child to hospital to have the object removed. Do not try to remove it yourself.

How to recognise and manage common eye injuries

Any injury to the eye could have serious consequences for the child's sight, so should be treated as soon as possible. Injuries include chemicals (such as household cleaning products) being splashed in the eyes, injuries resulting in a black eye and foreign bodies in the eye.

How to recognise a chemical burn to the eye

When a chemical is accidentally splashed in the eye, it can cause serious eye damage and even blindness. The child will:

- have a red, inflamed eye that will not stop watering
- be frightened and in severe pain
- have difficulty in opening the affected eye.

How to manage a chemical burn to the eye

- **Wash out the chemical immediately**: flush the affected eye under gently running cold water, keeping the side of the child's head with the unaffected eye uppermost. If holding the child over a basin is difficult, pour water from a jug over the eye. Reassure the child all the time.
- **Cover the injured eye**: use a clean pad of gauze to cover the eye and either call 999 for an ambulance or take the child to hospital.

Treating a black eye

Black eyes are caused by bruising of the skin and underlying tissues around the eye bones. Most of the time, black eyes are minor injuries that, just like any other bruise, will fade with time and disappear. Black eyes can, however, also be a sign of a more significant injury – especially if *both* eyes are black following an injury to the head.

- **Reduce the swelling and alleviate the pain**: place an ice pack wrapped in a soft cloth over the eye. A small bag of frozen peas works well.
- **Consult a doctor** if there appears to be serious damage to the eye itself or to the surrounding bone.

First aid for an infant or a child with a chronic medical condition or sudden illness

How to recognise and manage chronic medical conditions

Sickle cell anaemia

Sickle cell anaemia is an inherited blood condition caused by abnormal **haemoglobin**. Under certain conditions the red blood cells that contain the haemoglobin and are normally round become sickle- or crescent-shaped. They clump together and lodge in the smaller blood vessels, preventing normal blood flow and resulting in **anaemia** (a lack of haemoglobin). In the UK sickle cell anaemia is most common in people of African or Caribbean descent, but may also occur in people from India, Pakistan, the Middle East and the East Mediterranean. It affects about one in 2500 babies born every year.

The features of sickle cell anaemia

Children with sickle cell anaemia can almost always attend a mainstream school but are subject to **crises** that may involve the following:

- **Pain**: this is often severe, occurring in the arms, legs, back and stomach, and is due to the blockage of normal blood flow.
- **Infection**: children with sickle cell anaemia are particularly susceptible to coughs, colds, sore throats, fever and other infectious diseases.
- **Anaemia**: most children with sickle cell anaemia are anaemic; however, they will only feel lethargic and ill if the anaemia is severe.
- **Jaundice**: this may show as a yellow staining of the whites of the eyes.

General treatment and care

Blood transfusions may be necessary. Infections should be treated promptly, and immunisation against all the normal childhood diseases is recommended.

Guidelines for working with children who have sickle cell anaemia

- Make sure the child is always warm and dry. Never let a child become chilled after PE or swimming.
- Make sure the child does not become dehydrated. Allow them to drink more often and much more than normal.
- Give support. The child may find it difficult to come to terms with their condition; make allowances when necessary.

- Know how to recognise a sickle cell crisis – the child:
    - (a) suddenly becomes unwell or appears drowsy
    - (b) complains of severe abdominal or chest pain
    - (c) complains of headache or neck stiffness.
- Contact the parents or carers without delay because the child needs urgent hospital treatment.

Diabetes

Diabetes is a condition in which the amount of glucose (sugar) in the blood is too high because the body is not able to use it properly. Normally the amount of glucose in our blood is carefully controlled by the hormone **insulin**, which helps the glucose to enter the cells where it is used as fuel by the body. Most children who have diabetes will have **Type 1 diabetes**, meaning they can no longer produce insulin because the cells in the pancreas that produce it have been destroyed – and without insulin, the body cannot use glucose.

Signs and symptoms include the following:

- increased thirst
- **breath smells** of pear drops (acetone)
- **frequent passing of urine** – especially at night. Children who have previously been dry at night might start to wet the bed (this is called **enuresis** and is caused by the body trying to rid itself of excess glucose)
- **genital itching** – sometimes leading to thrush (a yeast infection)
- **extreme tiredness** and lack of energy
- loss of appetite
- blurred vision
- **loss of weight**: the amount of weight lost can be quite dramatic – up to 10 per cent of the child's total body weight can be lost in as little as two months. This is caused by the body breaking down protein and fat stores as an alternative source of energy.

Treatment and care

Diabetes cannot be cured, but it can be treated effectively. The aim of the treatment is to keep the **blood glucose** level close to the normal range, so it is neither too high (**hyperglycaemia**) nor too low (**hypoglycaemia**, also known as a **hypo**). Most children with diabetes will be treated by a combination of **insulin** and a **balanced diet**, with the recommendation of regular physical activity.

Insulin has to be injected. It is a protein that would be broken down in the stomach if it were swallowed like a medicine. The majority of children will take **two injections of insulin** a day, one before breakfast and one before the evening meal. They are unlikely to need to inject insulin at school, unless on a school trip. In most cases the equipment will be an **insulin 'pen'** rather than a syringe. The child's parents or carers or a Diabetes Specialist Nurse can demonstrate the device used and discuss where the pen and insulin should be kept while the child is in the setting.

Hypoglycaemia (Hypo)

Hypoglycaemia is the most common complication in diabetes where there is not enough sugar in the blood, usually because of too much insulin. It must be treated promptly to avoid possible brain damage from prolonged low blood sugar levels. **Hypoglycaemic attacks** – or **hypos** – are especially likely to happen **before meals**. They can also happen as a result of:

- too much **insulin**
- **too little food** at any stage of the day
- cold weather
- not enough food to fuel an **activity**
- a **missed meal** or delayed meal or snack
- the child **vomiting**.

How to recognise a hypo

Hypos happen quickly, but most children will have **warning signs** that will alert them, or people around them, to a hypo. Signs include:

- weakness or hunger
- confused or aggressive behaviour
- loss of concentration or coordination
- rapid, shallow breathing
- sweating
- dizziness
- glazed eyes and pallor
- headache
- trembling or shakiness.

First aid: how to manage a hypo

- Stay with the child – never leave them alone or expect them to go and get their own food or drink.
- Sit the child down and reassure him or her.
- Give the child a sugary drink (for example, fizzy non-diet drink) or sweet food.
- If the child recovers quickly after a sweet drink or food, give some more and allow the child to rest.
- If the child does not recover quickly or becomes unconscious, **call an ambulance immediately** and place the child in the recovery position.

Always inform the parents or carers of any hypoglycaemic attack, so that adjustments can be made to the treatment.

Guidelines for meeting the needs of a child with diabetes in an early years setting

- Children with diabetes should be treated as any other child. Diabetes is *not* an illness and children should be encouraged to take part in all the activities and daily routine.
- Make sure that all contact details are up to date – home contact numbers, GP, diabetic specialist nurse, etc.
- Always contact parents or carers immediately if the child becomes unwell, and keep them informed of the child's progress.

- Ensure that there is always a supply of glucose tablets or sweet drinks in the setting.
- When on outings, take a supply of sweet drinks or glucose tablets with you.
- Allow the child to take glucose tablets or snacks when required – most children with diabetes carry glucose tablets with them.
- Make sure all staff members know how to recognise and deal promptly with a child who has a hypoglycaemic attack.
- Always stay with the child if he or she feels unwell, and allow privacy if blood glucose testing is necessary during the day.
- Observe the child carefully during any vigorous exercise, such as swimming or climbing.
- Be understanding if the child shows emotional or behaviour problems caused by the necessary restrictions to their routine.
- Inform the child's parents or carers if you are planning an activity which might involve extra strains and excitement.
- Make sure that the child eats regularly and that cooks are consulted about the child's dietary needs.

How to recognise and manage serious sudden illnesses

Certain illnesses can develop suddenly and can have serious consequences. You need to know what signs to look out for and to get medical help quickly.

Meningitis

Meningitis is an inflammation of the lining of the brain. It is a very serious illness, but if it is detected and treated early, most children make a full recovery. The early symptoms of meningitis – such as fever, irritability, restlessness, vomiting and refusing feeds – are also common with colds and 'flu. However, a baby with meningitis can become seriously ill *within hours*, so it is important to act quickly if meningitis is suspected.

Symptoms of meningitis

Figure 12.04 shows the signs and symptoms of meningitis in babies and toddlers, as well as in children and adults.

The 'glass test'

Press the side or bottom of a glass firmly against the rash. You will be able to see if the rash fades and loses colour under the pressure. If it **does not** change colour, summon medical aid **immediately**. If spots are appearing on the child's body, this could be septicaemia, a very serious bacterial infection described as the 'meningitis rash'.

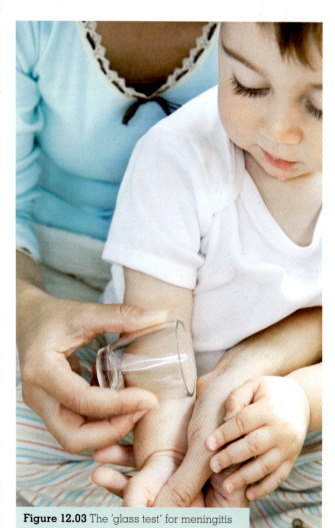

Figure 12.03 The 'glass test' for meningitis

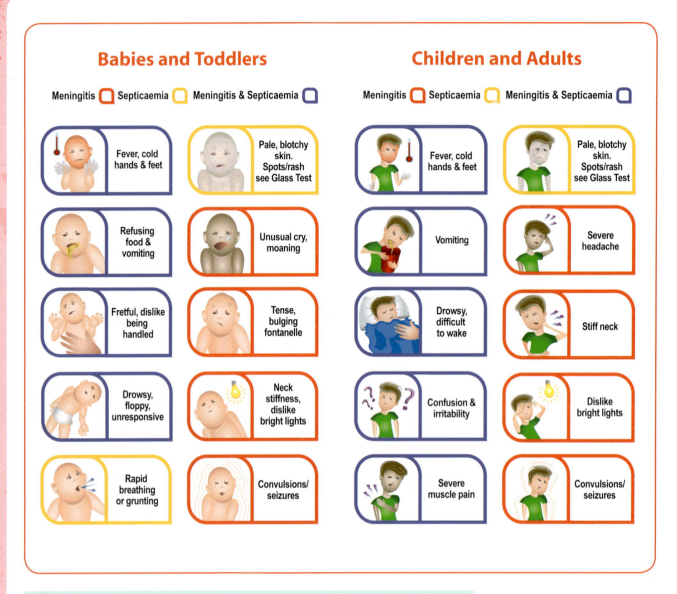

Figure 12.04 Signs and symptoms of meningitis. Image courtesy of the Meningitis Trust.

Febrile convulsions

Febrile convulsions can occur as a result of an illness that causes high temperature, for example, an ear infection or flu. A temperature over 39° C can be dangerous and lead to convulsions. Febrile convulsions are not epilepsy, and do not lead on to epilepsy in later life. They are frightening for parents and carers, but are not usually dangerous.

Signs and symptoms
The child may:

- be flushed and sweaty and her forehead will feel very hot to the touch
- stiffen her limbs, which will twitch or shake; this can go on for up to five minutes
- arch her back and clench her fists
- hold her breath, making her face look blue
- be incontinent of urine or faeces

- become unconscious from the violence of the twitching.

What to do

It is important to remain calm and to stay with the child until the convulsion is over.

- Remove any clothing and open the window.
- Lay the child down on her side somewhere where she cannot hurt herself – for example, on a carpeted floor. Provide support with a cushion or rolled-up blanket.
- Ask a colleague to call for a doctor at once. Call an ambulance if the convulsion lasts for longer than five minutes.
- Use tepid water to sponge over the child – she will soon start to become more alert. The convulsion will stop once she has cooled down.
- Contact the child's parents or carers to let them know what has happened.

Once recovered, encourage the child to drink plenty of water and give the recommended dose of paracetamol-based syrup. This will help to reduce her body temperature and relieve discomfort.

First aid for an infant or a child who is experiencing the effects of extreme heat or cold

Extremes of heat and cold affect babies and young children more than adults. This is because they are less efficient at regulating their body temperature and their sweat glands are not fully developed.

How to recognise and treat the effects of extreme cold for an infant or a child

Hypothermia is a serious condition that occurs when the body temperature drops below 35°C (95°F). It can be fatal if untreated as the vital organs – such as the heart and the liver – slow down and stop. Babies can contract hypothermia from sleeping in a cold room, being underdressed for the weather conditions or from prolonged contact with cold water. Children are most at risk when they have been active outside for a long time in low temperatures, or have become wet – for example, by falling into cold water.

Signs and symptoms in a baby

- unusually quiet and refusing to feed
- may not necessarily change colour.

What to do

- Call a doctor.
- Warm baby gradually by wrapping in a blanket.
- Cuddle to transfer your body warmth to baby.

Signs and symptoms in a child

- shivering
- cold, pale, dry skin
- listlessness or confusion
- weakening pulse
- failing consciousness
- slow, shallow breathing.

What to do

- Give the child a warm – but not hot – bath. When skin colour has returned to normal, help him out of the bath, dry him quickly and wrap him in warm towels or blankets.

- Dress the child warmly (including a hat) and put him to bed, covered with plenty of blankets.
- Ensure that the room is warm and give warm drinks.
- Stay with him until his temperature has returned to normal.

If the body temperature does not return to normal, get the child to hospital as soon as possible.

How to recognise and treat the effects of extreme heat for an infant or child

Heat exhaustion

Heat exhaustion is normally caused by an abnormally high loss of salt and water from the body through excessive sweating. It is not usually serious but the child needs to be cooled down as soon as possible to prevent the more serious condition – heatstroke – from occurring.

Signs and symptoms

The child may have:

- fatigue
- weakness
- clammy skin
- headache
- nausea and/or vomiting
- hyperventilation (rapid breathing).

What to do

- Bring the child indoors or into the shade.
- Undress the child and lay her down in a cool, airy room, if possible with a fan.
- Raise her legs to improve blood flow.
- Help the child to sit up and sip as much cool water as she can manage. Later give chilled water or diluted fruit juice to replace the salts lost from the body.

- Call the doctor for further advice. If the child is too exhausted or ill to eat or drink, intravenous (IV) fluids may be necessary.

If left untreated, heat exhaustion may escalate into heatstroke, which can be fatal.

Heatstroke

Heatstroke is the most serious form of heat illness in children and occurs when the body is unable to cope with prolonged exposure to heat (such as strong sun) and the child quickly becomes dehydrated. Factors that increase the risk for heatstroke include overdressing and extreme physical exertion in hot weather with inadequate fluid intake. Heatstroke can also occur when a child is left in, or becomes accidentally trapped in, a car on a hot day. The child's temperature can soar to 41.1°C (106°F) or even higher, leading to brain damage or even death if it is not quickly treated. Prompt medical treatment is required to bring the body temperature under control.

Signs and symptoms

The child may have:

- sudden headache
- dizziness and confusion
- hot, flushed and dry skin
- rapid deterioration in level of response
- high temperature (40°C (104°F) or above)
- loss of consciousness.

What to do

- Call for **emergency medical help** if the child has been outside in the sun exercising for a long time and shows any of the symptoms above.
- While waiting for help:
  (a) get the child indoors or into the shade
  (b) undress the child and sponge her with tepid water
  (c) do **not** give fluids unless the child is alert.

First aid for an infant or a child who has sustained an electric shock

An electric shock occurs when a person comes into contact with an electrical energy source. Electrical energy flows through a portion of the body, causing a shock. Exposure to electrical energy may result in no injury at all, or it could result in serious damage or death. Burns are the most common injury from electric shock.

Electrical accidents are usually linked with faulty wiring or appliances (such as a badly wired plug) or having wet hands when handling appliances. Another common cause is when children poke objects into plug sockets.

How to safely manage an incident involving electricity

An electric shock can cause burns not only at the point where the current enters the body, but also where it leaves. These burns often appear to be minor, but they may be deep and carry a serious risk of infection.

Signs and symptoms

The child may:

- become unconscious
- have burns
- have problems in breathing.

First aid treatments for electric shock incidents

If you touch a person who is still connected to the electricity supply, then you could suffer an electric shock yourself. The first thing to do therefore is to get the current away from the child – preferably by switching off at the mains.

What to do

- **Do not touch the child** if they are still in contact with the current.
- Break the contact between the child and the electrical supply by switching off the current at the mains, if it can be reached easily.
- If you cannot turn off the mains, you need to get the current away from the child *without* coming into contact with it yourself. For example:
  (a) Stand on some dry insulation material such as a telephone directory.
  (b) Use something made of non-conductive material (such as a wooden broom or a plastic tube) to push the electrical source away from the child.
  (c) Make sure that your hands are dry and that you are not standing on anything that is wet or made of metal.
- Check the child's breathing and for signs of life. Be prepared to begin rescue breaths if needed.
- Put a child who is unconscious but breathing into the **recovery position**.
- If the child has burns, treat these while you are waiting for help.

First aid for an infant or a child with burns or scalds

Almost all burns and scalds occur as the result of accidents, and most of these involve young children. Ten children under the age of five are admitted to hospital in the UK every day as the result of a burn or scald. Children playing with matches and lighters are a frequent cause of house fires, and 46 per cent of all fatal accidents to children take place in house fires.

Hot drinks cause most scalds to children under the age of five. A child's skin is much more sensitive than an adult's skin, and a hot drink can still scald a child 15 minutes after the drink has been made. Hot bathwater is responsible for the highest number of fatal and severe scalding injuries among young children.

Young children are also very vulnerable to sunburn because of their sensitive skin. Children can also suffer burns after contact with cigarettes, matches, cigarette lighters, open fires, ovens and cookers, irons and many other hot surfaces and hot liquids.

How to recognise the severity of burns or scalds to an infant or a child and respond accordingly

- **Burns** occur when the skin is exposed to direct heat or to chemicals, for example fire, sunburn, friction, acid, bleach or garden chemicals.
- **Scalds** occur when the skin is exposed to hot fluids, for example boiling water, steam or hot fat.

Burns and scalds are usually divided into three categories according to how much damage they cause to the skin and underlying tissues:

1. **First-degree or minor burns** are superficial and affect only the outer layer of the skin, making it red and sore.
2. **Second-degree or partial thickness burns** extend below the surface of the skin. The skin looks raw, and blisters form.
3. **Third-degree or full thickness burns** damage the entire layer of the skin and underlying tissues to affect nerves, muscle and fat. The skin looks pale, waxy and charred. Full thickness burns are painless, as the nerves carrying pain signals have been destroyed.

First-degree burns can be treated at home and usually heal in seven to ten days. Second- and third-degree burns are much more serious and require medical attention as there is a risk of infection and shock developing.

How to treat burns and scalds to an infant or a child
Severe burns and scalds

1. The priority is to cool the injury but this should not delay taking the child to hospital.
2. Call for an ambulance immediately.
3. Bathe the area in cold water for at least ten minutes.
4. While cooling the burn, check the child's breathing and level of consciousness and be prepared to resuscitate.

Minor burns and scalds

1. **Cool down the area** by running it under cool water for at least ten minutes or until the pain eases – or soak in cold water for ten minutes. This will prevent the burn from getting worse.
2. **Gently remove any constricting articles** from the injured area before it begins to swell.
3. **Lightly cover the burned area** with a sterile dressing – or you can use cling film, a clean plastic bag or cold, wet cloth (but not wrapping). This will help to protect the sore skin from further irritation and infection.
4. **Stay calm and watch for any signs of shock.** If the child loses consciousness, open the airway, check her breathing and be prepared to begin rescue breaths
5. **DO NOT:**

- use adhesive dressings
- apply lotions, ointments or grease to burn or scald
- break blisters or otherwise interfere.

First aid for an infant or a child who has been poisoned

How poisons enter the body

A poison is a substance that causes injury or illness when it gets into a person's body. Poisons can enter the body in a number of ways; see Table 12.3. Once in the body, poisons can enter the bloodstream and be carried to organs and tissues.

How to recognise and treat an infant or a child affected by common poisonous substances, including plants

Signs and symptoms

(The symptoms will differ depending on the poison and the amount taken.) If poison is swallowed, the child may:

- be red around the mouth
- have stomach pain
- have the smell of the poison on their breath (for example, alcohol)
- be nauseous or vomiting
- be unusually drowsy and possibly become unconscious

Figure 12.05 Treating a minor burn or scald

- have blistering or burns around the mouth and a burning sensation in the throat if a chemical has been swallowed.

If poison is inhaled, the child may:

- be breathing noisily
- have a headache.

Strong poisons can cause seizures or loss of consciousness and coma. The heart and breathing might also stop.

What to do

- Get medical attention immediately.
- Try to identify what the poison was. Try to find out what time the child took it and how much was consumed.
- Check inside the child's mouth and encourage him to spit out any berries or bits of leaf in the mouth. If possible, collect a sample to show the doctor.
- Check the child's circulation and breathing

Different ways in which poison can enter the body	
Swallowed: foods, alcohol, medication, household and garden items, and certain plants.	**Absorbed through the skin**: from plants such as poison ivy, fertilizers or pesticides.
Inhaled: gases, like carbon monoxide from car exhaust, carbon dioxide from sewers, and chlorine from a pool, or fumes from household products such as glue, paint, cleaners or drugs.	**Injected**: bites or stings of insects, spiders, marine life, snakes and other animals, or medications injected with a hypodermic needle.

Table 12.3 Different ways in which poison can enter the body

while waiting for the ambulance. Reassure him.

- If the child is unconscious but breathing, put him in the recovery position.

Important: Never try to make the child vomit if they have swallowed poison. Vomiting can make the condition worse by damaging the stomach and the tubes that carry the food to the stomach.

Sources of information that provide procedures for treating people affected by poisonous substances

Many poisonous products offer specific advice on the label about how to treat accidental swallowing of the contents, and some have a phone number which you can call for advice.

Figure 12.06 Label indicating danger if poison is accidentally swallowed

The **National Poisons Information Service (NPIS)** is approved by the Department of Health, and commissioned by the Health Protection Agency. It provides expert advice on all aspects of acute and chronic poisoning.

First aid for an infant or a child who has been bitten or stung
Animal bites

Any animal bite is hazardous and requires immediate attention. This is because a wide range of potentially dangerous bacteria is found in the saliva of all mammals, which can be passed into the skin and surrounding tissue during a bite. In adults, most animal bites are to their hands, arms, legs or feet. Due to children's smaller size, most bites are to their face and usually involve their lips, nose or cheek. Animal bites often occur as a result of a child becoming over-boisterous with a household pet – usually a dog or a cat.

Toddlers often bite each other when playing together, but the resulting injuries are usually minor and do not normally pose a serious risk to their health.

Insect stings

The most common insect stings are from wasps, bees and hornets. Other insects, such as mosquitoes and gnats, *bite* rather than sting and they do not require any specific first aid treatment. Bee and wasp stings are painful but rarely serious, unless the child has an extreme allergic reaction, also known as anaphylactic shock.

How to recognise the severity of bites and stings to an infant or a child and respond accordingly
Animal bites

An animal bite is minor if:

- the wound is superficial or skin-deep
- it has been caused by a human (such as another child) or a domestic animal that is vaccinated with anti-rabies.

An animal bite is serious if:

- there is a deep puncture wound that may have damaged bones, joints, muscles, tendons or nerves
- there is a possibility of a foreign body, such as a tooth, being embedded in the wound
- the wound is to an area that has a reduced blood supply, such as the nose or ears (wounds to these areas could take longer to heal and have a higher risk of infection)
- there are signs that the wound has become infected – for example, there is swelling and redness around the bite wound and possibly some discharge from the wound area.

Insect stings

All children will have an allergic reaction to a sting because it contains poison and goes directly into the child's body. Although it is rare to have an extreme allergic reaction (anaphylactic shock), it is important that you know what to look out for.

How to recognise and treat bites and stings

Animal bites

Most animal bites can be treated at home, but some more serious wounds require hospital treatment.

What to do

Always seek **immediate** medical attention:

- for all animal bites except very minor dog or cat bites
- if the child receives a bite to the:
  - (a) hands
  - (b) feet
  - (c) scalp or face
  - (d) genitals
  - (e) joint, tendon or ligament areas
  - (f) ears or nose.

For a minor bite wound, do the following:

- Calm and reassure the child, who may be very frightened.
- Wash the wound using warm water and soap, and rinse under running water for at least five minutes.
- Dry the wound carefully but gently with a clean gauze pad or tissue.
- Apply a plaster or sterile dressing.
- Check with the doctor as soon as possible to ensure that the bite is not infected or serious enough to carry the risk of **tetanus**.

For a serious and deep bite wound, you need to do the following:

- **Call an ambulance immediately** or take the child to the hospital.
- Calm and reassure the child.
- Cover the wound with a clean dressing or pad and apply pressure with your hand to stop the bleeding. If possible, raise the affected part above the level of the child's heart.

Insect stings

The following are signs and symptoms of an insect sting:

- child crying: stings from bees and wasps are painful and it is usually obvious that a baby or child has been stung as they will cry as a result of the pain
- a raised white area on an inflamed, reddened area of skin at the site of the sting
- itchiness
- there may be a sting left in the skin – sometimes so small it is not visible to the naked eye.

What to do

- Calm the child down and encourage him to stay as still as possible to slow down the rate of spreading the poison.

- If you can *see* a sting, scrape it off using a flat object such as a credit card or your fingernail. (The sting contains poison and if you use tweezers this may result in more poison being forced into the skin.)
- Once the sting has been removed, apply a cold compress to reduce the pain, swelling and itchiness. (A cold compress can be a flannel or towel soaked in very cold water or a pack of frozen peas wrapped in a dry cloth. Do not apply ice or frozen peas directly to the skin.)
- Leave the cold compress in place for up to ten minutes and reassure the child.

An insect sting in the mouth

A sting in the child's mouth often causes rapid swelling and can lead to breathing problems.

- **Call an ambulance immediately** if you notice this happening.
- If the child is over 12 months old, give him an ice cube to suck or cold water to drink to reduce the swelling.

Important: If the child has a severe allergic reaction to a sting, call an ambulance immediately (see p 208, Chapter 11, Unit PEFAP 001: Paediatric emergency first aid, for more information on anaphylactic shock).

Key term

Tetanus – Sometimes called lockjaw, tetanus can cause painful muscle spasms and stiffness. The bacteria that cause tetanus are found in soil and animal manure, and can enter the body through open wounds. Tetanus can also be caught through animal bites.

Assessment practice

Managing paediatric illness and injury

As you complete each section in this Unit, prepare materials to put in the folder required for assessment purposes.

13 Maintain and support relationships with children and young people: Unit TDA 2.7

Children and young people become confident, independent and most resilient when they are secure in the relationships around them. Relationships take time to become established, because they are based on a growing understanding of one another.

Effective communication helps children and young people to develop confidence, feelings of self-worth and positive relationships with others. It also helps them to grow into adults who have positive feelings about themselves and others.

Learning outcomes

By the end of this chapter you will be able to:

1. Communicate with children and young people.
2. Develop and maintain relationships with children and young people.
3. Support relationships between children and young people and others in the setting.

Communicating with children and young people

(The importance of communicating effectively is discussed in Chapter 1, Unit SHC 21: Introduction to communication in children and young people's settings.)

How parents and other significant adults speak to children and young people is extremely important. When talking with young children, adults tend to:

- emphasise key words
- slow their speech down

- repeat phrases if the child has not understood
- add gestures and expressions to help the child understand the meaning.

This is an example of 'scaffolding' children's learning (see p 88). When talking with babies, adults often talk in 'motherese' or 'parentese': this means they speak slowly, in a higher-pitched voice than usual, and use a lot of repetition (such as 'cootchie, cootchie coo'). Many people use this sort of 'baby talk' unconsciously when talking to very young babies – and often to their pets too!

Progress check

How to communicate with children and young people

- Make **eye contact** and show that you are listening – it is difficult to have a conversation with someone who never looks at you! Do remember, however, that certain cultures consider mutual eye contact to be disrespectful. When talking with very young children, it is usually necessary to stoop down to their level or to sit at a table with them.
- **Listen carefully** to the child's own spoken language and use it as a basis for conversation. Very young children tend to use one or two words to mean any of a number of things; for example, 'drink' can mean 'this is my drink,' 'I want a drink,' 'Where is my drink?' or 'You have got a drink.'
- **Repeat** the child's words in a correct form, or a complete sentence. This checks understanding and provides the child with an accurate model for the future. For example, young children often use speech such as 'feeded' instead of 'fed', 'runned' instead of 'ran'. In checking what they mean, the adult should use the correct term. For example:

  Child: I feeded carrots to my rabbit.
  Adult: Oh, you fed your rabbit some carrots.

- **Be a positive role model**: speak clearly and use correct grammar and patterns of speech.
- **Use open-ended questions**: encourage children and young people to speak by asking 'open' questions which require an answer in phrases and/or sentences rather than a simple 'yes' or 'no'; for example, 'Tell me about your party,' instead of 'Did you have a good time at your party?' This opens up opportunities for the child or young person to talk about a range of different things or one single event of his or her own choice. You can always ask more questions as the conversation progresses to check the information, supply additional vocabulary and correct grammar.
- **Use prompts**: these invite the child or young person to say more, to share ideas and feelings. They also communicate that you are really listening and interested, that their ideas are important, and that you accept and respect what is being said. Examples of prompts: 'Oh, I see.' 'Tell me more.' 'That's interesting.'
- **Listen attentively**: get rid of distractions and pay attention to what the child or young person is saying. At times, adults may need to stop whatever they are doing and just listen. It is difficult to pay close attention to what the child is saying if you are busy trying to read at the same time.
- **Respond sensitively**: remember the importance of **non-verbal communication**. Watch out for when a child or young person seems upset or looks sad; say, 'You seem upset – do you want to tell me about it?'
- **Say 'Please' and 'Thank You' to children and young people**: children and young people deserve the common courtesies that we as adults use with each other. They will learn by imitating the speech and behaviour of adults.
- **Use positive language to help promote self-esteem**: positive language helps give children and young people more self-confidence and helps them to behave better, try harder and achieve more. It communicates love and respect, and also creates an atmosphere in which problems can be discussed openly and understandings can be reached.
- For example: The child has spilt her orange juice on the floor. You could say, 'Look at the mess you've made!' But it would be better to say, 'Here's a cloth. Please wipe the juice up,' and later, 'Thank you for doing such a good job of cleaning the floor.'
- **Do not use inappropriate language that puts children down**: unkind words make the child feel bad, and they prevent effective communication. Avoid unkind words which:
  (a) *ridicule*: for example, 'You're acting just like a baby.'
  (b) *shame*: for example, 'I'm so ashamed of you.'
  (c) *label*: for example, 'You're a naughty boy.'
  Unkind words, spoken without thinking of their results, make the child or young person feel disliked – and result in low self-esteem. More importantly, unkind words do not help; they only make matters worse.
- **Always be positive**: tell children what to do instead of what *not* to do. For example, instead of 'Don't slam the door!' try 'Please shut the door quietly'; instead of 'Don't spill your drink!' try 'Try holding your beaker with both hands.'

Active listening

Listening should be an active process, involving not just hearing, but interpreting, understanding and responding. Being able to attend to and 'actively' listen to what children and young people are saying is important in the development of their self-esteem. When practitioners listen actively, they communicate to children and young people the message that they are important enough to have the adult's undivided attention. Active listening also supports children in solving problems and taking responsibility for their own learning. (Active listening is described in more detail on p 5, Chapter 1, Unit SHC 21: Introduction to communication in children and young people's settings.)

Key term

Active listening – The process of actively seeking to understand the meaning of another person's communication, whether the communication is spoken or conveyed in a different way. Active listening includes the use of verbal and non-verbal skills.

Check that children and young people understand what is communicated

As you may expect, young children *understand* more than they can *express* themselves. They may be able to follow simple instructions (especially if they are accompanied by a gesture, for example, pointing) such as 'give daddy a kiss' or 'fetch your teddy' long before they can actually use sentences. They learn new words – initially names of objects and important people – by listening carefully and copying. Many words which have unstressed syllables – such as 'important' and 'computer' – are learned as 'portant' and 'puter' because these are the sounds that they are able to hear easily.

In Practice

How to show a child or young person that you are actively listening

- ❏ **STOP**: Pay attention. When a child or young person approaches you with something to share, stop what you are doing and pay attention. This lets her know that you are listening and that you value what she is saying.

- ❏ **LOOK**: Make eye contact. Get down to her level, face her directly and make eye contact. Also show that you are listening through body language, such as by smiling and nodding.

- ❏ **LISTEN**: Listen attentively. Focus your attention on what she is saying by listening to her words and tone of voice. Listen carefully to what she *actually* says as well as what she might be *trying* to say.

- ❏ **RESPOND**: Respond appropriately. Having listened carefully to what has been said, respond appropriately. This could mean that you paraphrase what she has just said, ask open-ended questions, or prompt her to say more, by saying 'That's interesting' or 'Oh, I see.'

The developmental level of the individual child's understanding will vary in every group. Practitioners may have to simplify their language and use gestures or signs to help children who are struggling to understand.

Developing and maintaining relationships with children and young people

It is important to establish appropriate and effective relationships with all the people you encounter in your work. Relationships begin even before a baby is born. They begin with the care and attention that babies receive while they are in the womb. **Bonding** is the term that is commonly used to describe the strong attachment between a baby and the important people in the baby's life. It used to be thought that babies only truly bonded with their mothers, but research shows that babies can bond to a number of important or significant people. Babies can form an attachment with a variety of others, including:

Their grandparents

Their brothers and sisters

Their mother and father

Those who care for them outside the home

Their foster carer

Figure 13.01

Establishing rapport and respectful, trusting relationships

In line with the **CACHE values**, you need to ensure that the child or young person is at the centre of your practice – that their needs are **paramount**.

Treat children and young people with respect

- Give only essential directions and allow children and young people to make **choices**.
- Set **appropriate directions** which are realistic and consistent.
- Ask **open-ended questions** to encourage language development.
- **Avoid labelling** children and young people.
- Be **warm** and **positive** in a way which affirms children and young people.

Value and respect children and young people

- **Listen** to them.
- **Do not impose your own agendas** on them.
- **Do not single** out a child for special attention.
- Ensure that children **maintain control over their own play**.
- Be friendly, courteous and **sensitive to their needs**.
- Praise and **motivate** them; display their work.
- **Speak *to*** the child, not *at* the child; with young children, this means getting down to their level; with young people you should ensure you maintain eye contact.
- Respect their **individuality**.
- Develop a sense of **trust and caring** with each child and young person.

Early years practitioners are often concerned, or feel that parents are anxious, about young children becoming too attached to staff. However, babies and young children *need* to form close attachments with significant adults in their lives, and they cannot become too closely attached. Some young children spend many hours in group settings outside the home; they need and ought to develop attachments to their **key person**.

Parents who work long hours may experience a conflict of emotions. They want their child to be happy and secure in nursery care, but they do not want to feel forgotten or pushed out; parents often feel a real anxiety when their child shows affection for their key person.

Physical contact with babies, children and young people

Babies and very young children need physical contact – they need to be held and cuddled in order to develop emotionally. Hugging a baby, comforting a child when they are upset, putting a plaster on them, changing their wet pants – all of these are ways in which adults care for young children every day.

However, there is a growing concern among child care professionals about *touching* children in their care. Researchers say that there is anxiety and uncertainty about what is acceptable and what is not acceptable when it comes to innocent physical contact with children. If teachers and other child care professionals are no longer allowed to offer comforting hugs – or sometimes even to put on a plaster or sun cream – their relationship with the children they look after will certainly suffer. Your setting should have a **code of conduct** that will give clear guidelines on appropriate physical contact with the children or young people in your care. What is appropriate physical contact with a baby or toddler, such as hugging them when upset or sitting them on your lap to explain something, will not be seen as appropriate with an older child.

Giving individual attention

It is important to remember that your relationship with the children or young people in your care is a professional one. You should always be friendly and approachable but not try to take the place of the child's parents. Similarly, you should communicate with each child at a level which is appropriate to their stage of development and their holistic needs – you should not act as a child would when interacting with them. Children and young people need to feel safe and secure, and they need practitioners to react predictably to situations, showing fairness and consistency. If parents and staff are not consistent in their approaches, children become unsettled and confused, and they do not know what is expected of them. Behaviour then deteriorates, as they have no real understanding of the acceptable boundaries. All children and young people need care, attention, support and practical help, but as each person is unique, each will have different needs. It is important that practitioners do the following:

- **Address each child's needs**: for example, a confident, talkative child or a child with behavioural difficulties may take up a lot of your time, but it is important to watch out for the quiet child who seems not to need you when playing quietly alone.
- **Spend time with all the children in your care**: a team approach to planning activities will help to make sure that a balance is achieved for all, and that each child receives individual attention whenever possible.

Giving supportive and realistic responses

The basis of positive relationships with children and young people is effective communication. We have already seen how important it is to listen to children and young people. Practitioners should encourage children to interact with them, by encouraging two-way conversations – both listening and responding to children.

Case Study — A problem relationship in the nursery

Kate is a key person for six children in a day nursery. On Wednesdays, four of her key children attend nursery. One of the children, Jodie, has recently started at the nursery and was difficult to settle. Her mother spent a lot of time accompanying her and getting to know the staff, particularly Kate, to whom she warmed immediately and who struck up a trusting, professional relationship with her to help the family with their transition from using a childminder as efficiently as possible. As a result, Jodie relies heavily on Kate's presence in the room and will cry if she is handed over to another staff member in the morning.

Jodie has been used to one-to-one care for the first two years of her life. Throughout the day, she becomes tearful during noisy play and group activities. Outside, while the other children run around, Jodie holds Kate's hand and sucks her thumb, watching the other children in silence. Kate encourages Jodie to run around with her and the other children, but Jodie is not keen and Kate soon gives in, sitting on the garden bench with Jodie on her lap. The Nursery Manager sees this happen for a few days and reminds all the staff that they should not be sitting down when outside with the children; this is an active time for them, and they should be promoting physical play.

Other staff members begin to feel the strain as Jodie demands Kate's time and she neglects her other key children. Kate feels bad, but does not know what to do. One day, Kate is off work. Jodie spends the day following another staff member around, is very tearful and will not settle for her lunchtime nap. In the afternoon, she becomes so upset that her mum has to be called to take her home.

Note: Kate has a close bond with Jodie, which is a positive aspect of the relationship between key worker and the child. However, it is not a healthy bond, and Jodie is the person who seems worst affected.

1 Can you list
  a) the reasons why this is not a healthy bond in a nursery setting
  b) how it is affecting Jodie negatively
  c) what the consequences might be for her.
2 Who is affected by Kate's 'favouritism'? Think about outside the nursery setting as well. How is each of the people in your list affected?
3 What could Kate have done differently to avoid this happening?
4 What actions could be taken now by Kate, the Room Leader and the Nursery Manager to solve the problem?

Providing reasons for your actions

You should always be willing to give the reasons for your actions to the children and young people in your setting, unless there is an overriding concern, such as a safeguarding issue. If you need to refer a child or young person to your manager for assessment, then you should explain why you have done this. In the case of a baby or very young child, then you would still refer to your superior and he or she, in turn,

In Practice

Listening and responding to children and young people

- **Encourage children and young people to ask questions and make suggestions**: this will promote curiosity, extend the children's knowledge and help their understanding of new concepts. For example, you could say, 'I wonder what would happen if . . .?' 'Why do you think the train sank to the bottom of the water?'

- **Listen carefully to children and young people, and show interest**: this will help them to feel valued and appreciated, and to communicate well with you and with others.

- **Always thank them for their ideas**: respond positively, for example, saying, 'That's an interesting idea.'

- **Give your full attention to children and young people when they are expressing their ideas**: when a child is trying to explain something to you, make sure you give her your full attention and give her time to finish what she wants to say.

- **Teach children and young people how to listen attentively**: you should be a positive role model by showing through your own words and actions how to be an active listener, for example, at circle time.

- **Keep the conversation going in an interesting way**: use prompting questions and show empathy. For example, if a child tells you they are going to the seaside at the weekend, prompt them to express themselves further by saying: 'I think that is really exciting for you. Will you come in and tell me all about it on Monday?'

- **Avoid interrupting children or young people when they are telling you something**: if you *do* have to attend to something else, explain that you have to leave for a moment but that you would like to hear what they have to say – and remember to do this!

making process, you also need to let them know how and why you have reached a decision that concerns them. If you have to withdraw a piece of equipment from the outside play area – such as a trike that you notice is faulty – then you should explain why you have done so and reassure the children that it will be mended as soon as possible. If a young person confides in you about an aspect of sexual health such as teenage pregnancy or a sexually transmitted illness, you should not tell anyone else until you have told the young person what your intended actions are. Then you will need to consult your manager to find out about the rules of confidentiality.

Encouraging children and young people to make choices

So much of the day-to-day lives of children and young people is controlled and determined by adults – often with safety considerations in mind. Children need opportunities to make choices for themselves and to take control of some aspect of their lives, developing their preferences and dislikes. Children who are regularly encouraged to make decisions experience increased self-esteem and reduced feelings of frustration and aggression. They also learn to have self-confidence and to take on responsibility.

A detached youth work project

Detached youth work is a method of providing social education to young people who may not otherwise have access to youth services. The youth worker makes contact with young people in the places they choose to congregate and any resulting projects are negotiated between the worker and the young people. Youth workers in Surrey carried out a survey in an isolated small

would inform the child's parents or carers about the action taken. As you will be supporting children and young people in the decision-

In Practice

Involving children and young people in decision-making

By involving children in decision-making, practitioners are 'telling' them that they are important, and that what they think and feel is important to both the staff and the setting as a whole.

Practitioners could offer children and young people in their setting the following opportunities:

❏ select activities to put out for groups to play with

❏ choose the story at storytime

❏ decide what equipment to put outside

❏ choose how to reorganise resources

❏ consult young people about issues important to them.

town; they found that what the young people really wanted were opportunities to play football (mostly boys) and somewhere to practise street dancing (mostly girls). Arrangements were made to provide street dance sessions in a village hall and the evenings were always well attended.

Learning to negotiate

Learning to negotiate with others is a skill that children and young people will learn if given these kinds of opportunities, and children new to the setting may settle in more easily if they have been involved in making decisions. At first the decision-making could be a simple choice between two alternatives within the setting. For example, 'Would you like to build with these wooden blocks or do this jigsaw?' 'Would you like milk or water today?' Enabling children to make decisions in this way empowers them and they learn to consider the views and opinions of other children, to weigh them up and to use this knowledge to make an informed decision. These

are all important skills that we need throughout life.

Babies and young children

Babies and children under the age of two years are not generally able to negotiate. A toddler who has just snatched a toy from another child will not be able to appreciate the need for negotiation. In these circumstances, the best ploy is to distract the child with a different toy and to persuade them that the alternative is superior. Older children will appreciate games with rules and also boundaries when playing with others and sharing toys.

Using circle time to discuss questions about negotiation is a popular activity in many early years settings. Many practitioners use a story or puppets to discuss sharing and taking turns. Offering young children a scenario with a problem and asking them to come up with solutions helps their reasoning skills and encourages empathy, which is a vital factor within negotiation.

Supporting relationships between children and young people and others in the setting

Supporting effective communication

There are many advantages in involving children and young people in the organisation of the setting.

● **Services are appropriate for their needs**: insights gained from children can help adults work more effectively. It can also help to ensure that the services provided are relevant to children's needs.

- **Taking into account the needs of others**: children who learn to express their own needs also learn to consider the needs of others. They may develop skills of cooperation, negotiation and problem-solving.
- **Respect and understanding**: children and parents or carers often work together. This can make relationships stronger and promote greater understanding and respect
- **Promoting self-esteem and self-worth**: when you involve children and you respect their ideas and their capabilities, their confidence and self-esteem are boosted.

It is important to recognise that young people have a right to participate in the key decisions that affect their lives. Article 12 of the United Nations Convention on the Rights of the Child states that children and young people should have the opportunity to express their views on matters that concern them and to have those views taken into account when decisions are made. It is generally agreed that participation by young people results in real benefits for themselves and for the organisations that consult them. These benefits include:

- skills development – communication, negotiation and teamwork
- educational experience
- promoting a sense of responsibility for oneself and others
- being enjoyable and sociable
- raising self-esteem.

Recent research into consultation with pupils found that children's learning experiences could be enhanced if tasks were more closely aligned with the social worlds in which they lived – both inside and outside the classroom. Children said they found it helpful when teachers used materials, objects and images with which they were already familiar.

Understanding other people's individuality, diversity and differences

In order for children to be well integrated into the setting and into wider society, they need to

---

Case Study — An after-school club for children aged five to six

Practitioners wanted to find out how children felt about their after-school clubs. Although parents and carers had important views to contribute, the practitioners realised that children also had their own perspectives. When talking with the children, the practitioners found that:

- the children were unhappy about the lighting – it was too gloomy in some clubs
- some children said they became hungry and wished some food was provided
- some children felt tired and wished there was somewhere for them to have a quiet time, not just the structured activities

- they were also concerned about their environment – the paint on the walls, the lighting and their access to the garden and so on.

These were all legitimate and important insights that affected how those children experienced their care and which could have easily been overlooked by adults, who may have a different set of concerns. By placing the child at the centre of their practice, the practitioners developed a greater understanding of the sorts of factors that might affect children's lives.

learn to be tolerant and accepting of others, and to value differences between individuals. Practitioners can encourage children and young people to accept and value these differences in many ways.

Develop an understanding of each child or young person as an individual

Take every opportunity to find out more about the individual children in your care. Encourage general conversations about children's interests and home lives when supervising an activity.

Celebrate the individuality of each child or young person

You could organise a display that draws attention to each child's particular interests – for example, photos of each child doing their favourite activity with statements alongside, such as 'Hannah likes reading' or 'Bhavin likes to play on the computer.'

Help children and young people to understand their own feelings

A child who is showing signs of anger or frustration can be helped to understand these feelings if you respond by helping her to put those feelings into words; for example, 'I can see you are very cross right now. What's happened?'

Showing respect for other people's feelings and points of view

Only when children have learned that other people have feelings of their own can they start to develop empathy and concern for the wellbeing of others. They will then be able to share their feelings with other people and to show compassion to friends who are upset. This usually happens at around the age of three to four years.

Children show respect for others when they are treated with respect themselves. Adults should always model respectful and courteous behaviour

Case Study   The Youth Café Project

The Youth Café Project is for young people aged 13–19. Based aboard a specially customised double-decker bus, this is a place designed specifically with young people in mind. You can meet up with old friends, make some new ones, get involved in workshops from graffiti to music production, or just come and hang out. The bus is also a place which offers access to information and support on issues such as lifestyle, school and careers, to name but a few. We also offer information and support on issues such as sex, drugs and relationships, as well as providing free condoms where and when appropriate. The bus is also home to an onboard café, which

sells both hot and cold drinks, and snacks at a low cost. The bus exists because there are areas of the borough without dedicated youth clubs, centres or projects. The bus's mobility allows us to provide these important services to those who would otherwise miss out. Young people can choose what we do and how we spend our time. We welcome new ideas for activities or workshops that may not already be included but may be of interest to you. On the bus you can expect to be treated with respect by others and others should expect the same from you. We maintain a friendly environment here and everybody is welcome.

Figure 13.02 Young people enjoy relaxing together in an informal setting

– both to children and to their colleagues. You can show respect for others by following simple rules of courtesy; that is, by treating other people as you would wish to be treated yourself. From the earliest age, children can learn when to say 'please', 'thank you' and 'sorry' – all markers of respect for other people's feelings.

Key term

Empathy – Understanding how others feel.

Developing group agreements

Children and young people need to 'take ownership' of their interactions with one another. When developing group agreements they need to:

- Be able to share with others and to take turns
- Be able to negotiate – 'If you have your turn now then it's my turn next'
- Identify the positive aspects of the ways in which they interact with each other

In Practice

Building and maintaining relationships with young people

- ❏ Give them the opportunity to ask questions and listen to what they are saying.
- ❏ Find out whether they have any concerns.
- ❏ Ask them about the issues that affect and interest them.
- ❏ Tell them about potential work with young people's issues.
- ❏ Link young people into other services and agencies.
- ❏ Do nothing if they ask for nothing, just provide a listening ear and support.
- ❏ Provide emotional support.
- ❏ Learn from the young person.

- Consider the needs of other children and young people
- Be able to consider alternative ways of acting.

Supporting children to deal with conflict for themselves

Children need to be able to deal with conflict effectively. This is an important life skill and will help children and young people to resolve conflicts in an assertive but not aggressive manner. They will be more confident in situations if they feel they can stand up for themselves, without needing others to look out for them. If you see children arguing or fighting, try not to step in straightaway. Most conflicts in early childhood relate to sharing and taking turns. For example, if two children are arguing over whose turn it is to use the computer, stay nearby and observe, and allow the children time to sort the dispute out for themselves. (Only step in immediately if a child is being hurt – or is at risk of being hurt.)

If you *do* decide to intervene:

- Give both children the opportunity to be heard without interruption.
- Invite the children to come up with their own solutions to the problem.
- Acknowledge the feelings and emotions from *both* sides.
- Suggest one or two solutions – if necessary.

- Acknowledge the attempts made to resolve conflict: 'That's seems like a good idea, Tom. What do you think, Ivan?'

Supporting young people to resolve conflict

Conflict can often be constructive rather than destructive, if dealt with in the right way. Young people need to learn how to identify conflict and how to resolve it in a positive fashion. This involves learning the following interpersonal skills:

- *Identification of the problem*: What exactly is the conflict or issue and how did it occur?
- *Discussion:* What are the good options for conflict resolution and what are the bad ones?
- *Cooperation:* It helps to allow young people to act out their feelings in order to decide how these options will affect everyone involved.
- *Negotiation:* After considering everyone's viewpoint, which option is the best one to take?

Assessment for Unit MU10

This is a skills/competency unit only. Assessment by a CACHE task is not applicable.

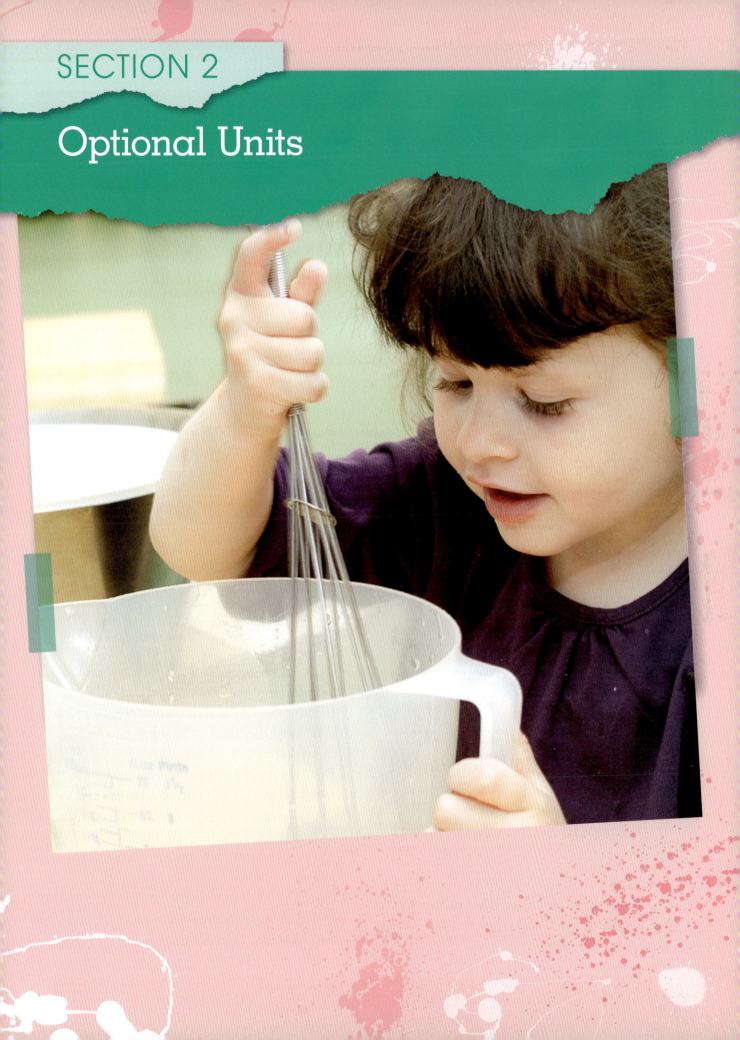

SECTION 2

Optional Units

14 Support children and young people with disabilities and special educational needs: Unit TDA 2.15

This chapter provides the knowledge and skills to support disabled children and young people and those with special educational needs. It explores their rights and needs, and methods of supporting their inclusion and participation in the full range of activities and experiences provided by the setting.

> ## Learning outcomes
>
> By the end of this chapter you will:
>
> 1. Know the rights of disabled children and young people and those with special educational needs.
> 2. Understand the disabilities and/or special educational needs of children and young people in own care.
> 3. Be able to contribute to the inclusion of children and young people with disabilities and special educational needs.
> 4. Be able to support disabled children and young people and those with special educational needs to participate in the full range of activities and experiences.

The rights of disabled children and young people and those with special educational needs

The human rights of disabled children

Like all children, disabled children have important rights under the **UN Convention on the Rights of the Child**. These rights can be summarised as follows:

- Disabled children have the human right to be included in their local community and to do the kinds of things that non-disabled children do. They have the right to support to help them do this.
- Disabled children have the human right to take part in play and leisure activities and to freely express themselves in cultural and artistic ways. They have the right to equal access to cultural, artistic, recreational and leisure activities.
- Disabled children have the human right to live with their parents unless this is not in their best interests. They have the right to services

Acts affecting the lives of children and young people with special needs	
The Education Act 1996	The Children Act 2004
The Disability Discrimination Act 2005	The Special Needs and Disability Act (SENDA) 2001
The Education (Additional Support for Learning) (Scotland) Act 2004	

Table 14.1 The main Acts relevant to children and young people with special needs

to make it possible for their families to look after them.

- Disabled children have the human right to express their views and for these to be taken into account. They also have the right to freedom of expression.
- Disabled children who spend time away from home because they need care or treatment have the human right to a review of the placement at regular intervals.
- Disabled children who do not live with their families, temporarily or permanently, have the human right to special protection and assistance which takes account of their ethnic, religious, cultural and linguistic background.

Every Disabled Child Matters

Every Disabled Child Matters is a campaign to make sure disabled children and their families get the same rights as everyone else. The aims of the campaign are for disabled children and their families to:

- have the same rights as everyone else so that they are fully included in society
- get the services and support they need to live their lives in the way they want
- stop living in poverty
- receive education that meets their needs
- have their say about services for disabled children.

The legal entitlements of disabled children and young people and those with special educational needs

A child or young person with **special needs** may need extra or different help at school or at home because of:

- physical difficulties or disability
- a visual or hearing impairment
- a serious medical condition
- communication problems
- emotional, social and behavioural difficulties
- **OR** a combination of any of these.

The main **Acts** that have shaped the way in which children and young people with special needs are cared for and educated today are shown in Table 14.1.

The Special Educational Needs Code of Practice 2002

The **SEN Code** includes the following principles:

- The special needs of children will be met in mainstream schools – wherever possible.
- Children with special educational needs should be offered full access to a broad, balanced and relevant education, including an appropriate curriculum for the EYFS Early Years Foundation Stage (in England) and the National Curriculum.

Every registered childcare setting must have a **Special Educational Needs Coordinator**

(SENCO) – a member of staff who takes responsibility for special education needs. The SENCO is responsible for:

- making sure that all children with special educational needs are being helped appropriately, ensuring liaison with parents and other professionals.
- talking to and advising any member of staff who is concerned about a child.
- coordinating provision for children with special needs.
- making sure all written records are completed and appropriate Individual Education Plans are in place.
- ensuring relevant background information about individual children is collected, recorded and updated.
- contacting the relevant Area SENCO at the earliest possible stage where there is a concern.

Special Educational Needs Policy

Every setting must have a Special Educational Needs policy. This should include information about:

- how they identify and make provision for children and young people with special educational needs
- the facilities they have, including those which increase access for pupils who are disabled, and access to the curriculum
- how resources are allocated to and among pupils with special educational needs
- how they enable pupils with special educational needs to engage in activities of the school, together with pupils who do not have additional needs
- how the governing body evaluates the success of the school's work with pupils with special educational needs
- their arrangements for dealing with complaints from parents.

Assessment and intervention frameworks

In the UK about 17 per cent of all schoolchildren have a special educational need. Most (around 60 per cent) are taught in **mainstream** schools, where they receive additional help from a range of services. Children with special educational needs but *without* a **statement** (see below) will have their needs met through intervention programmes called Early Years Action or Early Years Action Plus. When children reach school age, these are called School Action and School Action Plus.

Assessment

The Framework in England that enables assessment of the development and progress of all young children is the Early Years Foundation Stage (EYFS). The EYFS focuses on six areas of learning and development:

- personal, social and emotional development
- communication, language and literacy
- problem solving, reasoning and numeracy
- knowledge and understanding of the world
- physical development
- creative development.

Practitioners help to assess each child's development using the EYFS Profile.

The Statement of Special Educational Needs

The Statement of Special Educational Needs is a legal document produced by LEAs following multi-professional assessment and contributions from parents or carers. It specifies the precise nature of the child's assessed difficulties and educational needs, and the special or additional provision that would be made in order to meet that pupil's needs. Statements must then be reviewed at least annually.

An assessment must take account of the following five factors:

1. **Physical factors** – the child's particular illness or condition.

2. **Psychological and emotional factors** – the child's intellectual ability and levels of anxiety or depression will lead to different needs and priorities; for example, severe anxiety may adversely affect all daily activities, and therefore will need to be attended to first.

3. **Sociocultural factors** – the child's needs will be influenced by being part of a family, the family's background and the relationships within the family. The individual's wider community and the social class to which they belong are also influential.

4. **Environmental factors** – a child living in a cold, damp house with an outside toilet will have different needs from one who is more comfortably housed.

5. **Political and economic factors** – poverty or belonging to a disadvantaged group leads to less choice in day-to-day living.

Key term

Assessment – Through observing children and by making notes when necessary, practitioners can make professional judgements about children's achievements and decide on the next steps in learning. They can also exchange information with parents about how children are progressing.

The Common Assessment Framework for children and young people (CAF)

The government's aim is that every child will have the support they need to achieve the following Every Child Matters (ECM) outcomes – which can be remembered using the acronym SHEEP:

S   Stay **S**afe.

H   Be **H**ealthy.

E   **E**njoy and achieve.

E   Achieve **E**conomic wellbeing.

P   Make a **P**ositive contribution.

The CAF is an assessment designed for *universal* services (health, education and early years services). A practitioner's decision to undertake a common assessment is dependent on whether:

- the child or young person is not achieving one or more of the five priority ECM outcomes (SHEEP)
- there is uncertainty about the difficulty
- the support of another agency may be needed.

For more information about the CAF, see Chapter 10, Unit MU 2.9: Understand partnership working in services for children and young people.

If observation and assessment lead to concerns about any area of a child or young person's development, senior practitioners should always discuss these concerns with the child's parents or carers first. The SENCO can help settings to plan activities and experiences that will support specific areas of development. The SENCO will also advise settings if it is necessary to seek extra information and advice from other professionals, such as an educational psychologist or a speech and language therapist.

Intervention

If a child has a diagnosed special need or disability – or if assessment reveals a special need, they are likely to be in need of some kind of intervention – to offer support for them and for their family.

The Early Support programme

Early Support is an integral part of the delivery of the EYFS for babies and young children under five with disabilities or emerging special educational needs. It helps staff in early years settings to identify impairments early and to work in partnership with families and other services to provide the best possible care and support for young disabled children. An important part of the Early Support programme is the **Family File**, which the family holds. The Family File:

- is used by the professionals and the family together, to plan appropriate support to be provided for the child
- informs the family about the different professionals they may meet and what their role is
- explains how the different health, education and social services can provide support
- allows parents and carers to share information about their child with the professionals they meet, without having to say the same things to every new person
- provides information about sources of financial support and child care.

The benefits of early recognition and intervention

Sometimes parents are unaware that their child's development is delayed, especially in the case of their first or oldest child. On other occasions, parents may have felt that 'something is not quite right', but have either been anxious about sharing their worries, or have talked to other professionals but not been fully understood. Sometimes a child can appear to be developing well during a check-up, but have difficulties in less structured environments or in the company of other children. Early identification means that the child can be helped while still very young. In many cases, prompt intervention and support early on can prevent or minimise later difficulties.

Individual plans

Every child with special educational needs should have an **Individual Education Plan (IEP)**. The IEP's purpose is to detail the ways in which an individual child will be helped; for example:

- what special help is being given
- who will provide the help
- how often the child will receive the help
- targets for the child
- how and when the child's progress will be checked
- what help parents can give their child at home.

The child's teacher is responsible for the planning and should discuss the IEP with the parents or carers and with their child, whenever possible. IEPs are usually linked to the main areas of language, literacy, mathematics and behaviour and social skills. Sometimes the school or early education setting will *not* write an IEP but will record how they are meeting the child's needs in a different way, perhaps as part of the whole-class lesson plans. They will record the child's progress in the same way as they do for all the other children.

In addition, practitioners should:

- assess how accessible the setting is for children who use wheelchairs or walking frames or who are learning English as an additional language, and take appropriate action to include a wider range of children
- work together with professionals from other agencies, such as local and community health services, to provide the best learning opportunities for individual children.

Case Study   The importance of early recognition

When Matthew, Emma and their three-and-a-half-year-old daughter, Chloe, went on holiday to Portugal with another family, they found themselves in a nightmare situation. During the holiday, Chloe had not only pushed another child into the deep end of a swimming pool, where he had to be rescued by lifeguards, but she had also shoved an entire restaurant table into the harbour. For Matthew and Emma, it was the last straw. They had been concerned for some time that Chloe's development was slow, her hearing variable and her speech poor. But whenever they raised their anxieties with health professionals they were told not to worry. Chloe had failed her first hearing test but had passed a subsequent one and a speech test at 18 months. After the disastrous holiday, Matthew and Emma were so desperate that they consulted a child psychologist, who advised them to try removing their attention from Chloe for a short while every time she 'misbehaved'. After a few weeks, Chloe was transformed into a calm, compliant child. Now Emma believes it was the cruellest thing she has ever done and feels guilty about the whole episode.

What Matthew and Emma now know is that Chloe is deaf. In fact, she was born deaf. But even after numerous tests, Chloe's deafness was not diagnosed until she was nearly four years old. Chloe had somehow taught herself to lip-read. Matthew and Emma began to do their own hearing tests on Chloe; when they hid from her while speaking, they realised that she failed to respond – it was obvious she couldn't hear them. Chloe was just about to start school at four when she was diagnosed with a moderate-to-severe hearing loss after a thorough hospital hearing check. She was fitted with hearing aids. Matthew remembers the moment well: 'She smiled the most enormous smile of her whole life,' he says. Now six years old, Chloe is still struggling to catch up with her 'normal hearing' peers. Matthew and Emma just wish they had known what to look for in those early years.

(Chloe's is a true story. Since she was born, the otoacoustic emissions test (OET) – a hearing screen that might have identified her hearing impairment – has been routinely offered to all babies in the UK within a few days of birth.)

The principles of inclusive practice

All children have the right to have their needs met in the best way for them. It is important that they are seen as being part of the community, even if they need additional help to live a full life within the community. Inclusion refers to everyone, no matter the additional support needs of an individual, the gender or sexual preference, religion, race or cultural background.

Medical and social models of disability

The way you work with children and young people with learning difficulties and/or disabilities could be profoundly affected by the way you think about disability. It is important to appreciate the effects disability and impairment can have on the individual, by understanding the medical model and the social model of disability.

The medical model of disability:

- sees the person as deficient and focuses on the disability rather than the person
- treats the person as a sick patient
- focuses on how to 'fix' or 'cure' the impairment
- assesses the person by looking at all the things they 'can't do'
- seeks to 'adapt' the person to fit the non-disabled 'normal' environment, often by medical means
- often labels the person according to their impairment: for example, a Down's person, a diabetic, or an epileptic.

The social model of disability:

- views the discrimination and prejudice experienced by people who have a disability as a direct result of the barriers put up by society
- focuses on the child's or young person's strengths and abilities – what they 'can do' rather than what they 'can't do'
- sees disabled children and young people as active members of their families, settings and society
- focuses on the person, not on their disability.

Children and young people first

Although we are used to using the term 'special needs', the needs of children and young people are the same as those of all children. In other words, children are always children first, and the special need is secondary. This is why the social model of disability is important, as it encourages you to look at the child first, not the disability or impairment.

Every child – regardless of having a special need – needs to:

- feel welcome
- feel safe, both physically and emotionally
- have friends and to feel as if they belong

- be encouraged to live up to their potential
- be celebrated for his or her uniqueness.

In Practice

Inclusive practice

Inclusive practice is important in child care and education settings because:

- ❏ it promotes equality of opportunity for all children
- ❏ it encourages the development of more flexible attitudes, policies and everyday practices
- ❏ it promotes community integration through understanding of and respect for others
- ❏ it recognises and celebrates diversity.

Key term

Inclusion – 'Inclusion is a process of identifying, understanding and breaking down barriers to participation and belonging.' (Early Childhood Forum)

Progress check

Special educational needs

- Know how to define a special educational need (SEN).
- Understand how an individual plan helps a child with special needs.
- Know how to define inclusion.
- Understand the importance of using the social model of disability.

Disabilities and/or special educational needs of children and young people

Children with disabilities and/or special educational needs have needs that are 'in

THE INCLUSION CHARTER

Inclusion is a right

All children have the right to be included in every aspect of society. Disabled children should not have to ask or fight to be included in the things that other children do. Inclusion is a right in UK law (the Disability Discrimination Acts) and international law (UN Conventions on the Rights of the Child and the Rights of Persons with Disabilities).

Inclusion is about all of life

"We want to be part of society"

Inclusion is a process of change where all children are valued in every aspect of their life and in the life of their community.

Inclusion means no-one is left out

Inclusion means all children, whatever their impairment, wherever they live and however they communicate.

Inclusion starts early

From the very earliest age, disabled children should have the right to play and learn with other children, enjoying all the aspects of life and friendships that other children do.

Inclusion means everyone is heard

"We want to be respected"

All children have a right to communicate. Some express their views without using speech and services must respond.

Inclusion is everyone's responsibility

"We want to go where other children go"

Disabled children are not just the responsibility of specialist disability services. All services need to ensure that disabled children can take part in everything they do.

Inclusion is built in

Everyone who works with children must have training in disability equality to equip them with the skills to ensure disabled children are able to participate.

Inclusion benefits everyone

Inclusion benefits all children and young people, as well as adults. It promotes citizenship and helps create a society that celebrates difference and is at ease with itself.

Inclusion works

All over the country, right now, there are thousands of examples where inclusion is working. Disabled children can and should be included in every area of life.

Children & Young People Now

www.cypnow.co.uk

disabled

Every Child Matters

www.edcm.org.uk/inclusioncharter

Supported by
Contact a Family
Council for Disabled Children
Mencap
Special Educational Consortium

Figure 14.01 The Inclusion Charter

addition' to the general needs of children. Some children have a very obvious and well-researched **disability**, such as Down's syndrome or cerebral palsy; others may have a specific learning difficulty such as dyslexia. What defines them as children with special needs is the fact that they need *additional support* in some area of development, care or education compared with other children.

The range of disabilities and special needs is enormous, from severe to relatively minor, from temporary or short-lived to permanent. Children with special needs may be grouped into the following categories:

Main categories of special needs

- **Physical disability**: needs related to problems with mobility or coordination, such as cerebral palsy, spina bifida or muscular dystrophy.
- **Speech or communication difficulties**: needs related to communication problems such as delayed language, difficulties in articulation or stuttering.
- **Specific learning difficulties** (SLD): needs related to problems usually confined to the areas of reading, writing and numeracy; dyslexia is a term often applied to difficulty in developing literacy skills.
- **Medical conditions**: needs related to medical conditions such as cystic fibrosis, diabetes, asthma, chronic lung disease or epilepsy.
- **Sensory impairment**: needs related to problems with sight or hearing.
- **Complex needs**: needs related to problems many of which result from a genetic defect or from an accident or trauma.
- **Behavioural difficulties**: needs related to aggression, challenging behaviour, hyperactivity, attention deficit hyperactivity disorder (ADHD) or antisocial behaviour.

- **Life-threatening illness**: needs related to a serious or terminal illness, e.g. childhood cancer, HIV, AIDS and leukaemia.
- **Emotional and social difficulties**: needs related to conditions such as anxiety, fear, depression or autistic spectrum disorder (ASD).

Key term

Disability – Under the Equality Act 2010, a person has a disability if they have a physical or mental impairment, and if the impairment has a substantial and long-term adverse effect on their ability to perform normal day-to-day activities.

The relationship between disability and special educational needs

There is no absolute way of listing types of SEN, or of placing a child or young person into a single category. Many children will have needs that cross over one or more of the categories described above. Children and young people may also have specific areas of strength in addition to their special needs.

Special educational needs is a broad term to cover children and young people who need extra support, long term or temporarily. This might be because they have:

- a physical disability
- a learning disability
- sight and/or hearing problems
- specific behaviour problems
- some other disability or condition needing treatment over a long period.

It should also be noted that a child may also only have a *temporary* or short-term need. Examples include when a child's parent or sibling has died, when they are a victim of bullying or abuse, or when they have a temporary hearing loss after a common cold.

Special provision

You can often meet disabled children and young people's needs without using specialist aids and equipment. Special provision includes the following strategies:

- Position children and young people so that they learn effectively: for example, by making sure the light falls on the adult's face, so that a child wearing a hearing aid is able to lip-read and a child with a visual impairment can use any residual eyesight to see facial expressions.
- Provide the opportunity to learn sign languages: for example, Makaton or Signalong.
- Develop the self-esteem of children and young people: for example, by encouraging and praising effort as well as achievement.
- Allow children's behaviour and alternative ways of communicating to be acknowledged and understood.
- Provide appropriate therapies: for example, speech and language, occupational or physiotherapy. (Support from health services is generally set out as non-educational provision in a child's **statement**. However, speech and language therapy may be regarded as either educational or non-educational provision.)
- Plan the use of music, art, drama or movement therapy: these therapies may play a complementary role in the curriculum for individual children and young people and will need to be planned as part of the whole curriculum.
- Help children and young people to maintain good posture, appropriate muscle tone and ease of movement, and promote skills in independent mobility.
- Promote relaxation and support to help children and young people manage stress and anxiety: some settings use a sensory room, but a quiet, comfortable area will benefit all children.

Portage

It is useful to find out more about Portage if you are working with very young children. Although the teaching is usually carried out in the child's home, some Portage workers work closely with Children's Centres and other settings. Portage is a home-based teaching service for the families of pre-school children who show some delay in their development. The service aims to enable parents to teach their own children, in their own homes, supported by visits from a Portage home visitor supervised by an educational psychologist. Central to the Portage philosophy is the emphasis placed on the partnership between parents and professionals in the education and development of their own children.

How the Portage service normally works

- The family receives a weekly (or fortnightly) visit from a Portage home visitor.
- The home visitor discusses with the parents which new skill the parent would like their child to learn. The skills are usually chosen from the Portage checklist.
- The agreed skill and how to teach it are written down on an activity chart – on which the parent can record the child's progress throughout the week.
- The home visitor shows the parent how to teach the child the new skill.
- Throughout the week, the parent spends a few minutes teaching the child the new skill. The

parent records the outcome on the activity chart.

- On the next home visit, the home visitor checks whether the child can perform the skill.
- A new skill is then discussed and set for the following week.

Contributing to the inclusion of children and young people with disabilities and special educational needs

Obtaining information

Although schools in the UK are currently required to collect data on children with SEN, this does not capture information about all disabled children. In order to support children and young people with special needs, you need to find out the following information about the disabled children and young people in your setting:

- the nature of the child's disability
- the child's support needs.

Information about children's special needs can be obtained from:

- Observations
- Talking with the child's parents or carers
- Talking with colleagues – the nursery manager or class teacher, and other professionals such as the SENCO.

Observations

The EYFS states: 'Observe children to find out about their needs, what they are interested in and what they can do.' Observing children and young people is a very important part of your practice and can help you to identify when a

child's development is not following the normative pattern. You can actively observe children in many different ways, as shown below.

Practitioners identify children's needs by:

Figure 14.02

- talking with children
- watching children and young people when playing and working
- observing which activities they have difficulty with
- noting which activities they enjoy.

Talking with parents

Many parents who have a disabled child will have a lot of information about the nature of the disability, but – more importantly – they are the people who know their child best and will be able to tell you how the disability affects their own child. Every child will have needs that are specific to him or her – and their needs may change from day to day. For example, a child with asthma may be susceptible to specific 'triggers' that provoke an acute attack. Parents may be able to tell you what to look out for to help prevent an attack from occurring.

Colleagues and other professionals

It is important to value the contributions of other staff members and professionals. Each professional will have made his or her own observations and be able to offer useful information. For example, a physiotherapist will be able to help practitioners to think of practical methods to support a child with cerebral palsy in the setting.

Progress check

Supporting children with special needs

Practitioners need to:

- **be aware that all children and young people have different experiences**, interests, skills and knowledge which affect their ability to develop and learn.
- **provide a safe and supportive learning environment**, free from harassment, in which the contribution of all children and families is valued.
- **avoid all stereotypes** and expressions of discrimination or prejudice.

Barriers to participation

There are certain potential barriers to participation – or access to provision – for children or young people with special needs and their families.

Physical barriers

This does not refer only to the more obvious physical barriers, such as not having ramps or sufficiently wide doors for wheelchair access. It also refers to barriers such as inappropriate toilet and washing facilities or inappropriate signage for people with visual impairments.

Attitudes of staff

Settings may exclude children from participation in certain group activities because of their special needs. This exclusion can sometimes be justified on health and safety grounds, but usually could be remedied with some planning and communication with the child's family. Avoid making assumptions about individual children's special needs. These are based on stereotypes: for example, assuming that every child with Down's syndrome is always cheerful or assuming that a child with spina bifida will be clumsy.

Poverty

The cost of high-quality early years care is simply not affordable for those families living in poverty. Research shows that children are more likely to be living in poverty in:

- families with one or more disabled persons
- lone-parent households
- inner-city areas.

The following activities show how settings can present barriers to equality of access for children and young people and their families.

Supporting inclusion and inclusive practices in your own work

As we have seen in Chapter 3, Unit SHC 23: Introduction to equality and inclusion in children and young people's settings, stereotyping often leads to discrimination. It also matters a great deal how we 'label' people who are different from us. Many years ago, people who were obviously *different* – perhaps unable to walk or talk or were slow to understand – were believed to be in some way evil; some were even burnt to death as witches. Today we are much more aware of individual differences and have much more knowledge about diverse needs and abilities. It is still very important that we do not apply labels to anyone.

Activity

Excluded from an outing

The nursery manager at a private nursery explains to a child's parents that their son, Thomas, will not be able to join the rest of his group on a visit to a local children's theatre production of *The Gruffalo's Child*. Thomas has Down's syndrome and learning difficulties. The nursery staff had met to discuss the problem and had concluded that there was no point in Thomas going as he would not appreciate the show and would probably disrupt the other children. Thomas's mother is very unhappy with their decision and has accused the nursery of discriminating against Thomas on account of his disability.

Discuss the following questions in a group:

1 Do you think the nursery staff were justified in their decision?

2 Do you believe the nursery has discriminated against Thomas?

3 What could the nursery staff have done in order to enable Thomas to join the others?

Activity

A hearing problem

Carla, a baby of 15 months, has just been diagnosed with a severe hearing impairment. When Carla has her nappy changed, Mary, the Baby Room supervisor, notices that Laura, one of the early years practitioners, changes Carla's nappy in silence, although she always smiles, chats and plays with the other babies during nappy-changing routines. When Mary asks her why she does not do the same with Carla, Laura replies that she does not see the point because Carla cannot hear anything.

1 Why is Mary concerned about Laura's child care practice?

2 Discuss ways in which practitioners could promote Carla's development and meet her holistic needs.

Case Study   Barriers to leisure

Dan is 17 and has cerebral palsy, which causes problems with keeping his balance, shaky hand movements and irregular speech. Recently, he went out with a group of friends to a club. The bouncer barred him from entering because of the way he was walking. When his sister, Emma, objected to the bouncer's complaint that her brother 'can't walk because he's drunk' and explained that he had cerebral palsy, Dan was asked to produce a medical card as proof of his disability. One of the bouncers then used his radio to tell other nearby pubs not to let him in. Following his experience, his sister said that Dan had been 'upset and very withdrawn.'

The importance of realistic expectations of children's development

Having positive, realistic expectations for children's achievements and behaviour is something that parents, carers and practitioners should strive for. When expectations for children are set at the right level – not too high and not too low – then children can expect to have high self-esteem and also fulfil their potential.

A good understanding of child development is vital to your work with children. You need to be aware that every child varies as to when they pass through the normative stages of development described in Chapter 4, Unit TDA 2.1: Child and young person development.

You – and the child's parents or carers – need to have realistic expectations for each child, based on both the **child's stage of development**, his or her **temperament** and any **additional**

needs. For example, temper tantrums usually occur in children between one and three years of age, and are a normal developmental stage that reflects a child's inner struggle to establish his own sense of self. (Temper tantrums are often called 'the terrible twos' and may involve crying, screaming, head-banging, breath-holding, breaking objects and/or jumping up and down.) However, if you were to see a colleague behaving in this way, you would be very alarmed! Your realistic expectations fit with the boisterous two-year-old but not with an adult in his or her twenties.

You also need to take account of special or additional needs, where development may be very different from the norm. It is very important to promote the strengths of the children as well as assisting with their difficulties. You can achieve this by choosing some of the activities that you know the child is good at; for example, Child A may have difficulties tying her shoelaces, but may be very skilled at cutting out shapes, therefore do some cutting-out sessions and always offer plenty of praise and encouragement, both for *achievement* and for the *effort* the child has made.

Reflective practice: Supporting children and young people with special needs

- How well does your setting provide for the special needs of children?
- Is there effective communication between the child's parents or carers and the setting?
- Do the play experiences and activities avoid stereotyping and ensure that each child has an equal opportunity to take part in activities?

Types of adaptations to equipment and the environment	
Minor adaptations to the home such as grab rails and temporary ramps. **Bathing, feeding and walking equipment.**	**Major adaptations** including door widening for wheelchair access, lowering worktops, bathroom alterations and purpose-built extensions.
Providing ramps for wheelchair users.	**Providing thick pencils and brushes** for children with poor fine motor skills.
Adapting standard equipment: for example, by having a tray on the table so that objects stay on the table, and a child with a visual impairment does not 'lose' objects that fall off.	**Helping children to manage eating and drinking**: there is a wide range of specialist aids for eating and drinking, such as angled spoons and suction plates.
Using specialist environments: for example, ball pools, warm water pools or light and sound stimulation or sensory rooms.	**Promoting children's autonomy and independence** through the use of specialist aids and equipment: for example, hearing aids, non-slip table mats and special 'standing' chairs.

Table 14.2 Adaptations that may be required

Supporting disabled children and young people and those with special educational needs to participate in the full range of activities and experiences

Specialist aids and equipment

Many children with learning difficulties will have **personal priority needs** that are central to their learning and quality of life. Some children may need the provision of a specific **therapy** or paramedical care, for example supervising medication. Others need to have existing equipment or activities modified or adapted to suit their particular needs. Table 14.2 gives examples of required adaptations.

Safety when using aids and equipment

Using specialist aids and equipment safely is important – both for your health and that of

Figure 14.03 Using a spoon with a large easy-to-hold handle

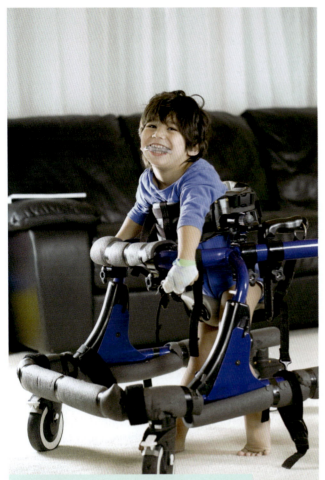

Figure 14.04 Using a walking frame or rollator

children and young people. Some equipment should not be moved without taking certain precautions.

- All equipment and furniture must be installed correctly and maintained adequately.
- Children and adults must know how to use the equipment correctly and follow the manufacturer's instructions.
- Help other non-disabled children to understand the importance specialist equipment has for disabled children and encourage them to treat it with respect: for example, a child who uses a hearing aid or who wears glasses needs to know that their valuable aids will be kept safely for them when not being used.

In Practice

Providing for Selma's needs

When Selma, a partially sighted baby, joined the nursery, her key person, Josh, discussed her needs with her parents and contacted the RNIB for information about ways of supporting her development. Josh decided to plan a set of activities that could be used by Selma – and by sighted babies too – based on his research, which found that for profoundly blind and partially sighted babies it is important to:

1. Offer as wide a range of *tactile experiences* as possible right from the beginning: Josh started collecting tactile objects, such as:

   ❏ a foil survival blanket to scrunch and reflect

   ❏ a flat silky cushion containing polystyrene beads

   ❏ pan scourer, lemon reamer, pasta strainer, dishwashing brush.

2. Encourage movement: Helping babies to become aware of whole body movements and to learn to tolerate different positions, such as being placed on their stomach. Josh:

   ❏ provided some brightly lit and sound-producing toys to provide the motivation to roll and reach

   ❏ rearranged the nursery furniture to provide a logical sequence to support the baby when moving – and to help 'mental mapping' of her environment.

3. Encourage exploration of sound, rhythm and timing. Josh provided:

   ❏ tactile nursery rhyme prompt cards: He made these using A4 cards and stuck on different fabrics to link touch to a particular song. For example, a piece of fur fabric stuck on card to make a link with 'Round and Round the Garden like a Teddy Bear', or a single shiny silver star stuck onto dark blue card to make a link with 'Twinkle, twinkle little star'.

   ❏ a handbell, rolling chime ball, musical xylophone and a drum.

Josh used some of the tactile objects in a treasure basket that could be enjoyed by all the babies in the setting.

How to use specific methods of communication

Many children and young people with special educational needs have difficulties with language and communication. They will often benefit from learning a sign language, such as Makaton, PECS, Signalong or British Sign Language/Signed English. These are discussed on p 11, Chapter 1, Unit SHC 21: Introduction to communication in children and young people's settings.

Working in partnership with children, young people and others to review and improve activities and experiences

Even when a setting has experience in providing inclusive care and education, it is still important that activities and experiences within the setting are regularly reviewed and evaluated. In order to ensure an inclusive approach, you should:

- **review the setting's policies**, procedures and codes of practice on equality of opportunity.

- **review activities and trips away from the setting** to determine whether the practice is inclusive and that there was no discrimination against disabled children (or adults).

- **be reflective in your practice**: this means that you are constantly learning from experience and learning how to improve your practice.

- **obtain feedback from the child or young person**: find out their views by listening to them as well as observing them. Ask them open-ended questions, such as 'What did you like about the activity? Which bits did you find easy and which difficult?' in order to gain valuable feedback.

- **encourage children and young people to participate**: show them that you value their

ideas and be ready to adapt your practice to suit their individual needs and preferences.

Working in partnership with families is particularly important when a child or young person has additional support needs. Each parent or carer should be made to feel welcome and valued as an expert on their child or young person, playing a vital role in helping practitioners to enable their child to participate and learn.

 Progress check

Working with parents, carers and families

It is important that practitioners work with parents, carers and families as they:

- have a unique knowledge and expertise regarding their children, and local authorities need this to help them to provide the best education possible.
- should be encouraged to participate in the decisions which affect their children and their education.
- should be provided with the information they need to be informed about changes to legislation and practice in education.
- should be given a named contact person for more detailed information; this person will provide them with details of local and national organisations that can offer more help, if required.

Parents or carers should also be able to choose the extent to which they are involved in their child's setting. Not all parents or carers have the time or the confidence to become involved in the setting's activities.

Providing support for children and families

Where factors that impact on a child's ability to learn and develop are just starting to become apparent, partnership working involving *all the adults* in a child's life becomes very important. The earlier a need for additional support is identified, the more likely it is that early intervention can prevent certain aspects of a child's development or behaviour developing into a persistent difficulty.

Information and advice

Parents and carers find that getting a diagnosis for their child is important. Being given a name for their child's condition or special need enables them to discuss their child's development needs with health, social services and education professionals.

Shared experiences

Parents and carers often find that the most helpful sources of information and advice come from others with shared experiences. There are many organisations which exist to provide support and answer questions: for example, Contact a Family, The Down's Syndrome Association, Mencap and The Royal Society for the Blind; there are many more – most with their own website and helpline.

Service provision

Getting information about what they and their children are entitled to, as early as possible, is very important. This applies to the **benefits** they are entitled to as well as the services.

Communicating with parents and carers

The principles of effective communication are discussed in Chapter 1, Unit SHC 21: Introduction to communication in children and young people's settings. One of the main purposes of communicating with parents and carers is to provide and to share information about the child or young person and about the setting – both about the care and education setting and the home. Practitioners need to build up a partnership with parents and carers, and to do this they need to promote a feeling of trust.

Providing flexible support

- **Parents and carers** want support which is flexible enough to respond to their particular family's needs, and which is both available in an emergency and can also be planned in advance.
- **Children and young people** want support which enables them to do the kinds of things their peers do: this can vary from going swimming with their siblings to spending time away from home with their friends.

The most popular services are generally those developed by parents or carers themselves, or by local disability organisations.

Parent partnership services

The Parent Partnership Scheme (PPS) is a statutory service that offers the following support:

- information, advice and support for parents or carers of children and young people with SEN
- putting parents or carers in touch with other local organisations
- making sure that the views of the parent or carer are heard and understood, and that these views inform local policy and practice.

Some parent partnerships are based in the voluntary sector although the majority of them remain based in their LEA or Children's Trust. All parent partnerships, wherever they are based, work separately and independently from the LEA; this means that they are able to provide impartial advice and support to parents and carers.

For more information, visit the NPPN (National Parent Partnership Network) website at: www. parentpartnership.org.uk.

Progress check

Support for the family

- What sort of difficulties might be experienced by the family of a child with a special need or disability?
- How can staff in early years settings and schools help the family?

Assessment practice

Identifying children or young people with special needs in your setting

Select a child or young person in your setting who has a special educational need or disability. Find out all you can about:

- the type of disability or special need
- the type of support that needs to be provided
- where to go for further information.

Useful websites and resources

www.cafamily.org.uk	**Contact a Family** Helps families who care for children with any disability or special need
www.ncb.org.uk	**Council for Disabled Children**
www.cftrust.org.uk	**Cystic Fibrosis Trust**
www.downssyndrome.org.uk	**Down's Syndrome Association**
www.mencap.org.uk	**MENCAP**
www.ndcs.org.uk	**National Deaf Children's Society**
www.parentpartnership.org.uk	**National Parent Partnership Network**
www.epilepsysociety.org.uk	**National Society for Epilepsy**
www.rnib.org.uk	**Royal National Institute of Blind People**
www.scope.org.uk	**SCOPE** For children with cerebral palsy
www.sense.org.uk	**SENSE** Supports and campaigns for children and adults who are deafblind

15 Support children and young people's play and leisure: Unit TDA 2.16

The Charter of Children's Rights (1989) states that every child in the world should have the right to play. Play is not the same as recreation or relaxation. Play is about high levels of learning, while recreation is about relaxing the body and mind.

Learning outcomes

By the end of this chapter you will:

1. Understand the nature and importance of play and leisure.
2. Be able to support children and young people's play and leisure.
3. Be able to support children and young people in balancing risk and challenge.
4. Be able to reflect on and improve your own practice

The nature and importance of play and leisure

Through play, children bring together and organise their ideas, feelings, relationships and their physical life. It helps them to use what they know and to make sense of the world and people they meet. Play brings together:

- ideas and creativity
- feelings
- relationships
- physical coordination
- spiritual development.

During play, children:

- control their world and deal with issues
- get ready for the future
- think about things that have happened.

There are different ideas about how to develop play, but although there are wide cultural variations, all children seem to develop and learn through play, including children with severe disabilities.

Your role will be important in providing opportunities that support and extend children's play and leisure. Leisure simply means a period spent doing things other than work. Active leisure involves energetic activities, such as sport, dancing, hiking etc. Passive leisure involves activities such as relaxation, socialising or reading.

Why is play important?

Play helps children to:

- **learn about the world in which they live**: they can investigate and discover, explore cause and effect, and find out about roles and

Features of self-directed play	
Freely chosen	Children choose *what* they do
Personally directed	Children choose *how* they do it
Intrinsically motivated	Children choose *why* they do it
Goal-less	They do it for no external goal or reward

Table 15.1 Self-directed play

values. Ideas and concepts expressed by children during play increase and become more complex as their play skills increase.

- **develop self-esteem**: children will often play at something they know they can do well, at which they can be successful.
- **develop social skills**: children learn to think of others through their play and leisure activities. They learn to behave in ways that are socially acceptable as they play. Social skills include communicating, sharing, turn-taking, listening and negotiating.
- **develop physically**: children learn how to control their bodies, develop their motor skills and improve their coordination and balance.
- **learn to express emotions**: children show a range of feelings when they are playing, learning to express and control their emotions and to resolve conflicts with others.
- **develop conversation skills**: children experiment with language during play and use words to express their thoughts and ideas, solve problems and communicate their wishes.
- **develop creativity**: children are able to stretch the limits of their world and experience the fun in make-believe.

The UN Convention on the Rights of the Child in relation to relaxation and play

Playing is integral to children's enjoyment of their lives, their health and their development. Children and young people – disabled and non-disabled – whatever their age, culture, ethnicity or social and economic background, need and want to play, indoors and out, in whatever way they can. Through playing, children are creating their own culture, developing their abilities, exploring their creativity and learning about themselves, other people and the world around them. The right to play is enshrined in the UN Convention on Rights of the Child:

Article 31 (Leisure, play and culture): Children have the right to relax and play, and to join in a wide range of cultural, artistic and other recreational activities.

The characteristics of freely chosen, self-directed play and leisure

Self-directed play takes place when children are in charge. It is sometimes called free play or unstructured play. Children are able to follow their interests and inclinations freely without the constraints that adults – and computers – place upon their world.

Self-directed play requires **minimal adult intervention**. For example, a child might be shown how to use a glue stick and paper and be minimally supervised while they explore those materials on their own and create a picture or model. The adult only intervenes if the child does something potentially dangerous – for example, putting the glue in their eye – and otherwise refrains from limiting the child's creativity.

How to encourage children and young people to direct their own play

Children of school age and over should be given both responsibility and choice in their play, according to their age. The play environment should support this by providing:

- a stimulating play environment which also promotes their physical safety and emotional wellbeing
- a wide range of opportunities for play, including an element of challenge and reasonable risk-taking
- minimal adult supervision so that the child feels in control
- opportunities to choose whether or not they want to be involved in certain play activities
- access to a wide range of materials and the freedom to choose how they use the resources, which will allow them to direct or determine their own play
- group activities that are not so large that children feel pressured and unable to enjoy the activity
- leisure opportunities for young people, such as youth clubs, sports clubs, uniformed organisations and places where they can socialise and just hang out together.

How to support children and young people's play and leisure

Your role in supporting children and young people's play and leisure activities

Children and young people have the right to be consulted and involved in decision-making about the type of play provision they have.

Involving children in making decisions is important because it helps them to develop:

- **independence** – which increases their feeling of confidence in their own abilities
- a sense of being in control of their own environment
- **trust**: knowing that adults trust their judgement and opinions
- **self-help skills**: for example, knowing that the adult will be patient in letting the child dress himself, even if it takes a long time and several attempts.

You can also support play by sensitive intervention. This means knowing when to supervise, but recognising when to stand back and supervise their play from a distance and when to intervene.

Young people need play

Young people need play, just as much as young children do. Older children and young people's play is more organised and structured as their enthusiasm for orderly thinking shows itself through games with rules and in organised sports. Winning becomes important as they begin to understand that winning means following the rules. This is the age when *team sports* become important. However, even when young people are just 'hanging out' together, they are learning – sharing information and knowledge and understanding social relationships.

Young people need leisure

Young people would probably not refer to their social activities as 'play', but surveys of the views of children and young people show that they want:

- opportunities to be physically active – indoors and outdoors
- the chance to meet with their friends
- the chance to be somewhere quiet
- choice and variety.

with disabilities may find it more challenging to play, and will need careful help from others.

Safety should always be in mind when working with young children so that accidents are prevented. This is called **risk assessment** because adults are thinking ahead about possible physical danger to children. It is important to check materials such as pens, crayons and felt pens for the safety mark. Remember, young children put objects into their mouths as part of the way in which they learn.

In Practice

Safety in play

❏ Worn equipment should be mended or replaced.

❏ Equipment should be checked for splinters, sharp edges or peeling paint.

❏ At the end of each day all aprons should be checked and wiped clean.

❏ Tables should be disinfected.

❏ Floors should be swept and washed once the rooms have been tidied.

❏ Carpets should be cleaned with a vacuum.

Guidelines for setting up materials and equipment

- Check large apparatus such as climbing frames and trucks for safety catches and safety surfaces. Do the children have enough space to move about safely?
- Heavy objects should not be on shelves in case they fall on children.
- All fire exits must be kept free at all times.
- Doors must not be left half open, especially if there are children with visual impairments as they might bump into them.

- Objects on shelves should not stick out at a child's head height in case they bump their head.

Emotional safety
Children need to feel emotionally safe or they will not be confident enough to play.

- They may sometimes need to play with or near an adult, especially if they are just settling in at the setting, or they have been upset.
- They may need to have a special friend with them in order to feel secure enough to play confidently.

Social safety
When children quarrel they often begin to shout at each other and even fight. Shouting means they are trying to put their feelings into words. Adults can help them by saying something like, 'I think you are angry. What shall we do about it? Do you want the bike? When Mary has finished with it, she will give you a turn.'

Children need to be supervised carefully. Careful supervision does not mean standing over children all the time. Much of the supervision you do can be at arm's length. However, it is important for adults never to sit with their back to the group, either indoors or outdoors. Without supervision, children might become involved in unacceptable or inappropriate behaviour, such as blocking the drains. If children rush about and become overexcited, it is sometimes best to join their play and help them to develop a storyline. Sometimes they may have lost their play ideas in the excitement.

Interacting during play

Showing you are interested
When interacting with children and young people during play and leisure activities,

practitioners should show that they are interested in what the children are saying and experiencing. This shows that their ideas and feelings are important to you – and that you value them. You can show your interest by:

- listening carefully to what they say
- maintaining eye contact
- sitting at their level
- nodding and smiling to encourage them to express their feelings
- praising them for achievements – and just as importantly – for their efforts
- responding to their questions and observations.

Respecting their need for privacy and to make choices

Even very young children show that they appreciate and need times when they can be alone – often choosing to sit quietly in the book corner when others are playing elsewhere. They also need to be able to talk with their friends and act out different roles without an adult presence. Older children and young people often show a greater need for privacy. Practitioners should always respect their need for privacy. The only time when it is appropriate to invade their privacy is when you believe the child to be at some sort of risk; then, your responsibility to protect them takes priority over their right to privacy. Encouraging children to make choices for themselves about how they play and spend their leisure time is also important. Practitioners should not try to impose their own ideas when children are involved in their activities.

Giving praise and encouragement

Praise is an expression of approval of a person's achievements or characteristics. Encouragement is when someone talks or behaves in a way that gives a person confidence to do something. Both praise and encouragement are very important as they help children and young people to:

- develop positive self-esteem
- become more confident in their own abilities
- keep trying and so develop their skills and abilities.

In Practice

How to praise and encourage children and young people

❏ Give praise and positive feedback for all achievements, however small.

❏ Be prompt in giving praise and encouragement: praise and encouragement work much better when delivered immediately after the effort or achievement.

❏ Encourage children to make choices and to try new things; sometimes they need to learn by their mistakes.

❏ Encourage young people to discover and develop their talents: Discovering something that they are good at will boost their confidence and self-esteem.

❏ Avoid making comparisons with another child. Always remember the child is an individual.

❏ Encourage them to feel included in decision-making and respond to their questions in a considerate way.

❏ Make sure the way you praise is appropriate to the age of the child or young person: young people might feel embarrassed by an effusive show of verbal praise and may prefer a high-five.

❏ Be specific about why you are praising them: Avoid general praise such as: 'You've done well today.' Instead say: 'Well done, Jack, for helping to clear away all the blocks.'

Supporting children and young people in balancing risk and challenge

From an early age, children are motivated to take risks. They want to learn to crawl, walk, climb, ride a tricycle, and they are not deterred from trying, even when they fall over and hurt themselves. Young children are particularly at risk because they:

- are still learning and do not always do things correctly
- may not yet understand safety instructions
- are easily distracted
- are adventurous and keen to try things out
- want to impress their friends.
- may not have adequate supervision.

Finding the right balance between providing a challenging environment and making sure that the risks are 'safe risks' requires the practitioner to do the following:

- **Understand the individual child or young person**: this includes knowing about the child's temperament, stage of development, and his or her abilities. For example, a timid or withdrawn child may find participating in group play socially challenging and emotionally risky, whereas a sociable and self-confident child may find listening, turn-taking or even playing alone emotionally risky and challenging.
- **Consider the play environment**: every environment has unique risk potentials which need consideration. For example, more adults might be required on outings, as children's behaviour can be different in new surroundings or when participating in new experiences.

All settings should have in place policies and procedures for keeping the play environment safe. Practitioners should:

- **Follow an inspection and maintenance programme**: this involves checking regularly for damage to equipment, and removing items from the setting for repair or disposal.
- **Have an overview**: be aware of what is happening in the whole area and move to areas where support is necessary. This is important if children are to be protected from avoidable risks.
- **Observe and support children's self-directed play**: be sensitive if you need to intervene to help children play together or to extend an activity.

The value of risk and challenge in children and young people's play and leisure

Play England states that:

> All children both need and want to take risks in order to explore limits, venture into new experiences and develop their capacities, from a very young age and from their earliest play experiences.

Everyday life always involves some degree of risk, and children need to learn how to cope with this. Being *told* about possible dangers is not enough – children need to *see* or *experience* the consequences of not taking care. Children who learn early on to make their own rational decisions instead of simply doing what they are told to do by others will be in a better position to resist the pressures they will inevitably face as adolescents and adults. Children who have been overprotected will probably lack the ability to make rational decisions, which could lead to them putting themselves at risk.

Taking small risks has a positive impact on a child's physical, intellectual, social and emotional development.

Physical development

Children learn how to move safely and to develop their coordination and balance. Physically challenging activities that involve safe risk-taking help children to build and extend their strength and fitness levels. Vigorous activities such as completing an obstacle course or running will also help to reduce obesity.

Intellectual development

Children learn how to negotiate, to solve problems and to make choices.

Emotional and social development

Children build resilience and social competence from taking risks when working or playing with others. Being able to make decisions from a range of choices is an important life skill that helps them to gain confidence and build their self-esteem.

Unacceptable risk and challenge in children and young people's play and leisure

Practitioners have a duty of care to keep children safe from harm. The need to support and extend children's abilities and learning about safe risk-taking has to be balanced with protecting them from harm. All experiences have some level of risk attached to them.

A **safe risk** means that:

- the benefits from the experience far outweigh the risk of possible harm
- the consequences of the potential risk are likely to be minor or insignificant
- the adults think carefully about the risks, know the children well and have taken appropriate action to minimise the risks.

Figure 15.03 A child enjoying the challenge of climbing and swinging

For example, if a child in your group is not ready – either physically or emotionally – to try a particular climbing experience, the relative risk that is to be found in any climbing activity would shift to being a dangerous – or **unsafe** – risk. In this situation, you would need to support the child physically as he climbs, or provide an alternative climbing experience to match the child's abilities.

The importance for children and young people of managing risk and challenge for themselves

Children's lives are often strictly controlled by adults, with after-school activities, playing in competitive sport teams and doing extra homework. Today, very few children walk or ride bikes to school, or are allowed to play freely in their local neighbourhoods. It is now even more important that practitioners provide children with opportunities to:

- make choices and engage in problem-solving and diverse creative experiences
- participate every day in physical unstructured and planned activities
- learn how to cope socially and emotionally as a member of a group.

Supporting children and young people to manage risk and challenge

Practitioners need to explain the value of challenging play to parents and carers, and involve them in developing policies on risk management. This helps parents to feel informed and positive about risky play and will allay any concerns they may have about the activities that are provided for their children. They also need to do the following:

- **Be positive role models**: by showing safe and sensible behaviour you can help children to understand how to behave outdoors and inside.
- Support children to learn about **personal safety**, risks and the safety of others.
- Support children in **problem-solving** and making choices.
- Encourage children to make **their own risk assessments**: children need to be encouraged to assess the risks of an activity and to think about the possible consequences of their actions. For example, when building with wooden blocks, children need to be helped to see how their building can be made stable and less likely to fall. This is more effective than telling children that they can only build to a certain height.

Reflective practice: Managing risks and challenges

Think about the way in which risks and challenges are managed in your setting.

- Have you encouraged a child to assess the risks involved in a particular activity, and to work out for themselves how to manage the risk? Did you have to intervene to support the child?
- Have you encouraged a child to try a more challenging activity?
- Have you helped a child to talk through potential problems during a play activity?
- How could you improve the way in which you support children to understand and assess risks?

Reflecting on your own practice in play and leisure

Being able to reflect on your practice in play and leisure will help you to understand which things have worked well – and which have not worked so well. This will help you to think of ways to improve your practice. There are various ways to reflect on your practice. These include:

- Observing the children's responses during play – their enjoyment and skill development
- Reviewing what worked well and what did not work so well – in terms of equipment provided, numbers of children involved and an assessment of how involved children were in their play
- Asking children and young people for feedback
- Asking colleagues for feedback
- Recording your reflections in a Reflective Diary.

Identifying your strengths and weaknesses and how to improve your practice

Practitioners need to reflect on their own contributions to good practice. This involves identifying their strengths and weaknesses. For example, here are three examples of practitioners identifying their own strengths and weaknesses and using them to improve their practice:

1. Robbie recognises that he is particularly effective when supporting young people to plan their own leisure opportunities. He finds it easy to build a rapport and to support their ideas. Identifying this strength will boost his confidence and enable him to model good practice within the team.

2. Leanne acknowledges a weakness when supporting young children during creative play. She admits to feeling frustrated, having prepared pretty paper flowers and scraps of lace for making Mother's Day cards, and then two of the children completely covered their decorated cards with crayon scribble. Identifying this weakness will help Leanne to cope with the feelings of frustration when not in control of a planned activity. She will revisit what she had read about one of the benefits of creative play being 'an end in itself' and discuss the issue with colleagues to decide how best to improve her practice in this area.

3. Jodie identified a strength when carrying out a cooking activity at the after-school club. She found that she got a real buzz out of working in a small team supporting the primary school children in making pizzas with lots of different toppings. Jodie received positive feedback from the adult team and from the children. This boosted her confidence and she plans to write some basic guidelines about the activity for newcomers to use.

Assessment practice

Supporting children and young people's play and leisure

Make a plan for the evidence file you are going to compile. You could take some photos of the children or young people in your setting (but remember to make sure that you have permission from their parent or carer before doing so). Use the photos to illustrate the information on the different assessment tasks.

Useful websites and resources

www.playengland.org.uk	**Play England** Promotes free play opportunities for all children and young people, and works to ensure that the importance of play for children's development is recognised. Find out about the national play organisations relevant to where you work: Play Scotland, Play Wales and the International Play Association.

16 Support children and young people at meal and snack times: Unit TDA 2.14

A good diet is essential for good health. It is important that children and young people are provided with a solid foundation for establishing lifelong healthy eating habits. Schools and early years settings can make a valuable contribution to improving the nutritional quality of children's diets and to promoting consistent messages about healthy eating.

Learning outcomes

By the end of this chapter you will:

1. Know the principles of healthy eating for children and young people.
2. Know the benefits of healthy eating for children and young people.
3. Know how to encourage children and young people to make healthier food choices.
4. Be able to support hygiene during meal and snack times.
5. Be able to support the code of conduct and policies for meal and snack times.

The principles of healthy eating for children and young people

Healthy eating (good nutrition) is one of the most important ways in which we can help ourselves to feel well and be well. We need food:

- to provide **energy** for physical activity and to maintain body temperature
- to provide material for the **growth** of body cells
- for the **repair and replacement** of damaged body tissues.

Children and young people need the right balance of food and **nutrients** to develop and grow. Healthy eating is about getting that balance right in order to provide enough of the important nutrients (such as vitamins, minerals and protein) and fibre without too much fat (especially saturated fat), sugar or salt.

The diet we offer children will not only have an impact on their future health, but it will also help to establish their feelings towards food and the food choices that they make as young people and then as adults.

Nutritional guidelines for children and young people are described on p 172, Chapter 9, Unit MU 2.8: Contribute to the support of positive environments for children and young people.

Key term

Nutrients – Essential dietary factors, such as carbohydrates, proteins, certain fats, vitamins and minerals.

Children have a high energy and nutrient requirement relative to their size. As they are growing and developing rapidly they need nutrient-dense foods. These include:

- fruits
- nuts
- seeds
- dairy foods such as milk, yoghurt and cheese
- cereals
- meat and fish.

A healthy diet should also be based on a variety of foods, with the emphasis on reducing intake of foods that are higher in fat and sugar (such as crisps, chips, chocolate and sweets) and increasing those that are more filling and nutrient-dense such as dairy foods, fruits and vegetables, wholegrain cereals and pulses.

Healthy meals and snacks for children and young people

How much food should children be given? Children's appetites vary enormously, so common sense is a good guide on how big a portion should be. Always be guided by the individual child:

- do not force them to eat when they no longer wish to, but
- do not refuse to give more if they really are hungry.

Some children always feel hungry at one particular mealtime. Others require food little and often. You should always offer food that is nourishing as well as satisfying their hunger.

Healthy meals

Three main meals a day should be encouraged, with healthy snacks between meals as needed.

Activity

The balanced daily diet

Look at the following daily diet:

- Breakfast   a glass of milk + scrambled egg and toast
- Mid-morning   a packet of crisps + a glass of blackcurrant squash
- Lunch   a cheese and egg flan + chips + baked beans; apple fritters and ice cream + apple juice
- Snack   chocolate mini-roll and orange squash
- Tea   fish fingers + mashed potatoes + peas + strawberry milkshake

1 Arrange the portions or servings into five columns (see example on p 174, Chapter 9, Unit MU 2.8: Contribute to the support of positive environments for children and young people: the four food groups and one extra column for extra fat and sugar) and assess the nutritional content of the diet.

2 How could you improve the menu to ensure a healthy balanced diet?

Breakfast	Orange juice Weetabix + milk 1 slice of buttered toast	Milk Cereal, e.g. corn or wheat flakes Toast and jam	Apple juice 1 slice of toast with butter or jam	Milk Cereal with slice of banana, or scrambled egg on toast	Yoghurt Porridge Slices of apple
Morning snack	Diluted apple juice 1 packet raisins	Blackcurrant and apple drink Cheese straws	1 glass fruit squash 1 biscuit	Peeled apple slices Wholemeal toast fingers with cheese spread	Diluted apple juice Chapatti or pitta bread fingers
Lunch	Chicken nuggets or macaroni cheese Broccoli Fruit yoghurt Water	Thick bean soup or chicken salad sandwich Green beans Fresh fruit salad Water	Vegetable soup or fish fingers/cakes Sticks of raw carrot Kiwi fruit Water	Sweet potato casserole Sweetcorn Spinach leaves Chocolate mousse Water	Bean casserole (or chicken drumstick) with noodles Peas or broad beans Fruit yoghurt Water
Afternoon snack	Diluted fruit juice Cubes of cheese with savoury biscuit	Milk shake Fruit cake or chocolate biscuit	Diluted fruit juice Thin-cut sandwiches cut into small pieces	Hot or cold chocolate drink 1 small packed dried fruit mix, e.g. apricots, sultanas	Lassi (yoghurt drink) 1 banana 1 small biscuit
Tea or supper	Baked beans on toast or ham and cheese pasta Lemon pancakes Milk or yoghurt	Fish stew or fish fingers Mashed potato Fruit mousse or fromage frais Milk or yoghurt	Baked potatoes with a choice of fillings Steamed broccoli Ice cream	Home-made beefburger or pizza Green salad Pancakes Milk	Lentil and rice soup Pitta or wholegrain bread Rice salad Milk

Table 16.1 Providing a balanced diet

Iron, calcium and vitamin D in children's diets

Iron is essential for children's health. Lack of iron often leads to **anaemia** which can affect both physical and mental development. Children most at risk of developing anaemia are those who are poor eaters or on restricted diets.

Iron
Iron comes in two forms. It is found in either:

- foods from animal sources (especially meat), which are easily absorbed by the body, or

- plant foods, which are not quite so easy for the body to absorb.

If possible, children should be given a portion of meat or fish every day, and kidney or liver once a week. Even a small portion of meat or fish is useful because it also helps the body to absorb iron from other food sources.

If children do not eat meat or fish, they must be offered plenty of **iron-rich alternatives**, such as egg yolks, dried fruit, beans and lentils, and green leafy vegetables. It is also a good idea to give foods or drinks that are high in vitamin C at mealtimes, as this helps the absorption of iron from non-meat sources.

Calcium and vitamin D

Children need calcium for maintaining and repairing bones and teeth. Calcium is found in milk, cheese, yoghurt and other dairy products, and is only absorbed by the body if it is taken with vitamin D.

The skin can make all the vitamin D that a body needs, when it is exposed to gentle sunlight. Sources of vitamin D include:

- milk
- fortified breakfast cereals
- oily fish
- meat
- fortified margarine
- soya mince, soya drink
- tahini paste (made from sesame seeds, which can cause an allergic reaction in a small number of children)
- tofu.

Vitamin drops provide vitamins A, C and D. Children under the age of five should be given vitamin drops as a safeguard *only* when their diets may be insufficient.

Dietary fibre and children's diets

Dietary fibre – or **roughage** – is found in cereals, fruits and vegetables. Fibre is made up of the indigestible parts or compounds of plants, which pass relatively unchanged through our stomach and intestines. A small amount of fibre is important for health in young children, but too much can cause problems as their digestive system is still immature. Some young children (under five years old) will not be able to consume enough food to meet their energy and nutrient needs if the fibre content is too high. This is because high-fibre foods tend to be very filling.

Providing a mixture of white bread and refined cereals, white rice and pasta as well as a few wholegrain varieties occasionally helps to maintain a healthy balance between fibre and nutrient intakes.

Children under five years: foods to avoid

Salt

There is no need to add salt to children's food. From the age of one to three, children should be having no more than 2 g a day. Even when buying processed food made specifically for children, remember to check the information given on the labels, and choose products which contain less salt.

Nuts

Do not give whole or chopped nuts to children under five years old because of the risk of choking.

Raw eggs

Avoid food that contains raw or partially cooked eggs because of the risk of **salmonella**, which causes food poisoning. Make sure that eggs are always cooked until both the white and yolk are solid.

Undiluted fruit juice

This contains natural sugars that are known to cause tooth decay; they are best only given at mealtimes and should be diluted when given to young children.

High-fibre foods

Foods such as brown rice and wholemeal pasta are too bulky for children under five; too much fibre can also make it more difficult for the body to absorb some essential nutrients, like calcium and iron.

Shark, swordfish and marlin

These types of fish should not be given because they contain relatively high levels of mercury, which might affect a child's developing nervous system.

Raw shellfish

This is a precaution to reduce the child's risk of contracting food poisoning.

Healthy snacks

Some children really do need to eat between meals. Their stomachs are relatively small and so they fill up and empty faster than adult stomachs. Sugary foods should not be given as a snack, because sugar is an appetite depressant and may spoil the child's appetite for the main meal to follow. For children between the ages of one and four, a routine of regular meals and snacks around their daytime sleeps should work well. Children do not eat well if they are tired or over-hungry. Planned snacks evenly spaced between meals will prevent their blood sugar levels from dropping too low and avoid the frustrations of being over-hungry. Offering both a savoury and sweet course at meals gives two opportunities for nutrients to be consumed, and increases the variety of foods which the toddler is eating. Puddings are a valuable part of the meal and should not be used only as a reward for eating the savoury course.

When to offer snacks

Snacks are best given to young children during a break in their normal activities when they can sit, eat and drink rather than continuing their activities with a snack in their hand. Sugary or savoury snack foods such as crisps, biscuits, sweets and chocolate can be part of the diet but should be treats rather than daily items.

Healthy snack foods include:

- breakfast cereal and milk
- toasted crumpet or teacake
- yoghurt or fromage frais

- glass of milk or home-made milkshake
- cheese and crackers or oatcakes
- crunchy muesli and yoghurt
- fresh fruit – such as pears, apple slices, satsuma, banana, seedless grapes, slices of mango, melon or pineapple
- cheese cubes and crackers/chapatti
- fruit smoothies
- slice of fruit loaf or malt loaf
- vegetable sticks, such as carrot, cucumber, pepper, baby corn
- plain biscuits, bread, toast, crumpets, scones, currant buns/teacakes, pitta bread.

Ideas for healthy packed lunches

Many children and young people take packed lunches to school. There are lots of different types of bread that can be used to add variety. You could offer pitta bread, chapattis, crusty rolls, muffins or bagels with one of these healthy fillings:

- banana
- tuna and tomato
- chicken with a low-fat dressing and salad
- salmon and cucumber
- cheese and pickle
- hummus and salad
- bacon, lettuce and tomato
- egg with low-fat mayonnaise.

Other ideas for items to supplement a lunchtime sandwich include:

- fresh or dried fruit
- cherry tomatoes
- cheese cubes
- fruit juice
- coleslaw
- soup in a flask
- sticks of raw vegetables
- hard-boiled egg
- small pot of potato salad
- pot of yoghurt or a yoghurt drink.

Crisps and other savoury snacks, chocolate or a muesli bar can be added as an occasional treat, depending on the setting's policy.

Healthy eating for young people

Adolescence is a time of increased nutrient needs. During the rapid growth of puberty, the body has increased need for **calories** and key nutrients including:

- protein
- calcium
- iron
- folate
- zinc.

Iron and calcium

Iron and calcium are particularly important nutrients during adolescence. Menstruation also increases a girl's need for iron. Iron:

- helps the blood to carry oxygen to all the muscles
- improves brain function
- helps the immune system to fight disease
- is found in liver, lean meats, poultry, oysters, tuna, salmon, molasses, dried beans and prunes, broccoli, spinach, eggs, almonds, raisins and apricots.

Calcium is important for strong bones and teeth. Children and teenagers who are still growing need to have extra calcium. Calcium is present in milk products, fish with bones, dried beans and some leafy green vegetables.

Providing drinks for children

You need to offer children drinks several times during the day. The best drinks for young children are water and milk.

The importance of water

It is important to ensure that all children and young people have regular drinks of water. Six to eight glasses of water a day helps to prevent dehydration and constipation, and quenches thirst without spoiling the appetite. If bottled water is used it should be still, not carbonated (fizzy) which is acidic. More water should be given in hot weather in order to prevent dehydration.

Milk

Milk is an excellent nourishing drink. Reduced-fat milks should not normally be given to children under the age of five because of their lower energy and fat-soluble content; however semi-skimmed milk may be offered from two years of age, provided that the child's overall diet is adequate.

Other drinks

All drinks that contain sugar can be harmful to teeth and can also take the edge off children's appetites. Examples are:

- flavoured milks
- fruit squashes
- flavoured fizzy drinks
- fruit juices (containing natural sugar).

Unsweetened diluted fruit juice is a reasonable choice for children (although not as good as water or milk), but ideally should only be offered at mealtimes. Low-sugar and diet fruit drinks contain artificial sweeteners and should be avoided. Tea and coffee should not be given to children under five years, as they prevent the absorption of iron from foods. They also tend to fill children up without providing nourishment.

Children aged one to four

- Offer around six to eight drinks per day from a beaker or cup (although more may be needed in very hot weather or when they are very active). One drink for this age group will be about 100–150 ml.
- Sweetened drinks, including diluted fruit juice, should only be consumed *with* rather than between meals, to reduce the risk of

dental decay. Consumption of sugar-free fizzy or fruit-based drinks, although not recommended, should also be confined to mealtimes because the high acidity level of these drinks can cause dental decay.

For school-aged children and young people

The following drinks are recommended: still water, milk (plain or flavoured), diluted pure fruit juice, fruit and milk/yoghurt smoothies, vegetable juices, and well-diluted squashes which contain no added sugar (sugar-free).

In between meals and snacks, water and plain milk are still the best drinks because they will not damage teeth as do acidic and sugary drinks.

Note: recent research shows that some parents never offer their children water to drink as they do not drink water themselves; some parents even consider it cruel to offer water in place of flavoured drinks.

How culture, religion and health conditions impact on food choices

The UK is the home of a multicultural and multi-ethnic society. Food is an important part of the heritage of any culture. Providing food from a wide range of cultures is an important way of celebrating this heritage. Children can learn to enjoy different tastes and to respect the customs and beliefs of people different from themselves.

The largest ethnic minority group in the UK belongs to the Asian community – about 1.25 million people. Asian dietary customs are mainly based on three religious groups: Hindus, Muslims (or Moslems) and Sikhs.

Hindu traditions

Orthodox Hindus are strict vegetarians as they believe in ahimsa – non-violence towards all living beings; some are vegans. Some Hindus will eat dairy products and eggs, while others will refuse eggs on the ground that they are a potential source of life. Even non-vegetarians do not eat beef as the cow is considered a sacred animal. It is also unusual for pork to be eaten, as the pig is considered unclean.

Wheat is the main staple food eaten by Hindus in the UK; it is used to make chapattis, puris and parathas. Ghee (clarified butter) and vegetable oil are used in cooking. Three festivals in the Hindu calendar are observed as days of fasting; these last from sunrise to sunset, during which Hindus eat only 'pure' foods such as fruit and yoghurt:

1. Mahshivrati – the birthday of Lord Shiva (March)
2. Ram Naumi – the birthday of Lord Rama (April)
3. Jan Mash Tami – the birthday of Lord Krishna (late August).

Muslim traditions

Muslims practise the Islamic religion, and their holy book, the Koran, provides them with their food laws. Unlawful foods (called haram) include pork, all meat that has not been rendered lawful (halal), alcohol and fish without scales. Halal meat has been killed in an approved way and must be bought from a halal butcher. Wheat, in the form of chapattis, and rice are the staple foods. During the lunar month of Ramadan, Muslims fast between sunrise and sunset. Children aged under 12 and elderly people are exempt from fasting.

Sikh traditions

Most Sikhs will not eat pork or beef. Some Sikhs are vegetarian, but many eat chicken, lamb and fish. Wheat and rice are staple foods. Devout Sikhs will fast once or twice a week, and most will fast on the first day of the Punjabi month or when there is a full moon.

Afro-Caribbean diets

The Afro-Caribbean community is the second-largest ethnic minority group in the UK. Dietary customs vary widely. Many people include a variety of European foods in their diet alongside the traditional foods of cornmeal, coconut, green banana, plantain, okra and yam. Although Afro-Caribbean people generally follow the Christian tradition, a minority are Rastafarians, which affects their diet.

Rastafarian diet

Dietary customs are based on laws laid down by Moses in the Bible, which state that certain types of meat should be avoided. The majority of followers will only eat ital foods, which are considered to be in a whole or natural state. Most Rastafarians are vegetarians and will not eat processed or preserved foods.

Jewish diets

Jewish people observe dietary laws which state that animals and birds must be killed by the Jewish method to render them kosher (acceptable). Milk and meat must never be cooked or eaten together, and pork in any form is forbidden. Shellfish are not allowed as they are thought to harbour disease.

The most holy day of the Jewish calendar is Yom Kippur (the Day of Atonement) when Jewish people fast for 25 hours.

Food and festivals

There are often particular foods that are associated with religious festivals, such as mince pies at Christmas and pancakes on Shrove Tuesday. Providing foods from different cultures within an early childhood setting is a very good way of celebrating these festivals.

Parents of children from ethnic minority groups are usually very pleased to be asked for advice on how to celebrate festivals with food, and may even be prepared to contribute some samples.

The different dietary requirements of children and young people

Most children on special diets are not ill. Often they simply require a therapeutic diet that replaces or eliminates some particular nutrient to prevent illness. Those with specific needs follow the diets listed in Table 16.2.

Vegetarian diets

Children and young people who are following a vegetarian diet need an alternative to meat, fish and chicken as the main sources of protein. These could include milk, cheese and eggs, pulses (lentils and beans).

They also need to consider their iron intake. As iron is more difficult to absorb from vegetable sources than from meat, a young child needs to obtain iron from sources such as:

- leafy green vegetables – such as spinach and watercress
- pulses (beans, lentils and chick peas)
- dried fruit (such as apricots, raisins and sultanas)
- some breakfast cereals.

It is easier to absorb iron from our food if it is eaten *with* foods containing vitamin C, such as fruit and vegetables or diluted fruit juices at mealtimes.

The vegan diet

A vegan diet completely excludes all foods of animal origin: animal flesh, milk and milk products, eggs, honey and all additives that may

Diets for specific needs

Diabetes mellitus

Diabetes mellitus occurs in one in every 500 children under the age of about 16 years, and results in difficulty in converting carbohydrate into energy due to the underproduction of insulin. Insulin is usually given by daily injection, and the hospital dietician will devise a diet sheet. It is important that mealtimes are *regular* and that some **carbohydrate** be included at every meal. Children with diabetes should be advised to carry **glucose** sweets whenever they are away from home in case of **hypoglycaemia** (low blood sugar).

Coeliac disease

Coeliac disease is a lifelong condition, and treatment is by gluten-free diet. All formula milks available in the UK are gluten-free, and many manufactured baby foods are also gluten-free. Any cakes, bread and biscuits should be made from gluten-free flour, and labels on processed foods should be read carefully to ensure that no wheat product is 'hidden' in the ingredients list.

Obesity

A child or young person who is diagnosed as being overweight will usually be prescribed a diet low in fat and sugar. High-fibre carbohydrates are encouraged, such as wholemeal bread and other cereals. The child who has to break the habit of eating crisps, chips and fatty snacks between meals will need much support and encouragement from carers.

Cystic fibrosis

The majority of children with cystic fibrosis have difficulty in absorbing fats. They need to eat 20 per cent more protein and more calories than children without the disease, and so require a diet high in fats and carbohydrates. They are also given daily vitamin supplements and pancreatic enzymes.

Galactosaemia

A child with galactosaemia cannot digest or use galactose – which, together with glucose, forms lactose, the natural sugar of milk. The dietician will issue a list of 'safe foods' with low galactose content, and food labels should be checked for the presence of milk solids and powdered lactose that contain large amounts of this sugar.

Children with difficulties with chewing and swallowing

Children with cerebral palsy can experience difficulties with either or both of these aspects of eating. Food has to be liquidised, but this should be done in separate batches so that the end result is not a pool of grey sludge. Presentation should be imaginative. Try to follow the general principle of making the difference in the meal as unobtrusive as possible.

Table 16.2 Diets for specific needs

be of animal origin. A vegan diet is based on cereals and cereal products, pulses, fruits, vegetables, nuts and seeds. Human breast milk is acceptable for vegan babies.

Supporting children and their families who have special diets

Any child or young person who has to follow a special diet for health reasons will occasionally feel like an outsider. Every health condition that requires a special diet has a support organisation where parents and carers can find information and often join in discussion forums on the internet.

Key terms

vegan – A vegan is a person who avoids using or consuming animal products. While vegetarians avoid flesh foods, vegans also avoid dairy and eggs, as well as fur, leather, wool, and cosmetics or chemical products tested on animals.

vegetarian – There are two types of vegetarianism: **lacto-ovo vegetarians** who exclude red meat, poultry and fish and **lacto-vegetarians** who exclude red meat, poultry, fish and eggs.

Variations in children and young people's diets

Parents or carers have a right to bring up their children and young people according to their own beliefs and cultural practices. Sometimes these preferences are difficult to accommodate within a group setting. An early years practitioner will need to ensure that the dietary needs and preferences of every child are recorded, and that every staff member knows how to follow these wishes. This is particularly important if a child has a **food allergy** or **intolerance**. Some nurseries have developed a system of personalised table placemats that include the child's name and photo along with their specific dietary requirements.

Occasionally, children may arrive at the setting with sweets and packets of crisps. Staff, parents and carers need to work together to formulate a policy that gives consistent guidelines about what is allowed in the setting, and to ensure that every child is offered a healthy and nutritious diet when away from home.

The benefits of healthy eating for children and young people

Eating a healthy diet during childhood makes it easier to maintain a healthy weight, and has been shown to improve children's concentration and behaviour. It can also help to reduce the risk of developing many common diseases, including heart disease, dental decay, diabetes and osteoporosis.

The possible consequences of an unhealthy diet

Imbalances in diet can contribute to children and young people developing a number of serious diet-related diseases and conditions over the course of their lifetime. In recent years there has been increasing public concern about the quality of children and young people's diets in the UK, rapidly increasing rates of **child obesity**, diet-related disorders and low consumption of fruit and vegetables by children. Several conditions can occur in childhood which are directly related to a poor or unbalanced diet; these are a result either of **malnutrition** or **under-nutrition,** and include:

- **failure to thrive** or faltering growth: poor growth and physical development
- **dental caries** or tooth decay: associated with a high consumption of sugar in snacks and fizzy drinks
- **obesity**: children who are overweight are more likely to become obese adults, and this can lead to a number of serious health conditions including some types of cancers, diabetes, coronary heart disease and stroke
- **nutritional anaemia**: due to an insufficient intake of iron, folic acid and vitamin B12
- **increased susceptibility to infections**: particularly upper respiratory infections, such as colds and bronchitis.

Key terms

Malnutrition – A person's diet is lacking the necessary amounts of certain elements which are essential to growth, such as vitamins, salts and proteins.

Under-nutrition – People do not receive enough food to eat.

Childhood obesity

Obesity is where there is excess fat in the body to the extent that it may have an adverse affect on health. Obesity results from taking in more energy from food than is used up by the body in daily activity. Some children and young people appear to inherit a tendency to put on weight very easily, and some parents and carers offer more high-calorie food than their children need. Some associated dietary problems are listed here.

- **Changing lifestyles**: the consumption of fast food is overtaking the eating of traditionally prepared meals. Many convenience meals involve coating the food with fatty sauces or batters.
- **Foods high in sugar and fat**: children eat more sweets and crisps and drink more fizzy drinks than in the past. This is partly because of advertising, but also because such foods are more widely available.
- **Poor fruit and vegetable consumption**: despite fresh fruit and vegetables being more readily available, many children do not eat enough of these, preferring processed varieties that often contain added sugar and fat.

Obesity can lead to emotional problems as well as to the physical problem of being more prone to infections. An obese child may be taunted by others, and will be unable to participate in the same vigorous play as their peers.

Support for overweight and obese children and young children

MEND is a community-based programme for overweight and obese children aged between seven and 13, and their families. The multi-disciplinary programme places equal emphasis on **(M)ind, (E)xercise, (N)utrition**. It comprises 18 two-hour sessions, typically run in the early evening hours across a nine-week period during the school term. (The MEND programme emphasises the word **programme** – they do not use the word diet.)

Food allergies and intolerances

Food allergy and food intolerance are both types of 'food sensitivity'. The main differences between them are the length of time it takes for symptoms to appear and the type of symptoms involved.

Food allergy

The **immune system** reacts to a particular food as if it is not safe. This causes *immediate* symptoms such as itchiness, rash and swelling. Sometimes this reaction is so severe that people can experience life-threatening reactions known as **anaphylaxis**, which affects the whole body, often within minutes of eating the food (see below).

Research Activity

Childhood obesity

As a group, prepare a factfile for your school or college on childhood obesity. Include the following information:

1 What is obesity? What causes it? What are the problems associated with it?

2 Find out the prevalence of obesity in children and young people in the UK. Present the information in chart form (pie charts, bar graphs, etc.), showing your results by gender and age group.

3 Research the latest government initiatives into tackling childhood obesity.

4 How does the MEND programme work? (See p 291 for the website address.)

Food intolerance

This does *not* involve the immune system. Some reactions are caused by an inability to digest a particular food, but often the reason behind the reaction is not understood. Usually symptoms are not immediate, but there are some preservatives and flavour enhancers that can cause flushing or wheezing in people with asthma soon after eating them.

Common food allergies

Up to 5 per cent of children in the UK have food allergies. Most children outgrow their allergy, although an allergy to peanuts and some other tree nuts is considered lifelong.

There are eight foods that cause 90 per cent of all food allergic reactions:

- peanuts
- soy
- tree nuts (such as almonds, walnuts, pecans)
- wheat
- milk
- shellfish
- eggs
- fish.

Milk is the most common cause of food allergies in children, but peanuts, nuts, fish and shellfish commonly cause the most severe reactions.

Recognising an allergic reaction

Symptoms of an allergic response can include:

- vomiting
- difficulty in breathing
- itching or swelling of the lips, tongue or mouth
- hives (or urticaria) – an itchy raised rash usually found on the trunk or limbs
- itching or tightness in the throat
- diarrhoea
- eczema
- cramps
- wheezing.

Allergic symptoms can begin *within minutes* or up to one hour after ingesting the food.

Anaphylaxis

In rare cases of food allergy, just one bite of a particular food can bring on **anaphylaxis**. This is a severe reaction that involves various areas of the body simultaneously. In extreme cases, it can cause death.

Anaphylaxis is a sudden and severe, potentially life-threatening allergic reaction. It can be caused by insect stings or medications, as well as by a food allergy. Although any food can potentially cause anaphylaxis, peanuts, nuts, shellfish, fish and eggs are foods that most commonly cause this reaction.

Symptoms of anaphylaxis may include all of those listed above for food allergies. In addition, the child's breathing is seriously impaired and the pulse rate becomes rapid.

Anaphylaxis is fortunately very rare, but is also very dangerous:

- Symptoms can occur in as little as five to fifteen minutes.
- As little as half a peanut can cause a fatal reaction in severely allergic individuals.
- Some severely allergic children can have a reaction if milk is splashed on their skin.
- Being kissed by somebody who has eaten peanuts, for example, can cause a reaction in severely allergic individuals.

Emergency treatment of anaphylaxis

1 **Summon medical help immediately**. The child will need **oxygen** and a life-saving injection of **adrenaline**.

2 **Place the child in a sitting position** to help relieve any breathing difficulty.

3 **Be prepared to resuscitate** (CPR) if necessary.

In some settings attended by a child or children known to be at risk from anaphylaxis, the staff may be trained to give the adrenaline injection.

Managing food allergies

- The only way to manage food allergies is strictly to **avoid** the foods to which the child is allergic. It is important to learn how to interpret ingredients on food labels and how to spot high-risk foods.
- If either parent or any siblings suffer hay fever, asthma, eczema or food allergies, a child should not be given peanuts in any form until they are at least three years old. This may help reduce the risk of the child developing a peanut allergy.

Many children outgrow earlier food-allergic symptoms as they get older, but parents will need professional support and advice to ensure that their child is receiving a safe, balanced diet.

Where to find advice on dietary concerns

When parents or carers register their child at nursery or school, they are asked to detail any special dietary requirements that their child may have. Some children may need special diets

In Practice

Recording and reporting allergies and intolerances

All staff should be aware of which children suffer from an allergy, to which food, and of the policy regarding first aid and administering medication. Practitioners involved in the care of a child with a food allergy must do the following:

- ❑ Be aware of the foods and ingredients being offered to the child.

- ❑ Take care in the preparation and serving of food so as not to cross-contaminate food being served to a child with an allergy.

- ❑ Seek medical advice **immediately** if you notice swelling of a child's mouth or face or breathing difficulties when eating. Symptoms such as a rash or vomiting after eating may also suggest that there has been a reaction to a food. Always inform the parent or carer.

- ❑ Never try to diagnose allergies or cut out foods without medical advice, as this may compromise the quality of the diet and result in nutritional deficiencies.

To reduce the risk of peanut allergies, foods containing peanuts should not be given to children under three years of age if the child has a parent or sibling with a diagnosed allergy. Whole nuts should not be given to any child under the age of five years because of the risk of choking.

Activity

Special dietary requirements

Find out about the policy in your work setting covering special dietary requirements. In particular, find out about:

- special diets (which have been medically advised)

- preference diets (where there is no degree of risk attached)

- food allergies.

How does your setting ensure that any special dietary requirements are identified, and that each child is offered the appropriate food and drink?

because of an underlying medical condition; others may require a vegetarian or vegan diet. It is important that all child care and education settings are aware of any particular allergies or problems with eating that a child or young person may have. If a parent or carer expresses any concern to you about the food provided within your nursery or school, refer them to the person in charge or the child's key person for guidance. See also the Food Standards Agency website: www.eatwell.gov.uk.

Making healthier food choices

Some children and young people can be choosy about the food they eat, and this can be a source of anxiety for parents and for those who work with children. However, as long as children eat some food from each of the five food groups – even if they are the same old favourites – there is no cause for worry.

Guidelines: Encouraging children to make healthier food choices

- **Offer a wide variety of different foods** – give babies and young children a chance to try a new food more than once; any refusal on first tasting may be due to dislike of the *new* rather than of the food itself.
- **Set an example** – children will imitate both what you eat and how you eat it. Be relaxed, patient and friendly. It will be easier to encourage a child to eat a stick of raw celery if you eat one too! If you show disgust at certain foods, young children will notice and copy you.
- **Be prepared for messy mealtimes!** Present the food in a form that is fairly easy for children to manage by themselves (for example, easy to chew).

- **Do not use food as a punishment, reward, bribe or threat** – for example, do not give sweets or chocolates as a reward for finishing savoury foods. To a child this is like saying, 'Here is something nice after eating those nasty greens.' Reward them instead with a trip to the park or a story session.
- **Give healthy foods as treats**, such as raisins and raw carrots, rather than sweets or cakes.
- **If a child rejects the food**, never force-feed him; simply remove the food without comment. Give smaller portions next time and praise the child for eating even a little.
- **Encourage children to feed themselves** – either using a spoon or by offering suitable finger foods.
- **Introduce new foods in stages** – for example, if switching to wholemeal bread, try a soft-grain white bread first. Always involve the children in making choices as far as possible.
- **Teach children to eat mainly at mealtimes** and avoid giving them high-calorie snacks (biscuits and sugary drinks) which might take the edge off their appetite for more nutritious food. Most young children need three small meals and three snacks a day.
- **Be imaginative with presentation** – for example, cut slices of pizza into interesting shapes. Use ideas from children's food manufacturers. Using these tactics can make mealtimes more fun.
- **Avoid adding salt to any food** – too much salt can cause dehydration in babies and may predispose certain people to hypertension (high blood pressure) if taken over a lifetime.
- Allow children to follow their own individual appetites when deciding how much they want to eat.
- **Never give a young child whole nuts to eat – particularly peanuts**. Children can very easily choke on a small piece of the nut or even inhale it, which can cause a severe type

Figure 16.01 Enjoying a healthy meal

of pneumonia. Rarely, a child may have a serious allergic reaction to nuts.

- **Respect individual preferences**. Some families prefer to eat with their fingers, while others use chopsticks or cutlery. Whatever tool is preferred, be patient, as children need time to get used to them.

As an early years practitioner, you are ideally placed to ensure that **stereotyping** in relation to eating habits is not practised. Mealtimes and the choice of food can be used in a positive sense to affirm a feeling of cultural identity.

Eating disorders in children and young people

The most common eating disorders affecting children and adolescents are obesity, anorexia nervosa and bulimia nervosa. All three have profound implications for the successful development of the individual's self-concept and resulting self-esteem. (Obesity is discussed above on pp 280–1.)

Anorexia nervosa

People with anorexia nervosa have an extreme fear of gaining weight; they feel fat, even when they have lost so much weight that it becomes obvious to others. Those affected are predominantly adolescent girls from the higher social classes in the developed world, but recent evidence points to problems in children as young as seven years old, with a slight increase in the number of boys affected.

Features of the disorder are:

- regularly skipping meals and obsessively counting calories
- disappearing from the table directly after meals (in order to make themselves vomit)
- eating only low-calorie food
- showing a keen interest in buying or cooking food for others
- wearing very loose clothes to hide the body
- an obsession with exercise
- dramatic weight loss or gain
- saying they are unhappy with their body
- lanugo (baby-like hair on the body; thinning of hair on the head).

There are various theories on the causes of anorexia, including the following:

- Affected individuals do not wish to grow up and are trying to keep their childhood shapes. In part, this may be influenced by the media obsession with achieving the 'perfect' (i.e. slim) body, and also by the desire to defer the 'storm and stress' of adolescence.
- Those affected see anorexia as a way of taking control over their lives.
- Some specialists see it as a true phobia about putting on weight.
- It may be due to an attempt to avoid adult sexual feelings and behaviours.
- The affected individual is over-involved in their own family, so that when they enter adolescence, there is a confrontation between the peer group and the family.
- It may be a physical illness caused in part by **hormonal** changes or a disorder of the hypothalamus (the part of the brain concerned with hunger, thirst and sexual development).
- It is caused by depression, a personality disorder or, rarely, schizophrenia.

Bulimia nervosa

People with bulimia nervosa eat large amounts of food in 'binges' and then make themselves sick to get rid of the food. They may also:

- take large amounts of laxatives.
- not look overweight or underweight, and because of this their eating problems are often difficult to detect.
- eventually do serious harm to their bodies; in severe cases, repeated vomiting leads to dehydration and loss of the body's vital salts, especially potassium – this may result in weakness and cramps. The acid present in stomach juices may damage tooth enamel.
- become clinically depressed or even suicidal.

As with anorexia, there is no single cause to account for the disorder. Many of the theories about bulimia are closely linked to those above, and include a morbid fear of fatness and a constant craving for food, developed after months or years of fasting. Without help, eating disorders can take over young people's lives, leaving them feeling guilty and bad about themselves. Life can become lonely and depressing and young people often become isolated from their friends. There is a small but definite risk of suicide. The future health of young people is also affected; for example, anorexia nervosa in the teenage years can cause, among other problems, permanent infertility and osteoporosis (brittle bones) in adult life.

Children and young people's eating disorders

Discuss the prevalence of ultra-slim models in the media – on film, in television and in magazines. Try to collect articles and advertisements in which photos of very slim models are used and analyse their appeal.

Teenage dolls – such as Barbie and Bratz – promote an idealised role model which is unhealthy and can damage the self-concept of the child. Discuss this statement.

Supporting hygiene during meal or snack times

Careful preparation of food and correct food handling techniques are important, to avoid the risk of infection or food poisoning. Settings must observe the following principles:

- Cooks and staff must be trained in **correct food service techniques**.
- **Correct food handling** by children and staff.
- **Adequate hand washing** by staff and children.
- Correct use of **serving utensils**.
- **Correct sharing of food** at tables (for example, when fruit platters are shared).
- **Correct storage and reheating of food** and drinks is important for food safety. Settings that serve food should provide the following:

Healthy eating: Parents and carers versus practitioners?

Government guidelines state:

> If parents provide packed lunches, providers should inform them about what can be stored safely and about appropriate food content.

Cassie is in reception class and brings a packed lunch to school every day. Staff are concerned because the lunchbox nearly always contains the same things: a packet of crisps, a chocolate spread sandwich, a chocolate fudge bar and an apple. When Cassie's teacher mentioned to Cassie's mother that children were not allowed to bring crisps or chocolate into the school, she said that Cassie point-blank refused to take anything else and would simply bring it home again, uneaten. She assured the teacher that Cassie ate very healthily at home, and that she did not regard the contents of Cassie's lunchbox as any of the school's business.

1. Do you think it is the practitioner's job to ensure that children are provided with nutritious food in their lunchboxes?
2. What about the rights of the child and the parents?

(a) safe food storage
(b) safe use of microwave ovens for heating food and drinks.

- See also food hygiene on p 173–76, Chapter 9, Unit MU 2.8: Contribute to the support of positive environments for children and young people.

Activity

Food and drink policy

Find out what is contained in your setting's Food and Drink policy (or Healthy Eating Policy).

- Who is responsible for ensuring that lunchboxes contain appropriate foods?
- How does the setting ensure that appropriate drinks and snacks are offered to children?

Promoting children's personal hygiene at meal and snack times

Practitioners should always model and promote good hygiene procedures. Make sure you follow the guidelines on p 122–23 for when and how to wash your hands. Ensure that children in your care understand the need for hygiene, and supervise them when they wash their hands after going to the toilet and before meals and snacks.

Supporting the code of conduct and policies for meal and snack times

Each setting should have a code of conduct and policies for meal and snack times. Apart from the hygiene procedures described above, the code of conduct should also cover:

- entry to and exit from the dining area
- noise levels
- conduct at the table
- collecting/ serving food
- conduct in the dining area
- clearing away.

Reflective practice: Code of conduct

Find out what is contained in your setting's code of conduct for meal and snack times.

- Do you find snack and meal times relaxing?
- How could these sessions be made more enjoyable? What could you do personally to improve the social experience?

Skills and techniques to promote positive behaviour in the dining area

The atmosphere at meal and snack times and the attitude and behaviour of practitioners are important to the development of healthy eating practices and positive behaviour. Practitioners should do the following:

- Develop and encourage healthy eating patterns and positive attitudes to food.
- Ensure that the children or young people are relaxed and happy when they are eating.
- Be consistent in their expectations of children's behaviour at mealtimes. Children need to understand what is expected of them.
- You could involve the children in drawing up some mealtime 'golden rules'.
- You should act as a positive role model, sitting, eating and talking with the children, instead of hurrying around, sorting out the room or passing plates of food around.
- Encourage children to talk to each other and to enjoy themselves – but not to shout or leave their seats!
- Encourage children to serve themselves as this promotes self-reliance and confidence.

Dealing with inappropriate behaviour in the dining area

When children behave inappropriately at meal and snack times, they can spoil what should be a pleasurable experience for the other children and adults in the room. Some children do not regularly eat with their family at home, so it might seem strange for them to have to sit down with others to eat a meal.

Figure 16.02 Children develop self-reliance when encouraged to serve themselves with food

Food refusal

Many children go through phases of refusing to eat certain foods or not wanting to eat anything much at all. This is particularly common in children up to the age of five, and is a normal part of growing up and asserting their independence. Eating can quickly become a focus for conflict and tension at home, with parents feeling anxious and out of control. Food refusal often starts because it is one of the few ways in which children can exert influence over their parents.

Reflective practice: A learning environment

Describe an activity using a meal or snack time as a learning situation for children. What did the children learn? How could you adapt the activity for a different age group?

Activity

Food refusal
- Give some reasons why a child may refuse food.
- Find out what to do if a child continually refuses to eat when at your setting.

Useful websites and resources

www.nutrition.org.uk	**British Nutrition Foundation** For information on healthy eating and the Balance of Health pictorial guide
www.schoolfoodtrust.org.uk	**The School Food Trust** The School Food Trust promotes the education and health of children and young people and the quality of food in schools.
www.mendprogramme.org	**MEND programme**

Communication, language and literacy are at the heart of learning for children and young people, as well as being important for promoting their social and emotional development. The learning environment should reflect the importance of language and literacy through books, labels and signs. Practitioners should provide a wide variety of songs, stories, rhymes and poems on a daily basis.

Learning outcomes

By the end of this chapter you will:

1. Understand the importance of communication, language and literacy for children's learning and development.

2. Be able to contribute to children's learning in communication, language and literacy.

3. Be able to evaluate your own contribution to children's learning in communication, language and literacy.

The importance of communication, language and literacy for children's learning and development

Communication, language and literacy

The Early Years Foundation Stage (EYFS) in England places an emphasis on the importance of communication by including it as a statutory requirement under the Learning and Development theme. It is divided into six aspects.

Six aspects of communication for EYFS

Language for communication

This is about how children become communicators. Learning to listen and speak emerges out of non-verbal communication, which includes facial expression, eye contact and hand gesture.

Aims: children listen with enjoyment, and respond to stories, songs and other music, rhymes and poems. They make up their own stories, songs, rhymes and poems. They speak clearly and audibly with confidence and control and show awareness of the listener; for example, the use of convention such as greetings, 'please' and 'thank you'.

Language for thinking

How children learn to use language to clarify their thinking and ideas, or to refer to events they have observed.

Aims: children use talk to organise, sequence and clarify thinking, ideas, feelings and events. They use language to imagine and recreate roles and experiences.

Linking sounds and letters

How children develop the ability to distinguish between sounds and become familiar with rhyme, rhythm and **alliteration**.

Aims: children link sounds to letters, naming and sounding the letters of the alphabet. They use their **phonic** knowledge to write simple regular words, and make phonetically plausible attempts at more complex words.

Reading

This aspect is about children understanding and enjoying stories, books and rhymes.

Aims: children explore and experiment with sounds, words and texts. They read a range of familiar and common words and simple sentences independently, and know that print carries meaning. They also know that, in English, print is read from left to right and top to bottom.

Writing

How children build an understanding of the relationship between the spoken and written word, and how through making marks, drawing and personal writing, children ascribe meaning to text and attempt to write for various purposes.

Aims: children attempt writing for different purposes, using features of different forms such as lists, stories and instructions. They write their own names and other things such as labels and captions, and begin to form simple sentences, sometimes using punctuation.

Handwriting

The ways in which children's random marks, lines and drawings develop and form the basis of recognisable letters.

Aims: children use a pencil and hold it effectively to form recognisable letters, most of which are correctly formed.

Key term

Alliteration – When two or more words begin with the same letter or sound – for example, **R**abbits **R**unning over **R**oses.

Why communication skills are important for children's development

We have already seen in Chapter 13, Unit TDA 2.7: Maintain and support relationships with children and young people, how important communication is for maintaining and supporting relationships with children. Communication must always be a two-way process. It is not just about you telling the children something or giving advice, but rather listening to their viewpoints and accepting their emotions.

The importance of language

Language is the key to learning. Our ability to use language lies at the centre of the development and expression of our:

- emotions
- thinking
- learning
- sense of personal identity.

The importance of literacy

The importance of literacy is evident. Everywhere you look, you see words – on signs and labels, in training manuals, on buses, in books. Adults who can't read risk becoming isolated from society. Research shows that people with well-developed literacy skills are more likely to have positive self-esteem and are generally more able to take advantage of the opportunities that life may offer them.

Key term

Literacy – The ability to read and write.

Talk to Your Baby campaign

Talk To Your Baby is a campaign run by the National Literacy Trust to encourage parents and carers to talk more to children from birth to three. Talking and listening to young children help them to develop effective language and communication skills, which enable them to express themselves, listen, learn, read, write and socialise better. It also helps children to feel

Research Activity

Campaigns for literacy

Find out more about the Talk to Your Baby campaign and the 2011 Hello campaign, run by The Communication Trust. (See p 308, Useful websites and resources section at the end of this chapter.)

Pushchairs and buggies – which way should they face?

Young children spend a considerable amount of time each day strapped into buggies – and most children's buggies face away from the pusher. Research shows that this makes eye contact between the adult and the child impossible and leads to difficulties in communication.

1. Discuss how buggies that face the pusher can aid communication between adult and child.
2. What kind of communication problems might develop if the adult is pushing a forward-facing buggy and also constantly using a mobile phone?

valued, builds their confidence and helps parents and children to bond.

How communication, language and literacy link with other areas of learning and development

Child development should always be viewed holistically. This is because each area of development is linked with and affects every other area of development.

You will need to look at the early years framework used in your setting:

England	Early Years Foundation Stage (EYFS) Communication, language and literacy
Wales	Foundation Phase Language, literacy and communication skills Children are likely to be learning both Welsh and English
Scotland	Curriculum for Excellence Languages Literacy not identified as a separate area. Practitioners have access to resources to embed literacy into activities.
Northern Ireland	Language and literacy (for children in school) No formal framework for early years but **Early Years (0-6) Strategy** in draft form (2011)

EYFS area of learning	Themes	Links with communication, language and literacy
Personal, social and emotional development	Dispositions and attitudes, self-confidence and self-esteem, making relationships, behaviour and self-control, self-care and sense of community	Language used to talk about feelings and emotions Language helps children to socialise and show positive behaviour
Problem-solving, reasoning and numeracy	Numbers as labels and for counting, calculating, shape, space and measures	Children develop the language of mathematics in order to solve problems, remember concepts and make sense of their world
Knowledge and understanding of the world	Exploration and investigation, designing and making, ICT, time, place and communities	Language used to talk about what they are seeing, doing and experiencing
Physical development	Movement and space, health and bodily awareness and using equipment and materials	Skills of hand–eye coordination and fine manipulative skills to enable children to write
Creative development	Being creative – responding to experiences, expressing and communicating ideas, exploring media and materials, creating music and dance, developing imagination and imaginative play	Early mark-making promotes self-expression Language to talk about what they have been doing Awareness of sound and making music – rhythm and beat

Table 17.1 Links to communication, language and literacy

Table 17.1 shows how in England the EYFS's areas of development and learning link with communication, language and literacy. If your setting does not work with the EYFS, then the second column, Themes, will help you to find out how the links are made in the relevant framework.

Contributing to children's learning in communication, language and literacy

Communicating with children

You need to pay close attention to your own non-verbal messages, and adapt them accordingly to meet the needs of children. You can help children by:

- **making eye contact**: give your attention to the child, and use a friendly facial expression. This will make the child feel that he or she is important to you and that you are respectful of his or her needs.
- **supporting them in how to manage their emotions**, control their impulses and express feelings of anger with words.
- **talking them gently through** the experience when they have just had a tantrum.
- **questioning the child sensitively** – try to find out what he or she was feeling. You could ask, 'How did that make you feel?' Children need to be taught how to 'label' and manage their feelings, especially anger.
- **getting down to their level**: if the child has been aggressive – punching, biting or kicking others – try to prompt the child to think about how she would feel if someone else had done the same thing to her.

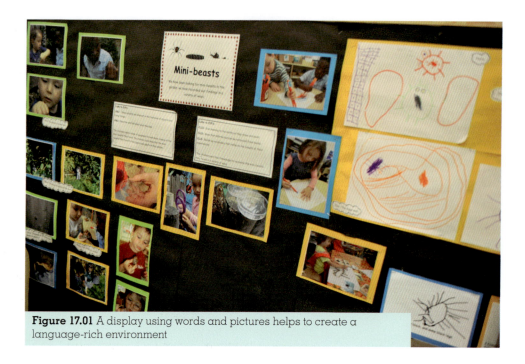

Figure 17.01 A display using words and pictures helps to create a language-rich environment

The importance of a language-rich environment

Children learn speech and language through listening, watching, exploring, copying, initiating, responding, playing and interacting with others. During children's early years most of the important interaction is between the child and their parents, carers and maybe siblings. Parents and practitioners should provide a language-rich environment. This environment should be:

- **nurturing**: giving children love and affection and building their self-confidence
- **a place of learning**: creating a place where language and learning can take place together
- **language-rich**: using every opportunity to use language, interact, share a common focus, talk and take turns.

One of the biggest things to be aware of when using language around young children is the level and complexity of the language you use. A young child will generally understand more words than he uses in speech.

Let the child take the lead

Children do not learn language by having an adult continually asking them to name various items. Children learn by hearing words and linking them to things. It is a good idea to *add* language into the child's play, rather than asking

Case Study   Harry and the train

Harry is sitting in the nursery playing with a train. Phoebe is Harry's key person and is sitting next to him. Harry makes a 'Brrm' noise and says, 'Train,' as he pushes the train along the floor. Phoebe smiles and nods and says, 'That's right, it's a train, a blue train.' Harry stops pushing the blue train and picks up a red car. He says, 'Car,' and shows Phoebe, who says, 'Yes, that's right. It's a car, a red car.'

By simply commenting, rather than asking questions, Phoebe is allowing Harry to be in control of his own play and he is not under any pressure to communicate.

the child to name every toy she is playing with. For example, you could:

- comment on what the child sees or what she is doing
- expand on what she has said.

In this way you are building the child's confidence and promoting language development.

Activities and equipment that are used to support children's communication, language and literacy

Activities that encourage children to communicate by listening and talking

Young children need to be encouraged to **learn through play** and to focus on an activity rather than on practising a specific language skill. The following activities encourage children to listen and talk to others.

Role play

Children use a rich variety of language to communicate during role play. They enjoy being someone else and acting out a situation; for example, at the shop, at the post office or driving a car. Children naturally use role play in their own language situations; for example, 'I'll be Mummy and you be Daddy.' They also use props in their play – such as dressing-up clothes, hats, wooden blocks, etc.

Reading aloud

Reading aloud to children is a natural way to encourage two-way communication. Talking and listening to young children develop their literacy skills and the social skills of sharing and taking turns. Reading books aloud has many benefits:

- It is an important source of new vocabulary – words for characters and objects.
- It introduces children to the exciting world of stories and helps them to learn how to express their own thoughts and emotions.
- It provides topics for discussion, with many opportunities for learning the *context* of language.
- It provides parents and practitioners with a structure to help them talk aloud to children and listen to their responses.
- It combines the benefits of talking, listening and storytelling within a single activity and helps to build the foundation for language development.

Choose stories with repetition like 'The Three Little Pigs', or 'The Very Hungry Caterpillar'.

Puppets and props

Children often use puppets or dolls to express themselves verbally, and props like masks or dressing-up clothes help them to act out roles in their own pretend play. Playing with hand puppets offers great opportunities to develop listening and talking skills. Children usually find it easy to talk to their own and other people's puppets, and this gives them confidence to express their ideas and feelings.

Games and puzzles

Children quickly learn to use the language necessary to take part in simple games, such as I Spy, Spot the difference, etc. As they get older, children enjoy board games such as Ludo® and Junior Scrabble®.

Songs and rhymes

These help children to learn new words in an enjoyable way. Songs and rhymes are also a good way to help children's talking and listening skills. When singing rhymes and songs:

- **Make them fun**: change the sound of your voice, make up some actions or add the children's names. Make up alternative endings and encourage the children to supply the last word of the nursery rhyme.
- **Encourage them to join in**: when a child joins in, show that you have noticed him by giving lots of encouragement.
- **Link language with physical movement**: use action songs and rhymes, such as 'The wheels on the bus' or 'We're going on a bear hunt'.
- **Talk about similarities** in rhyming words, and draw attention to the similarities in sounds at the beginning of words, emphasising initial sounds.

Speaking and listening activities in group settings

These range from individual conversations between adult and child to whole-class or group 'news' times. In addition, there are many games and activities that provide ideal opportunities for children to use and practise their speaking and listening skills. For very young children, sharing rhymes (traditional nursery, finger and action), songs and books with an adult are both valuable and enjoyable.

As language and listening skills develop, older children will be able to play games that involve 'active' listening such as those listed below.

What (or who) am I?
This involves the adult (or a child, perhaps with help) giving clues until the animal/person/object is identified. For example: 'I have sharp teeth. I have a long tail. I have a striped coat. I eat meat.' Answer: 'I'm a tiger or a tabby cat.'

Taped sounds
These can be environmental (a kettle boiling, a doorbell, someone eating crisps) or related to a particular topic – farm animals, pet animals, and machines – or of familiar people's voices.

Taped voices
Reception or Year 1 children tape their own voices, giving clues about themselves but without saying who they are. For example: 'I have brown eyes. I have two brothers. I have a Lion King® lunchbox. I have short, dark hair. Who am I?' This activity works best with a small group so that they are not guessing from among the whole class! They may find it difficult not to say their own names, but will love hearing themselves and their friends. The enjoyment factor makes it valuable and ensures concentrated listening once the excitement has died down.

Feely box
Use varied objects for children to feel (without being able to see) and encourage them to describe the shape, size, texture, surface, etc. This can be topic-related such as fruit or solid shapes, and is a very good activity for extending children's vocabulary.

Snowball
These are games that involve active listening and memory – 'I went to market and I bought . . .' There are many versions of this. It can be used for **number** (one cabbage, two bananas, three flannels, etc.) or to reinforce the **alphabet** (an apple, a budgie, a crane, etc), or it could be **topic-related** (food items, transport items, clothing, etc.)

Chinese whispers
This is appropriate for older children who are more able to wait patiently for their turn. A child whispers a word or phrase into the ear of another child, who whispers in the ear of the next child, and so on. The last child in the row has to repeat what they think is the word or phrase.

Circle activities

Children and the practitioner/s sit in a circle and the person who is speaking holds a 'special' object. The rule is are that only the person holding the object is allowed to speak. The object is passed around in turn or to whoever wants to say something; adult supervision may be needed! Alternatively a large ball can be rolled across the circle and the person rolling the ball makes a contribution (this can be on a theme – favourite foods/colours/games, etc.); the person who receives the ball makes the next contribution.

These **group activities** encourage children to:

- take turns
- use language to express their thoughts, feelings and ideas, and
- gain confidence as communicators.

The circle activities are particularly good for encouraging shy or withdrawn children who may not otherwise be heard in the group.

Progress check

Your role in promoting children's communication skills

- Know how to 'tune into' the different messages which babies and young children are attempting to convey.
- Model the correct use of key words, rather than correcting what children say.
- Talk about things that interest young children, both indoors and outdoors.
- Support children in using a variety of communication strategies, including gestures and signing where appropriate.
- Take time to listen to children and respond with interest to what they say.
- Help children to expand on what they say, introducing and reinforcing their vocabulary.

How to engage children's interest and attention

Children who have had a lack of social interaction or inappropriate role modelling in the early years of their lives may present with listening and attention difficulties. It is important to build their confidence early on by providing activities that are relatively easy to start with, offering quick success and rewards. They can then be adapted and developed as the children's listening and attention skills improve. Suitable activities to engage children's interest and attention are:

- matching games, such as Lotto
- 'spot the difference' games that require the child to observe closely and to respond when a difference is noticed
- board games that require the child to take turns and to know what to do when it is her turn
- musical games where the child has to complete the song.

Factors that particularly affect language development and/or communication

These include:

- any hearing impairments – permanent or temporary
- physical impairments such as cleft palate and hare lip
- stammers and stutters
- other medical conditions which affect other aspects of development and, as a consequence, a child's confidence or self-esteem
- disorders which affect learning such as autism
- an additional language – children's home language must be valued. Adults should recognise that these children are probably competent communicators at home, and need support to develop an additional vocabulary

which, for the very young child, may only apply in the early childhood setting

- lack of language input (conversations) with an interested adult or positive role model
- emotional factors which can result in shyness, low self-esteem and a lack of confidence.

Learning to read

Almost all children can learn to read and most really want to learn. The majority of children learn to read between the ages of four and a half and six years old. Research shows that pre-school children who are exposed to plenty of language (books and conversation) tend to do better at school.

In order to learn to read, children must recognise that a certain pattern of letters represents a particular sound. They need to build up a set of skills to help them make sense of words, signs and symbols.

These early reading skills are shown in Table 17.2.

The importance of books

Unlike learning to talk, children are not born with the instinct to read. Reading must be intentionally learned, and the best place to start is in the child's home. Children who are familiar with books and stories before they start school are better prepared to cope with the demands of formal literacy teaching. Children learn by example, so if they see an adult reading, they are likely to want to join in. Reading books with children is important because:

- books contain new words that will help to build children's language and understanding
- reading together is fun and helps to build relationships
- reading with children, or talking about what they have read, is a good way of showing that both reading and talking about books are

valued by the family or setting, as a good way to spend their time

- children learn about make-believe worlds, true stories and folk stories, which introduce them to different cultures.

Choosing books for babies and children

The variety of children's books is enormous. They come in all shapes and sizes – big board books, squashy books, interactive books that make noises, books with 'touchy-feely' bits, 'lift-the-flap' books.

Babies and toddlers

Very young children enjoy books that:

- **are well made and durable**. Babies like to really explore their favourite books, carrying them around, tugging on the pages, and even 'mouthing' them, so cloth, plastic or cardboard books are ideal.
- **contain bright, bold pictures** to help with focusing and identification.
- **may safely be left in the pram cot**, so that the baby develops a 'taste' for books. (Check safety labels carefully.)
- **have just a few words on each page,** or books which label objects in the pictures.
- **have rhyming verse or a repetitive theme**. A great favourite for many young children is 'Each Peach, Pear, Plum' by Allan Ahlberg and Janet Ahlberg.

Children aged between three and five years

Popular books for this age range:

- **have good stories** with interesting characters and a plot with lots of action.
- **have stories with a moral**: children like to see rules being obeyed and right to triumph.
- **are based on everyday experiences** and use the child's vocabulary.

Early reading skill	Activities to promote the skill
Shape recognition and matching: the ability to recognise shapes and to differentiate between them is important. Children learn to match shapes and patterns first, and this helps them to match letters and, finally, words.	• Snap (with cards) • shape sorter • picture pairs • Lotto • jigsaws • dominoes.
Rhyming: Research shows that children who can understand about rhyming words have a head start in learning to read and, even more, to spell.	• Rhyming games such as 'I Spy with my little eye, something that rhymes with cat' (hat or mat). • Leave off the end of rhymes for the child to complete, e.g. 'Humpty Dumpty sat on a wall, Humpty Dumpty had a great . . . ?' • Reading simple poetry.
Language skills: The more experience children have of language, the more easily they will learn to read. Children need to hear and join in conversations (with adults and children), and to listen to stories and poetry of all sorts.	• talking • reading stories • encouraging children to talk • share their favourite stories again and again: repeating phrases helps to build children's language.
Concepts of print: This means 'how we look at books' and includes following print from left to right, turning the pages, looking at pictures.	Children need to learn practical skills: • how to hold a book (the right way up!) • how to turn pages singly • let the child see your finger following the print when reading.
Letter skills: Children need to learn what sounds the letters can make.	• Begin with letters with an interesting shape that makes them easy to recognise, or a letter which is important to the child, such as their own initial. • Use the letter *sounds* rather than letter *names*; e.g. 'ah for ant', 'ay for ape'. • Try a letter hunt: looking for objects which begin with a particular letter.
Motor skills: since reading and writing are best taught together, pencil control is important.	• Encourage creativity: drawing and painting with lots of different tools and materials to encourage pencil and brush control. • Playing with small toys, especially construction sets, helps to develop fine motor skills.
Looking at a variety of printed materials: newspapers, magazines, packaging, street and shop names	• Point out words in the environment: e.g. 'Push', 'Pull', 'Open', 'Closed', etc. • Visit the library to encourage familiarity with the idea of books for everyone.
Memory skills: words are made up of sequences of letters and sounds, and children need to remember this before they can read.	• Memory games: such as 'I went to the shops and I bought a . . .' and pairs (Pelmanism) all help to improve children's memory skills and to increase their attention span. • Sequencing: book page layout can be reinforced by, for example, laying out the child's clothes to be selected first from left then to the right: vest, pants, top, trousers, socks, shoes.

Table 17.2 Activities to promote early learning skills

Figure 17.02 Sharing stories is important

Children also enjoy storybooks accompanied by a tape, so that they can follow the pages while listening to the story. Many libraries now offer board books as well as picture books for babies and young children. Parents can set up a book exchange to avoid unnecessary expense.

Bookstart is a national programme which encourages all parents and carers to enjoy books with their children from as early an age as possible. It offers the gift of free books to all children at three key ages before they start school, to inspire, stimulate and create a love of reading.

Figure 17.03 Bookstart packs. Pack contents correct at February 2011 – contents of packs may vary. Courtesy of Booktrust, used with permission.

Learning to write

Writing and spelling are more difficult to learn than speaking and reading. The child's first word written from memory is usually his or her own name. Most of the activities shown to promote early reading skills will also help children to learn to write. Children also need to develop the following basic skills:

- control the pen or pencil (this involves fine manipulative skills)
- form letters including upper and lower case
- recognize letter direction, such as b, d and p, q
- write in a straight line and space out words
- punctuate – understanding when writing needs a comma or full stop
- plan what they are going to write in advance
- sit still for some time with the correct posture for writing.

Children learn how to copy letters from as early as two years, and the skills of learning to write develop gradually as they become competent readers.

How writing develops

It is important to remember that children progress through the different stages at different rates and ages, depending on their experiences and developmental abilities. All children begin their journey into writing by **making marks**. This early writing follows a sequence:

Stage one

- The child holds the pencil or crayon in the palm of the hand in a palmar (fist-like) grasp.
- She makes early attempts at mark-making which feature lots of random marks, often made over other marks. This is often described by adults as scribbling.
- She cannot usually distinguish between her writing and her picture.

Stage two

- She may hold the pencil or crayon in a pincer grip between the thumb and index finger.
- She makes a definite attempt to make individual marks.
- She attempts to close shapes, making an inside and an outside. These shapes are often circular.

Figure 17.04 Mark-making

Figure 17.05 A colourful result of mark-making

- She combines shapes and lines. These marks will often represent one word.

Stage three

- The child copies adults and makes marks going across the page. These are often zigzags and curvy lines.
- She has a clearer idea of the marks which she wants to make.
- She may use either hand for writing.

Stage four

- The child forms symbols and some recognisable familiar letters that follow on next to each other.
- She is becoming aware of the left-to-right direction of print, and can point to where the print begins.
- She is becoming aware that writing conveys meaning, and she may 'read' her own writing.

Stage five

- The child writes a message using familiar letters.
- She writes some upper and lower case letters.
- She writes her name reliably.

Stage six

- The child writes most of the alphabet correctly, using upper and lower case letters.
- She writes first one or two letters correctly, then finishes with a jumbled string of letters.
- She begins to include capital letters and full stops at the beginning and end of work.
- She writes a longer sentence and can read it back.
- She attempts familiar forms of writing such as letters and lists.

Stage seven

- The child makes individual marks and uses some letters from her own name to communicate a message.
- She begins to understand that drawing and writing are different.

> ### Key term
>
> **Mark-making** – When children realise that marks can be used symbolically to carry meaning, in much the same way as the spoken word, they begin to use marks as tools to make their thinking visible.

- She is becoming aware that print carries a message.

How to promote mark-making and writing skills

Settings should provide the following:

- **Materials for mark-making**: these can include a range of pencils, felt-tip pens, different-sized paper, envelopes, little books and recycled cards. Also useful are other materials such as alphabet friezes, name cards and magnetic letters.
- **Meaningful contexts**: a writing-rich environment where writing and mark-making are encouraged for a wide variety of purposes, or when adults take part in writing with children.
- **Examples of other people writing**: these can include activities such as staff completing records, parents and carers leaving messages, and visits to the local environment to see adults writing in shops, banks or post offices.
- **Encouragement and praise**: all attempts at writing made by children should be positively encouraged. Practitioners help children to understand that their writing is important and valuable if they take time to discuss with children what marks mean.

Using clear language to support children's learning

It is important that practitioners use clear language when helping children to learn. Children are great mimics and they unconsciously pick up on everything you say.

Case Study   Early writing skills

According to official data, more than one in six boys cannot write his own name or simple words such as 'mum', 'dad' or 'cat' after a year of school. Half as many girls have the same problem. Nurseries and childminders are to be told to encourage three- and four-year-old boys to write using materials such as chocolate powder and coloured sand in a bid to stop them falling behind girls. Government guidance being sent out next month will include advice to set up role-play activities specially designed to interest the youngest boys, such as builders taking phone messages and writing up instructions, post office workers filling in forms and waiters taking orders.

(Adapted news article from the *Guardian*, December 2009)

When talking with a child, make sure that you have the child's attention, maintain eye contact (usually this means getting down to their level) and speak in short, simple sentences using appropriate vocabulary. Repeat your statement or question if necessary, using non-verbal communication also – nodding and smiling. A good way of expanding children's vocabulary is to describe what you are doing when involved in a shared activity, such as cooking. Ask open-ended questions so that the child will have to think before answering. Using clear language also involves developing the following skills:

- **Being grammatically correct**: Adults should express themselves clearly and use correct grammar. This does not mean that you should correct children's grammar, rather you should 'model' the correct grammar. For

example, a two-year-old child might say: 'I falled down.' The adult replies: 'Yes, you did, didn't you – you fell down. Never mind – I'll help you up.'

- **Adapting the way you speak to the individual child:** The language you use should be appropriate to the child's stage of development. With babies and toddlers this will involve repeating key words and keeping your sentences fairly short.
- **Checking for comprehension:** Adults need to use different ways of checking that a child has understood them. This will often be clear from the child's facial expression. With older children, you can ask a question and receive verbal feedback.
- **Using appropriate body language – gestures and facial expressions:** Children learn about body language and non-verbal cues by observing and imitating other people. One of the first conscious facial expressions learned by a baby is the smile; this is because adults tend to smile at infants a great deal. It is important to have a friendly, relaxed posture and to smile when talking with children. You can help children's understanding by using gestures, such as pointing and waving, to clarify what you are saying.

Reflective practice:
Communicating with children

- Do you encourage repetition, rhythm and rhyme by reciting poems and rhymes and singing?
- Do you encourage playfulness and turn-taking with babies, using games such as peek-a-boo?
- Do you use different voices to tell stories and get young children to join in, sometimes using puppets, soft toys or real objects?

Using encouragement and praise when supporting children's learning

Practitioners should always recognise young children's competence, and appreciate their efforts when they show their understanding of new words and phrases. Make sure that children understand what they are being praised for by responding immediately; saying, for example, 'Well done, Sasha, you told that story very well.' It is important to use encouraging words when a child is putting in a lot of effort, even if he has not managed to achieve his aim. Children need to receive positive feedback in order to develop confidence and good self-esteem. Then, they will be more likely to try again and to persevere until they succeed.

Reflective practice: Praise and encouragement

- To what extent do you regard yourself as a positive practitioner?
- Do you feel you could use praise more effectively, for example by distinguishing between praise for a task well done, behaviour-related praise and praise of personal qualities?

Evaluating your own contribution to children's learning in communication, language and literacy

The National Strategies for Early Years contain guidelines for how practitioners should work to promote children's development in communication, language and literacy. Many questions are asked of practitioners, to enable them to critically evaluate how they are doing. These include the following:

As a practitioner, do you do the following:

- Comment on what is happening during activities, rather than questioning children?
- Use talk to describe what children are doing by providing a running commentary alongside activities?
- Help children to predict and order events or make up stories, by providing props and materials to re-enact stories?
- Set up displays that remind children of what they have experienced?
- Provide opportunities to reflect on and recount past events and stories?
- Plan effectively for the next steps in learning?
- Talk about and value the random marks which young babies and children make?
- Make books with activities the children have been doing?
- Write poems and short stories with the children?
- Encourage children to draw and paint, and talk to them about what they have done?
- Provide opportunities for children to see practitioners using writing for a purpose, for example writing lists and messages?
- Include opportunities for writing in role play and other activities?

For more information on supporting children's learning in this area, visit the Standards website at www.nationalstrategies.standards.dcsf.gov.uk.

Reviewing your own working practice

Reflection on your own practice is important because it allows you to assess what you are doing well, and to identify areas where you might like or need more training or guidance to ensure that:

- you are performing to the best you can
- you are meeting all standards and expectations within the setting's policies and procedures.

It also helps you to think about what you are doing and to be aware at all times of how you work with the children, families and colleagues.

Reviewing your practice

Using the questions above, try to think of three examples of something that you have done of which you are proud. Similarly, you can use the questions to prompt you to explore areas where you feel you have not done so well, and think of reasons for this.

Adapting your own practice to meet individual children's needs

Every setting is different, and of course every child is unique. You may have children in your setting for whom English is not their primary language. There may also be a child with specific communication difficulties, because of autism or a hearing impairment. Children who are left-handed will need strategies to help them learn to write that are different from strategies needed by children who are right-handed. It is important that you know how to adapt your own practice to meet the needs of each individual child.

In Practice

Meeting individual needs

1. Choose a child in your setting who requires additional help with some aspect of communication, language and literacy.
2. Make an assessment of the child's needs.
3. Plan a programme or activity that will help to meet those needs.
4. Implement the activity.
5. Evaluate the activity.

Key terms

Evaluate – Examine strengths and weaknesses; make points for and against.

Review – Look back over the topic or activity and make or identify adjustments, changes or additions that would improve the topic or activity.

Assessment practice

The importance of communication, language and literacy

How is the development and learning area of communication, language and literacy promoted in your setting? Are parents involved in coming into the setting to help with communication, language and literacy activities, such as reading or musical activities with the children?

Useful websites and resources

www.literacytrust.org.uk	**The National Literacy Trust** Provides up-to-date information, articles and research about all aspects of literacy, including how to support children with their reading and writing.
www.thecommunicationtrust.org.uk	**The Communication Trust** The purpose of the Trust is to raise awareness of the importance of speech, language and communication across the children and young people's workforce, and to enable practitioners to access the best training and expertise to support all children's communication needs.

This unit looks at the ways that you can contribute to children's creative development. Practitioners can promote children's creative development by providing them with opportunities to explore and share their thoughts, ideas and feelings, for example, through a variety of creative activities.

Learning outcomes

By the end of this chapter you will:

1. Understand the importance of creative development.
2. Be able to contribute to children's creative development.
3. Be able to evaluate your own contribution to children's creative development.

The importance of creative development

What is creative development?

It is often thought that being creative is about being artistic. It is, but it is also possible to be creative in scientific and problem-solving ways. Creative development is strongly linked to **play**, and involves children:

- taking risks and making connections
- exploring their own ideas and expressing them through movement
- making and transforming things using media and materials such as crayons, paints, scissors, words, sounds, movement, props and make-believe

- making choices and decisions about their own learning
- responding to what they see, hear and experience through their senses.

The requirements of the Early Years Foundation Stage (in England) state:

Children's creativity must be extended by the provision of support for their curiosity, exploration and play. They must be provided with opportunities to explore and share their thoughts, ideas and feelings, for example, through a variety of art, music, movement, dance, imaginative and role-play activities, mathematics, and design and technology.

Aspects of creative development

Being creative

Children respond in different ways to their sensory experiences – what they see, hear, smell, touch or feel. Being creative is also about expressing and communicating their ideas, thoughts and feelings.

Exploring media and materials

Children find out about and explore a widening range of media and materials (by themselves or under guidance), thinking about and working with colour, texture, shape, space and form in two and three dimensions.

Creating music and dance

Children explore sound, movement and music (by themselves or under guidance), focusing on how sounds can be made and changed, and recognised and repeated from a pattern. This aspect of creative development includes ways of exploring movement, matching movements to music and singing simple songs from memory.

Developing imagination and imaginative play

Children are supported to develop and build their imaginations through stories, role plays, imaginative play, dance, music, design and art.

How creative development links to other areas of learning and development

Creative play helps children to express their feelings and ideas about people and objects and events. It helps children to:

- be physically coordinated (**physical** development)
- develop language (**language and communication** development)
- develop ideas or concepts (**intellectual** – or **cognitive** – development)
- develop relationships with people (**social** development)
- be more confident and increase levels of self-esteem (**emotional** development).

Activity to promote creative development (CD)	Links to areas of learning and development	
A group of four-year-old children are using a variety of recycled materials for model-making - Exploring materials - Responding to experiences - Solving problems - Making designs - Expressing ideas - Developing imagination	CLL: PSED: PSRN: PD: KUS:	interacting, speaking, listening and communicating ideas expressing feelings, taking turns concepts of size, weight, space awareness, solve practical problems use scissors, brushes, fine manipulative skills, awareness of personal space choose different tools and materials, exploring and investigating
A group of three-year-old children are in the role play area, using a variety of play props - Exploring materials - Responding to experiences - Expressing ideas - Developing imagination	CLL: PSED: PSRN: PD: KUS:	interacting, making stories, learning new words relationships, expressing feelings and ideas, taking turns use numbers ideas, e.g. 2 hats, 3 places at the table use range of materials and equipment find out about materials, exploring and investigating

Key:
CD = Creative Development; **CLLL** = Communication, Language and Literacy; **PSED** = Personal, Social and Emotional Development; **PSRN** = Problem-Solving, Reasoning and Numeracy; **KUS** = Knowledge and Understanding of the World; **PD** = Physical Development

Contributing to children's creative development

The Early Years Foundation Stage and creative development

The Early Years Foundation Stage (EYFS) guidance for effectively implementing creative development asks practitioners to pay particular attention to these themes: positive relationships, enabling environments, learning and development.

Positive relationships

- Ensure that children feel secure enough to 'have a go', to learn new things and to be adventurous.
- Value what children can do and their own ideas, rather than expecting them to reproduce someone else's picture, dance or model, for example.
- Give opportunities for children to work alongside artists and other creative adults so that they see at first hand different ways of expressing and communicating ideas, and different responses to media and materials.
- Take account of children's specific religious or cultural beliefs relating to particular forms of art or methods of representation.

Enabling environments

- Provide a stimulating environment in which creativity, originality and expressiveness are valued.
- Include resources from a variety of cultures to stimulate new ideas and different ways of thinking.
- Offer opportunities for children with visual impairment to access and have physical contact with artefacts, materials, spaces and movements.
- Provide opportunities for children with hearing impairment to experience sound through physical contact with instruments and other sources of sound.
- Encourage children who cannot communicate by voice to respond to music in different ways, such as gestures.

Learning and development

- Present a wide range of experiences and activities that children can respond to by using many of their senses.
- Allow sufficient time for children to explore and develop ideas, and finish working through these ideas.
- Create opportunities for children to express their ideas through different types of representation.

Key term

Artefact – Man-made object.

Equipment and activities used to support creative development

Children learn about play from natural and recycled materials as well as specially designed toys and equipment. They need a balance of the two, for example, hollow wooden blocks and cardboard boxes.

Natural materials

These should be attractively presented. They are important for children living in a world where plastic is found everywhere. Natural materials help children to learn about sand, water, wood and clay. They also show children how they can

Figure 18.01 Working alongside creative artists in a woodworking activity

find materials for themselves, and are cheap to provide.

Recycled materials

These cost nothing to provide. Margarine tubs, bottle corks and plastic bottles, for example, need to be set out in attractive containers, which are easy to reach and use. Children need enough space and table room for creative play with these materials.

Commercially made equipment

These can be expensive and need to be carefully chosen. Look at Chapter 7, Unit MU 2.4: Contribute to children and young people's health and safety, which emphasises safety of equipment, non-toxic materials and cleanliness.

Many toys are pre-structured, which means that children can only use them in a narrow way. Open-ended equipment which can be used in a variety of ways is better value for money, such as wooden blocks, Lego®, Duplo®. Children benefit greatly if there are plenty of these, so that they can build exciting models. It is a good idea to have all the same brand of wooden blocks, or Lego® or Duplo®, so that these can be added to over the years.

In Practice

Equipment for creative play

❑ Check equipment for safety marks.

❑ Can the equipment be cleaned easily?

❑ Can it be mended easily, or are there replacement parts?

❑ Is it open-ended so that it can be used in many different ways, such as a doll's house, farm, home area equipment, wooden blocks?

Choosing play materials

Adults need to choose play materials carefully and to create:

- play opportunities
- time to play
- space for play indoors and outdoors
- places for dens, physical play, manipulative play and creative play
- **play props** and clothes for dressing up and role play
- an adapted play environment for children with disabilities.

Adults who provide **open-ended** materials create more play possibilities for children. You should provide:

- recycled junk materials (string, boxes, wood)
- natural materials (clay, woodwork, sand, water, twigs, leaves, feathers)

Figure 18.02 Playing with recycled materials allows children the choice of what to make

- traditional areas (home area, wooden blocks, workshop area with scissors, glue, etc).

Providing a variety of resources

A painting (or drawing) activity that allows children to develop their creativity and fine manipulative skills can be adapted to provide variety by using:

- different-quality papers – such as sugar, cartridge, 'newsprint', wall-lining paper
- paper of different colours
- different sizes of paper
- different media – such as pastels, wax crayons, colouring crayons, chalk
- paint – such as ready-mixed, powder, thick, thin, fluorescent, pearlised
- different techniques – such as finger, bubble, printing, marble rolling, string.

While using such a variety the children are also learning about textures and colours, and developing concepts about materials – how runny paint 'behaves', how chalk smudges. Other types of activity – construction, water, sand, small world, role play – can easily be varied to broaden children's experience.

Creative activities with children

When children are playing creatively – or being creative – they must not be expected to 'make something'. Creative play is about experimenting with materials and music. It is not about producing things to go on displays, or to be taken home; for example, when children are involved with messy finger play with paint, nothing is left at the end of the session once it has been cleared away.

Adults can encourage creative play by offering children a range of materials and play opportunities in:

- dance
- music
- drawing
- collage
- paintings
- model-making and woodwork
- sand (small world scenarios)
- water (small world scenarios)
- miniature garden scenarios
- drama and imaginative play.

Providing well-planned play for the EYFS

The EYFS applies to children from birth to five years of age. During this Foundation Stage, children might be attending a play group, pre-school, nursery school, nursery class, day care setting, reception class, private nursery or be with a childminder or nanny. Well-planned play, both indoors and outdoors, is an important part of the Early Years Foundation Stage. There are six areas of learning:

- personal, social and emotional development
- problem-solving, reasoning and numeracy
- physical development
- communication, language and literacy
- knowledge and understanding of the world
- creative development.

The following pages look more closely at seven different types of play provision and at the way in which they link to the six areas of learning and development in this stage. These types of play are:

- wooden block play
- sand and water play
- role play area
- dressing-up clothes
- small world play
- clay, dough and mud patches
- painting and drawing.

Wooden blocks

Indoors

Wooden blocks are best if they are free standing. They never wear out and can easily be reconditioned (sanded). There are three kinds of blocks:

- unit blocks
- mini hollow bricks
- large hollow bricks.

All these link with each other. To use wooden blocks, children need:

- enough space to build
- to play with the blocks away from 'traffic' of people walking through the area
- to have the blocks set out on shelves with outlines of shapes showing each type of block, so that children know where different types of blocks should be stored; children need to see them and to choose which they will use

Figure 18.03 A girl playing with wooden blocks

- a complete set of blocks (and not to lose any!); they should be easily tidied away
- to have blocks available each day.

Outdoors

Blocks could also be milk crates or wooden boxes, which can be stored outside along the wall and used each day. Children can make stepping-stones and build with them.

Safety

Children must be supervised closely. If they build blocks too high there is a risk that blocks could fall on them.

Progression in block play

- **At one to two years**: children mainly build towers and put blocks in rows.

- **At two to three years**: children make enclosures, towers become taller and blocks are put in rows. Balance is important now. They sometimes call their models something, such as a house.
- **At three to five years**: children begin to put together a variety of patterns. They begin to create play scenarios with more complicated stories. They make many patterns and achieve quite difficult balancing. They are interested in how to balance and build blocks.
- **At five to seven years**: the stories and buildings become very complex and are highly coordinated.

Figure 18.04 Water play

Construction

Construction is similar to block play except that all the pieces connect with each other, whereas blocks balance. Ideally, a variety of construction sets should be available, such as Lego®, Duplo®, Stickle Bricks®, Construct-O-Straws®. However, it is important that whatever sets you have should contain enough pieces to interest a group of children. Younger children find Duplo® easier than Lego® because the pieces are larger and easier to hold as they develop muscle control in their hands. As they develop their pincer movement, they enjoy practising it.

Sand and water play

Indoors

Sand can be offered in a commercial sand tray, in seed boxes from a garden shop or in washing-up bowls on tables. It can be poured on to a plastic mat and used as a 'beach' experience with shells, buckets, spades and pebbles. The mat can be rolled up at the end of the session and the sand poured into a sand tray to use again.

There should always be both wet and dry sand on offer, such as dry sand in bowls on tables, or wet sand in a sand tray. Provide jugs, scoops, funnels, sponges, small world scenarios, farms, tubes, spades, small buckets and rakes.

Miniature gardens can be made adding twigs, moss, and leaves.

Outdoors

Sand and water play outside is similar to indoors. However, the following equipment can also be used outdoors:

- hoses
- watering cans
- water-washable paint for use on the tarmac (using buckets of water and giant brushes)
- large, covered sandpit where several children can play.

Safety

- Make sure that sand and water play is carefully supervised.
- Be alert as children can drown in very shallow water, get sand in their eyes or slip on wet floors.

- Outdoor sandpits need covers to keep animals and insects out.
- Place the indoor water tray near to the sink (because it is heavy and in case people slip).
- Change the water every day.
- Always sweep the floor after sand play.
- Use a mop to ensure that floors are not slippery after water play.

Progression in sand and water play

- **At one to two years**: children begin by pouring and carrying water and sand, and by putting these materials in and out of containers.
- **At three to five years**: children begin to enjoy practical problems, and to solve them as they develop their learning; for example, how to make a strong jet of water, how to make sand keep its shape.
- **At five to seven years**: children's play scenarios have more of a story than previously. They use a variety of play people and cooperate more with other children.

Role play area

Indoors

The role play area is one of the most important areas in early childhood settings. Ideally it should have:

- some things in it that are like those in the child's home, such as cups, cooking pots
- some things that are from different cultures, such as a wok, chopsticks
- a proper place for everything, with children being encouraged to tidy up carefully
- a large dresser with hooks for cups and cupboards to store dishes and saucepans
- big, middle-sized and small dolls, representing children of different cultures
- a cooker (this can be home-made, for example from a cardboard box)

Figure 18.05 Role play

- wooden boxes which can be used as beds, tables, chairs
- food can be pre-structured (plastic fruit), transformable (dough), real food (a salad) or pretend food
- clothes can be kept in a chest of drawers, labelled with pictures and words
- magazines, notepads and writing implements which can be put by the telephone, and perhaps a bookcase with books
- adaptations for children with disabilities; for example, a child who is a wheelchair user may need a higher or lower table so that they can use the bowls and plates.

This area can be adapted to follow children's interests; for example, a till and some baskets would turn it into a shop; some toy pets could be visiting a vet, etc.

Outdoors

The home area outside is a den. Children at home enjoy playing in outside dens.

- Old furniture can be used outside to make a home area; an old airer (clothes horse) with a sheet or blanket over it makes good walls.
- Children can make pretend food using sand, water and messy materials (but supervision may be required to ensure that they do not actually eat it).
- A rug can be put in the den and furniture can be made by collecting spare cardboard boxes; they can become tables or beds for dolls.
- Cushions can make seats or beds.
- A box on its side can become a cupboard, with flaps as the cupboard doors.
- Cups and saucers can be made out of old yoghurt pots and margarine containers.

Safety

- Wooden equipment should be checked regularly for rough edges and splinters.
- Cutlery must be carefully introduced. Ask your supervisor for advice.
- Glass and china break easily. If used, close supervision is essential.

Progression in role play

- **At one to two years**: children carry materials (pots, pans, dolls) about; put them in and out of boxes and prams; put them in rows.
- **At two to three years**: they begin to make play scenarios, often about food.
- **At three to five years**: more of the story develops about a wider range of events and people.

Dressing-up clothes

Indoors and outdoors

Children wear dressing-up clothes indoors, but enjoy wearing them outdoors too.

- The clothes need to be simple and flexible in use.
- A basic cape and some basic hats are useful, including 'uniform' hats such as a firefighter's helmet, scarves and drapes, sari, tunic, shoes and baggy trousers to help children in role playing. They need to reflect different cultures.
- Fastenings should be varied to give children different experiences of connecting clothes together, such as zips, buttons, tying bows, buckles and Velcro.
- The clothes need to be hanging on a rack, with separate boxes for shoes and hats. A large safety mirror at child height is useful.

Safety

- There should be no strings, ribbons or purses on strings around the neck, which might strangle a child.
- Beware of children tripping over clothes that are too long.
- Make sure children wear suitable footwear – for example, no high heels when playing on climbing frames or running out of doors.
- Clothes should be washed regularly.

Progression in dressing-up clothes play

- **At one to two years**: children wear hats and shoes.
- **At two to three years**: children wear hats, shoes, capes and scarves.
- **At three to five years**: children are more adventurous – they begin to wear whole outfits and want more accuracy to look right for the role they play.

Figure 18.06 Dressing-up clothes play

Small world play

Garages, railway tracks, farms, zoos, space scenes, houses, hospitals, boats and castles all feature in small world play.

Indoors

Children can easily create play scenarios with pretend people and make up imaginative stories

Figure 18.07 Small world play

using small world materials to help them. These should be set out on a floor mat or carpet, or in a sand tray (see sand and water play).

- Miniature gardens make a good play scene; these can be made in seed trays from garden centres and put on tables.
- Children can make their own gardens and make up stories using them – pots of moss, gravel, twigs, pebbles and feathers.
- They can also make paths, trees, grass and hills.
- Older children begin to use doll's houses, garages and castles.

Outdoors

Small animals can transform a part of the garden into a jungle. Be careful to collect everything at the end of the play session, as small world materials are easily lost outside.

Safety

Check that the pieces are not so small that a younger child might choke.

Progression in play

- **At one to two years**: children mainly put toys in rows and make constructions.
- **At two to four years**: they make more complex constructions, such as a house, simple everyday stories.
- **At four to six years**: children use play scenarios such as going shopping, or develop a story with different people such as hospital scenes, outer space, garage scenes.

Clay, dough and mud patches

Indoors

Children often do not make anything in particular because this is creative play. There is

no need to have any sort of result or finished product. It is important not to force children into this. For a simple play dough recipe, please see the end of the chapter.

Storing clay

Clay can be brown or grey. It is stored by rolling it into a ball, the size of a large orange, pressing a thumb into it, pouring water into the hole, and covering the hole full of water with clay. It should then be stored in a bin with a well-fitting lid.

Outdoors

A mud patch for digging is a popular area outdoors. Spades and rakes with short handles are useful. Children love to bury things and fill holes with water. They enjoy planting flowers and vegetables.

Safety

Dough must be made using salt and cream of tartar if it is to be stored and used more than once.

Deter children from putting the dough in their mouths. Be extra vigilant with children who have coeliac disease as they must not consume any gluten (present in ordinary flour).

Progression in play

- **At one to three years**: children bash and bang clay.
- **At three to five years**: they learn to pinch, pull and roll it, and can also:
  - (a) make shapes
  - (b) choose their tools or use their hands more carefully
  - (c) begin to design and make models, which they sometimes like to keep and display, but not often.

Painting and drawing

Indoors

For **drawing**: children need a variety of materials to draw with (fat and thin felt pens,

Figure 18.08 Being creative with dough

Figure 18.09 Children enjoy expressing themselves through painting

chubby crayons, pastels, chalks, charcoal and pencils). Paper of different size, texture, shape and colour is also required. It should be attractively set out and stored on shelves or in boxes or trays.

For **painting**, provide a variety of paints (commercially produced or freshly mixed every day) and brushes, clean water, non-spillable paint containers, and pots to mix colours.

- Children need a range of paintbrushes (thick, middle and thin), ideally made from good-quality hog's hair. Poor-quality brushes lead to poor-quality paintings and are frustrating to use.
- Flat tables are easier for younger children to use than easels.
- Children should choose which paper and tools to use.

- A well-designed paint dryer which stacks paintings while allowing them to dry is ideal, but you can spread paintings out on the floor under a radiator, or hang with pegs to dry from a washing line.
- Mixing colours: it is best to provide only primary colours (red, blue and yellow paints) and to make shades by adding white or black to lighten or darken the colours.

Red + blue = purple

Red + yellow = orange

Blue + yellow = green

Red + white = pink

All colours mixed together = **brown**

- It is important that young children are given the opportunity to mix different colours

Singing

Songs can be well-known rhymes or games that involve the children in imitating a short tune sung by an adult (or a child, with older, confident children). Regular singing games develop children's listening skills and their ability to discriminate sound, particularly helping them to pitch a note more accurately.

Playing instruments

This involves many skills – physical, listening, social and intellectual. The best and most available instrument is the body. Body percussion involves hitting, flicking, tapping or thumping different parts of the body to produce a wide range of sounds; try chests, fingernails, teeth, cheeks with mouths open – in fact, anything, not forgetting the human voice! Children learn to control their movements to create loud and soft sounds, fast and slow rhythms.

Any bought instruments should be of good quality and produce pleasing sounds; cheap ones are not sufficiently durable and often create a poor sound. Although tuned percussion items (such as xylophone, glockenspiel, metallophone) are likely to be found in schools, individual, child-friendly instruments are better for younger children who may not be ready to share. A good range could include untuned percussion: tulip blocks, cabasa, guiro (or scraper), maracas, tambour (hand-held drum), tambourine (a tambour but with the metal discs around the side), castanets (on a hand-held stick), claves (or rhythm sticks), click-clacks, bongo drums, Indian bells, triangle and beater, individual chime bars and beaters, cow bells and hand-held bells. A group of instruments can be placed in a 'sound' corner for children to experiment with on their own or in pairs; perhaps all wooden instruments on one occasion or 'ones which are struck with a beater' another time.

Playing musical instruments in a group

Large group sessions can be difficult to organise but some *simple rules* can make them enjoyable for all and worthwhile:

- **Sitting in a circle** and reinforcing the names of instruments as they are given out help to keep things under control. Even three-year-old children can understand that they must leave their instrument on the floor in front of them until asked to pick it up, although this is not easy in the first instance.
- **Having a go**: it is usually a good idea to allow children to 'have a go' with their instruments before doing a more focused activity. The whole point of the games is for children to experience music-making, so there must be plenty of playing and experimenting and not too much sitting around waiting!
- **Taking turns to listen** to each child make as many different sounds on her instrument in as many ways as she can, is a good way of building her confidence and understanding that there is no right or wrong way.
- **Offer choices:** children can then choose the sounds they like best. Similarly, work can focus on dynamics (loud and soft) and children can be asked to play as loudly as they can and as quietly as they can. Which instruments were difficult to do this with? Why?
- **Taking turns to play**: another activity involves each child having an instrument. This time make sure there are some which resonate (continue sounding after they have been played or struck) as well as the wooden percussion instruments. Going around the group, one child plays her instrument and the next child cannot play until the sound has died away. Discuss which instruments had 'long' sounds and which 'short' ones.

Figure 18.11 Making music

Moving to music

This allows children to respond creatively to different sounds and rhythms. A wide variety should be available, as for listening. Circle singing games such as 'The farmer's in his den', 'Ring-a-ring o' roses' and 'Here we go round the mulberry bush' all encourage children to move in time with the pulse or beat.

Composing music

Choosing sounds and putting them together in patterns to create their own tunes and rhythms can develop children's listening and intellectual skills.

Using **home-made instruments** adds variety and interest. The most successful of these are shakers made from 'found materials' using different containers – tins, plastic pots, boxes (these must be clean and have close-fitting lids) – and choosing contents which will produce interesting sounds. These could be rice grains, lentils, chickpeas, black-eyed beans, runner bean seeds, dried pasta, stones and sand.

Under supervision, children can experiment and choose the contents, the amount and the container. If they are to be used continually it is a good idea to glue the lids on to avoid the danger of children putting small items in their mouths. They can also be decorated or covered in patterned sticky-backed plastic.

The opportunities for drama and imaginative play in a variety of settings

In imaginative play, children use their own real-life experiences and rearrange them. It provides opportunities for children to express emotions, such as jealousy, frustration or anger, in a safe and unthreatening way. Imaginative play links with:

- creative play
- role play
- dramatic play
- domestic play
- fantasy play
- play with dolls and small world objects.

Activities to promote imaginative play

Role play (or pretend play)

Children act out roles, sometimes pretending to be parents or characters from television programmes or books. They benefit from having access to a home area, with scaled-down cooker, table and chairs, etc.

Small world play

Small-scale models of people, animals, cars, doll's houses and fake food are useful in imaginative play; children are familiar with these objects, and playing with them helps them to relax and also to extend their language skills.

Dressing-up activities

Playing with dressing-up clothes stimulates imaginative play, and pretending to be an adult (parent, superhero, king or queen) allows children to feel in control and empathise with others.

Puppets and dolls (or teddies)

These can often help a withdrawn or shy child to voice their hidden feelings, by using the puppet's voice. This type of play may also help children to vent their powerful emotions (such as jealousy of a new baby) by shouting at the teddy.

Using clear language to support children's creative development

One of the best ways to help children to develop their creative skills is to talk about what they have done. By talking with children about their activity, you are showing that you value their art. Adults should not interrupt the child during his activity, or make suggestions. It is not helpful to ask a child, 'What is it?' when he brings a model or drawing to show you. However, encouraging children to talk about what they have already done will promote language development, as well as letting children knowing that you appreciate their art.

Using encouragement and praise when supporting children's creative development

Children need confidence to learn anything, and knowing that you value what they do can help them to be more adventurous. Most settings display children's work or put them in a personal folder. This helps children to feel that their work is valued, and encourages them to try the experience again.

Evaluating your own contribution to children's creative development

The National Strategies for Early Years contain guidelines for how practitioners should work to promote children's creativity and creative play. Many questions are asked of practitioners, to enable them to critically evaluate their work. These include the following; as a practitioner, do you:

- Ensure that there is enough time for children to express their thoughts, ideas and feelings in a variety of ways, such as in role play, by painting and by responding to music?
- Encourage children to discuss and appreciate the beauty around them in nature and the environment?
- Provide a wide range of materials, resources and sensory experiences to enable children to explore colour, texture and space?
- Provide a place where work-in-progress can be kept safely?
- Introduce vocabulary to enable children to talk about their observations and experiences, for example: smooth, shiny, rough, prickly, flat, patterned, jagged, bumpy, soft and hard?
- Provide experiences that involve all the senses and movement?

Reviewing your own working practice

Reflection on your own practice is important because it allows you to assess what you are doing well and to identify areas where you might like or need more training or guidance, to ensure that you are:

- performing to the best of your ability
- meeting all standards and expectations within the setting's policies and procedures.

It also helps you to think about what you are doing and to be aware at all times of how you work with the children, families and colleagues.

Reflective practice: Creative development

1. What open-ended activities do you provide for children in your setting?
2. Do you give children the experience of playing with paint and glue, before expecting them to use them to make a product such as a greetings card?
3. Have you ever taped your interactions with children to see how you support their creative development?

Adapting your own practice to meet individual children's needs

Every setting is different and of course, every child is unique. Most children love the opportunity to be creative, but you may have children in your setting who have particular difficulties in one area or more. For example, some children might not like getting dirty when painting or modelling with clay. Others might be too angry or fearful to act out their feelings through dramatic play, but they may be able to draw a picture that expresses their emotions. A child with poor fine motor skills may become frustrated when trying to express herself creatively. It is important that you know how to adapt your own practice to meet the needs of each individual child.

Progress check

Reviewing your practice

1. Using the questions above, try to think of three examples of some creative play that you have initiated which were successful.
2. Explain why those particular activities were successful.
3. Similarly, you can use the questions to prompt you to explore areas where you feel activities were not successful, and think of reasons for this.

In Practice

Meeting individual needs

1. Choose a child in your setting who requires additional help with some aspect of creative play.

2. Make an assessment of the child's needs.

3. Plan a programme or activity that will help to meet those needs.

4. Implement the activity.

5. **Evaluate** the activity.

Assessment practice

The importance of creative play

Using the information on well-planned play in the Foundation Stage on p 314, explain how each category of play promotes creative development and how creative play is promoted in your own setting.

Key terms

Evaluate – Examine strengths and weaknesses; make points for and against.

Review – Look back over the topic or activity and make or identify adjustments, changes or additions that would improve the topic or activity.

Useful websites and resources

www.5x5x5creativity.org.uk **5x5x5=creativity** An independent, arts-based action research organisation that supports children in their exploration and expression of ideas, helping them to develop creative skills for life.

Bruce, T. (2004) *Cultivating creativity: babies, toddlers and young children* (London: Hodder Arnold).

A simple play dough recipe

Ingredients

- 1 cup of plain flour (gluten-free flour can also be used)
- ½ cup of salt
- 2 tablespoons of oil
- 1 cup of water
- 2 tablespoons of cream of tartar
- Food colouring

Method

1. Mix together the dry ingredients
2. Add the water
3. Mix until smooth
4. Add the food colouring followed by the oil
5. Cook on a medium heat, stirring constantly, until the dough leaves the side of the pan and forms a ball
6. Allow to cool before use

Notes:

This is a non-toxic recipe, but because of its high salt content, children should be discouraged from eating it. The recipe makes about twice the amount of dough that comes in the average-sized tub of commercially prepared dough. You can vary the dough by changing the food colouring to make different tubs of play dough in a variety of colours. The dough will dry out if left exposed to the air for too long. To keep it in good condition for longer, keep it in a sealed plastic bag or container, and put it in the fridge when not in use.

Acronyms

ADD	Attention Deficit Disorder
ADHD	Attention Deficit Hyperactivity Disorder
ASBO	Anti-Social Behaviour Order
ASD	Autistic Spectrum Disorder
BASW	British Association of Social Workers
BEST	Behaviour and Education Support Team
BME	Black and Minority Ethnic
BTEC	Business and Technology Education Council
C&G	City and Guilds
CAB	Citizens Advice Bureau
CACHE	Council for Awards in Care, Health and Education
CAF	Common Assessment Framework
CAFCASS	Children and Family Court Advisory and Support Service
CAMHS	Child and Adolescent Mental Health Services
CCLD	Children's Care Learning and Development
CCW	Care Council for Wales
CRE	Commission for Racial Equality
CWDC	Children's Workforce Development Council
CWN	Children's Workforce Network
CYP	Children and young people
DCS	Director of Children's Services
DH	Department of Health
DTI	Department for Trade & Industry
EBSD	Emotional, Behavioural and Social Difficulties
ECAT	Every Child a Talker
ECM	Every Child Matters
ELPP	Early Learning Partnership Project
EPPE	Effective Provision of Pre-School Education Project
EWO	Education Welfare Officer
EYFS	Early Years Foundation Stage
EYP	Early Years Professional
EYPS	Early Years Professional Status
FPI	Family and Parenting Institute
FSW	Family Support Worker
FYJ	Forum for Youth Justice
GP	General Practitioner
IQF	Integrated Qualifications Framework
LLUK	Lifelong Learning UK
LP	Lead Professional
LRN	Learning Resource Network

LSC	Learning and Skills Council
LWS	Local Workforce Strategy
MAT	Multi-agency Team
NACP	National Association of Connexions Partnerships
NASWE	National Association of Social Workers in Education
NCB	National Children's Bureau
NCERCC	National Centre for Excellence in Residential Child Care
NCH	National Children's Home (The Children's Charity)
NCMA	National Childminding Association
NCVCCO	National Council of Voluntary Child Care Organisations
NDNA	National Day Nurseries Association
NEET	Not in Education Employment or Training
NGfL	National Grid for Learning
NISCC	Northern Ireland Social Care Council
NOS	National Occupational Standards
NVQ	National Vocation Qualification
OCW	One Children's Workforce
Ofsted	Office for Standards in Education
PHCT	Primary Health Care Team
PLA	Pre-school Learning Alliance
PRU	Pupil Referral Unit
QCA	Qualification and Curriculum Authority
QTS	Qualified Teacher Status
RNIB	Royal National Institute for the Blind
RNID	Royal National Institute for the Deaf
SEAL	Social and Emotional Aspects of Learning
SEN	Special Educational Needs
SENCO	Special Education Needs Co-ordinator
SSDA	Sector Skills Development Agency
SSSC	Scottish Social Care Council
TAC	Team around the Child
UCAS	University and Colleges Admission Service
VRQ	Vocationally Related Qualification
YCPS	Youth Crime Prevention Strategy
YCS	Youth & Community Service
YISP	Youth Inclusion and Support Panel
YJB	Youth Justice Board
YOS	Youth Offending Service

Index